적중100

영어 기출 문제집

중 3

천재 | 이재영

Best Collection

구성과 특징

교과서의 주요 학습 내용을 중심으로 학습 영역별 특성에 맞춰 단계별로 다양한 학습 기회를 제공하여
단원별 학습능력 평가는 물론 중간 및 기말고사 시험 등에 완벽하게 대비할 수 있도록 내용을 구성

Words & Expressions

Step1 Key Words 단원별 핵심 단어 설명 및 풀이
      Key Expression 단원별 핵심 숙어 및 관용어 설명
      Word Power 반대 또는 비슷한 뜻 단어 배우기
      English Dictionary 영어로 배우는 영어 단어

Step2 실력평가 단원별 수시평가 대비 주관식, 객관식 문제풀이

Step3 서술형 대비 학업성취도 및 수행능력평가 대비 서술형 문제풀이

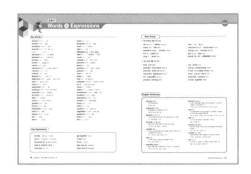

Conversation

Step1 핵심 의사소통 소통에 필요한 주요 표현 방법 요약
      핵심 Check 기본적인 표현 방법 및 활용능력 확인

Step2 대화문 익히기 교과서 대화문 심층 분석 및 확인

Step3 교과서 확인학습 빈칸 채우기를 통한 문장 완성 능력 확인

Step4 기본평가 시험대비 기초 학습 능력 평가

Step5 실력평가 단원별 수시평가 대비 주관식, 객관식 문제풀이

Step6 서술형 대비 학업성취도 및 수행능력평가 대비 서술형 문제풀이

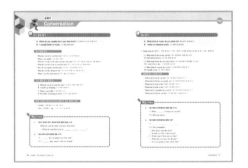

Grammar

Step1 주요 문법 단원별 주요 문법 사항과 예문을 알기 쉽게 설명
      핵심 Check 기본 문법사항에 대한 이해 여부 확인

Step2 기본평가 시험대비 기초 학습 능력 평가

Step3 실력평가 단원별 수시평가 대비 주관식, 객관식 문제풀이

Step4 서술형 대비 학업성취도 및 수행능력평가 대비 서술형 문제풀이

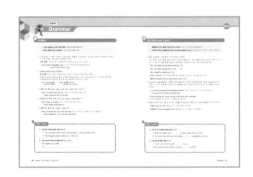

Reading

Step1 구문 분석 단원별로 제시된 문장에 대한 구문별 분석과 내용 설명
      확인문제 문장에 대한 기본적인 이해와 인지능력 확인

Step2 확인학습A 빈칸 채우기를 통한 문장 완성 능력 확인

Step3 확인학습B 제시된 우리말을 영어로 완성하여 작문 능력 키우기

Step4 실력평가 단원별 수시평가 대비 주관식, 객관식 문제풀이

Step5 서술형 대비 학업성취도 및 수행능력평가 대비 서술형 문제풀이
      교과서 구석구석 교과서에 나오는 기타 문장까지 완벽 학습

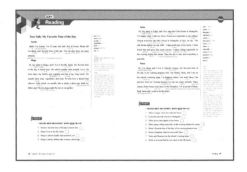

Composition

|영역별 핵심문제|

단어 및 어휘, 대화문, 문법, 독해 등 각 영역별 기출문제의 출제 유형을 분석하여 실전에 대비하고 연습할 수 있도록 문제를 배열

|단원별 예상문제|

기출문제를 분석한 후 새로운 시험 출제 경향을 더하여 새롭게 출제될 수 있는 문제를 포함하여 시험에 완벽하게 대비할 수 있도록 준비

|서술형 실전 및 창의사고력 문제|

학교 시험에서 점차 늘어나는 서술형 시험에 집중 대비하고 고득점을 취득하는데 만전을 기하기 위한 학습 코너

|단원별 모의고사|

영역별, 단계별 학습을 모두 마친 후 실전 연습을 위한 모의고사

on the textbook

교과서 파헤치기

- **단어Test1~3** 영어 단어 우리말 쓰기, 우리말을 영어 단어로 쓰기, 영영풀이에 해당하는 단어와 우리말 쓰기
- **대화문Test1~2** 대화문 빈칸 완성 및 전체 대화문 쓰기
- **본문Test1~5** 빈칸 완성, 우리말 쓰기, 문장 배열연습, 영어 작문하기 복습 등 단계별 반복 학습을 통해 교과서 지문에 대한 완벽한 습득
- **구석구석지문Test1~2** 지문 빈칸 완성 및 전문 영어로 쓰기

Contents

Be Positive, Be Happy

🎙 의사소통 기능

- 주제 소개하기
  A: I'd like to talk about Frida Kahlo.

- 이유 묻고 답하기
  A: I want to spend more time on social media.
  B: What makes you say that?
  A: I can make more friends from around the
     world.

🎙 언어 형식

- 현재완료진행형
  Jake **has been sleeping** all afternoon.

- so ~ that ... 구문
  It was **so** cold **that** I put on my coat.

Words & Expressions

Key Words

- **appearance** [əpíərəns] 명 외모, 출현
- **argue** [ɑ́ːrgjuː] 동 주장하다
- **artificial** [ɑ̀ːrtəfíʃəl] 형 인공적인
- **as** [əz] 접 ~처럼
- **besides** [bisáidz] 부 그 외에도
- **boring** [bɔ́ːriŋ] 형 지루한
- **bother** [báðər] 동 성가시게 하다
- **cause** [kɔːz] 명 원인
- **chemical** [kémikəl] 명 화학물질
- **common** [kámən] 형 흔한
- **effect** [ifékt] 명 효과
- **focus** [fóukəs] 동 집중하다
- **friendship** [fréndʃip] 명 우정
- **gloomy** [glúːmi] 형 우울한
- **grade** [greid] 명 성적
- **helpful** [hélpfəl] 형 도움이 되는
- **improve** [imprúːv] 동 개선하다
- **leave** [liːv] 동 남겨두다
- **left-handed hitter** 좌타자

- **matter** [mǽtər] 동 문제가 되다, 중요하다
- **media** [míːdiə] 명 매체
- **method** [méθəd] 명 방법
- **nervous** [nɔ́ːrvəs] 형 불안한
- **patient** [péiʃənt] 형 인내하는
- **positive** [pázətiv] 형 긍정적인
- **produce** [prədjúːs] 동 생산하다
- **relieve** [rilíːv] 동 덜다
- **relieved** [rilíːvd] 형 안심이 되는
- **salty** [sɔ́ːlti] 형 짠
- **scary** [skɛ́əri] 형 무서운
- **schoolwork** [skúlwərk] 명 학교 공부
- **scream** [skriːm] 동 소리를 지르다
- **sleepy** [slíːpi] 형 졸리는
- **spend** [spend] 동 쓰다, 소비하다
- **stressed** [strest] 형 스트레스 받은
- **tidy** [táidi] 형 깔끔한
- **well-known** 형 유명한
- **work** [wəːrk] 동 효과가 있다

Key Expressions

- **according to** ~에 따르면
- **as long as** ~하는 한
- **at bat** 타석에
- **at the same time** 동시에
- **at the top of my lungs** 있는 힘껏
- **break a promise** 약속을 어기다
- **deal with** ~을 다루다, 처리하다
- **decide on** ~에 대하여 결정하다
- **feel like ~** ~하고 싶은 기분이 들다
- **feel low** 우울하게 느끼다
- **forget to** ~할 것을 잊어버리다
- **get stressed** 스트레스 받다
- **get upset** 속이 상하다
- **have difficulty -ing** ~에 어려움이 있다

- **in other ways** 다른 방식으로
- **instead of ~** ~ 대신에
- **make sense** 의미가 통하다
- **put down** 내려놓다
- **put on** 입다
- **something else** 다른 어떤 것
- **stress ~ out** 스트레스를 받아 지치게 하다
- **take a deep breath** 심호흡을 하다
- **take time out** 시간을 내다, 쉬다
- **thanks to ~** ~ 덕택에
- **that way** 그런 식으로
- **the next time** 다음 번 ~할 때
- **used to** ~하곤 했다
- **work on a team** 한 팀으로 일하다

Word Power

※ 서로 비슷한 뜻을 가진 어휘

- ☐ **artificial** 인공적인 : **manufactured** 제조된
- ☐ **bother** 성가시게 하다 : **disturb** 방해하다
- ☐ **common** 흔한 : **normal** 보통의
- ☐ **gloomy** 우울한 : **cheerless** 활기 없는
- ☐ **nervous** 불안한 : **unstable** 불안한
- ☐ **relieve** 덜다 : **ease** 편하게 하다
- ☐ **scream** 소리를 지르다 : **shout** 소리치다
- ☐ **tidy** 깔끔한 : **neat** 깨끗한

- ☐ **boring** 지루한 : **dull** 지루한
- ☐ **cause** 원인 : **reason** 이유
- ☐ **effect** 결과 : **outcome** 결과
- ☐ **improve** 개선하다 : **develop** 개발하다
- ☐ **patient** 인내하는 : **tolerant** 참을성 있는
- ☐ **matter** 중요하다 : **count** 중요하다
- ☐ **sleepy** 졸리는 : **drowsy** 졸리는
- ☐ **produce** 생산하다 : **manufacture** 제작하다

※ 서로 반대의 뜻을 가진 어휘

- ☐ **agree** 동의하다 ↔ **disagree** 동의하지 않다
- ☐ **cause** 원인 ↔ **effect** 결과
- ☐ **gloomy** 우울한 ↔ **cheerful** 활발한
- ☐ **positive** 긍정적인 ↔ **negative** 부정적인
- ☐ **relieved** 안심이 되는 ↔ **worried** 걱정되는
- ☐ **tidy** 깔끔한 ↔ **messy** 어질러진

- ☐ **artificial** 인공적인 ↔ **natural** 자연적인
- ☐ **common** 흔한 ↔ **rare** 흔하지 않은
- ☐ **nervous** 불안한 ↔ **calm** 차분한
- ☐ **produce** 생산하다 ↔ **consume** 소모하다
- ☐ **patient** 인내하는 ↔ **impatient** 조바심을 내는

English Dictionary

- ☐ **appearance** 외모
  → the way someone or something looks to other people
  어떤 사람 또는 어떤 것이 다른 사람에게 보여지는 방식

- ☐ **argue** 주장하다
  → to disagree with someone in words, often in an angry way
  말로 또는 종종 화가 나서 다른 사람의 의견에 반박하다

- ☐ **artificial** 인공적인
  → not made of natural things
  자연적인 것들로 만들어지지 않은

- ☐ **bother** 성가시게 하다
  → to make someone feel slightly worried, upset, or concerned
  다른 사람이 좀 걱정되거나 불편하게 느끼도록 만들다

- ☐ **cause** 원인
  → a person, event, or thing that makes something happen
  무엇인가가 일어나도록 만드는 사람, 사건 또는 사물

- ☐ **effect** 효과
  → a change that is caused by an event, action, etc.
  사건이나 행위 등에 의해서 생겨난 변화

- ☐ **gloomy** 우울한
  → sad because you think the situation will not improve
  상황이 나아지지 않을 것이라고 생각해서 슬픈

- ☐ **improve** 개선하다
  → to make something better, or to become better
  어떤 것을 더 좋게 만들거나 더 좋아지다

- ☐ **positive** 긍정적인
  → expressing support, agreement, or approval
  지지, 동의, 찬성을 표현하는

- ☐ **tidy** 깔끔한
  → neatly arranged with everything in the right place
  모든 것이 제자리에 단정하게 정돈된

서답형

[01~02] 다음 짝지어진 단어의 관계가 같도록 빈칸에 알맞은 말을 쓰시오. (주어진 철자로 시작할 것)

01

cause : effect = a_____ : natural

02 중요

patient : impatient = n_____ : calm

03 다음 영영풀이에 해당하는 단어를 고르시오.

to disagree with someone in words, often in an angry way

① argue   ② grow

③ destroy   ④ support

⑤ produce

04 중요 다음 중 밑줄 친 부분의 뜻풀이가 바르지 <u>않은</u> 것은?

① I'd like to talk about true <u>friendship</u>. (우정)

② I think it's going to be a <u>boring</u> talk show. (지루한)

③ What makes you feel the most <u>stressed</u>? (스트레스를 받은)

④ Problems with friends <u>took</u> second place with 15.3%. (차지했다)

⑤ I understand. I <u>used to</u> feel that way, too. (사용했다)

05 다음 대화의 빈칸에 들어갈 말로 적절한 것을 고르시오.

A: I'd like to talk about the effects of artificial light.

B: Oh, I have _____ problems at night.

① eating   ② reading

③ running   ④ driving

⑤ sleeping

06 중요 문장의 빈칸에 알맞은 것으로 짝지어진 것은?

• Jane put _____ a new skirt.

• This book deals _____ educational problems.

① on – with   ② on – to

③ in – with   ④ to – for

⑤ for – from

07 중요 다음 중 〈보기〉에 있는 단어를 사용하여 자연스러운 문장을 만들 수 <u>없는</u> 것은?

┌─ 보기 ─┐

scary   spend   bothering   gloomy

① What's _____ you the most these days?

② We have _____ to eat.

③ Good horror movies are so _____ that I scream a lot.

④ Some people _____ time with friends when they feel low.

⑤ This is a very _____ situation.

01 다음 빈칸에 공통으로 들어갈 단어를 쓰시오.

> • I'm studying for the math test, Mom. Grades stress me _____.
> • "Me Time" on her calendar. This means she takes some time _____ for herself.

➡ _____

02 다음 밑줄 친 단어와 의미상 반대가 되는 단어를 주어진 철자로 시작하여 쓰시오.

> His brother has a <u>rare</u> disease.

➡ c_____

03 다음 주어진 단어를 이용해 빈칸을 완성하시오.

> What makes you feel the most _____?

➡ _____ (stress)

04 다음 우리말에 맞게 빈칸에 알맞은 말을 쓰시오.

(1) 오늘 학급 티셔츠에 대하여 이야기합시다. 우리는 디자인을 정해야 합니다.
   ➡ Today, let's talk about the class T-shirt. We have to _____ on the design.
(2) 나는 인공조명의 효과에 대하여 이야기하고 싶습니다.
   ➡ I'd like to talk about the effects of _____ light.
(3) 시험 공부가 나를 졸리게 만들어.
   ➡ Studying for tests makes me _____.

05 다음 영영풀이에 해당하는 단어를 쓰시오. (주어진 철자로 시작할 것)

> not real or not made of natural things but made to be like something that is real or natural

➡ a_____

06 다음 빈칸에 공통으로 들어가기에 적절한 한 단어를 쓰시오.

> • I try to forget about problems. It is a good way to deal _____ my feelings.
> • Some people spend time _____ friends when they feel low.

➡ _____

07 다음 중 〈보기〉의 적절한 단어를 넣어 의미상 자연스러운 문장을 완성하시오.

> ── 보기 ──
> drinking relax happy deep counting

(1) I'd like to talk about some good ways to _____ when you get upset.
(2) First, it's good to take _____ breaths.
(3) Second, _____ to ten is a great idea.
(4) Also, _____ cold water helps.
(5) Lastly, thinking _____ thoughts can help.

Conversation

1 주제 소개하기

A **I'd like to talk about Frida Kahlo.** Frida Kahlo에 대하여 이야기하겠습니다.

■ 무엇인가를 하려고 할 때 'I'd like to ~'라고 한다. 지금부터 상대에게 새로운 주제를 소개하려고 할 때 '~에 대하여 말씀드리겠습니다.'라는 의미로 'I'd like to talk about ~'라고 한다.

• I'd like to talk about true friendship. 진정한 우정에 관하여 말씀드리겠습니다.

• Today, I'd like to talk to you about teen stress. 오늘 청소년의 스트레스에 관하여 말씀드리겠습니다.

■ 주제를 소개할 때 'I'd like to talk about ~'라고 할 수도 있지만 'Let's talk about ~'라고 하거나 'would like to' 대신 will, want to를 사용하여 'Today, I will talk about ~' 또는 'I want to talk about ~'라고 할 수도 있다.

■ 격식을 차려서 소개할 때는 'I'd like to give a presentation about ~'나 'I'd like to give you an introduction about ~'라고 할 수도 있다.

주제 소개하는 여러 가지 표현

• I'd like to talk about ~. ~에 대하여 말씀드리겠습니다.

• I want to talk about ~. ~에 대하여 말씀드리고 싶습니다.

• I will talk about ~. ~에 대하여 말씀드리겠습니다.

• Let's talk about ~. ~에 대하여 이야기해 봅시다.

핵심 Check

1. 다음 우리말과 일치하도록 빈칸에 알맞은 말을 쓰시오.

(1) **A:** I'd like to _____ about Spanish art. (스페인 예술에 대하여 말씀드리겠습니다.)

B: Okay, I'm ready. You may start. (좋아요. 준비됐습니다. 시작하세요.)

(2) **B1:** Today, _____ talk about the class T-shirt. We have to decide on the design.

(오늘 학급 티셔츠에 대하여 이야기해 보자. 우리는 디자인을 정해야 해.)

G: Let me show you some designs on the screen. (화면으로 디자인을 몇 개 보여줄게.)

B2: We have to choose a T-shirt with short sleeves. (우리는 반팔 티셔츠를 골라야 해.)

B1: What makes you say that? (무슨 이유로 그렇게 말하는 거야?)

B2: _____ we'll wear the T-shirt on Sports Day. It's in June.

(우리가 체육대회 때 티셔츠를 입기 때문이야. 그건 6월에 열려.)

G: That makes _____. What about this green one?

(그 말이 맞아. 이 초록색 티셔츠는 어때?)

② 이유 묻고 답하기

A I want to spend more time on social media. 나는 소셜 미디어에 시간을 더 쓰고 싶어.

B What makes you say that? 왜 그런 말을 하니?

A I can make more friends from around the world.
나는 전 세계로부터 더 많은 친구를 사귈 수 있어.

■ 상대방의 말을 듣고 그 이유를 묻는 표현은 'What makes you say that?'이나 'What makes you say so?'이다. '무엇 때문에 그런 말을 하니?'의 의미로 상대방이 한 말의 이유를 확인하기 위하여 묻는 표현이다.

• M: I'd like to talk about true friendship. 진정한 우정에 대하여 말씀드리겠습니다.

• B: I think it's going to be a boring talk show. 지루한 토크쇼가 되겠군.

• G: What makes you say so? 왜 그런 말을 하니?

■ 이유를 물어볼 때는 'What makes you say that?'/ 'What makes you say so?'/ 'What makes you think so?' 등으로 물어볼 수 있다. 대답할 때는 단순히 자기 생각이나 이유를 말하면 되고, Because를 붙여서 말해도 된다.

이유 묻고 답하기

이유 묻기 • What makes you say that? 무엇 때문에 그런 말을 하니?

• What makes you say so?

• What makes you think so? 무엇 때문에 그렇게 생각하니?

• I wonder what makes you say that. 무엇 때문에 그런 말을 하는지 궁금해.

대답 • Because ~

핵심 Check

2. 다음 우리말과 일치하도록 빈칸에 알맞은 말을 쓰시오.

W: What are you doing, Oliver?

B: I'm studying for the math test, Mom. Grades stress me (A)_____.
(성적 때문에 스트레스를 받아 지쳐요.)

W: I understand. I (B)_____ to feel that way, too. (나도 또한 그렇게 느꼈지.)

B: Really? I didn't know that.

W: Yeah, but a little stress was helpful for me.

B: (C)_____ makes you say that? (무엇 때문에 그렇게 말씀하세요?)

W: I got stressed when I had an exam, but at the same time it made me (D)_____
and try harder. (동시에 그것이 집중하고 더 열심히 공부하도록 만들었지.)

 Listen & Answer Dialog 1

W: Today, ❶I'd like to talk to you about teen stress. ❷What makes you feel the most stressed? ❸About 9,000 teens answered this question. ❹As you can see, schoolwork was the most common cause of stress. Over half of the students said schoolwork stresses them the most. Problems with friends ❺took second place with 15.3%. ❻Next came family and worries about the future. 8.2% of the students said they ❼get stressed because of their appearance.

W: 오늘, 저는 여러분에게 십 대들의 스트레스에 관해 말씀드리려고 합니다. 여러분에게 가장 많이 스트레스를 주는 것은 무엇인가요? 약 9,000명의 십 대들이 이 질문에 답했습니다. 보시다시피, 학업이 스트레스의 가장 흔한 원인이었습니다. 절반이 넘는 학생들은 학업이 스트레스를 가장 많이 준다고 말했습니다. 친구들과의 문제는 15.3%로 2위를 차지했습니다. 다음은 가족, 그리고 장래에 대한 걱정 순이었습니다. 8.2%의 학생들은 외모 때문에 스트레스를 받는다고 말했습니다.

❶ would like to ~ = ~하고 싶다, ~하겠다
❷ 'What makes you ~?'는 '무엇이 ~하도록 만들었느냐?'의 의미로 이유를 물어보는 표현이다. Why를 사용할 수도 있지만 직설적인 느낌을 주어서 대화가 어색한 느낌을 줄 수도 있을 때는 'What ~?'으로 물어보는 것이 자연스럽다.
❸ about ~ = 약 ~
❹ As ~ (접속사) = ~다시피
❺ take ~ place = ~째 자리를 차지하다
❻ 부사 Next로 시작하는 문장에서 '부사+동사+주어'의 순서로 도치되어 있다. 주어는 'family and worries about the future'이다.
❼ 'get stressed'는 be동사 대신 get을 사용하여 수동의 의미로 사용하고 있다.

Check(√) True or False

(1) Schoolwork was the most common cause of stress. T ☐ F ☐

(2) Problems with friends were the second common cause of stress. T ☐ F ☐

 Listen & Answer Dialog 2

W: What are you doing, Oliver?

B: I'm studying for the math test, Mom. Grades stress me out.

W: I understand. I used to feel that way, too.

B: Really? I didn't know that.

W: Yeah, but a little stress was helpful for me.

B: What makes you say that?

W: I got stressed when I had an exam, but at the same time it made me ❶focus and try harder.

B: I see. Did stress help you in other ways?

W: Yes, ❷it helped improve my memory.

W: 뭐 하고 있니, Oliver?
B: 수학 시험이 있어서 공부하고 있어요, 엄마. 성적이 제게 스트레스를 줘요.
W: 이해한단다. 나도 그렇게 느끼곤 했거든.
B: 정말요? 그러신 줄 몰랐어요.
W: 그래, 하지만 약간의 스트레스는 내게 도움이 되기도 했단다.
B: 왜 그렇게 말씀하세요?
W: 나는 시험이 있을 때 스트레스를 받았지만, 동시에 그 스트레스가 나를 집중하고 더 열심히 노력하게 했거든.
B: 그렇군요. 스트레스가 다른 방식으로 엄마에게 도움이 된 적이 있나요?
W: 그럼, 내 기억력을 높이는 데 도움을 주었단다.

❶ 사역동사 made의 목적격보어로 focus와 try는 원형부정사로 사용되었다.
❷ = it helped (me) (to) improve my memory.

Check(√) True or False

(3) The boy is studying for the math test. T ☐ F ☐

(4) Mom didn't get stressed when she had an exam. T ☐ F ☐

Listen More

B1: Today, let's talk about the class T-shirt. We have to ❶decide on the design.

G: ❷Let me show you some designs on the screen.

B2: We have to choose a T-shirt with short sleeves.

B1: ❸What makes you say that?

B2: Because we'll wear the T-shirt on Sports Day. It's in June.

G: That ❹makes sense. ❺What about this green one?

B2: I like it. The bee on the T-shirt is so cute.

G: And it's not expensive.

B1: Yes. I think it's the best one.

❶ decide on ~ = ~에 대하여 결정하다
❷ Let me ~. = ~하겠습니다.
❸ 'What makes you ~?'는 이유를 묻는 질문이기 때문에 대답에 Because를 사용해서 대답할 수 있다.
❹ make sense = 의미가 통하다, 말이 되다
❺ 'What about ~?'는 '~은 어때?'의 의미로 상대의 의견을 묻거나 권유할 때 쓰는 표현이다.

 Speak – Talk in groups.

Hi. Today, I'd like to talk about Frida Kahlo. She was a Mexican painter. ❶One of her most ❷well-known paintings is *Viva la Vida*.

❶ 'one of the[소유격]+최상급 복수명사'의 형태로 '가장 ~한 것 중 하나'의 의미이다.
❷ well-known은 '잘 알려진'의 의미로 famous와 동의어이다.

 Speak – Talk in pairs.

A: I want to ❶spend more time on social media.

B: What makes you say that?

A: I can ❷make more friends from around the world.

B: That makes sense.

❶ 보통 'spend 시간 -ing'의 구문으로 쓰지만 명사와 함께 사용할 때는 'spend 시간 on 명사'의 형태로 쓰기도 한다.
❷ make friends = 친구를 사귀다

 My Speaking Portfolio Step 3

I'd like to talk about some good ways ❶to relax when you ❷get upset. First, ❸it's good to take deep breaths. Second, ❹counting to ten is a great idea. Also, drinking cold water helps. Lastly, thinking happy thoughts can help.

❶ to relax는 명사 ways를 수식하는 부정사의 형용사적 용법이다.
❷ get upset = 화가 나다, 속상하다
❸ 'it is ~ to부정사'의 형태로 가주어, 진주어의 구문이다.
❹ 'counting to ten', 'drinking cold water', 'thinking happy thoughts'는 모두 동명사가 주어로 사용되었다.

 Wrap Up – Listening & Speaking 1

W: Hello, teens. I'm Dr. Broccoli. Last time, I talked about different foods ❶that are good for your health. Today, I'd like to talk about healthy eating habits. First, ❷try to eat slowly. Second, ❸it's important to ❹stop eating when you're full.

❶ that은 주격 관계대명사로 선행사는 different foods로 복수이다.
❷ try to ~ = ~하려고 노력하다, 애쓰다
❸ it is ~ to부정사의 가주어, 진주어 구문이다.
❹ stop -ing = ~하기를 중단하다

 Wrap Up – Listen & Speaking 2

G: ❶Why don't we make a sport club?

B: ❷Sounds good. Let's make a baseball club.

G: Well, I think a basketball club is a better idea.

B: ❸What makes you say that?

G: ❹All we need is a ball to play basketball.

❶ Why don't we ~? = 우리 ~하는 게 어때? (권유나 제안의 표현이다.)
❷ '(It) sounds good.'에서 It을 생략한 말이다.
❸ 상대방의 말에 대하여 이유를 물어보고 있다.
❹ 'All we need'는 'all that we need'에서 목적격 관계대명사 that을 생략하고 쓴 단수 주어이다. '우리가 필요한 것이라고는 ~뿐이다.'의 의미로 쓴다.

● 다음 우리말과 일치하도록 빈칸에 알맞은 말을 쓰시오.

Listen and Answer – Dialog 1

W: Today, I'd like to _____ to you _____ teen stress. _____ makes you _____ the most _____? _____ 9,000 teens _____ this question. _____ you can _____, schoolwork was the most _____ _____ of stress. _____ half of the students said schoolwork _____ them the most. _____ with friends _____ second place _____ 15.3%. _____ came family and _____ about the future. 8.2% of the students said they _____ _____ because of their _____.

Listen and Answer – Dialog 2

W: _____ are you doing, Oliver?

B: I'm _____ _____ the math test, Mom. _____ stress me out.

W: I understand. I _____ _____ feel that _____, too.

B: Really? I didn't _____ that.

W: Yeah, but a little _____ was _____ for me.

B: _____ makes you say that?

W: I _____ _____ when I had an exam, but _____ the same time it made me _____ and try harder.

B: I see. Did stress _____ you in other ways?

W: Yes, it helped _____ my memory.

Listen More – Listen and choose.

B1: Today, let's _____ about the class T-shirt. We have to _____ on the design.

G: _____ me show you some _____ on the screen.

B2: We have to _____ a T-shirt with _____ sleeves.

B1: What makes you _____ that?

B2: _____ we'll _____ the T-shirt on Sports Day. It's in June.

G: That _____ _____. What _____ this green one?

B2: I like it. The bee on the T-shirt is so _____.

G: And it's not _____.

B1: Yes. I think it's the best one.

W: 오늘, 저는 여러분에게 십 대들의 스트레스에 관해 말씀드리려고 합니다. 여러분에게 가장 많이 스트레스를 주는 것은 무엇인가요? 약 9,000명의 십 대들이 이 질문에 답했습니다. 보시다시피, 학업이 스트레스의 가장 흔한 원인이었습니다. 절반이 넘는 학생들은 학업이 스트레스를 가장 많이 준다고 말했습니다. 친구들과의 문제는 15.3%로 2위를 차지했습니다. 다음은 가족, 그리고 장래에 대한 걱정 순이었습니다. 8.2%의 학생들은 외모 때문에 스트레스를 받는다고 말했습니다.

W: 뭐 하고 있니, Oliver?

B: 수학 시험이 있어서 공부하고 있어요, 엄마. 성적이 제게 스트레스를 줘요.

W: 이해한단다. 나도 그렇게 느끼곤 했거든.

B: 정말요? 그러신 줄 몰랐어요.

W: 그래, 하지만 약간의 스트레스는 내게 도움이 되기도 했단다.

B: 왜 그렇게 말씀하세요?

W: 나는 시험이 있을 때 스트레스를 받았지만, 동시에 그 스트레스가 나를 집중하고 더 열심히 노력하게 했거든.

B: 그렇군요. 스트레스가 다른 방식으로 엄마에게 도움이 된 적이 있나요?

W: 그럼, 내 기억력을 높이는 데 도움을 주었단다.

B1: 오늘은 학급 티셔츠에 관해 이야기해 보자. 우리는 디자인을 정해야 해.

G: 화면으로 몇 가지 디자인을 보여 줄게.

B2: 우리는 반팔 티셔츠를 골라야 해.

B1: 무슨 이유로 그렇게 말하는 거야?

B2: 우리가 체육대회 때 티셔츠를 입기 때문이야. 그건 6월에 열려.

G: 그 말이 맞아. 이 초록색 티셔츠는 어때?

B2: 나는 마음에 들어. 티셔츠 위의 벌 그림이 정말 귀여워.

G: 그리고 비싸지 않아.

B1: 맞아. 그게 제일 좋겠어.

Speak – Talk in groups.

Hi. Today, I'd like to _____ about Frida Kahlo. She was a Mexican painter. _____ of her most _____ paintings is *Viva la Vida*.

해석

안녕하세요. 오늘은 Frida Kahlo에 대하여 이야기하겠습니다. 그녀는 멕시코인 화가입니다. 그녀의 가장 유명한 그림 중 하나는 Viva la Vida입니다.

Speak – Talk in pairs.

A: I want to _____ more time on social media.

B: What _____ you say that?

A: I can _____ more friends from around the world.

B: That _____ sense.

A: 나는 소셜 미디어에 더 많은 시간을 쓰고 싶어.
B: 왜 그렇게 생각하니?
A: 나는 전 세계로부터 더 많은 친구를 사귈 수 있어.
B: 옳은 말이야.

My Speaking Portfolio Step 3

I'd _____ to talk about some good ways to _____ when you get _____. First, it's good to _____ _____ breaths. Second, _____ to ten is a great idea. Also, _____ cold water helps. _____, thinking happy thoughts can help.

여러분이 화가 났을 때 긴장을 풀 수 있는 방법에 관하여 이야기하겠습니다. 첫째, 심호흡을 하는 것이 좋습니다. 둘째, 열까지 세는 것은 좋은 생각입니다. 또한 차가운 물을 마시는 것도 도움이 됩니다. 마지막으로 행복한 생각을 하는 것이 도움이 됩니다.

Wrap Up – Listening & Peaking 1

W: Hello, teens. I'm Dr. Broccoli. Last time, I _____ about different _____ that _____ _____ for your health. Today, I'd _____ _____ talk about _____ _____ habits. First, try to eat _____. Second, it's important to stop _____ when you're full.

여: 안녕하세요, 십 대 여러분. 저는 Broccoli 박사입니다. 지난 시간에, 건강에 좋은 다양한 음식에 관해 이야기했죠. 오늘은 건강한 식습관에 관해 이야기하고자 합니다. 먼저, 천천히 먹으려고 노력하세요. 둘째, 배가 부르면 그만 먹는 것이 중요합니다.

Wrap Up – Listening & Speaking 2

G: Why _____ we _____ a sport club?

B: Sounds good. Let's _____ a baseball club.

G: Well, I think a _____ club is a better idea.

B: What makes you _____ that?

G: All _____ _____ is a ball to play basketball.

G: 우리 운동 동아리를 만드는 게 어때?
B: 좋아. 야구 동아리를 만들자.
G: 글쎄, 농구 동아리가 더 좋은 생각인 것 같아.
B: 왜 그렇게 말하는 거야?
G: 농구를 하기 위해 우리에게 필요한 건 농구공뿐이잖아.

[01~02] 다음 대화의 빈칸에 들어갈 말을 고르시오.

01

> M: I'd like to talk _____ true friendship.
> A: I think it's going to be a boring talk show.
> B: What makes you say so?

① to   ② with   ③ for
④ about   ⑤ by

02

> A: I want to spend more time on social media.
> B: _____ makes you say that?
> A: I can make more friends from around the world.
> B: That makes sense.

① Why   ② What   ③ When
④ Who   ⑤ Which

[03~04] 다음 글을 읽고 물음에 답하시오.

Hello, teens. I'm Dr. Broccoli. Last time, I ___(A)___ about different foods that are good for your health. Today, I'd like to talk about healthy eating habits. First, try to eat slowly. Second, it's important to stop eating when you're full.

03 빈칸 (A)에 들어갈 알맞은 말을 고르시오.

① studied   ② talked   ③ chose
④ took   ⑤ thought

04 위 글의 내용과 일치하지 <u>않는</u> 것은?

① The speaker's name is Broccoli.
② The speaker is a doctor.
③ He will talk about different foods.
④ We should eat slowly for our health.
⑤ When we feel full, we had better stop eating.

[01~03] 다음 대화를 읽고 물음에 답하시오.

W: What are you doing, Oliver?

B: I'm studying for the math test, Mom. Grades stress me out.

W: I understand. I used to feel (A)that way, too.

B: Really? I didn't know that.

W: Yeah, but a little stress was helpful for me.

B: (B)왜 그렇게 말씀을 하세요? (what, say, that)

W: I got stressed when I had an exam, but at the same time it made me focus and try harder.

B: I see. Did stress help you in other ways?

W: Yes, it helped improve my memory.

01 밑줄 친 (A)가 가리키는 것을 우리말로 쓰시오.

➡ _____

02 (B)의 주어진 우리말을 영어 문장으로 쓰시오. (주어진 단어 반드시 포함)

➡ _____

03 According to the dialogue, which one is NOT true?

① Oliver is studying for the math test.

② Oliver's mom also felt stressed about grades.

③ Oliver knew a little stress was helpful.

④ Stress helped Oliver's mom try harder.

⑤ Oliver's mom got stressed when she had an exam.

04 다음 글의 내용과 일치하지 <u>않는</u> 것은?

W: Today, I'd like to talk to you about teen stress. What makes you feel the most stressed? About 9,000 teens answered this question. As you can see, schoolwork was the most common cause of stress. Over half of the students said schoolwork stresses them the most. Problems with friends took second place with 15.3%. Next came family and worries about the future. 8.2% of the students said they get stressed because of their appearance.

① The topic of this talk is 'teen stress.'

② The largest number of students feel stressed about schoolwork.

③ Problems with friends are the most common cause of stress.

④ Over half of the students get stressed because of schoolwork.

⑤ 8.2% of the students get stressed because of their appearance.

05 다음 대화의 순서가 바르게 배열된 것을 고르시오.

(A) I can make more friends from around the world.

(B) I want to spend more time on social media.

(C) What makes you say that?

① (A) – (C) – (B)　　② (B) – (A) – (C)

③ (B) – (C) – (A)　　④ (C) – (A) – (B)

⑤ (C) – (B) – (A)

[06~07] 다음 대화를 읽고 물음에 답하시오.

> G: Why don't we make a sport club?
> B: _____(A)_____ Let's make a baseball club.
> G: Well, I think a basketball club is a better idea.
> B: What makes you say that?
> G: All we need is a ball to play basketball.

06 빈칸 (A)에 들어가기에 적절하지 <u>않은</u> 것은?

① That's a good idea.
② Sounds good.
③ Yes, I agree.
④ I can't agree with you more.
⑤ I'm not with you.

07 Which one is true about the dialogue?

① The girl suggests making a sport club.
② The girl wants to make a baseball club.
③ The boy suggests making a basketball club.
④ The girl agrees with the boy's idea.
⑤ Just a ball is needed to play baseball.

[08~09] 다음 대화의 빈칸에 들어갈 말을 고르시오.

08

> W: What are you doing, Oliver?
> B: I'm studying for the math test, Mom. Grades _____ me out.
> W: I understand. I used to feel that way, too.

① stress   ② take
③ get   ④ work
⑤ bring

09

> W: A little stress was _____ for me.
> B: What makes you say that?
> W: I got stressed when I had an exam, but at the same time it made me focus and try harder.
> B: I see. Did stress help you in other ways?
> W: Yes, it helped improve my memory.

① hopeful   ② helpful   ③ careful
④ stressful   ⑤ tiring

서답형

10 다음 대화의 빈칸에 들어갈 말을 <보기>에서 골라 순서대로 배열하시오.

> B1: Today, let's talk about the class T-shirt. We have to decide on the design.
> G: Let me show you some designs on the screen.
> B2: _____
> B1: _____
> B2: Because we'll wear the T-shirt on Sports Day. It's in June.
> G: That makes sense.
> _____
> B2: I like it. The bee on the T-shirt is so cute.
> G: _____
> B1: Yes. I think it's the best one.

┤ 보기 ├
(A) What makes you say that?
(B) We have to choose a T-shirt with short sleeves.
(C) And it's not expensive.
(D) What about this green one?

➡ _____

[01~03] 다음 글을 읽고 물음에 답하시오.

W: Today, I'd like to talk to you about teen stress. (A)여러분에게 가장 많이 스트레스를 주는 것은 무엇인가요? About 9,000 teens answered this question. As you can see, schoolwork was the most common cause of stress. Over half of the students said schoolwork stresses them the most. Problems with friends took second place with 15.3%. (B)다음은 가족, 그리고 장래에 관한 걱정 순이었습니다. 8.2% of the students said they get stressed because of their appearance.

01 (A)에 주어진 우리말에 해당하는 영어 문장을 완성하시오. 〈보기〉의 단어를 포함할 것) (7 words)

┌─ 보기 ┐
stressed   make   feel
└────────────────────┘

➡ _____

02 다음 단어를 배열하여 (B)의 의미에 해당하는 영어 문장을 완성하시오.

┌──────────────────────────┐
│ (1) Next로 시작할 것.   │
│ (2) family, the future, about, worries, │
│   came, and를 배열할 것.   │
└──────────────────────────┘

➡ _____

03 위 글을 읽고 다음 질문에 대한 답을 완성하시오.

┌──────────────────────────┐
│ What is the most common cause of stress │
│ for teens?   │
└──────────────────────────┘

➡ The most common cause of stress for teens is _____.

[04~05] 다음 대화를 읽고 물음에 답하시오.

W: What are you doing, Oliver?
B: I'm studying for the math test, Mom. Grades stress me out.
W: I understand. I used to feel that way, too.
B: Really? I didn't know ⓐthat.
W: Yeah, but a little stress was helpful for me.
B: What makes you say that?
W: I got stressed when I had an exam, but _____ⓑ_____ the same time it made me focus and try harder.
B: I see. Did stress help you in other ways?
W: Yes, it helped improve my memory.

04 위 대화의 밑줄 친 ⓐ가 가리키는 것을 우리말로 쓰시오.

➡ _____

05 위 대화의 빈칸 ⓑ에 알맞은 전치사를 쓰시오.

➡ _____

06 다음 밑줄 친 우리말을 영어로 쓰시오. (it으로 시작하고 breaths를 포함할 것)

┌──────────────────────────┐
│ I'd like to talk about some good ways to │
│ relax when you get upset. First, 심호흡을 │
│ 하는 것이 좋습니다. Second, counting to ten │
│ is a great idea. Also, drinking cold water │
│ helps. Lastly, thinking happy thoughts │
│ can help.   │
└──────────────────────────┘

➡ _____

Grammar

① 현재완료진행형

> • Jake **has been sleeping** all afternoon. Jake는 오후 내내 자고 있다.

■ 형태: have/has been -ing
   의미: ~하고 있다

■ 현재완료진행형은 과거에서 지금까지 계속된 현재완료의 상황과 지금도 지속되고 있는 진행형을 결합한 것으로 '과거에 시작해서 지금까지 계속되었고, 지금도 진행하고 있는 동작'을 나타낸다. 현재완료진행형에서 '~ 이래로'는 since로 나타내고, '~ 동안'은 for로 나타낸다.

   • I've **been using** this method for the past several months. 나는 지난 몇 달 동안 이 방법을 사용하고 있다.

   • She **has been waiting** for his call for two hours. 그녀는 두 시간 동안 그의 전화를 기다리고 있다.

■ 현재완료진행형은 현재까지 계속되고 있는 동작을 나타낼 때 사용한다. 상태 동사는 진행 시제를 쓸 수 없기 때문에 현재완료진행형으로 나타내지 않는다. 현재완료진행형은 현재완료와 마찬가지로 명백한 과거 표현과는 같이 쓸 수 없다.

   • I **have been learning** English since I was 10. 나는 10살 이후로 영어를 배우고 있다.

   • Ann **has been living** in this city since she was born. Ann은 태어난 이래로 이 도시에 살고 있다.

핵심 Check

1. 다음 주어진 단어를 적절한 형태로 쓰시오.

   (1) He's been _____ for a job since last month. (look)

   (2) I've been _____ 'Me Time' on my calendar for two months. (write)

   (3) Plum has been _____ with us since last winter. (live)

2. 다음 주어진 문장을 한 문장으로 적절하게 완성하시오.

   (1) They have waited for him to arrive and they are still waiting.

   ➡ They _____ for him to arrive.
      (그들은 그가 도착하기를 기다리고 있다.)

   (2) He started to read the book two hours ago. He is still reading the book.

   ➡ He _____ the book for two hours.
      (그는 두 시간 동안 그 책을 읽고 있다.)

❷ so ~ that ... 구문

- It was **so** cold **that** I put on my coat. 날씨가 너무 추워서 나는 코트를 입었다.

■ 형태: so 형용사/부사 that 주어+동사

　의미: 너무 ~해서 …하다

■ 'so ~ that …' 구문은 '너무 ~해서 …하다'의 의미로 원인과 결과를 나타내는 표현이다. so와 that 사이에는 형용사나 부사를 써야 한다.

　• Good horror movies are **so** scary **that** I scream a lot.
　　좋은 공포 영화는 너무 무서워서 나는 소리를 많이 지른다.

　• While I fish, I'm **so** focused **that** I can leave all my worries behind.
　　낚시를 하는 동안 나는 너무 집중하여 걱정을 뒤로 미뤄놓을 수 있다.

　• When she's **so** stressed **that** her life looks gloomy, she cleans her room.
　　그녀가 너무 스트레스를 받아 삶이 우울해 보일 때, 그녀는 방청소를 한다.

■ so와 that 사이에는 형용사나 부사를 써야 하지만, 명사구를 써야 할 때는 so가 아니라 such를 써서 'such (a)+형용사+명사 that ~'의 형태가 된다.

　• It was **such** an interesting novel **that** I finished reading it last night.
　　그것은 너무 재미있는 소설이어서 나는 어젯밤에 그것을 다 읽었다.

　• It was **such** a delicious cake **that** he wanted to have some more.
　　그것은 너무 맛있는 케이크여서 그는 좀 더 먹기를 원했다.

■ 'so that'은 '그래서 ~'의 의미로 결과를 나타내는 부사절을 유도한다. 'so that 주어 can/will ~'은 '~하기 위하여'의 의미로 목적을 나타내는 부사절을 유도한다.

핵심 Check

3. 다음 주어진 문장에서 적절한 것을 고르시오.

　(1) The book was (so / such) interesting that he read it again.

　(2) It was (so / such) a heavy bag that I couldn't move it.

4. 다음 주어진 문장을 'so ~ that'을 이용하여 한 문장으로 다시 쓰시오.

　(1) Because it was too cold, we didn't go out.

　　= It was ＿＿＿＿ ＿＿＿＿ ＿＿＿＿ ＿＿＿＿ ＿＿＿＿ go out.

　(2) Since the jacket was very expensive, he didn't buy it.

　　= The jacket was ＿＿＿＿ ＿＿＿＿ ＿＿＿＿ ＿＿＿＿ ＿＿＿＿ buy it.

　(3) Because the wind was very strong, they stopped fishing.

　　= The wind was ＿＿＿＿ ＿＿＿＿ ＿＿＿＿ ＿＿＿＿ ＿＿＿＿ fishing.

01 다음 빈칸에 어법상 적절한 것은?

> I have been _____ in this city since I was born.

① lived   ② lives   ③ live
④ to live   ⑤ living

02 다음 중 어법상 어색한 것은?

① Today, I'd like to talk to you about teen stress.
② What makes you feel the most stressed?
③ Let me show you some designs on the screen.
④ It's so noisy that she wants to shut the window.
⑤ French fries are so salty that I won't eat.

03 다음 〈보기〉의 두 문장을 현재완료진행형을 사용하여 한 문장으로 연결하시오. (단, 숫자는 한 단어로 취급하며, 총 12단어로 주어진 문장을 완성하시오.)

> ┤ 보기 ├
> • James started teaching English 20 years ago.
> • He is still teaching at this middle school.

➡ James _____ .

04 다음 문장의 빈칸에 들어갈 알맞은 말을 차례대로 쓰시오.

> I was _____ tired _____ I fell asleep on the bus.

05 다음 빈칸에 어법상 적절한 것은?

> It was so _____ that they stopped sailing.

① windy   ② fog   ③ wind
④ rain   ⑤ rained

서답형

01 〈보기〉를 참고하여 주어진 단어를 이용하여 두 문장을 한 문장으로 쓰시오.

┤ 보기 ├
- They started to play basketball two hours ago.
- They are still playing basketball. (for)
➡ They have been playing basketball for two hours.

(1) • She sat on the bench an hour ago.
   • She is still sitting on the bench. (for)
   ➡ _____
   _____

(2) • She began to work at the store in 2010.
   • She is still working at the store. (since)
   ➡ _____
   _____

(3) • Tom started cleaning the room this morning.
   • He is still cleaning the room. (since)
   ➡ _____
   _____

02 다음 중 빈칸에 들어갈 be동사의 형태가 다른 하나는?

① I have _____ living in this city since I was born.
② The house _____ painted red yesterday.
③ She has _____ reading a book for two hours.
④ They have _____ playing soccer for forty minutes.
⑤ We have _____ running along the river for an hour.

03 다음 빈칸에 어법상 적절한 것은?

Sam has _____ sleeping all afternoon.

① be   ② being
③ been   ④ was
⑤ are

서답형

04 다음 괄호 안에 주어진 어구들을 바르게 배열하여 문장을 완성하시오.

(I've / 'Me Time' / my calendar / been / for / writing / on / two months)

➡ _____
   _____

05 다음 〈보기〉에서 어법상 어색한 문장의 개수는?

┤ 보기 ├
ⓐ My sister is old enough to ride a bike.
ⓑ My fathet was too sleepy to drive.
ⓒ It was such fine that we went outside.
ⓓ Thinking happy thoughts can help.
ⓔ She has been lived here for 5 years.

① 1개   ② 2개   ③ 3개   ④ 4개   ⑤ 5개

06 다음 밑줄 친 부분의 쓰임이 나머지와 다른 하나는?

① It's so noisy that he closed the door.
② The food is so salty that I don't want it.
③ I am so hungry that I will eat a whole pizza.
④ I know the boy that is walking to me.
⑤ The line is so long that I won't wait in line.

07 다음 중 밑줄 친 부분이 어법상 어색한 것은?

① It's good <u>to take</u> deep breaths.
② She <u>has been running</u> for an hour.
③ <u>Counting</u> to ten is a great idea.
④ <u>Drink</u> cold water helps.
⑤ Some people spend time with friends when they feel <u>low</u>.

서답형

08 〈보기〉를 참고하여 주어진 두 문장을 한 문장으로 연결하여 쓰시오.

┌─ 보기 ─┐
- She bought the flowers.
- The flowers were very beautiful.
➡ <u>The flowers were so beautiful that she bought them.</u>

(1) • She went to bed early.
   • She was very tired.
➡ _____

(2) • The cake looked very delicious.
   • He decided to buy it.
➡ _____

(3) • The story was very interesting.
   • He read it in a day.
➡ _____

서답형

09 다음 우리말을 영어로 옮길 때 빈칸에 알맞은 말을 쓰시오.

방이 너무 더워서 그는 창문을 열었다.

➡ It was so hot in the room _____ he opened the window.

10 다음 우리말을 영어로 옮긴 것 중 어색한 것은?

① 청소년들의 스트레스에 관하여 말씀드리겠습니다.
  ➡ I'd like to talk to you about teen stress.
② 무엇이 가장 스트레스를 받게 했습니까?
  ➡ What makes you feel the most stressed?
③ 그는 한 시간 동안 방에서 음악을 듣고 있다.
  ➡ He was been listening to music in the room for an hour.
④ 약 9천 명의 청소년이 이 질문에 대답을 했다.
  ➡ About 9,000 teens answered this question.
⑤ 날씨가 너무 추워서 나는 두꺼운 코트를 입었다.
  ➡ It was so cold that I wore a thick coat.

11 다음 중 밑줄 친 부분의 쓰임이 어색한 것을 고르시오.

① It was <u>so</u> a nice day that he went out for a walk.
② He felt <u>so</u> tired that he went home early.
③ The cake was <u>so</u> delicious that I wanted to have some more.
④ It was <u>so</u> hot that I drank some cold water.
⑤ The mountain was <u>so</u> high that we couldn't climb it.

서답형

12 다음 괄호 안에서 알맞은 말을 고르시오.

(1) They have [being / been] eating lunch.
(2) He has been [cleaned / cleaning] the room.
(3) The bag was [so / such] heavy that he couldn't move it.
(4) He was [so / such] busy that he couldn't help her.

13 다음 중 어법상 <u>어색한</u> 것을 고르시오.

① She has been watching TV for an hour.

② He has been living here since 2010.

③ They have known each other since 20 years.

④ The weather was so hot that we went to the lake.

⑤ She spoke so fast that we couldn't understand her.

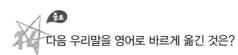

14 다음 우리말을 영어로 바르게 옮긴 것은?

> 그는 너무 고통스러워 잠을 잘 수가 없었다.

① He was very painful that could sleep.

② He was so painful that he couldn't sleep.

③ It was so painful that he can't sleep.

④ He was such painful that he couldn't sleep.

⑤ He couldn't sleep so that he was painful.

15 다음 중 밑줄 친 부분의 쓰임이 <u>어색한</u> 것을 고르시오.

① They have been married <u>for</u> 2005.

② We have been waiting for him <u>since</u> last January.

③ They have been eating lunch <u>for</u> 30 minutes.

④ She has been living here <u>since</u> 2011.

⑤ She has been doing the dishes <u>since</u> she finished dinner.

16 다음 우리말을 영어로 바르게 옮긴 것은?

> 그 차는 너무 오래 되어서 빨리 달릴 수 없었다.

① It was such an old car that it couldn't run fast.

② It was so old car that it could run fast.

③ It was such old a car that it couldn't run fast.

④ It ran so fast that it was very old car.

⑤ It was so an old car that it couldn't run fast.

17 다음 중 어법상 <u>어색한</u> 것은?

① I've been using this method for a long time.

② I know that he hasn't finished the work yet.

③ My uncle graduated from college two years ago.

④ He has been looking for a job since last year.

⑤ She has finished reading a book yesterday.

18 다음 두 문장을 한 문장으로 쓸 때 빈칸에 알맞은 말을 쓰시오.

> • He began watching TV five hours ago.
> • He is still watching TV now.
> ➡ He _____ _____ _____ TV for five hours.

01 다음 우리말에 맞게 괄호 안에 주어진 어휘를 바르게 배열하시오.

(1) 그녀는 이 학교에서 10년 동안 영어를 가르치고 있다.

(teaching, she, been, 10 years, has, English, for, at this school)

➡ _____

_____

(2) 어젯밤부터 비가 내리고 있다.

(it, raining, since, has, last, been, night)

➡ _____

_____

(3) 그가 차를 너무 빠르게 몰아서 그의 아버지가 그에게 차를 천천히 운전하라고 말했다.

(he, his father, drove the car, so, told, that, him, fast, slowly, to drive)

➡ _____

_____

02 다음 주어진 문장을 아래와 같이 바꾸어 쓸 때 적절한 말을 쓰시오.

The mountain was so high that they couldn't climb it.
= It was such _____ _____ _____ that they couldn't climb it.

03 다음 문장의 빈칸에 우리말의 의미에 맞게 채우시오.

(1) Mike has been doing his homework all day.

➡ _____ his homework all day?

(Mike는 하루 종일 그의 숙제를 하고 있는 중이니?)

(2) Jack has been playing the computer game since last night.

➡ _____ the computer game since last night.

(Jack은 지난밤부터 지금까지 계속해서 컴퓨터 게임을 해오고 있지는 않다.)

04 다음 빈칸에 주어진 단어를 적절한 형태로 쓰시오.

(1) She has been _____ on the phone for an hour. (talk)

(2) He has _____ lying on the bed since this morning. (be)

05 다음 두 문장을 한 문장으로 만들 때 빈칸을 완성하시오. (단, 반드시 been을 사용할 것)

• Chris started playing tennis two hours ago.
• He is still playing tennis.
➡ Chris _____

_____.

06 다음 주어진 두 문장을 한 문장으로 연결할 때 빈칸에 알맞은 말을 쓰시오.

He is very rich. He can buy anything
= He is _____ _____ that he can buy anything.

07 다음 우리말을 〈조건〉에 맞게 영작하시오.

> 그녀는 매우 친절해서 모두가 그녀를 좋아한다.

> ┤ 조건 ├
> 1. 'so ... that' 구문을 활용할 것.
> 2. 8단어의 완전한 문장으로 쓸 것.

➡ _____

08 다음 괄호 안에서 알맞은 단어를 골라 〈보기〉와 같이 두 문장을 한 문장으로 바꿔 쓰시오.

> ┤ 보기 ├
> • My father started repairing his car two hours ago.
> • He is still repairing it now. (for/since)
> ➡ My father has been repairing his car for two hours.

> • Ann and I started studying Chinese last week.
> • We are still studying it now. (for/since)

➡ _____

_____

09 다음 빈칸에 알맞은 말을 넣어 문장을 완성하시오.

(1) He felt too tired. He stopped working.
　➡ He felt _____ _____ that he stopped working.

(2) Because the box was too heavy, the child couldn't move it.
　➡ The box was so _____ _____ the child couldn't move it.

(3) Since the pizza was very delicious, they wanted more.
　➡ The pizza was so delicious _____
　_____ _____ _____ .

10 다음 두 문장을 한 문장으로 만들 때 빈칸에 들어갈 알맞은 말을 쓰시오.

> • My brother started using a computer two hours ago.
> • He is still using it.
> ➡ My brother _____ a computer for two hours.

11 다음 괄호 안에 주어진 단어들을 바르게 배열하여 문장을 다시 쓰시오.

> Some people (with / spend / when / time / feel / they / friends / low).

➡ _____

_____

12 다음 주어진 문장이 같은 의미가 되도록 so, that을 사용하여 다시 쓰시오.

(1) She is too hungry. She can't swim any more.
　➡ _____

_____

(2) Because the car was very old, it couldn't run fast.
　➡ _____

_____

(3) Since it was very cold, he put on his coat.
　➡ _____

_____

Say Goodbye to Stress

Some people spend time with friends when they feel low. Others
eat special foods to feel better. Still others simply sleep for a while.
How do you deal with stress? Here are some stories about people who
suggest different ways.

Mina (15, Daejeon)

Sometimes my friends give me stress by saying bad things about me,
breaking promises, or arguing over small things. When this happens, I
watch horror movies! Good horror movies are so scary that I scream a
lot. I guess that screaming at the top of my lungs helps me feel better.
Also, thanks to scary scenes and sound effects, I can forget about what
bothers me. I've been using this method for the past several months,
and it really works.

Junho (14, Yeosu)

My uncle graduated from college two years ago. He lives with my
family, and he's been looking for a job for some time. I know that
he's stressed out, but he always tries to be positive by going fishing.
He never gets upset when he doesn't catch any fish. He says, "While I
fish, I'm so focused that I can leave all my worries behind. Besides, it
teaches me to be patient." I'm sure that focusing on one thing helps us
forget about something else.

feel low 기운이 없다, 무기력하다	
for a while 잠깐, 잠시 동안	
suggest 제안하다, 제시하다	
break (약속 등을) 어기다	
argue over ~을 두고 논쟁하다	
scream 비명을 지르다	
thanks to ~덕분에	
scene 장면	
effect 효과	
bother 괴롭히다	
method 방법	
work 효과가 나다[있다]	
graduate 졸업하다	
stress out 스트레스를 받다	
focused 집중한, 집중적인	
worry 걱정거리, 걱정(되는 일)	
patient 참을성[인내심] 있는	

📎 **확인문제**

- 다음 문장이 본문의 내용과 일치하면 T, 일치하지 않으면 F를 쓰시오.

1 When Mina's friends give her stress, she watches horror movies. ☐

2 Screaming at the top of her lungs prevents Mina from feeling better. ☐

3 Junho's uncle has been looking for a job for some time. ☐

4 Junho's uncle gets upset when he doesn't catch any fish. ☐

Dobin (16, Seoul)

My sister, a second-year student in high school, has a wonderful way
to stay free from stress. She feels a lot of stress from schoolwork, but
my mother seems to like the situation for a good reason. It is because
cleaning is my sister's number-one way to make life better! When
she's so stressed that her life looks gloomy, she cleans her room. She
says, "As I clean my room, I feel like I'm also relieving stress. When
my room looks tidy, my life looks brighter."

Yulia (14, Ansan)

Let me tell you what my mother does about her stress. She feels
stressed by all the things she has to do at work and at home. When
she's under stress, she writes "Me Time" on her calendar. This means
she takes some time out for herself. She reads a book, watches a
movie, or talks with her friends. She says, "It doesn't really matter
what I do, as long as it's something I like. I've been writing 'Me Time'
on my calendar for two months, and I feel much better."

Which methods will work for you? Try some of these ideas yourself,
and find your best way to say goodbye to stress.

way 방법

stay free from ~으로부터 벗어나다

schoolwork 학교 공부

situation 상황

reason 이유

gloomy 우울한

relieve 없애[덜어]주다

tidy 깔끔한

bright 밝은

feel stressed 스트레스를 받다

take some time out 잠깐 시간을 갖다

matter 중요하다

method 방법

 확인문제

● 다음 문장이 본문의 내용과 일치하면 T, 일치하지 <u>않으면</u> F를 쓰시오.

1 Dobin's sister is a second-year student in high school.

2 Dobin's sister doesn't have any ways to stay free from stress.

3 When Dobin's mother is so stressed, she cleans her room.

4 Yulia's mother feels stressed by all the things she must do at work and at home.

5 When Yulia's mother is under stress, she writes "Me Time" on her calendar.

6 It really matters what Yulia's mother should do as it's something she doesn't like.

● 우리말을 참고하여 빈칸에 알맞은 말을 쓰시오.

1 Say _____ to Stress

2 Some people spend time with friends when they _____ _____.

3 _____ eat special foods _____ _____ _____.

4 _____ _____ simply sleep for a while.

5 How do you _____ _____ stress?

6 Here are some stories about people who _____ _____ _____.

Mina (15, Daejeon)

7 Sometimes my friends give me stress by _____ bad things about me, _____ promises, or _____ over small things.

8 _____ _____ _____, I watch horror movies!

9 Good horror movies are _____ scary _____ I scream a lot.

10 I guess that screaming _____ _____ _____ _____ _____ _____ helps me feel better.

11 Also, _____ _____ scary scenes and sound effects, I can forget about _____ _____ _____.

12 _____ _____ _____ this method for the past several months, and it really _____.

Junho (14, Yeosu)

13 My uncle _____ _____ college two years ago.

14 He lives with my family, and _____ _____ _____ _____ a job for some time.

15 I know that _____ _____ _____, but he always tries to be positive _____ _____ _____ _____.

16 He never _____ when he doesn't catch any fish.

17 He says, "While I fish, I'm _____ focused _____ I _____ all my worries _____.

18 _____, it teaches me _____ _____ patient."

---

2 어떤 사람들은 울적할 때 친구들과 시간을 보낸다.

3 다른 사람들은 기분이 좋아지도록 특별한 음식을 먹는다.

4 또 다른 사람들은 그저 잠시 잠을 자기도 한다.

5 여러분은 스트레스를 어떻게 다루는가?

6 여기 다양한 방법을 제안하는 사람들의 이야기가 있다.

미나 (15살, 대전)

7 때때로 내 친구들은 나에 관해 나쁜 말을 하거나, 약속을 어기거나, 혹은 사소한 일을 두고 언쟁을 하며 내게 스트레스를 준다.

8 이럴 때, 나는 공포 영화를 본다!

9 훌륭한 공포 영화는 너무 무서워서 나는 소리를 많이 지르게 된다.

10 있는 힘껏 소리 지르는 것은 내 기분이 나아지는 데 도움이 된다고 생각한다.

11 또한, 무서운 장면과 음향 효과 덕분에 나를 괴롭히는 것들을 잊을 수 있다.

12 나는 지난 몇 달간 이 방법을 써오고 있는데, 효과가 아주 좋다.

준호 (14살, 여수)

13 우리 삼촌은 2년 전에 대학을 졸업했다.

14 삼촌은 우리 가족과 함께 살고 있고, 얼마 전부터 직장을 구하고 있다.

15 나는 삼촌이 스트레스를 받고 있지만 낚시를 다니며 긍정적으로 지내려고 항상 노력한다는 것을 안다.

16 물고기를 한 마리도 잡지 못했을 때에도 삼촌은 절대 속상해 하지 않는다.

17 삼촌은 "낚시하는 동안, 나는 아주 몰입해서 모든 걱정을 잊을 수 있어.

18 게다가 낚시는 나에게 인내를 가르쳐 준단다."라고 말한다

---

19 I'm sure that _____ _____ one thing helps us _____ about something else.

Dobin (16, Seoul)

20 My sister, a _____ student in high school, has a wonderful way to stay _____ _____ stress.

21 She feels a lot of stress from schoolwork, but my mother _____ _____ _____ the situation _____ _____ _____ _____.

22 It is because cleaning is my sister's _____ _____ to make life better!

23 When she's _____ stressed _____ her life looks gloomy, she cleans her room.

24 She says, "As I clean my room, I _____ _____ I'm also _____ stress.

25 When my room _____ _____ , my life _____ _____."

Yulia (14, Ansan)

26 Let me tell you _____ my mother does about her stress.

27 She feels stressed by _____ _____ _____ _____ _____ _____ _____ at work and at home.

28 When _____ _____ _____ , she writes "Me Time" on her calendar.

29 This means she _____ _____ _____ _____ for herself.

30 She _____ a book, _____ a movie, or _____ with her friends.

31 She says, "It doesn't really _____ what I do, _____ _____ it's something I like.

32 _____ _____ _____ 'Me Time' on my calendar for two months, and I feel much better."

33 Which methods will _____ _____ _____ ?

34 Try some of these ideas yourself, and find your best way _____ _____ _____ _____ _____.

19 한 가지 일에 집중하는 것이 다른 무언가를 잊는 데 도움이 된다고 나는 확신한다.

도빈 (16살, 서울)

20 고등학교 2학년인 우리 누나에게는 스트레스에서 벗어나는 훌륭한 방법이 있다.

21 누나가 학업 때문에 많은 스트레스를 받지만, 그럴 만한 이유로 우리 어머니는 그 상황을 좋아하시는 것 같다.

22 그것은 바로, 청소가 누나의 삶을 향상하는 최고의 방법이기 때문이다.

23 스트레스를 너무 많이 받아서 인생이 우울해 보일 때, 누나는 방을 청소한다.

24 누나는 "방을 청소하면서 스트레스도 해소되는 것 같아.

25 내 방이 깔끔해 보이면 내 삶도 더 밝아 보여."라고 말한다.

Yulia (14살, 안산)

26 우리 어머니께서 스트레스를 어떻게 다루시는지 소개하려고 한다.

27 어머니는 직장과 집에서 해야 하는 온갖 일로 인해 스트레스를 받으신다.

28 스트레스를 받을 때면 어머니는 달력에 '나만의 시간'이라고 적으신다.

29 이것은 어머니 자신을 위해 잠깐 시간을 낸다는 의미이다.

30 어머니는 책을 읽거나, 영화를 보거나, 친구들과 이야기를 나누신다.

31 어머니는 "내가 좋아하는 것이라면, 무엇을 하는지는 별로 중요하지 않아.

32 나는 두 달째 달력에 '나만의 시간'을 적어 왔고, 기분이 훨씬 좋아졌어."라고 말씀하신다.

33 어떤 방법이 여러분에게 효과가 있을까?

34 이 아이디어 중 몇 개를 직접 해 보고, 스트레스와 이별하는 자신만의 최고의 방법을 찾아라.

● 우리말을 참고하여 본문을 영작하시오.

1 ▶ 스트레스와 이별하라

➡ _____

2 ▶ 어떤 사람들은 울적할 때 친구들과 시간을 보낸다.

➡ _____

3 ▶ 다른 사람들은 기분이 좋아지도록 특별한 음식을 먹는다.

➡ _____

4 ▶ 또 다른 사람들은 그저 잠시 잠을 자기도 한다.

➡ _____

5 ▶ 여러분은 스트레스를 어떻게 다루는가?

➡ _____

6 ▶ 여기 다양한 방법을 제안하는 사람들의 이야기가 있다.

➡ _____

미나 (15살, 대전) Mina (15, Daejeon)

7 ▶ 때때로 내 친구들은 나에 관해 나쁜 말을 하거나, 약속을 어기거나, 혹은 사소한 일을 두고 언쟁을 하며 내게 스트레스를 준다.

➡ _____

_____

8 ▶ 이럴 때, 나는 공포 영화를 본다!

➡ _____

9 ▶ 훌륭한 공포 영화는 너무 무서워서 나는 소리를 많이 지르게 된다.

➡ _____

10 ▶ 있는 힘껏 소리 지르는 것은 내 기분이 나아지는 데 도움이 된다고 생각한다.

➡ _____

11 ▶ 또한, 무서운 장면과 음향 효과 덕분에 나를 괴롭히는 것들을 잊을 수 있다.

➡ _____

12 ▶ 나는 지난 몇 달간 이 방법을 써 오고 있는데, 효과가 아주 좋다.

➡ _____

준호 (14살, 여수) Junho (14, Yeosu)

13 ▶ 우리 삼촌은 2년 전에 대학을 졸업했다.

➡ _____

14 ▶ 삼촌은 우리 가족과 함께 살고 있고, 얼마 전부터 직장을 구하고 있다.

➡ _____

15 ▶ 나는 삼촌이 스트레스를 받고 있지만 낚시를 다니며 긍정적으로 지내려고 항상 노력한다는 것을 안다.

➡ _____

16 ▶ 물고기를 한 마리도 잡지 못했을 때에도 삼촌은 절대 속상해 하지 않는다.

➡ _____

17 삼촌은 "낚시하는 동안, 나는 아주 몰입해서 모든 걱정을 잊을 수 있어.

➡ _____

18 게다가 낚시는 나에게 인내를 가르쳐 준단다."라고 말한다.

➡ _____

19 한 가지 일에 집중하는 것이 다른 무언가를 잊는 데 도움이 된다고 나는 확신한다.

➡ _____

도빈 (16살, 서울) Dobin (16, Seoul)

20 고등학교 2학년인 우리 누나에게는 스트레스에서 벗어나는 훌륭한 방법이 있다.

➡ _____

21 누나가 학업 때문에 많은 스트레스를 받지만, 그럴 만한 이유로 우리 어머니는 그 상황을 좋아하시는 것 같다.

➡ _____

22 그것은 바로, 청소가 누나의 삶을 향상하는 최고의 방법이기 때문이다.

➡ _____

23 스트레스를 너무 많이 받아서 인생이 우울해 보일 때, 누나는 방을 청소한다.

➡ _____

24 누나는 "방을 청소하면서 스트레스도 해소되는 것 같아.

➡ _____

25 내 방이 깔끔해 보이면 내 삶도 더 밝아 보여."라고 말한다.

➡ _____

Yulia (14살, 안산) Yulia (14, Ansan)

26 우리 어머니께서 스트레스를 어떻게 다루시는지 소개하려고 한다.

➡ _____

27 어머니는 직장과 집에서 해야 하는 온갖 일로 인해 스트레스를 받으신다.

➡ _____

28 스트레스를 받을 때면 어머니는 달력에 '나만의 시간'이라고 적으신다.

➡ _____

29 이것은 어머니 자신을 위해 잠깐 시간을 낸다는 의미이다.

➡ _____

30 어머니는 책을 읽거나, 영화를 보거나, 친구들과 이야기를 나누신다.

➡ _____

31 어머니는 "내가 좋아하는 것이라면, 무엇을 하는지는 별로 중요하지 않아.

➡ _____

32 나는 두 달째 달력에 '나만의 시간'을 적어 왔고, 기분이 훨씬 좋아졌어."라고 말씀하신다.

➡ _____

33 어떤 방법이 여러분에게 효과가 있을까?

➡ _____

34 이 아이디어 중 몇 개를 직접 해 보고, 스트레스와 이별하는 자신만의 최고의 방법을 찾아라.

➡ _____

[01~03] 다음 글을 읽고 물음에 답하시오.

Mina (15, Daejeon)

Sometimes my friends give me stress by ①saying bad things about me, ②breaking promises, or ③arguing over small things. When this happens, I watch horror movies! Good horror movies are so scary that I scream a lot. I guess that ④screaming at the top of my lungs helps me feel better. Also, thanks to scary scenes and sound effects, I can forget about what bothers me. I've been ⑤using this method for the past several months, and it really ⓐworks.

01 위 글의 밑줄 친 ①~⑤ 중에서 문법적 쓰임이 나머지 넷과 다른 것은?

① ② ③ ④ ⑤

02 위 글의 밑줄 친 ⓐworks와 같은 의미로 쓰인 것을 고르시오.

① He works for an engineering company.
② This medicine works pretty well.
③ I like the works of Tolstoy.
④ They didn't finish the public works.
⑤ This machine works by electricity.

03 According to the passage, which is NOT true?

① Sometimes Mina feels stressed when her friends say bad things about her.
② When Mina feels stressed, she watches horror movies.
③ Good horror movies are too scary to make Mina scream a lot.
④ Screaming at the top of her lungs helps Mina feel better.
⑤ Scary scenes and sound effects in horror movies help Mina forget about what bothers her.

[04~06] 다음 글을 읽고 물음에 답하시오.

Junho (14, Yeosu)

My uncle graduated ____ⓐ____ college two years ago. He lives with my family, and (A)he's been looking for a job for some time. I know that he's stressed out, but he always tries to be positive by going fishing. He never gets upset when he doesn't catch any fish. He says, "While I fish, I'm so focused that I can leave all my worries behind. Besides, it teaches me to be patient." I'm sure that focusing ____ⓑ____ one thing helps us forget about something else.

04 위 글의 빈칸 ⓐ와 ⓑ에 들어갈 전치사가 바르게 짝지어진 것은?

	ⓐ ⓑ		ⓐ ⓑ
①	at – for	②	from – on
③	in – on	④	at – to
⑤	from – for		

05 위 글에서 알 수 있는 준호의 삼촌 성격으로 가장 알맞은 것을 고르시오.

① passive ② impatient
③ optimistic ④ generous
⑤ negative

06 위 글의 밑줄 친 (A)에 쓰인 것과 같은 용법의 현재완료가 쓰인 문장을 모두 고르시오.

① How many times have you considered moving to New York?
② She has been studying English for five years.

③ It has just stopped snowing.

④ Have you ever practiced playing the piano?

⑤ I have been cleaning the house since this morning.

[07~10] 다음 글을 읽고 물음에 답하시오.

Dobin (16, Seoul)

  My sister, a second-year student in high school, has (a)a wonderful way to stay free from stress. She feels a lot of stress from schoolwork, but my mother seems to like the situation for a good reason. It is (A)[because / why] cleaning is my sister's number-one way to make life better! When she's so stressed that her life (B)[looks / looks like] gloomy, she cleans her room. She says, "(b)As I clean my room, I feel like I'm also (C)[increasing / relieving] stress. When my room looks ____ⓐ____, my life looks brighter."

서답형

07 주어진 영영풀이를 참고하여 빈칸 ⓐ에 철자 t로 시작하는 단어를 쓰시오.

> neat and arranged in an organized way

➡ _____

서답형

08 위 글의 밑줄 친 (a)a wonderful way가 가리키는 것을 본문에서 찾아 쓰시오.

➡ _____

서답형

09 위 글의 괄호 (A)~(C)에서 문맥이나 어법상 알맞은 낱말을 골라 쓰시오.

➡ (A) _____ (B) _____ (C) _____

10 위 글의 밑줄 친 (b)As와 같은 의미로 쓰인 것을 고르시오.

① Do in Rome as the Romans do.

② He runs as fast as you.

③ As he entered the room, he cried.

④ As I was tired, I soon fell asleep.

⑤ It can be used as a knife.

[11~13] 다음 글을 읽고 물음에 답하시오.

Yulia (14, Ansan)

  Let me tell you what my mother does about her stress. She feels stressed by all the things she has to do at work and at home. When she's under stress, she writes "Me Time" on her calendar. This means she takes some time out for herself. She reads a book, watches a movie, or talks with her friends. She says, "ⓐIt doesn't really matter what I do, as long as ⓑit's something I like. I've been writing 'Me Time' on my calendar for two months, and I feel much better."

서답형

11 위 글의 밑줄 친 ⓐIt과 ⓑit이 공통으로 가리키는 것을 본문에서 찾아 쓰시오.

➡ _____

12 위 글의 제목으로 알맞은 것을 고르시오.

① Causes of Yulia's Mom's Stress

② Yulia's Mom's Ways to Deal with Stress

③ How to Write "Me Time" on the Calendar

④ What Really Matters When You Feel Stressed?

⑤ How to Spend "Me Time" Effectively

13 Which question CANNOT be answered after reading the passage?

① By what does Yulia's mother feel stressed?

② When Yulia's mother is under stress, what does she do?

③ What's the meaning of writing "Me Time" on the calendar?

④ How often does Yulia's mother have "Me Time"?

⑤ How long has Yulia been writing 'Me Time' on her calendar?

[14~17] 다음 글을 읽고 물음에 답하시오.

Mina (15, Daejeon)

Sometimes my friends give me stress by saying bad things about me, breaking promises, or arguing over small things. (①) Good horror movies are so scary that I scream a lot. (②) I guess that ⓐ있는 힘껏 소리 지르는 것은 helps me feel better. (③) Also, thanks to scary scenes and sound effects, I can forget about ⓑwhat bothers me. (④) I've been using this method for the past several months, and it really works. (⑤)

14 위 글의 흐름으로 보아, 주어진 문장이 들어가기에 가장 적절한 곳은?

> When this happens, I watch horror movies!

①   ②   ③   ④   ⑤

15 위 글의 밑줄 친 ⓐ의 우리말에 맞게 주어진 어휘를 이용하여 7단어로 영작하시오.

> top, lungs

➡ _____

16 위 글의 밑줄 친 ⓑwhat과 문법적 쓰임이 같은 것을 모두 고르시오.

① What kind of music do you like?

② He knows what it is to be in debt.

③ What you need is a good meal.

④ He is not what he was.

⑤ What are you looking at?

17 위 글의 주제로 알맞은 것을 고르시오.

① many causes of stress

② friends saying bad things

③ how to deal with stress

④ the benefit of horror movies

⑤ scary sound effects in horror movies

[18~20] 다음 글을 읽고 물음에 답하시오.

Junho (14, Yeosu)

My uncle graduated from college two years ago. He lives with my family, and he's been looking for a job for some time. I know that he's stressed out, but he always tries to be positive by going ____ⓐ____. He never gets upset when he doesn't catch any fish. He says, "While I fish, I'm so focused that I can leave all my worries behind. ____ⓑ____, it teaches me to be patient." I'm sure that focusing on one thing helps us forget about something else.

서답형

18 위 글의 빈칸 ⓐ에 fish를 알맞은 형태로 쓰시오.

➡ _____

19 위 글의 빈칸 ⓑ에 들어갈 알맞은 말을 고르시오.

① Instead   ② Besides

③ However   ④ For example

⑤ By contrast

서답형

20 다음 빈칸 (A)~(C)에 알맞은 단어를 넣어 준호의 삼촌에 대한 소개를 완성하시오.

Junho's uncle has been looking for (A)_____ _____ for some time. Though he is stressed out, he always tries to be optimistic by (B)_____ _____, and he never (C)_____ _____ when he catches no fish.

[21~23] 다음 글을 읽고 물음에 답하시오.

Dobin (16, Seoul)

My sister, a second-year student in high school, has a wonderful way ⓐto stay free from stress. She feels ⓑa lot of stress from schoolwork, but ⓒmy mother seems to like the situation for a good reason. It is because cleaning is my sister's number-one way to make life better! When she's so stressed that her life looks gloomy, she cleans her room. She says, "As I clean my room, I feel like I'm also relieving stress. When my room looks tidy, my life looks brighter."

21 아래 〈보기〉에서 위 글의 밑줄 친 ⓐto stay와 to부정사의 용법이 다른 것의 개수를 고르시오.

┌─ 보기 ─┐
① His mother lived to be ninety years old.
② I don't have any friends to talk with.
③ My dream is to travel around the world.
④ It is important to use your time well.
⑤ She came here to meet Jake.
└────────┘

① 1개 ② 2개 ③ 3개 ④ 4개 ⑤ 5개

22 위 글의 밑줄 친 ⓑa lot of와 바꿔 쓸 수 없는 말을 모두 고르시오.

① many   ② much
③ a number of   ④ lots of
⑤ a great deal of

서답형

23 다음 빈칸 (A)와 (B)에 알맞은 단어를 넣어 밑줄 친 ⓒ의 이유를 완성하시오.

It's because when Dobin's sister is so stressed that her life looks gloomy, she (A)_____ _____ _____.
Cleaning is her number-one way to (B)_____ _____ _____.

[24~25] 다음 글을 읽고 물음에 답하시오.

Which methods will ⓐwork for you? ⓑTry some of these ideas yourself, and find your best way to say hello to stress.

24 위 글의 밑줄 친 ⓐwork와 의미가 같은 것을 모두 고르시오.

① Taking care of a baby is hard work.
② Do you know how to work the coffee machine?
③ The pills the doctor gave me don't work on me.
④ She had been out of work for a year.
⑤ My plan didn't work well in practice.

서답형

25 위 글의 밑줄 친 ⓑ에서 흐름상 어색한 부분을 찾아 고치시오.

_____ ➡ _____

[01~03] 다음 글을 읽고 물음에 답하시오.

Mina (15, Daejeon)

  Sometimes my friends give me stress by ___ⓐ___ bad things about me, ___ⓑ___ promises, or ___ⓒ___ over small things. When this happens, I watch horror movies! ⓓ훌륭한 공포 영화는 너무 무서워서 나는 소리를 많이 지르게 된다. I guess that screaming at the top of my lungs helps me feel better. Also, thanks to scary scenes and sound effects, I can forget about what bothers me. I've been using this method for the past several months, and it really works.

01 위 글의 빈칸 ⓐ~ⓒ에 say, break, argue를 각각 알맞은 형태로 쓰시오.

➡ ⓐ _____ ⓑ _____ ⓒ _____

02 위 글의 밑줄 친 ⓓ의 우리말에 맞게 주어진 어휘를 알맞게 배열하시오.

> I / so / are / a lot / scary / scream / good horror movies / that

➡ _____

03 다음 빈칸 (A)와 (B)에 알맞은 단어를 넣어 미나의 스트레스 해소 방법에 대한 소개를 완성하시오.

> When Mina feels stressed, she watches (A)_____ _____ and screams at the top of (B)_____ _____.

[04~06] 다음 글을 읽고 물음에 답하시오.

Junho (14, Yeosu)

  My uncle graduated from college two years ago. He lives with my family, and he's been looking for a job (A)[for / since] some time.

I know that he's stressed out, but he always tries to be (B)[positive / negative] by going fishing. He never gets upset when he doesn't catch any fish. He says, "While I fish, I'm (C)[so / such] focused that I can leave all my worries behind. ⓐBesides, it teaches me being patient." I'm sure that focusing on one thing helps us forget about something else.

04 위 글의 괄호 (A)~(C)에서 문맥이나 어법상 알맞은 낱말을 골라 쓰시오.

➡ (A) _____ (B) _____ (C) _____

05 위 글의 밑줄 친 ⓐ에서 어법상 틀린 부분을 찾아 고치시오.

_____ ➡ _____

06 다음 문장에서 위 글의 내용과 <u>다른</u> 부분을 찾아서 고치시오.

> Junho's uncle has no difficulty finding a job.

_____ ➡ _____

[07~09] 다음 글을 읽고 물음에 답하시오.

Yulia (14, Ansan)

  Let me tell you ___ⓐ___ my mother does about her stress. She feels stressed by all the things she has to do at work and at home. When she's under stress, she writes "Me Time" on her calendar. This means she takes some time out for herself. She reads a book, watches a movie, or talks with her friends. She says, "It doesn't really matter ___ⓑ___ I do, ⓒas long as it's something I like. ⓓI've been writing 'Me Time' on my calendar for two months, and I feel much better."

07 위 글의 빈칸 ⓐ와 ⓑ에 공통으로 들어갈 알맞은 단어를 쓰시오.

➡ _____

08 위 글의 밑줄 친 ⓒas long as와 바꿔 쓸 수 있는 말을 쓰시오.

➡ _____

09 위 글의 밑줄 친 ⓓ를 다음과 같이 바꿔 쓸 때 빈칸에 들어갈 알맞은 단어를 쓰시오.

➡ I started to write 'Me Time' on my calendar _____ _____ ago, and I am still _____ it on my calendar.

[10~12] 다음 글을 읽고 물음에 답하시오.

Dobin (16, Seoul)

My sister, a second-year student in high school, has a wonderful way to stay ⓐfree from stress. She feels a lot of stress from schoolwork, but my mother seems to like ⓑ the situation for a good reason. It is because cleaning is my sister's number-one way to make life better! When she's so stressed that her life looks gloomy, she cleans her room. She says, "As I clean my room, I feel like I'm also relieving stress. When my room looks tidy, my life looks brighter."

10 위 글의 밑줄 친 ⓐfree from과 바꿔 쓸 수 있는 한 단어를 쓰시오.

➡ _____

11 위 글의 밑줄 친 ⓑ가 가리키는 상황을 우리말로 쓰시오.

➡ _____

12 본문의 내용과 일치하도록 다음 빈칸 (A)와 (B)에 알맞은 단어를 쓰시오.

- Cause of Dobin's Sister's Stress:
  (A) _____
- Dobin's Sister's Method to Relieve Stress:
  (B) _____ _____ _____

[13~15] 다음 글을 읽고 물음에 답하시오.

Yulia (14, Ansan)

Let me (A)[tell / telling] you what my mother does about her stress. She feels stressed by all the things she has to do at work and at home. When she's (B)[over / under] stress, she writes "ⓐMe Time" on her calendar. This means she takes some time out for (C)[her / herself]. She reads a book, watches a movie, or talks with her friends. She says, "It doesn't really matter what I do, as long as it's something I like. I've been writing 'Me Time' on my calendar for two months, and I feel ⓑmuch better."

13 위 글의 괄호 (A)~(C)에서 문맥이나 어법상 알맞은 낱말을 골라 쓰시오.

➡ (A) _____ (B) _____ (C) _____

14 위 글의 밑줄 친 ⓐMe Time의 의미를 우리말로 쓰시오.

➡ _____

15 위 글의 밑줄 친 ⓑmuch와 바꿔 쓸 수 있는 말을 쓰시오. (두 개)

➡ _____

해석

Words in Action

1. Tests stress me out. Grades give me more stress.
   stress ~ out (스트레스로) ~을 지치게 하다
2. Worry less, smile more. Worry never helps.
   worry (동사) 걱정하다   (명사) 걱정
3. I work hard. I have a lot of work to do.
   work (동사) 일하다   (명사) 일
4. I need a change. I will change my hairstyle.
   change (명사) 변화   기분전환 (동사) 바꾸다
5. I caught just a few fish. I want to fish some more.
   fish (명사) 물고기   (동사) 낚시하다

구문해설 • need a change 기분 전환이 필요하다

1. 시험은 나를 지치게 해. 성적은 나에게 더 많은 스트레스를 준다.
2. 걱정은 줄이고 더 많이 웃어라. 걱정은 전혀 도움이 되지 않아.
3. 나는 열심히 일한다. 나는 할 일이 많다.
4. 나는 기분 전환이 필요하다. 나는 헤어스타일을 바꿀 것이다.
5. 나는 겨우 물고기 몇 마리를 잡았다. 나는 몇 마리 더 낚고 싶다.

Speak – Get ready.

1. I want to spend more/less time on social media.
   spend time on ~ = ~에 시간을 쓰다
2. Working on a team can be difficult/helpful.
   difficult/helpful 어려운/유익한
3. I like watching/playing sports better.
4. Having a part-time job as a teen can be good/bad.
   십대일 때   좋은/나쁜

구문해설 • working on a team 팀을 이루어 일하는 것

1. 나는 소셜미디어에 더 많은/적은 시간을 보내기를 원한다.
2. 팀을 이루어 일하는 것은 어려울 수 있다/도움이 될 수 있다.
3. 나는 스포츠 보는 것을/하는 것을 더 좋아한다.
4. 십대일 때 아르바이트를 하는 것은 좋다/나쁘다.

Wrap Up – Reading

Are you stressed or feeling low? Then here is some good news for you. A few simple steps can help you! First, go outdoors and get plenty of sunlight.
= measures   = much
According to scientists, this helps produce a special chemical in your brain,
= to produce
and the chemical makes you feel happy! Another thing you can do is exercise.
사역동사 make+목적어+동사원형   = to exercise
This helps produce even more of the "happiness chemical." Try these simple
= to produce 비교급 강조(훨씬)
tips the next time you feel low. Instead of sitting in front of a screen, go
다음에 ~할 때에는   Instead of+동명사
outdoors and run around in the sun!

구문해설 • low: 기분이 저조한 • step: 조치 • outdoors: 옥외[야외]에서
• according to: ~에 따르면 • chemical: 화학 물질 • instead of: ~ 대신에

스트레스를 받았거나 기분이 우울한가? 그렇다면 여기 당신에게 좋은 소식이 있다. 간단한 몇 가지 절차가 도움이 될 것이다! 첫째, 밖에 나가서 충분한 양의 햇볕을 쬐라. 과학자들에 따르면 이것이 뇌 속에 특별한 화학물질을 만드는 데 도움을 주고, 이 화학물질은 당신을 행복하게 만든다고 한다! 당신이 할 수 있는 또 다른 일은 운동이다. 이것은 훨씬 더 많은 '행복 화학물질'을 만드는 데 도움을 준다. 다음에 당신이 우울하다면 이 간단한 조언을 시도해 보라. 화면 앞에 앉아 있는 대신, 밖에 나가 태양 아래에서 뛰어다녀라!

영역별 핵심문제

01 다음 영영풀이에 해당하는 단어를 고르시오.

> the way someone or something looks to other people

① appearance   ② program
③ patient   ④ view
⑤ scene

02 다음 짝지어진 단어의 관계가 같도록 빈칸에 알맞은 말을 쓰시오. (주어진 철자로 시작할 것)

> agree : disagree = a_____ : natural

03 다음 대화의 빈칸에 들어갈 말로 적절한 것을 고르시오.

> A: I want to spend more time on social media.
> B: What makes you say that?
> A: I can _____ more friends from around the world.

① invite   ② make
③ help   ④ visit
⑤ call

04 다음 밑줄 친 단어와 의미가 가장 가까운 것을 고르시오.

> He looked quite <u>cheerless</u>.

> A: This is a very ①gloomy situation.
> B: What's ②bothering you?
> A: We ③have nothing to eat.
> B: Don't ④worry. We can have ⑤free pizza.

05 다음 대화의 순서가 바르게 배열된 것을 고르시오.

> G: Why don't we make a sport club?
> B: Sounds good. Let's make a baseball club.
> (A) What makes you say that?
> (B) Well, I think a basketball club is a better idea.
> (C) All we need is a ball to play basketball.

① (A) – (C) – (B)   ② (B) – (A) – (C)
③ (B) – (C) – (A)   ④ (C) – (A) – (B)
⑤ (C) – (B) – (A)

06 다음 글의 내용과 일치하는 것은?

> I'd like to talk about some good ways to relax when you get upset. First, it's good to take deep breaths. Second, counting to ten is a great idea. Also, drinking cold water helps. Lastly, thinking happy thoughts can help.

① 글의 주제는 화를 푸는 방법이다.
② 심호흡을 하는 것은 건강에 좋다.
③ 열까지 세는 것은 소화를 도와준다.
④ 화가 났을 때는 말을 하지 마라.
⑤ 행복한 생각은 명상에 도움이 된다.

07 다음 대화의 빈칸에 들어가기에 적절한 단어를 주어진 철자로 시작하여 쓰시오.

> A: I want to spend more time on social media.
> B: What makes you say that?
> A: I can make more friends from around the world.
> B: That m_____ sense.

08 다음 빈칸 ⓐ~ⓔ에 들어갈 말로 가장 어색한 것은?

> B1: Today, let's talk about the class T-shirt. We have to decide on the design.
> G: _____ ⓐ _____
> B2: We have to choose a T-shirt with short sleeves.
> B1: _____ ⓑ _____
> B2: Because we'll wear the T-shirt on Sports Day. _____ ⓒ _____
> G: _____ ⓓ _____ What about this green one?
> B2: I like it. The bee on the T-shirt is so cute.
> G: And _____ ⓔ _____
> B1: Yes. I think it's the best one.

① ⓐ Let me show you some designs on the screen.

② ⓑ What makes you say that?

③ ⓒ It's in November.

④ ⓓ That makes sense.

⑤ ⓔ it's not expensive.

[09~11] 다음 대화를 읽고 물음에 답하시오.

> W: What are you doing, Oliver?
> B: I'm studying for the math test, Mom. ___(A)___ stress me out.
> W: I understand. I used to feel that way, too.

> B: Really? I didn't know that.
> W: Yeah, but a little stress was helpful for me.
> B: (B)What makes you say that?
> W: I got stressed when I had an exam, but at the same time it made me focus and try harder.
> B: I see. Did stress ___(C)___ you in other ways?
> W: Yes, it helped improve my memory.

09 빈칸 (A)에 들어갈 가장 알맞은 말을 고르시오.

① Homework   ② Grades

③ Clothes   ④ Friends

⑤ Foods

10 밑줄 친 (B)와 바꿔 쓸 수 있는 것을 고르시오.

① What makes you think so?

② Why do you study so hard?

③ What is the cause of your stress?

④ How can you avoid this stress?

⑤ When will the stress be away?

11 빈칸 (C)에 알맞은 말을 쓰시오.

➡ _____

Grammar

12 다음 빈칸에 어법상 적절한 것은?

> I am _____ hungry that I want to eat *ramyeon*.

① such   ② very

③ too   ④ so

⑤ quite

[13~14] 다음 괄호 안에 주어진 단어들을 바르게 배열하여 문장을 완성하시오.

13

[I guess / screaming / that / of my lungs / at the top / me / helps / feel better].

➡ _____

_____

14

Let me [what / you / my mother / tell / about / does / her stress].

➡ Let me _____

_____ .

15 다음 〈보기〉에서 어법상 <u>어색한</u> 문장의 개수는?

┌─── 보기 ───┐

ⓐ My sister has a wonderful way to stay free from stress.

ⓑ She feels a lot of stress from schoolwork.

ⓒ My mother seems to like the situation for a good reason.

ⓓ She has been using this method when she was a child.

ⓔ She was so happy that she sang out.

① 1개　② 2개　③ 3개　④ 4개　⑤ 5개

[16~17] 다음 빈칸에 들어가기에 적절한 것은?

16

Tom has been living with us _____ last winter.

① after　　② before　　③ while
④ since　　⑤ for

17

It was so cloudy _____ he took his umbrella.

① that　　② what　　③ which
④ while　　⑤ when

18 다음 우리말을 영어로 바르게 옮긴 것은?

그는 너무 기뻐서 마음껏 소리를 질렀다.

① She was so happy what she screamed loudly.

② She felt so pleased that she screamed at the top of her lungs.

③ She was such happy that she screamed at the top of her lungs.

④ She screamed at the top of her lungs that she was so happy.

⑤ She was happy so that she screamed at the top of her lungs.

19 다음 대화에서 어법상 <u>어색한</u> 것을 2개 찾아 고치시오.

W: Little stress was helpful for me.

B: What makes you say that?

W: I got stressed when I had an exam, but at the same time it made me focus and try harder.

B: I see. Did stress help you in other ways?

W: Yes, it helped improving my memory.

(1) _____ ➡ _____

(2) _____ ➡ _____

영역별 핵심문제　**43**

20 다음 중 어법상 어색한 것은?

① Problems with friends took second place with 15.3%.
② Next family and worries about the future came.
③ My mother takes some time out for herself.
④ They eat special foods to feel better.
⑤ I'd like to talk about some good ways to relax when you get upset.

21 다음 우리말을 영어로 옮긴 것 중 어색한 것은?

① 또 다른 사람들은 단지 잠시 잠을 잔다.
 → Still others simply sleep for a while.
② 집이 너무 조용해서 그는 TV를 켰다.
 → The house was so quiet that he turned on the TV.
③ 왜 그런 생각을 하십니까?
 → Why makes you think so?
④ 당신은 스트레스를 어떻게 처리합니까?
 → How do you deal with stress?
⑤ 이 녹색은 어떻습니까?
 → What about this green one?

22 다음 중 문장의 의미가 나머지와 다른 하나는?

① She was so honest that she couldn't tell a lie.
② She was too honest to tell a lie.
③ She couldn't tell a lie because she was very honest.
④ She was very honest, so she couldn't tell a lie.
⑤ She was very honest though she told a lie.

Reading

[23~26] 다음 글을 읽고 물음에 답하시오.

_____ⓐ_____ people spend time with friends when they feel low. Others eat special foods (A)to feel better. _____ⓑ_____ others simply sleep for a while. (B)What do you deal with stress? Here are some stories about people _____ⓒ_____ suggest different ways.

23 위 글의 빈칸 ⓐ~ⓒ에 들어갈 알맞은 단어를 각각 쓰시오.

➡ ⓐ _____ ⓑ _____ ⓒ _____

24 위 글의 밑줄 친 (A)to feel과 to부정사의 용법이 같은 것을 모두 고르시오.

① I worked hard to pass the test.
② There are many books to read.
③ It is hard for me to study English.
④ She must be mad to say so.
⑤ I don't know where to go.

25 위 글의 밑줄 친 (B)에서 어법상 틀린 부분을 찾아 고치시오.

_____ ➡ _____

26 위 글의 뒤에 올 내용으로 가장 알맞은 것을 고르시오.

① 스트레스의 주된 원인들
② 스트레스를 다루는 방법들 소개
③ 친구들과 즐거운 시간을 보내는 방법들
④ 스트레스를 없애는 음식들 소개
⑤ 효과적인 수면 방법들

[27~28] 다음 글을 읽고 물음에 답하시오.

Junho (14, Yeosu)

My uncle graduated from college two years ago. He lives with my family, and he's been looking for a job for some time. I know that he's stressed out, but he always tries to be positive by going fishing. He never gets upset when he doesn't catch any fish. He says, "While I fish, I'm so focused that I can leave all my worries behind. Besides, it teaches me to be patient." I'm sure that ⓐ한 가지 일에 집중하는 것이 다른 무엇인가를 잊는 데 도움이 된다.

27 위 글의 밑줄 친 ⓐ의 우리말에 맞게 한 단어를 보충하여, 주어진 어휘를 알맞게 배열하시오.

> helps / thing / about / focusing / us / else / something / one / forget

➡ _____

_____

28 According to the passage, which is NOT true?

① Junho's uncle lives with Junho's family.

② Junho's uncle has not found a job yet.

③ Junho's uncle is stressed out and has a negative attitude.

④ While Junho's uncle fishes, he's so focused that he can leave all his worries behind.

⑤ Fishing teaches Junho's uncle to be patient.

[29~30] 다음 글을 읽고 물음에 답하시오.

Dobin (16, Seoul)

My sister, a second-year student in high school, has a wonderful way to stay free ___ⓐ___ stress. She feels a lot of stress from schoolwork, but my mother seems to like the situation for a good reason. It is because cleaning is my sister's number-one way to make life better! When she's so stressed that her life looks gloomy, she cleans her room.

She says, "As I clean my room, I feel like I'm also relieving stress. ⓑ내 방이 깔끔해 보이면 내 삶도 더 밝아 보여."

29 위 글의 빈칸 ⓐ에 알맞은 것은?

① from   ② to   ③ over

④ with   ⑤ along

30 위 글의 밑줄 친 ⓑ의 우리말에 맞게 주어진 어휘를 이용하여 9단어로 영작하시오.

> When, tidy, brighter

➡ _____

[31~32] 다음 글을 읽고 물음에 답하시오.

**Use Your Five Senses
and Stay Free from Stress**

Eye	Look at the sky when you are outdoors.
___ⓐ___	Drink some tea.
Hand	Give your friend a high-five.
___ⓑ___	Smell fresh flowers.
Ear	Listen to your favorite song.

31 Fill in the blanks ⓐ and ⓑ with suitable words.

➡ ⓐ _____ ⓑ _____

32 위 글의 '오감을 사용한 스트레스 해소법'에 해당하지 않는 것은?

① 야외에 있을 때는 식물들을 보아라.

② 약간의 차를 마셔라.

③ 친구에게 하이 파이브를 해주어라.

④ 신선한 꽃 냄새를 맡아라.

⑤ 좋아하는 노래를 들어라.

출제율 90%

01 다음 짝지어진 단어의 관계가 같도록 빈칸에 알맞은 말을 쓰시오. (주어진 철자로 시작할 것)

> bright : clever = b_____ : dull

출제율 90%

02 다음 영영풀이에 해당하는 단어를 고르시오.

> to make someone feel slightly worried, upset, or concerned

① bother
② produce
③ please
④ depress
⑤ frighten

출제율 95%

03 다음 문장의 빈칸에 알맞은 것으로 짝지어진 것은?

> • Did you decide _____ the menu?
> • I met a lot of nice people, thanks _____ you.

① to – on
② for – at
③ to – from
④ on – to
⑤ on – with

출제율 100%

04 다음 중 〈보기〉에 있는 단어를 사용하여 자연스러운 문장을 만들 수 <u>없는</u> 것은?

> ┌ 보기 ┐
> positive   graduated   forget   focused

① My uncle _____ from college two years ago.
② I know that he's _____ out by the work.
③ He always tries to be _____ by going fishing.
④ While I fish, I'm so _____ that I can leave all my worries behind.
⑤ I'm sure that focusing on one thing helps us _____ about something else.

[05~06] 다음 빈칸에 들어갈 말로 적절한 것을 고르시오.

출제율 95%

05
> Good horror movies are so _____ that I scream a lot.

① boring
② scary
③ gloomy
④ patient
⑤ difficult

출제율 95%

06
> I guess that screaming at the top of my _____ helps me feel better. Also, thanks to scary scenes and sound effects, I can forget about what bothers me.

① nose
② height
③ sizes
④ fingers
⑤ lungs

출제율 95%

07 다음 짝지어진 단어의 관계가 같도록 빈칸에 알맞은 말을 쓰시오. (주어진 철자로 시작할 것)

> cause : effect = tidy : m_____

출제율 95%

08 다음 중 밑줄 친 부분의 뜻풀이가 바르지 <u>않은</u> 것은?

① <u>Grades</u> stress me out. (학년)
② Yeah, but a little stress was <u>helpful</u> for me. (유익한)
③ At the same time it made me <u>focus</u> and try harder. (집중하다)
④ I <u>see</u>. Did stress help you in other ways? (이해하다)
⑤ Yes, it helped <u>improve</u> my memory. (향상하다)

09 다음 영영풀이에 해당하는 단어를 고르시오.

> able to wait calmly for a long time or to accept difficulties without becoming angry

① patient ② stressed
③ sleepy ④ gloomy
⑤ positive

10 다음 우리말에 맞게 빈칸에 알맞은 말을 쓰시오.

(1) 고등학교 2학년인 누나는 스트레스를 없애는 좋은 방법을 가지고 있다.
➡ My sister, a second-year student in high school, has a wonderful way to stay _____ from stress.

(2) 엄마는 그 상황을 정당한 이유로 좋아하는 것 같다.
➡ My mother seems to like the situation for a good _____.

(3) 그녀는 너무 스트레스를 받아서 삶이 우울해 보일 때 방을 청소한다.
➡ When she's so stressed that her life looks _____, she cleans her room.

11 다음 대화의 내용과 일치하는 것은?

> G: Why don't we make a sport club?
> B: Sounds good. Let's make a baseball club.
> G: Well, I think a basketball club is a better idea.
> B: What makes you say that?
> G: All we need is a ball to play basketball.

① The girl wants to make a sport club.
② The boy doesn't like to make a sport club.
③ The girl wants to make a baseball club.
④ The girl agrees with the boy about a baseball club.
⑤ The girl and the boy like baseball a lot.

[12~14] 다음 대화를 읽고 물음에 답하시오.

> B1: Today, let's talk about the class T-shirt. We have to decide on the design.
> G: Let me show you some designs on the screen.
> B2: We have to choose a T-shirt ___(A)___ short sleeves.
> B1: What makes you say that?
> B2: Because we'll wear the T-shirt on Sports Day. It's in June.
> G: That makes sense. What about this green one?
> B2: I like it. The bee on the T-shirt is so cute.
> G: _____(B)_____
> B1: Yes. I think it's the best one.

12 위 대화의 빈칸 (A)에 알맞은 것은?

① on ② with ③ for
④ from ⑤ over

13 위 대화의 흐름으로 보아 (B)에 들어가기에 적절한 것은?

① And it's so large.
② But it's too colorful.
③ But how about this one?
④ And it's very dark.
⑤ And it's not expensive

출제율 95%

14 위 대화의 내용과 일치하지 <u>않는</u> 것은?

① They are talking about the T-shirt.

② They are choosing the design.

③ They chose a T-shirt which has short sleeves.

④ They will wear the T-shirt in spring.

⑤ They may choose a green T-shirt.

출제율 90%

15 다음 빈칸에 어법상 적절한 것은?

> He lives with my family, and he's been _____ for a job for some time.

① looked　　　② looks

③ to look　　　④ being looked

⑤ looking

출제율 90%

16 다음 중 어법상 <u>어색한</u> 것은?

① How do you deal with stress?

② Here are some stories about people who suggest different ways.

③ The girl has been playing the piano since an hour.

④ As you can see, schoolwork was the most common cause of stress.

⑤ About 9,000 teens answered this question.

출제율 90%

17 다음 〈보기〉에서 어법상 <u>어색한</u> 문장의 개수는?

> ─┤ 보기 ├─
> ⓐ I was so busy that I didn't eat lunch.
> ⓑ She has been running around the playground for an hour.
> ⓒ The bag was so expensive that she couldn't buy.
> ⓓ He was such tired that he stopped working.
> ⓔ He was reading a book since this morning.

① 1개　② 2개　③ 3개　④ 4개　⑤ 5개

[18~20] 다음 글을 읽고 물음에 답하시오.

Mina (15, Daejeon)

Sometimes my friends give me stress by saying bad things about me, breaking promises, or arguing over small things. When (A)<u>this</u> happens, I watch horror movies! Good horror movies are so scary that I scream a lot. I guess that screaming at the top of my lungs helps me feel better. Also, thanks to scary scenes and sound effects, I can forget about what bothers me. I've been ___(B)___ this method for the past several months, and it really works.

출제율 95%

18 위 글의 밑줄 친 (A)this가 가리키는 내용을 우리말로 쓰시오.

➡ _____

_____

출제율 95%

19 위 글의 빈칸 (B)에 use를 알맞은 형태로 쓰시오.

➡ _____

출제율 95%

20 What TWO things in horror movies help Mina forget about the thing which bothers her? Answer in English.

➡ ① _____　② _____

[21~22] 다음 글을 읽고 물음에 답하시오.

Junho (14, Yeosu)

My uncle (A)[graduated / graduated from] college two years ago. He lives with my family, and he's been looking for a job for some time. I know that he's stressed out, but he always tries to be positive by going fishing. He never gets (B)[relaxed / upset] when he doesn't catch any fish. He says, "While I fish, I'm so focused that I can leave all my worries behind. ⓐBesides, it teaches me to be (C) [patient / impatient]." I'm sure that focusing on one thing helps us forget about something else.

21 위 글의 괄호 (A)~(C)에서 문맥이나 어법상 알맞은 낱말을 골라 쓰시오.

➡ (A) _____ (B) _____ (C) _____

22 위 글의 밑줄 친 ⓐBesides와 바꿔 쓸 수 없는 말을 모두 고르시오.

① Therefore
② In addition to
③ Moreover
④ What's more
⑤ Furthermore

[23~25] 다음 글을 읽고 물음에 답하시오.

Yulia (14, Ansan)

Let me tell you what my mother does about her stress. She feels stressed by all the things she has to do at work and at home. When she's under stress, she writes "Me Time" on her calendar. (A)This means she takes some time out for her. She reads a book, watches a movie, or talks with her friends. She says, "(B)It doesn't really matter what I do, as long as it's something I like. I've been writing 'Me Time' on my calendar for two months, and I feel much better."

23 위 글의 밑줄 친 (A)에서 어색한 것을 고치시오.

_____ ➡ _____

24 위 글의 밑줄 친 (B)를 다음과 같이 바꿔 쓸 때 빈칸에 들어갈 알맞은 단어를 쓰시오.

➡ It isn't really _____

25 위 글의 내용과 일치하도록 다음 빈칸 (A)와 (B)에 알맞은 단어를 쓰시오.

- Cause of Yulia's Mother's Stress:
  (A) _____ _____ _____ _____
  _____ _____ _____ at work and at home
- Yulia's Mother's Method to Relieve Stress:
  (B) having " _____ _____ "

[26~27] 다음 글을 읽고 물음에 답하시오.

Are you stressed or feeling low? Then here is some good news for you. A few simple steps can help you! First, go outdoors and get plenty of sunlight. According to scientists, (A)this helps produce a special chemical in your brain, and the chemical makes you feel happy! Another thing you can do is exercise. (B)This helps produce even more of the "happiness chemical." Try these simple tips the next time you feel low. _____ⓐ_____ sitting in front of a screen, go outdoors and run around in the sun!

26 위 글의 빈칸 ⓐ에 들어갈 알맞은 말을 고르시오.

① Besides
② Instead of
③ Along with
④ In spite of
⑤ In addition

27 위 글의 밑줄 친 (A)this와 (B)This가 가리키는 것을 각각 본문에서 찾아 쓰시오. ((A)는 동명사를 사용하여 답하시오.)

➡ (A) _____
   (B) _____

[01~02] 다음 짝지어진 단어의 관계가 같도록 빈칸에 알맞은 말을 쓰시오. (주어진 철자로 시작할 것)

01
> bother : disturb = cause : r_____

02
> cheap : expensive = relieved : w_____

03 다음 영영풀이에 해당하는 단어를 주어진 철자로 시작하여 쓰시오.

> a change that is caused by an event, action, etc.

➡ e_____

[04~06] 다음 대화를 읽고 물음에 답하시오.

W: What are you doing, Oliver?
B: I'm studying for the math test, Mom. Grades stress me out.
W: I understand. I used to feel ⓐthat way, too.
B: Really? I didn't know that.
W: Yeah, but a little stress was ⓑhelp for me.
B: What ____ⓒ____ you say that?
W: I got stressed when I had an exam, but at the same time it made me focus and try harder.
B: I see. Did stress help you in other ways?
W: Yes, it helped improve my memory.

04 위 대화의 밑줄 친 ⓐ를 본문에 나오는 한 단어로 바꿔 쓰시오.

➡ _____

05 위 대화의 밑줄 친 ⓑ를 알맞은 형으로 고치시오.

➡ _____

06 위 대화의 빈칸 ⓒ에 알맞은 말을 쓰시오.

➡ _____

[07~08] 다음 글을 읽고 물음에 답하시오.

W: Today, I'd like to talk to you about teen stress. What makes you feel the most stressed? About 9,000 teens answered ⓐthis question. As you can see, schoolwork was the most common cause of stress. Over half of the students said schoolwork stresses them the most. Problems with friends took second place with 15.3%. Next came family and worries about the future. 8.2% of the students said they get stressed because of their ⓑappear.

07 위 글의 밑줄 친 ⓐthis question의 내용을 우리말로 구체적으로 쓰시오.

➡ _____

08 밑줄 친 ⓑappear를 알맞은 형으로 고치시오.

➡ _____

09 다음 〈보기〉의 두 문장을 현재완료진행시제를 사용하여 한 문장으로 연결하시오.

> ┤ 보기 ├
> • My mother started cooking dinner at 6:00.
> • My mother is still cooking dinner.

➡ _____

10 다음 〈보기〉의 두 문장을 적절한 단어를 사용하여 한 문장으로 쓰시오.

> ┌─ 보기 ─┐
> • He was very excited.
> • He shouted for the team.

➡ He was _____ excited _____ he shouted for the team.

[11~13] 다음 글을 읽고 물음에 답하시오.

Mina (15, Daejeon)

Sometimes my friends give me stress by saying bad things about me, breaking promises, or arguing over small things. When this (A)[happens / is happened], I watch horror movies! Good horror movies are ____ⓐ____ scary ____ⓑ____ I scream a lot. I guess that screaming at the top of my lungs (B)[help / helps] me feel better. Also, thanks to scary scenes and sound effects, I can forget about (C)[that / what] bothers me. I've been using this method for the past several months, and ⓒit really works.

11 Fill in the blanks ⓐ and ⓑ with the suitable words.

➡ ⓐ _____ ⓑ _____

12 위 글의 괄호 (A)~(C)에서 어법상 알맞은 낱말을 골라 쓰시오.

➡ (A) _____ (B) _____ (C) _____

13 위 글의 밑줄 친 ⓒit이 가리키는 것을 본문에서 찾아 쓰시오.

➡ _____

[14~16] 다음 글을 읽고 물음에 답하시오.

Junho (14, Yeosu)

My uncle graduated from college two years ago. He lives with my family, and ⓐhe's been looking for a job for some time. I know that he's stressed out, but he always tries to be positive by going fishing. He never gets upset when he doesn't catch any fish. He says, "While I fish, ⓑI'm so focused that I can leave all my worries behind. Besides, it teaches me to be patient." I'm sure that focusing on one thing helps us forget about something else.

14 위 글의 밑줄 친 ⓐ를 다음과 같이 바꿔 쓸 때 빈칸에 들어갈 알맞은 단어를 쓰시오.

➡ he started to look for a job some time _____, and he _____ still _____ for a job

15 위 글의 밑줄 친 ⓑ를 단문으로 고칠 때, 빈칸에 들어갈 알맞은 단어를 쓰시오.

➡ I'm focused _____ _____ leave all my worries behind.

16 다음 빈칸 (A)와 (B)에 알맞은 단어를 넣어 준호 삼촌의 구직 활동으로 인한 스트레스 해소 방법을 완성하시오.

> Junho's uncle goes (A)_____, which enables him to have a (B)_____ attitude though he has a hard time finding a job.
>
> *attitude: 태도

창의사고력 서술형 문제

01 다음 대화의 빈칸에 알맞은 말을 넣어 대화를 완성해 봅시다.

A: What's the matter?

B: I've been _____ all day.

A: You need a _____. Why don't you go to the river and fish?

B: That's a good idea.

......

A: What's the matter this time?

B: I haven't caught a _____. It _____ me out.

A: Don't _____. You'll catch one soon.

02 다음 항목들을 'have been -ing'를 사용하여 말해 봅시다.

since I was ten -
- live in this city
- hang out with my best friend
- learn English
- play the guitar
- use this computer

➡ I _____ since I was ten.

03 다음 그림을 바탕으로 오감을 사용한 스트레스 해소법을 소개하는 포스터를 완성하시오.

Use Your Five Senses and Stay Free from Stress

(A)_____ : Look at the sky when you are outdoors.

(B)_____ : Drink some tea.

(C)_____ : Give your friend a high-five.

(D)_____ : Smell fresh flowers.

(E)_____ : Listen to your favorite song.

단원별 모의고사

01 다음 짝지어진 단어의 관계가 같도록 빈칸에 알맞은 것은?

> tidy : neat = _____ : shout

① affect　　② scream　　③ laugh
④ sense　　⑤ weep

02 다음 영영풀이에 해당하는 단어를 고르시오.

> to make something better, or to become better

① produce　　② present　　③ stress
④ improve　　⑤ decide

03 다음 중 밑줄 친 부분의 뜻풀이가 바르지 않은 것은?

① This is a very gloomy situation. (우울한)
② What's bothering you? (괴롭히는)
③ We can have free pizza here. (공짜의)
④ I'm so relieved. (안심이 되는)
⑤ Let's be patient and wait for our food. (조바심이 나는)

04 다음 대화의 순서가 바르게 배열된 것을 고르시오.

> A: I want to spend more time on social media.
> (A) I can make more friends from around the world.
> (B) What makes you say that?
> (C) That makes sense.

① (A) – (C) – (B)　　② (B) – (A) – (C)
③ (B) – (C) – (A)　　④ (C) – (A) – (B)
⑤ (C) – (B) – (A)

05 다음 대화의 문맥상 또는 어법상 어색한 것을 찾아 고치시오.

> W: What are you doing, Oliver?
> B: I'm ①studying for the math test, Mom. Grades stress me out.
> W: I understand. I ②used to feel that way, too.
> B: Really? I didn't know that.
> W: Yeah, but a little stress was ③helpful for me.
> B: What makes you ④say that?
> W: I got ⑤stress when I had an exam, but at the same time it made me focus and try harder.
> B: I see. Did stress help you in other ways?
> W: Yes, it helped improve my memory.

_____ ➡ _____

06 다음 대화의 내용과 일치하지 않는 것은?

> B1: Today, let's talk about the class T-shirt. We have to decide on the design.
> G: Let me show you some designs on the screen.
> B2: We have to choose a T-shirt with short sleeves.
> B1: What makes you say that?
> B2: Because we'll wear the T-shirt on Sports Day. It's in June.
> G: That makes sense. What about this green one?
> B2: I like it. The bee on the T-shirt is so cute.
> G: And it's not expensive.
> B1: Yes. I think it's the best one.

① 오늘의 주제는 티셔츠 디자인 결정이다.

② 그들은 안내책자를 보고 디자인을 결정할 것이다.

③ 소매가 짧은 셔츠 디자인을 결정할 것이다.

④ 고르려고 하는 셔츠는 비싸지 않다.

⑤ 티셔츠에는 꿀벌 그림이 있다.

07 다음 중 어법상 <u>어색한</u> 문장은?

① He has been working for two hours.

② It was so cold that we stayed home.

③ He is a such kind boy that I like him.

④ He has been singing for two hours.

⑤ She has lived here for ten years.

08 다음 〈보기〉와 같이 주어진 두 문장을 한 문장으로 바꾸어 쓰시오.

┤ 보기 ├

• I started working at the Chinese restaurant six months ago.

• I am still working there.

➡ I have been working at the Chinese restaurant for six months.

• My father started repairing his car this morning.

• He is still repairing it now.

➡ _____

_____

09 다음 빈칸에 어법상 적절한 것은?

I've been using this method _____ the past several months, and it really works.

① for   ② since

③ before   ④ after

⑤ during

10 다음 문장에 들어가기에 적절한 것은?

Because the soup was too hot, he decided to eat it later.

= The soup was _____ _____

_____ he decided to eat it later.

11 다음 괄호 안에 주어진 어구를 바르게 배열하여 문장을 완성하시오.

(1) I'd (to / some / talk / ways / like / about / you / good / when / relax / upset / to / get).

➡ I'd _____

_____ .

(2) While I (focused / fish, / I / I'm / so / that / all my worries / can leave / behind).

➡ While I _____

_____ .

12 다음 중 어법상 <u>어색한</u> 문장은?

① She has been doing the dishes since half an hour.

② He has been playing the piano for two hours.

③ We have been waiting for him since this morning.

④ He has been living in the house for three years.

⑤ They have been studying for the test for three hours.

13 다음 〈보기〉에서 어법상 어색한 문장의 개수는?

> ─── 보기 ───
> ⓐ Last time, I talked about different foods that are good for your health.
> ⓑ Ann was such hungry that she wanted to eat *ramyeon*.
> ⓒ Today, I'd like to talk about healthy eating habits.
> ⓓ First, it's important to stop eating when you're full.
> ⓔ The weather is so fine which I can go to the park today.
> ⓕ I have been read this novel for three hours.

① 1개 ② 2개 ③ 3개 ④ 4개 ⑤ 5개

[14~15] 다음 글을 읽고 물음에 답하시오.

Mina (15, Daejeon)

ⓐSometimes my friends give me stress by saying bad things about me, keeping promises, or arguing over small things. When this happens, I watch horror movies! Good horror movies are so scary that I scream a lot. I guess that screaming at the top of my lungs helps me feel better. Also, thanks to scary scenes and sound effects, I can forget about ⓑwhat bothers me. I've been using this method for the past several months, and it really works.

14 위 글의 밑줄 친 ⓐ에서 흐름상 어색한 부분을 찾아 고치시오.

_____ ➡ _____

15 위 글의 밑줄 친 ⓑwhat을 3 단어로 바꿔 쓰시오.

➡ _____

[16~17] 다음 글을 읽고 물음에 답하시오.

Junho (14, Yeosu)

My uncle graduated from college two years ago. He lives with my family, and he's been looking for a job for some time. I know that he's stressed out, but he always tries to be positive by going fishing. He never gets upset when he doesn't catch any fish. He says, "ⓐWhile I fish, I'm so focused that I can leave all my worries behind. Besides, ⓑit teaches me to be patient." I'm sure that focusing on one thing helps us forget about something else.

16 위 글의 밑줄 친 ⓐWhile과 같은 의미로 쓰인 것을 모두 고르시오.

① I fell asleep while I was reading.
② Where have you been all this while?
③ The walls are green, while the ceiling is white.
④ Did anyone call while I was away?
⑤ Some are rich, while others are poor.

17 위 글의 밑줄 친 ⓑ가 가리키는 것을 한 단어로 쓰시오.

➡ _____

[18~19] 다음 글을 읽고 물음에 답하시오.

Dobin (16, Seoul)

My sister, a second-year student in high school, has a wonderful way to stay free _____ⓐ_____ stress. She feels a lot of stress _____ⓑ_____ schoolwork, but my mother seems to like the situation for a good reason.

It is because cleaning is my sister's number-one way to make life better! When she's so stressed that her life looks gloomy, she cleans her room. She says, "As I clean my room, I feel like I'm also relieving stress. When my room looks tidy, my life looks brighter."

18 위 글의 빈칸 ⓐ와 ⓑ에 공통으로 들어갈 알맞은 전치사를 쓰시오.

➡ _____

19 According to the passage, which is NOT true?

① Dobin's sister is a second-year student in high school.

② When Dobin's sister feels much stress, Dobin's mother doesn't like it.

③ Cleaning is Dobin's sister's number-one way to make life better.

④ When Dobin's sister is so stressed that her life looks gloomy, she cleans her room.

⑤ As Dobin's sister cleans her room, she feels like she's also relieving stress.

[20~22] 다음 글을 읽고 물음에 답하시오.

Yulia (14, Ansan)

Let me tell you what my mother does about her stress. She feels stressed by all the things she has to do at work and at home. When she's under stress, she writes "Me Time" on her calendar. This means she takes some time out for herself. She reads a book, watches a movie, or talks with her friends. She says,

ⓐThis doesn't really matter what I do, as long as it's something I like. ⓑI've been writing 'Me Time' on my calendar for two months, and I feel much better."

20 위 글의 밑줄 친 ⓐ에서 어법상 틀린 부분을 찾아 고치시오.

_____ ➡ _____

21 위 글의 밑줄 친 ⓑ에 쓰인 것과 같은 용법의 현재완료가 쓰인 문장의 개수를 고르시오.

┤ 보기 ├
① Have you ever seen it before?
② She has gone to Paris.
③ I have just solved the problem.
④ How long have you known each other?
⑤ He hasn't finished it yet.

① 1개　② 2개　③ 3개　④ 4개　⑤ 5개

22 위 글의 내용으로 보아 대답할 수 없는 질문은?

① What does Yulia tell you about?

② What kind of job does Yulia's mother have?

③ What does Yulia's mother do when she is stressed?

④ What does Yulia's mother write on her calendar?

⑤ How long has Yulia been writing 'Me Time' on her calendar?

Lesson 4

Opening a Window to the World

 의사소통 기능

- 궁금한 점 표현하기
  A: I wonder if there's a bank around here.
  B: I'm sorry, but we don't have one near here.

- 도움 제안하기
  A: Do you want me to play *baduk* with you?
  B: That'd be great. Thank you.

언어 형식

- 관계부사
  Friday evening is the time **when** my family likes to go for a walk.

- 접속사 if/whether
  I wonder **if** they are angry.

Words & Expressions

Key Words

- **add** [æd] 동 더하다
- **alive** [əláiv] 형 살아 있는
- **architect** [ɑ́:rkətèkt] 명 건축가
- **attract** [ətrǽkt] 동 끌어들이다, 끌어당기다, 매혹하다
- **bill** [bil] 명 계산서
- **carry** [kǽri] 동 운반하다
- **cart** [kɑ:rt] 명 수레
- **covered** [kʌ́vərd] 형 지붕이 덮인
- **culture** [kʌ́ltʃər] 명 문화
- **design** [dizáin] 동 설계하다
- **digest** [didʒést] 동 소화하다
- **directly** [diréktli] 부 곧장, 바로, 직접적으로
- **disappear** [dìsəpíər] 동 사라지다
- **discover** [diskʌ́vər] 동 발견하다, 알아내다
- **effective** [iféktiv] 형 효과적인, 실질적인
- **electric-powered** 형 전기로 동력이 주어지는
- **environment** [inváiərənmənt] 명 환경
- **experience** [ikspíəriəns] 명 경험
- **fishing pole** 낚싯대
- **float** [flout] 동 뜨다
- **follow** [fálou] 동 따르다
- **gardening** [gɑ́:rdniŋ] 명 원예
- **house** [hauz] 동 살 곳을 주다, 거처를 제공하다
- **imaginable** [imǽdʒənəbl] 형 상상할 수 있는
- **insect** [ínsekt] 명 곤충
- **last** [læst] 동 지속하다, 오래가다
- **local** [lóukəl] 형 현지의, 지역의
- **mostly** [móustli] 부 주로, 대부분

- **natural** [nǽtʃərəl] 형 천연의, 자연스러운
- **notice** [nóutis] 동 주목하다
- **pick** [pik] 동 고르다, 뽑다, 수확하다
- **planet** [plǽnit] 명 지구, 행성
- **plant** [plænt] 명 식물
- **popular** [pɑ́pjulər] 형 인기 있는
- **present** [préznt] 명 선물
- **producer** [prədjú:sər] 명 생산자
- **recipe** [résəpi] 명 조리법
- **relax** [rilǽks] 동 쉬다
- **send** [send] 동 보내다
- **share** [ʃɛər] 동 공유하다
- **ship** [ʃip] 동 운송하다, 실어 나르다
- **spider** [spáidər] 명 거미
- **suggest** [səgdʒést] 동 제안하다
- **taste** [teist] 동 맛보다
- **therefore** [ðɛ́ərfɔ̀:r] 부 그러므로, 따라서
- **tourist** [túərist] 명 관광객
- **trade** [treid] 명 무역
- **tradition** [trədíʃən] 명 전통
- **translate** [trænsléit] 동 번역하다
- **transportation** [trænspərtéiʃən] 명 운송, 교통
- **try** [trai] 동 맛보다
- **way** [wei] 명 방식
- **whether** [hwéðər] 접 ~인지 아닌지
- **wholesale** [hóulseil] 형 도매의
- **wonder** [wʌ́ndər] 동 궁금하다
- **work** [wə:rk] 동 작동하다, 효과가 있다

Key Expressions

- **all corners of the world** 세계의 곳곳
- **be crowded with** ~로 붐비다, 꽉 차다
- **be good for** ~에 유익하다
- **be rich in** ~이 풍부하다
- **chat with** ~와 잡담하다
- **floating market** 수상 시장

- **have ~ in common** ~한 공통점이 있다
- **Here you are.** 여기 있습니다.
- **make an appointment** 약속하다
- **make sure to** 반드시 ~하다
- **take a nap** 낮잠을 자다
- **best-before date** 유효 기한, 유통 기한

Word Power

※ 서로 비슷한 뜻을 가진 어휘

☐ **attract** 끌어들이다, 끌어당기다 : **draw** 끌다

☐ **disappear** 사라지다 : **vanish** 사라지다

☐ **mostly** 주로, 대부분 : **largely** 주로

☐ **suggest** 제안하다 : **propose** 제안하다

☐ **carry** 운반하다 : **transport** 운반하다

☐ **local** 현지의, 지역의 : **regional** 지역의

☐ **pick** 수확하다 : **harvest** 수확하다

☐ **tourist** 관광객 : **traveler** 여행자

※ 서로 반대의 뜻을 가진 어휘

☐ **add** 더하다 ↔ **subtract** 빼다

☐ **directly** 직접적으로 ↔ **indirectly** 간접적으로

☐ **effective** 효과적인 ↔ **ineffective** 효과가 없는

☐ **alive** 살아 있는 ↔ **dead** 죽은

☐ **disappear** 사라지다 ↔ **appear** 나타나다

☐ **float** 뜨다 ↔ **sink** 가라앉다

※ 동사 → 형용사

☐ **select** 고르다 → **selective** 선택적인

☐ **impress** 인상을 주다 → **impressive** 인상적인

☐ **create** 창조하다 → **creative** 창조적인

☐ **invent** 발명하다 → **inventive** 독창적인

☐ **defense** 방어하다 → **defensive** 방어적인

☐ **attract** 끌다 → **attractive** 매력적인

※ 명사 → 형용사

☐ **emotion** 감정 → **emotional** 감정적인

☐ **person** 개인 → **personal** 개인적인

☐ **cost** 비용 → **costly** 많은 돈이 드는

☐ **time** 시간 → **timely** 시기적절한

☐ **courage** 용기 → **courageous** 용감한

☐ **fame** 명성 → **famous** 유명한

☐ **magic** 마법 → **magical** 마법 같은

☐ **season** 계절 → **seasonal** 계절적인

☐ **friend** 친구 → **friendly** 친한

☐ **adventure** 모험 → **adventurous** 모험적인

☐ **danger** 위험 → **dangerous** 위험한

☐ **humor** 유머 → **humorous** 유머가 있는

English Dictionary

☐ **disappear** 사라지다
→ to see no longer 더 이상 보이지 않다

☐ **discover** 발견하다
→ to find out 찾아내다

☐ **imaginable** 상상할 수 있는
→ possible to think of in your mind
마음 속에서 생각해 내는 것이 가능한

☐ **tourist** 여행자
→ a person who is traveling for pleasure
즐거움을 위해 여행하는 사람

☐ **attract** 끌다, 매혹하다
→ to make someone interested in something and cause them to come to it
누군가가 어떤 것에 관심을 갖게 하고 그것에게 오도록 하다

☐ **tradition** 전통
→ cultural beliefs and customs passed down through generations 세대에 걸쳐 전해지는 문화적 신념과 관습

☐ **wholesale** 도매의
→ the action of selling things in large amounts and at low prices 대량으로 그리고 낮은 가격으로 물건을 판매하는 행위

☐ **ship** 운송하다
→ to send people or things somewhere by ship, truck, and so on 선박, 트럭 등으로 사람이나 물건을 보내다

☐ **floating market** 수상 시장
→ the market which buys and sells things directly on a boat 보트 위에서 물건을 직접 사고파는 시장

☐ **directly** 직접적으로
→ without stopping; with nothing in between
멈추지 않고; 중간에 개입하는 것 없이

 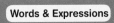

 01 다음 짝지어진 단어의 관계가 같도록 빈칸에 알맞은 말을 쓰시오.

> float : sink = alive : _____

02 다음 영영풀이가 가리키는 것을 고르시오.

> the action of selling things in large amounts and at low prices

① wholesale   ② retail
③ buyer   ④ store
⑤ seller

 03 다음 중 밑줄 친 부분의 뜻풀이가 바르지 않은 것은?

① He loves to visit the local markets and eat food there. (현지의, 지역의)
② Did you eat something before the meal? (식사)
③ Milk is rich in calcium. (부자인)
④ Babies cannot digest meat well. (소화하다)
⑤ Let me write a recipe for you. (조리법)

04 다음 문장에 공통으로 들어갈 말을 고르시오.

> • The school is _____d in two buildings.
> • My _____ looks south, so it is warm.
> • Most of _____s are built of woods.

① share   ② house
③ trade   ④ taste
⑤ notice

05 다음 짝지어진 단어의 관계가 나머지와 다른 것은?

① person – personal
② friend – friendly
③ humor – humorous
④ advent – adventure
⑤ cost – costly

06 다음 주어진 문장의 밑줄 친 covered와 같은 의미로 쓰인 것은?

> It is the largest covered market in the world.

① Did you remember the covered area of the stadium with seats?
② The survey covers all aspects of the business.
③ I think $100 can cover your expenses.
④ The lecture covered a lot of strategy in the game.
⑤ My grandparents didn't cover my father's tuition fees.

서답형
07 다음 우리말에 맞게 빈칸을 완성하시오.

(1) 몇몇 앱들은 효과적인 가르침의 도구들로서 사랑받는다.
  ➡ Some apps are loved as _____ teaching tools.

(2) 내 친구들과 나는 대부분 시험 후에 영화관에 간다.
  ➡ My friends and I _____ go to the movies after exams.

(3) 서울의 대중교통 시스템은 깨끗하고, 빠르고 안전하다.
  ➡ The public _____ system in Seoul is clean, fast and safe.

01 다음 짝지어진 단어의 관계가 같도록 빈칸에 알맞은 말을 쓰시오.

> appear : disappear = add : _____

02 다음 영영풀이가 가리키는 것을 쓰시오.

> the market which buys and sells things directly on a boat

➡ _____

03 주어진 단어에 -al이나 -ive를 붙여 형용사를 완성하시오.

(1) select → _____
(2) invent → _____
(3) magic → _____
(4) impress → _____
(5) person → _____
(6) collect → _____
(7) emotion → _____
(8) season → _____

04 다음 우리말을 주어진 단어를 이용하여 영작하시오.

(1) 영화가 다소 길다. 그것은 두 시간 반 동안 지속된다. (two and a half)
➡ The movie is a bit long. It _____
   _____.

(2) 나는 몇 시에 가게 문을 닫는지 궁금합니다. (to, going)
➡ I wonder _____
   _____.

(3) 만약 당신이 비로부터 상품들을 보호하고 싶다면, 당신은 반드시 지붕이 덮인 트럭을 사용해야 합니다. (must)
➡ If you want to protect your goods from the rain, _____
   _____.

서답형

05 다음 우리말에 맞게 빈칸에 알맞은 말을 쓰시오.

(1) 모든 초콜릿은 최소 6개월의 유통 기한이 있다.
➡ All chocolate has a _____ of at least 6 months.

(2) 여러분은 여기서 세계 곳곳의 음식을 맛볼 수 있다.
➡ You can taste food from _____ _____ here.

(3) 대부분의 고양이는 우유를 잘 소화하지 못한다는 것을 유념해라.
➡ Remember most cats cannot _____ milk very well.

(4) 과학자들은 암에 대한 약을 발견하기 위해 연구하고 있다.
➡ Scientists are working to _____ medicine for cancers.

(5) 그랜드 캐니언은 세계 자연 경관 중의 하나이다.
➡ The Grand Canyon is one of the _____ wonders of the world.

06 다음 〈보기〉의 단어들을 이용하여 빈칸을 완성하시오.

> ┤ 보기 ├
> local   transportation   last   tourist   discover

> Are you a _____ in a new city? Do you want to _____ its beauty? Then, use public _____. Your memory of the new place will _____ longer. You should visit local market too. If you try some food there, you can enjoy the _____ culture.

Conversation

1 궁금한 점 표현하기

> **A** I wonder if there's a bank around here. 이 근방에 은행이 있는지 궁금해요.
> **B** I'm sorry, but we don't have one near here. 유감스럽게도 이 근방에 은행이 없어요.

■ 자신의 궁금함을 상대방에게 나타내는 표현은 wonder(궁금하다), curious(궁금한, 호기심이 많은), want to know(알고 싶다) 등의 표현을 이용하여 나타낼 수 있다. 궁금함을 나타낼 때, 궁금한 내용이 '주어+동사'의 절의 형태이면 접속사 if[wether]를 사용하여 'I wonder if[wether] 주어+동사 ~.'(~인지 궁금하다) 또는 'I wonder+의문사+주어+동사 ~.'로 나타내고, 궁금한 내용이 명사구이면 'I wonder+명사구'의 구문을 이용한다.

■ 궁금함을 나타낼 때 'I wonder ~.' 대신에 쓸 수 있는 표현으로는 'I'm curious ~.' 또는 'I want to know ~.' 등이 있다. 'I'm curious'와 명사구를 같이 쓸 때는 'I'm curious about+명사구'이고, 명사절과 함께 쓸 때는 'I'm curious if/whether ~.' 또는 'I'm curious+의문사+주어+동사'이다.

■ 'I want to know'를 명사구와 함께 사용할 때는 'I want to know+명사구'이고, 명사절과 함께 사용할 때는 'I want to know+명사절'이다. 그 외에 궁금증을 나타낼 때는 'Do you know ~?' 또는 'Can you tell me ~?' 등을 사용할 수도 있다.

궁금한 점 표현하기

- I wonder if/whether+주어+동사. ~인지 궁금하다
- I wonder+의문사절.
- I wonder+명사구.
- I'm curious if/whether+주어+동사. ~가 궁금하다
- I'm curious about+명사구.
- I want to know+명사구/명사절. ~을 알고 싶다
- I'd be very interested to ~. 나는 ~이 알고 싶다.
- Can you tell me about ~? ~에 대해 말해 줄 수 있니?

핵심 Check

1. 다음 우리말과 일치하도록 주어진 표현을 포함하여 빈칸에 알맞은 말을 쓰시오.

   M: Welcome to the Tourist Information Office! How may I help you?

   W: Hi, _____. (a tourist map of the town)
   (여행자가 이용할 수 있는 마을 지도가 있는지 궁금해요.)

   M: Is there a special place you're looking for?

   W: Yes. I'd like to try some local food.

   M: Then go to Jeongseon Market. It opens every five days, and it's open today.

2 도움 제안하기

A Do you want me to play *baduk* with you? 제가 바둑을 같이 두기를 원하세요?

B That'd be great. Thank you. 그거 좋지. 고마워.

■ 일반적으로 도움을 제안하는 표현은 help(도움을 주다), give a hand(도움을 주다) 등을 사용하여 'May I help you?', 'How may I help you?', 'Do you need any help?' 등으로 나타낸다. 'give ~ a hand'는 '~를 돕다'라는 관용적 표현이다. 도움을 제공하고자 할 때는 'Can I give you a hand?'라고 물어볼 수 있다. 이는 레스토랑, 호텔, 기내 등과 같이 서비스를 제공받을 수 있는 공간에서 흔히 쓸 수 있는 표현이다.

■ 상대방이 지루해 하거나 힘들어 하는 등, 현재 처해 있는 상황을 보고 구체적인 도움을 제안할 때는 'Do you want me to ~?'(제가 ~해드리기를 원하세요?)라고 물어본다. 상대방에게 닥친 어려움이나 힘든 일을 도와준다고 제안할 때 'Let me help you with ~.'(내가 너에게 ~하도록 도와줄게.)와 같은 표현을 쓸 수 있다. 도와 달라는 표현은 'Can you help me with ~?'(~ 좀 도와주시겠어요?)이다.

도움 제안하기

- Do you want me to+동사원형? 당신은 내가 ~해 주기를 원합니까?
- May/Can I help you? 도와 드릴까요?
- How may I help you? 어떻게 도와드릴까요?
- What can I do for you? 무엇을 도와 드릴까요?
- Do you need any help? 도움이 필요하세요?
- Let me give you a hand. 제가 도와드리겠습니다.
- Can I give you a hand? 도와 드릴까요?
- Is there anything that I can help you? 도와드릴 일이 있을까요?
- Let me help you. 내가 도와줄게.

핵심 Check

2. 다음 우리말과 일치하도록 빈칸에 알맞은 말을 쓰시오.

W: Excuse me. Can _____? (with this milk)
   (이 우유 (사는 것) 좀 도와주겠니?)

B: Sure. What is it?

W: Read me the date, please.

B: Oh, _____? (want, the best-before date)
   (유통 기한을 말씀드리길 원하세요?)

W: Yes, I forgot my glasses.

Listen – Listen & Answer Dialog 1

M: Welcome to the Tourist Information Office! ❶How may I help you?

W: Hi, ❷I wonder ❸if there's a tourist map of the town.

M: Sure. Is there a special place you're ❹looking for?

W: Yes. I'd like to try some local food.

M: Then go to Jeongseon Market. It opens every five days, and it's open today.

W: I'm so lucky. How can I get ❺there?

M: You can walk there. It takes about 10 minutes.

W: Great. Will you mark the way on the map, please?

M: Sure. Try *gondrebap* when you get ❺there.

남: 관광 안내소에 오신 것을 환영합니다! 무엇을 도와드릴까요?

여: 안녕하세요. 저는 마을 관광 지도가 있는지 궁금합니다.

남: 물론이죠. 특별히 찾으시는 곳이 있나요?

여: 네. 이 지역 음식을 먹어 보고 싶어요.

남: 그렇다면 정선 시장에 가 보세요. 시장이 5일마다 열리는데, 오늘 열렸네요.

여: 제가 정말 운이 좋군요. 그곳에 어떻게 가나요?

남: 거기까지 걸어갈 수 있어요. 10분 정도 걸려요.

여: 잘됐군요. 지도에 길을 표시해 주시겠어요?

남: 물론이죠. 거기에 가면 곤드레밥을 드셔 보세요.

❶ 도움을 제안하는 표현으로 'May I help you?', 'Can I give you a hand?' 또는 'Do you need any help?' 등으로 바꾸어 쓸 수 있다.
❷ 궁금함을 나타내는 표현으로 'I wonder ~' 대신에 쓸 수 있는 표현으로는 'I'm curious ~.' 또는 'I want to know ~.' 등이 있다.
❸ if는 '~인지 아닌지'를 뜻하며 whether와 바꾸어 쓸 수 있다.
❹ look for: ~을 찾다
❺ there = to Jeongseon Market

Check(√) True or False

(1) The woman wants to try some local food. T ☐ F ☐

(2) Jeongseon Market opens once a week. T ☐ F ☐

Listen – Listen & Answer Dialog 2

W: Can I have the ❶bill, please?

M: Here you are. Did you enjoy the meal?

W: It was great. I liked the *gondrebap* very much.

M: Thanks. ❷It's also good for your health.

W: Oh, really?

M: Yes. *Gondre* ❸is rich in vitamins A and C. It also ❹digests well.

W: Good. I wonder if I could buy some *gondre* here.

M: Sure. Do you want me to give you the recipe for *gondrebap*?

W: Yes, that'd be great.

여: 계산서 좀 주시겠어요?

남: 여기 있습니다. 식사는 맛있게 하셨나요?

여: 아주 훌륭했어요. 저는 곤드레밥이 정말 좋았어요.

남: 고맙습니다. 그것은 건강에도 좋답니다.

여: 오, 정말이요?

남: 네. 곤드레는 비타민 A와 C가 풍부합니다. 그리고 소화도 잘돼요.

여: 그렇군요. 여기서 곤드레를 좀 살 수 있을까요?

남: 물론이죠. 제가 곤드레밥 조리법을 드릴까요?

여: 네. 그러면 정말 좋겠어요.

❶ bill: 계산서   ❷ be good for: ~에 좋다, 유익하다   ❸ be rich in: ~이 풍부하다   ❹ digest: 소화하다

Check(√) True or False

(3) The woman is satisfied with *gondrebap*. T ☐ F ☐

(4) The man knows how to make *gondrebap*. T ☐ F ☐

Listen More – Listen and complete

W: Excuse me. ❶Can you help me with this milk?

B: Sure. What is it?

W: Read me the date, please.

B: Oh, do you want me to tell you ❷the best-before date?

W: Yes, I forgot my glasses.

B: Let me see. You should drink ❸it by June 7.

W: That's too soon. I wonder ❹if there's one that ❺lasts longer.

B: Wait. I found one. This one is good until June 11.

W: Oh, I'll take that one. Thank you very much.

B: You're welcome.

❶ 도움을 요청하는 표현으로 'Would you do me a favor?' 또는 'Could you give me a hand?'로 바꾸어 쓸 수 있다.
❷ the best-before date: 유효 기한
❸ it은 the milk를 가리킨다.
❹ if는 '~인지 아닌지'를 뜻하며 'whether'로 바꾸어 쓸 수 있다.
❺ last: 지속하다, 오래가다

Speak – Talk in pairs. 1

A: Excuse me. ❶I wonder if there's a bank around here.

B: I'm sorry, but we don't have ❷one near here.

A: That's all right. Thanks.

❶ 궁금함을 나타내는 표현으로 'I'm curious if there's a bank around here.' 또는 'I want to know if there's a bank around here.'로 바꾸어 쓸 수 있다.
❷ one은 a bank를 가리킨다.

Speak – Talk in pairs. 2

A: ❶What's wrong, Grandpa?

B: I'm ❷bored.

A: Do you want me to play *baduk* with you?

B: That'd be great. Thank you.

❶ 'What's the matter?', 'What's the problem?' 등으로 바꾸어 쓸 수 있다.
❷ 감정을 나타내므로 과거분사 형태이다.

Wrap Up 1

G: I feel hungry.

B: I'll make *ramyeon* for you.

G: ❶How nice!

B: Do you want me to ❷add an egg?

G: ❸That'd be great.

❶ 'How nice you are!'의 줄임말이다.
❷ add: 더하다
❸ That's good! 또는 'Sounds great.' 등으로 바꾸어 말할 수 있다.

Wrap Up 2

G: Dad, look at ❶that cute bag. I wonder ❷how much it is.

M: ❸Why don't we go in and check?

G: Really? Thanks, Dad.

M: I didn't say I will buy ❹it for you. We're just asking the price.

G: Of course.

❶ 지시형용사로 사용되었다.
❷ 간접의문문 어순으로 '의문사+주어+동사' 순서로 이어진다.
❸ 들어가서 확인해 볼 것을 제안하는 표현으로 'How[What] about going in and checking?' 또는 'Let's go in and check.'로 바꾸어 쓸 수 있다.
❹ it은 the cute bag을 가리킨다.

● 다음 우리말과 일치하도록 빈칸에 알맞은 말을 쓰시오.

Listen – Listen & Answer Dialog 1

M: _____ _____ the Tourist Information Office! How may I _____ you?

W: Hi, I wonder _____ there's a _____ _____ of the town.

M: Sure. _____ _____ a special place you're _____ _____?

W: Yes. I'd _____ _____ _____ some _____ food.

M: Then go to Jeongseon Market. It opens every _____ _____, and it's _____ today.

W: I'm so _____. _____ _____ _____ _____ _____?

M: You can walk there. It _____ _____ 10 _____.

W: Great. Will you _____ the way on the map, please?

M: Sure. _____ *gondrebap* _____ you _____ there.

Listen – Listen & Answer Dialog 2

W: Can I have the _____, please?

M: _____ you are. Did you enjoy the _____?

W: It was great. I liked the *gondrebap* very much.

M: Thanks. It's also _____ _____ your health.

W: Oh, really?

M: Yes. *Gondre* is _____ in vitamins A and C. It also _____ well.

W: Good. I _____ _____ I could buy some *gondre* here.

M: Sure. Do you want me _____ _____ you the _____ for *gondrebap*?

W: Yes, that'd be great.

Listen More – Listen and complete

W: Excuse me. Can you _____ _____ _____ this _____?

B: Sure. What is it?

W: _____ me the date, please.

B: Oh, do you want me to tell you _____ _____ _____?

W: Yes, I forgot my _____.

B: _____ me _____. You should drink it _____ June 7.

해석

남: 관광 안내소에 오신 것을 환영합니다! 무엇을 도와드릴까요?

여: 안녕하세요, 저는 마을 관광 지도가 있는지 궁금합니다.

남: 물론이죠. 특별히 찾으시는 곳이 있나요?

여: 네. 이 지역 음식을 먹어 보고 싶어요.

남: 그렇다면 정선 시장에 가 보세요. 시장이 5일마다 열리는데, 오늘 열렸네요.

여: 제가 정말 운이 좋군요. 그곳에 어떻게 가나요?

남: 거기까지 걸어갈 수 있어요. 10분 정도 걸려요.

여: 잘됐군요. 지도에 길을 표시해 주시겠어요?

남: 물론이죠. 거기에 가면 곤드레밥을 드셔 보세요.

여: 계산서 좀 주시겠어요?

남: 여기 있습니다. 식사는 맛있게 하셨나요?

여: 아주 훌륭했어요. 저는 곤드레밥이 정말 좋았어요.

남: 고맙습니다. 그것은 건강에도 좋답니다.

여: 오, 정말이요?

남: 네. 곤드레는 비타민 A와 C가 풍부합니다. 그리고 소화도 잘돼요.

여: 그렇군요. 여기서 곤드레를 좀 살 수 있을까요?

남: 물론이죠. 제가 곤드레밥 조리법을 드릴까요?

여: 네, 그러면 정말 좋겠어요.

여: 미안하지만, 이 우유 (사는 것) 좀 도와주겠니?

남: 그럼요. 뭔데요?

여: 날짜를 좀 읽어 주렴.

남: 아, 유통 기한을 말씀드리길 원하세요?

여: 그래, 내가 안경을 두고 왔단다.

남: 잠깐만요. 6월 7일까지 드셔야 해요.

W: That's too soon. _____ _____ _____ there's one that _____ _____.

B: Wait. I found one. This _____ is good _____ _____ _____.

W: Oh, I'll take that _____. Thank you very much.

B: You're _____.

Speak – Talk in pairs. 1

A: _____ me. I _____ if there's a bank _____ _____.

B: I'm sorry, _____ we _____ _____ _____ near here.

A: That's _____ _____. Thanks.

Speak – Talk in pairs. 2

A: What's _____, Grandpa?

B: I'm _____.

A: Do you _____ _____ _____ play *baduk* _____ you?

B: That'd _____ _____. Thank you.

Wrap Up 1

G: I feel _____.

B: I'll make *ramyeon* for you.

G: _____ nice!

B: Do you _____ me _____ _____ an egg?

G: That'd be great.

Wrap Up 2

G: Dad, _____ _____ that cute bag. _____ _____ _____ _____ _____ _____ _____ _____.

M: _____ _____ we _____ _____ and _____?

G: Really? Thanks, Dad.

M: I didn't say I will _____ _____ _____ _____. We're just _____ the _____.

G: Of _____.

해석

여: 그건 너무 짧네. 기한이 더 긴 게 있는지 궁금하구나.
남: 잠깐만요. 하나 찾았어요. 이것은 6월 11일까지 드실 수 있어요.
여: 오, 그걸로 사야겠다. 정말 고맙구나.
남: 천만에요.

A: 실례합니다. 이 근처에 은행이 있는지 궁금합니다.
B: 미안하지만 이 근처에는 없어요.
A: 괜찮아요. 고맙습니다.

A: 무슨 일이세요, 할아버지?
B: 지루하구나.
A: 제가 함께 바둑을 두길 원하세요?
B: 그러면 좋겠구나. 고맙구나.

여: 나 배고파.
남: 내가 널 위해 라면을 끓여 줄게.
여: 좋아!
남: 달걀을 넣길 원하니?
여: 그러면 정말 좋겠어.

여: 아빠, 저 귀여운 가방을 보세요. 얼마인지 궁금해요.
남: 들어가서 확인해 보는 게 어떻겠니?
여: 정말요? 고마워요, 아빠.
남: 사 주겠다고는 말하지 않았단다. 그냥 가격만 물어보는 거야.
여: 물론이죠.

01 다음 대화의 빈칸에 주어진 단어를 사용하여 대답을 완성하시오.

> A: How do you want to travel? I wonder if you want to travel with friends or family.
> B: Well, _____. (friends)

➡ _____

02 다음 대화가 자연스럽게 이어지도록 순서대로 배열하시오.

> (A) Do you want me to add an egg?
> (B) How nice!
> (C) I'll make *ramyeon* for you.
> (D) I feel hungry.

> That'd be great.

➡ _____

[03~04] 다음 대화를 읽고 물음에 답하시오.

> Jane: Dad, look at ⓐthat cute bag. I wonder ⓑhow much it is.
> Dad: Why don't we go in and ⓒchecking?
> Jane: Really? Thanks, Dad.
> Dad: I didn't say I ⓓwill buy it for you. We're just ⓔasking the price.
> Jane: Of course.

03 위 대화의 밑줄 친 ⓐ~ⓔ 중 어법상 어색한 것을 찾아 바르게 고치시오.

_____ ➡ _____

04 위 대화를 읽고 대답할 수 <u>없는</u> 것은?

① What is Jane looking at?
② What does Jane want to know?
③ What does Dad suggest doing?
④ Where are Dad and Jane going to go?
⑤ How much is the cute bag?

[01~03] 다음 대화를 읽고 물음에 답하시오.

M: Welcome to the Tourist Information Office! How may I help you?

W: Hi, (a)I wonder if there's a tourist map of the town.

M: Sure. Is there a special place you're looking for?

W: Yes. I'd like to try some local food.

M: Then go to Jeongseon Market. It opens every five days, and it's open today.

W: I'm so lucky. How can I get there?

M: You can walk there. It takes about 10 minutes.

W: Great. _____(A)_____, please?

M: Sure. Try *gondrebap* when you get there.

서답형

01 위 대화의 빈칸 (A)에 들어갈 말을 주어진 어구를 배열하여 영작하시오.

> the way / the map / you / will / on / mark

➡ _____

서답형

02 위 대화에서 주어진 영영풀이가 나타내는 말을 찾아 쓰시오.

> a person who is traveling for pleasure

➡ _____

03 위 대화의 밑줄 친 (a)와 바꾸어 쓸 수 있는 것을 <u>모두</u> 고르시오.

① I'm curious whether there's a tourist map of the town.

② I believe there's a tourist map of the town.

③ I want to know if there's a tourist map of the town.

④ I doubt if there's a tourist map of the town.

⑤ I'm sure there's a tourist map of the town.

[04~05] 다음 대화를 읽고 물음에 답하시오.

W: Can I have the ___(A)___, please?

M: Here you are. Did you enjoy the meal?

W: It was great. I liked the *gondrebap* very much.

M: Thanks. It's also good for your health.

W: Oh, really?

M: Yes. *Gondre* is rich in vitamins A and C. It also digests well.

W: Good. I wonder if I could buy some *gondre* here.

M: Sure. Do you want me to give you the recipe for *gondrebap*?

W: Yes, that'd be great.

서답형

04 위 대화의 빈칸 (A)에 다음 영영풀이가 나타내는 말을 쓰시오.

> a document that shows how much you owe somebody for goods or services

➡ _____

05 위 대화의 내용과 일치하지 <u>않는</u> 것은?

① The woman asked the bill after having *gondrebap*.

② The woman was satisfied with her meal.

③ *Gondrebap* is good for the health.

④ It is easy to digest *gondre*.

⑤ The woman wants to know where to buy some *gondre*.

[06~08] 다음 대화를 읽고 물음에 답하시오.

Grandma: Excuse me. Can you help me with this milk?

Brian: Sure. What is it?

Grandma: Read me the date, please.

Brian: Oh, do you want me to tell you the best-before date?

Grandma: Yes, I forgot my glasses. ⓐ

Brian: Let me see. ⓑ

Grandma: That's too soon. I wonder if there's one that lasts longer. ⓒ

Brian: Wait. I found one. This one is good until June 11. ⓓ

Grandma: Oh, I'll take that one. Thank you very much. ⓔ

Brian: You're welcome.

 06 위 대화의 ⓐ~ⓔ 중 주어진 문장이 들어가기에 적절한 곳을 고르시오.

> You should drink it by June 7.

① ⓐ 　② ⓑ 　③ ⓒ 　④ ⓓ 　⑤ ⓔ

07 위 대화가 이루어지는 곳을 고르시오.

① Airport
② Tourist information office
③ Post office
④ Restaurant
⑤ Grocery store

 08 위 대화를 읽고 대답할 수 <u>없는</u> 것은?

① What's the matter with the grandma?
② What does the grandma want Brian to do?
③ What did the grandma forget?
④ Which milk is the grandma going to take?
⑤ What date is it today?

[09~11] 다음 대화를 읽고 물음에 답하시오.

Jane: Dad, look at that cute bag. (A)<u>I wonder how much is it.</u>

Dad: (B)<u>Why don't we go in and check?</u> (let)

Jane: Really? Thanks, Dad.

Dad: I didn't say I will buy it for you. We're just asking the price.

Jane: Of course.

서답형
09 위 대화의 밑줄 친 (A)를 어법에 맞게 고치시오.

➡ _____

서답형
10 위 대화의 밑줄 친 (B)와 의도가 같도록 주어진 어휘를 사용하여 다시 쓰시오.

➡ _____

서답형
11 What are Jane and Dad going to do together?

➡ _____

12 다음 대화가 자연스럽게 이어지도록 순서대로 배열하시오.

> W: Can I have the bill, please?
> (A) Oh, really?
> (B) It was great. I liked the *gondrebap* very much.
> (C) Here you are. Did you enjoy the meal?
> (D) Thanks. It's also good for your health.
> (E) Yes. *Gondre* is rich in vitamins A and C. It also digests well.
> W: Good. I wonder if I could buy some *gondre* here.

➡ _____

01 다음 대화의 밑줄 친 우리말을 주어진 단어를 사용하여 영작하시오.

> A: Excuse me. <u>저는 이 근처에 은행이 있는지 궁금합니다.</u> (if, wonder, around)
> B: I'm sorry, but we don't have one near here.

➡ _____

02 다음 대화를 읽고 Brian이 박물관을 방문하고 싶은 이유를 서술하시오.

> Amy: Do you want to visit museums or markets?
> Brian: I want to visit museums. It's a great way to learn about the local culture.

➡ _____

_____

[03~04] 다음 대화를 읽고 물음에 답하시오.

Grandma: Excuse me. Can you help me with this milk?

Brian: Sure. What is it?

Grandma: Read me the date, please.

Brian: Oh, do you want me to tell you the best-before date?

Grandma: Yes, I forgot my glasses.

Brian: Let me see. You should drink it by June 7.

Grandma: That's too soon. (A)<u>기한이 더 긴 게 있는지 궁금하구나.</u>

Brian: Wait. I found one. This one is good until June 11.

Grandma: Oh, I'll take that one. Thank you very much.

Brian: You're welcome.

03 위 대화의 밑줄 친 (A)의 우리말을 주어진 단어를 모두 배열하여 영작하시오.

> if / longer / that / there's / I / lasts / wonder / one

➡ _____

04 위 대화의 내용과 일치하도록 할머니가 쓴 일기의 빈칸을 완성하시오.

> Friday, June 5th, 2020.
> Today, I didn't bring (A)_____ to the grocery store. It was hard for me to read (B)_____ because it was too small. I asked a boy to tell it to me. I didn't buy the first milk that I picked up because its best-before date was too soon. Fortunately, the boy found the one that its best-before date (C)_____. I think I can finish it until (D)_____. I really appreciate him.

05 다음 대화가 자연스럽게 이어지도록 순서대로 배열하시오.

> (A) Of course.
> (B) I didn't say I will buy it for you. We're just asking the price.
> (C) Really? Thanks, Dad.
> (D) Dad, look at that cute bag. I wonder how much it is.
> (E) Why don't we go in and check?

➡ _____

Grammar

① 관계부사

> • Friday evening is the time **when** my family likes to go for a walk. 금요일 저녁은 우리 가족이 산책하기를 좋아하는 시간이다.
>
> • Lake Park is the place **where** my family likes to go for a walk. 호수 공원은 우리 가족이 산책하기를 좋아하는 장소이다.

■ 관계부사는 두 문장을 연결하는 접속사의 역할과 부사의 역할을 동시에 한다. 관계부사 앞에 오는 수식을 받는 명사를 선행사라 하고, 그 선행사에 따라 관계부사 when(시간), where(장소), why(이유), how(방법)를 쓴다.

  • Summer is a time **when** a lot of rain comes down. 여름은 비가 많이 내리는 시기이다.

  • Is this the place **where** it happened? 여기가 그 일이 일어난 장소인가요?

■ 관계부사 how는 선행사 the way와 함께 쓰지 않고 둘 중의 하나만 써야 하며 how 대신 the way that이나 the way in[by] which를 쓸 수 있다. 다른 관계부사의 경우 the time, the place, the reason과 같은 선행사가 나올 경우 선행사나 관계부사 중 하나를 생략할 수 있다.

  • He loved **the way**[또는 **how**] she smiled. (○) 그는 그녀가 미소 짓는 모습이 너무 좋았다.

  He loved the way how she smiled. (×)

■ 관계부사는 '전치사+관계대명사(which)'로 바꿔 쓸 수 있으며, which를 쓸 때는 전치사를 which 바로 앞에 쓰거나 관계사절의 끝에 쓴다.

  • This is the house **where** I was born. 이곳이 내가 태어난 집이다.
    = This is the house **in which** I was born. = This is the house **which** I was born **in**.

■ 선행사에 따른 관계부사

	선행사	관계부사	전치사+관계대명사
때	the time	when	in/on/at which
장소	the place	where	in/on/at which
이유	the reason	why	for which
방법	the way	how	in/by which

■ 주의: 관계대명사는 관계사절에서 주어나 목적어의 역할을 하므로 주어나 목적어가 빠진 불완전한 절이 나오지만 관계부사는 부사 역할을 하므로 완전한 절이 나온다.

핵심 Check

1. 다음 괄호 안에서 알맞은 말을 고르시오.

  (1) There are days (when / where) I can't do my homework.

  (2) I remember the house (when / where) I was born.

  (3) I cannot think of one reason (why / how) we should accept his proposal.

② 접속사 if/whether

- I wonder **if** they are angry. 나는 그들이 화가 났는지 궁금하다.
- Can you tell me **whether** they speak Chinese? 그들이 중국어를 할 수 있는지 내게 말해 줄래?

■ if나 whether는 '~인지 (아닌지)'라는 의미의 접속사로 어떠한 사실의 여부를 확인하거나 불확실함을 나타낼 때 쓰이며, 주로 ask, be not sure, find out, know, see, tell, wonder 등의 동사의 목적어 역할을 하는 명사절을 이끈다. if[whether] 뒤에 오는 절은 의문사가 없는 간접의문문으로 'if[whether]+주어+동사'의 어순으로 쓴다.

- I'm not sure **if** I can do it. 내가 그것을 할 수 있을지 모르겠어. 〈목적어〉
- **Whether** Jack will come or not is another matter. Jack이 올지 안 올지는 다른 문제이다. 〈주어〉
- My chief concern is **whether** or not they are alive. 나의 주요 관심사는 그들의 생사 여부다. 〈보어〉
- I wonder. + Can you help me?
  → I wonder **if** you can help me. 나를 도와주실 수 있는지 궁금하네요.

■ if가 명사절을 이끄는 접속사로 그 명사절이 문장 내에서 동사의 목적어로 쓰일 때는 whether로 바꿔 쓸 수 있다. whether가 이끄는 절이 주어 역할을 할 경우에는 if로 바꿔 쓸 수 없으며, whether 다음에는 or not을 바로 붙여 쓸 수 있지만, if는 바로 붙여 쓸 수 없다.

- I can't tell **if** he is happy or not. 그가 행복한지 아닌지 모르겠다.
  = I can't tell **whether** he is happy or not.
- **Whether** he will come or not is doubtful. 그가 올지 안 올지 의심스럽다.
  = If he will come or not is doubtful. (×)
- I was anxious about **whether** or not I would fail the exam. 나는 시험에 떨어질까봐 마음을 졸였다.
  = I was anxious about if or not I would fail the exam. (×)

cf. 보통 if가 조건의 부사절을 이끌 때는 '만약 ~라면'이라는 의미로 쓰이며, whether가 부사절을 이끌 경우에는 '~이든 (아니든)'이라는 '양보'의 의미로 쓰인다.

- Is it OK **if** I leave now? 제가 지금 떠나도 될까요? 〈조건〉
- **Whether** or not we're successful, we will do our best. 우리가 성공을 하든 못 하든, 우리는 최선을 다할 것이다. 〈양보〉

핵심 Check

2. 다음 빈칸에 들어갈 말을 〈보기〉에서 골라 쓰시오.

┤ 보기 ├

whether   if   that

(1) She asked me _____ I was alright.

(2) I wasn't sure _____ I could handle such a powerful car.

(3) It's questionable _____ or not the news is true.

01 다음 빈칸에 들어갈 말로 알맞은 것은?

> I remember the day _____ I got my first cell phone.

① when   ② where   ③ why
④ how   ⑤ which

02 다음 괄호 안에서 알맞은 말을 고르시오.

(1) This is the library (when / where) I met her for the first time.
(2) The day (when / where) I start for my journey is drawing near.
(3) Nick wonders (if / that) she likes roses.
(4) The question arises as to (if / whether) or not he knew about the situation.

03 다음 빈칸에 들어갈 말로 알맞은 것은?

> Tell us _____ you know the answer.

① that   ② what   ③ which
④ if   ⑤ unless

04 다음 우리말에 맞게 주어진 어휘를 바르게 배열하시오.

(1) 네가 늦은 이유를 내게 말해.
(the reason, you, me, late, tell, were, why)
➡ _____

(2) 그는 자신이 도울 수 있는지를 물었다.
(he, he, could, asked, help, whether)
➡ _____

(3) 그분이 지금 시간이 있는지 알아봐 주시겠어요?
(he, you, available, find, can, is, now, if, out)
➡ _____

01 다음 중 어법상 어색한 것은?

① This is the town where I was born.

② Can you tell me the reason how he got angry?

③ He cares for the children on the days when he's not working.

④ I remember the restaurant where I met her first.

⑤ Winter is the season when it snows.

02 다음 중 어법상 바르지 않은 것은?

① Thanks for your suggestion, but I'm not sure if it's realistic.

② Food will last longer if it is kept in an airtight container.

③ I asked her if she wanted to join my birthday party.

④ I asked her that she wanted to marry me, but she wouldn't answer.

⑤ Every child needs to know that he is loved.

03 다음 빈칸에 알맞은 말이 바르게 짝지어진 것은?

> • I wonder _____ he can help me.
> • May 5 is the day _____ I visit the children's home in my neighborhood with my parents.

① if – when

② that – when

③ if – where

④ that – where

⑤ whether – how

서답형

04 다음 괄호 안에서 알맞은 말을 고르시오.

(1) Penguin Snack is the place (when / where) I like to go with my friends.

(2) Do you know the reason (how / why) she didn't come?

(3) Shirley will go to the restaurant (which / where) she can have delicious *samgyupsal* with her friends.

(4) I asked her (whether / that) she was ready to go.

(5) She asked me (if / that) I would be able to finish my work.

(6) Decide (whether / if) or not you're going to continue the job.

05 주어진 두 문장을 한 문장으로 바꿀 때 옳지 않은 것은?

> • This is the way.
> • I solved the math problem in the way.

① This is how I solved the math problem.

② This is the way I solved the math problem.

③ This is the way in which I solved the math problem.

④ This is the way that I solved the math problem.

⑤ This is the way how I solved the math problem.

06 빈칸 (A)와 (B)에 알맞은 것으로 바르게 짝지어진 것은?

> • I wonder ___(A)___ Jane can come to the party.
> • I want you to tell me ___(B)___ or not he is a good person.

	(A)	(B)
①	whether	if
②	that	if
③	if	whether
④	that	whether
⑤	if	that

07 다음 문장의 밑줄 친 부분 중 어법상 어색한 것은?

> I ⓐhave been ⓑto ⓒthe house ⓓwhen Mozart ⓔwas born.

① ⓐ   ② ⓑ   ③ ⓒ   ④ ⓓ   ⑤ ⓔ

08 다음 밑줄 친 부분과 바꿔 쓸 수 있는 것은?

> She asked me if I would give her English lessons.

① unless   ② that
③ what   ④ which
⑤ whether

서답형

09 다음 두 문장을 한 문장으로 바꿔 쓸 때 빈칸에 들어갈 알맞은 말을 쓰시오.

> • This is a country.
> • Trading on boats has a long history in this country.
> ➡ This is a country _____ trading on boats has a long history.

10 밑줄 친 부분의 쓰임이 주어진 문장과 같은 것은?

> Apr. 26 is the day when I confessed my love to her.

① When did you last see him?
② Do you remember the moment when you decided to become a singer?
③ I loved history when I was a student.
④ I was standing there lost in thought when I was called from behind.
⑤ I will contact you later to advise you when to come.

11 다음 우리말을 바르게 영작한 것을 고르시오.

> 오늘 밤에 비가 올지 안 올지 확실하지 않다.

① It is not certain whether it will rain tonight or not.
② It is certain whether it will not rain tonight or not.
③ It is not certain that it will rain tonight or not.
④ It is certain because it will not rain tonight.
⑤ It is not certain if or not it will rain tonight.

서답형

12 다음 문장에서 생략할 수 있는 것을 찾아 쓰시오.

(1) This is the time when the government should take action.
➡ _____

(2) I'd like to know the reason why you're so late.
➡ _____

13 주어진 문장의 틀린 부분을 찾아, 올바르게 고치지 <u>않은</u> 것을 고르시오.

> He didn't know that he could win the race or not.

① He didn't know whether he could win the race or not.

② He didn't know whether or not he could win the race.

③ He didn't know if he could win the race or not.

④ He didn't know if or not he could win the race.

⑤ He didn't know whether he could win the race.

서답형

14 다음 문장에서 어법상 <u>어색한</u> 것을 바르게 고쳐 다시 쓰시오.

(1) Sandra wonders if it is fine tomorrow.

   ➡ _____

   _____

(2) If he stays or goes doesn't matter that much.

   ➡ _____

   _____

(3) That is the place when I buy food for the coming week.

   ➡ _____

   _____

(4) The reason which he did it is complicated.

   ➡ _____

   _____

(5) The way how it was done was the best they could do at the time.

   ➡ _____

15 다음 우리말을 바르게 영작한 것을 고르시오.

> 우리는 작년에 갔던 해변에 다시는 가지 않을 것이다.

① We will never go back to the beach when we went last year.

② We will never go back to the beach why we went last year.

③ We will never go back to the beach which we went last year.

④ We will never go back to the beach which we went last year for.

⑤ We will never go back to the beach to which we went last year.

16 다음 중 어법상 <u>어색한</u> 것을 고르시오. (2개)

① I'm not sure if I'm qualified enough or not.

② They are arguing about if they should begin the project.

③ It is a place which you can experience the traditional type of house in Korea.

④ I don't understand the reason why he's gone.

⑤ The time when we can drive flying cars will come soon.

서답형

17 다음 두 문장을 한 문장으로 바꿔 쓰시오.

> • Will you tell me?
> • Do I still have a place in your heart?

   ➡ _____

   _____

01 다음 두 문장을 관계부사를 써서 한 문장으로 바꿔 쓰시오.

(1) • March 14 is the day.
   • People around the world celebrate Pi Day on the day.

   ➡ _____
   _____

(2) • School is the place.
   • I learn, eat, and have fun with my friends at the place.

   ➡ _____
   _____

(3) • Tell me the reason.
   • You were late for the reason.

   ➡ _____
   _____

(4) • This is the way.
   • He killed the big bear in the way.

   ➡ _____
   _____

02 if를 이용하여 다음 두 문장을 한 문장으로 바꿔 쓰시오.

(1) • Please let me know.
   • Is the movie fun?

   ➡ _____

(2) • Ask him.
   • Is it true?

   ➡ _____

(3) • I'm not sure.
   • Can I do this?

   ➡ _____

03 다음 우리말에 맞게 주어진 어구를 바르게 배열하시오.

(1) 내가 시험에 통과할 수 있을지 나는 잘 모르겠다. (I, I'm, the exam, if, can, sure, pass, not)

   ➡ _____
   _____

(2) 비가 곧 올 것인지는 농부들에게 중요하다. (farmers, it, whether, rain, is, will, important, soon, to)

   ➡ _____
   _____

(3) 펭귄 분식은 우리 학교 학생들이 가기 좋아하는 장소이다. (Penguin Snack, students, the place, my school, like, go, is, where, to, in)

   ➡ _____
   _____

(4) 네가 기차를 타러 가야 할 시간을 잊지 마라. (the time, the train, you, forget, leave, don't, should, when, for)

   ➡ _____
   _____

04 다음 문장에서 잘못된 것을 알맞게 고치시오.

(1) If you win the fight or not is important.

   _____ ➡ _____

(2) Decide if or not you're going to continue the job.

   _____ ➡ _____

(3) You'll have to choose if to buy it or not.

   _____ ➡ _____

05 그림을 보고 주어진 어휘를 이용하여 빈칸을 알맞게 채우시오.

(1) She wonders _____

_____. (he, help, that milk)

(2) The hair dresser asked my brother

_____.

(he, like, done)

06 알맞은 단어 하나를 추가하여 주어진 두 문장을 하나의 문장으로 쓰시오.

(1) • I'm not sure.

• I should tell you the news.

➡ _____

_____

(2) • I don't know.

• He will get better.

➡ _____

_____

(3) • Turkey is a country.

• East meets West in Turkey.

➡ _____

_____

07 다음 우리말을 괄호 안의 지시대로 영작하시오.

(1) 이곳은 Ben 삼촌이 매주 토요일에 빵을 사는 빵집이다.

➡ _____

_____ (관계부사를 써서)

➡ _____

_____ (관계대명사를 써서)

(2) 그의 행동 방식은 나를 화나게 만든다.

➡ _____

(관계부사를 생략해서)

➡ _____

(선행사를 생략해서)

➡ _____

(that을 써서)

08 다음 문장에서 어법상 어색한 것을 바르게 고쳐 다시 쓰시오.

(1) I am just considering if to go or not.

➡ _____

_____

(2) Please let me know if you are late tonight.

➡ _____

_____

(3) The way how he worked has left much to be desired.

➡ _____

_____

(4) This is the hospital which I was born.

➡ _____

_____

Reading

교과서

Leah's Travel Story

I am Leah. I have been writing a travel blog since I was 18. I go
places and share my experiences with my readers.

Must-Visit Markets Around the World   July 15, 20**

Visiting markets is a good way to learn about the culture of a country.
Markets are places where you can meet people, learn history, and
taste local food. I wonder whether there is any better way to discover
another culture.

1 Grand Bazaar, Turkey

Turkey is a country where East meets West, so it has a long tradition
of trade. It is a natural place for large markets like the Grand Bazaar.
The market was built in 1455 in Istanbul. Back then, the market had
two big buildings, and people traded goods like cloth and gold there.
Today the Grand Bazaar is much bigger, and it is the largest covered
market in the world. It has 64 streets and more than 4,000 shops under
one roof. The market attracts over 250,000 visitors every day. You can
buy almost any imaginable item there.

---

whether ~인지 아닌지

discover 발견하다, 알아내다

attract 끌어들이다, 끌어당기다

imaginable 상상할 수 있는

📎 **확인문제**

● 다음 문장이 본문의 내용과 일치하면 T, 일치하지 않으면 F를 쓰시오.

1 Leah has been writing a travel blog since she was 18. ☐

2 Visiting museums is a good way to learn about the culture of the country. ☐

3 Markets are places where you can meet people, learn history, and taste local food. ☐

4 Turkey is a country where East meets West, so it has a long tradition of art. ☐

5 The Grand Bazaar was built in 1455 in Istanbul. ☐

6 Today the Grand Bazaar is much bigger, and it is the largest outdoor market in the

   world. ☐

Extra Tip Ask shop owners if they carry *nazar boncuğu*, a traditional
_{if는 명사절을 이끄는 접속사로 '~인지 아닌지'라는 의미}   _{nazar boncuğu와 이어지는 명사구는 동격 관계}

Turkish symbol for good luck. Also, if you want a nice snack,

make sure to try *lokum*, a traditional Turkish candy.
_{반드시 (…하도록) 하라[(…을) 확실히 하라]}

2 Damnoen Saduak Floating Market, Thailand

In the past, Thai people traded goods on rivers. This was the
_{This는 앞 문장 전체 내용(과거에, 태국인들은 강 위에서 물건을 사고팔았다)을 받는 대명사}

beginning of floating markets in Thailand. With better road

transportation, many floating markets disappeared. Since the late
_{were disappeared(×)}

1960s, however, some of them have come back and kept the tradition
_{앞 문장에 언급된 '도로 교통 개선으로}   _{have come back: 재기했다. kept the tradition}

alive.
_{인해 사라진 많은 수상 시장 중 몇 개'}   _{alive: (물 위에서 무역하던) 전통을 사라지지 않게 실려왔다}
_{O.C. living(×)}

Today, one of the most popular floating markets is Damnoen Saduak

Floating Market. It is always crowded with tourists from all over the
_{Damnoen Saduak Floating Market}

world. You can buy local foods and traditional gift items directly from

boats.
_{if not: '그렇지 않다면'(If you haven't had a meal on water). if: 조건의 부사절을 이끄는 접속사}

Extra Tip I wonder if you have ever had a meal on water. If not, try
_{'~인지 아닌지'(접속사)   경험을 나타내는 현재완료}

noodles like *pad thai*. The sellers will cook them on their boats and
_{noodles like pad thai}

pass them to you with a long fishing pole.
_{noodles like pad thai}

---

carry (가게에서 물품을) 팔다

transportation 운송. 교통

disappear 사라지다

keep ~ alive ~을 존속시키다. 살려
두다

crowded with ~으로 붐비는

directly 직접

fishing pole 낚싯대

확인문제

● 다음 문장이 본문의 내용과 일치하면 T, 일치하지 않으면 F를 쓰시오.

1   *Nazar boncuğu* is a traditional Turkish symbol for good luck. ☐

2   In the past, Thai people usually traded goods on lands. ☐

3   As the road transportation got better, many floating markets disappeared. ☐

4   Since the late 1960s, some of the floating markets have come back but lost their

　　tradition. ☐

5   Damnoen Saduak Floating Market is always crowded with tourists from all over the

　　world. ☐

6   The sellers of noodles will cook them on their boats and pass them to you with their

　　hands. ☐

3 Aalsmeer Flower Market, The Netherlands

The Netherlands means "low lands." As the name suggests, about
'~하듯이'라는 의미로 부사절을 이끄는 접속사

70% of the country sits below sea level. Thus, the Dutch built up the
문장의 주어(나라의 약 70%)가 단수이므로 3인칭 단수형 동사인 sits 사용

land, and one effective way to use it was to grow flowers and sell
형용사적 용법의 to부정사   명사적 용법의 to부정사(보어)

them. It is, therefore, no surprise that the country has the largest flower
It: 가주어   that이 이끄는 절: 진주어
    It is no surprise that: '~라는 것은 놀라운 일이 아니다'

market in the world: the Aalsmeer Flower Market.

The building where the market is housed is bigger than 120 soccer
주어   선행사 The building을 수식하는 관계부사

fields. The market is busy with thousands of flower-filled carts.
명사와 과거분사가 하이픈(-)으로 연결되어 하나의 의미를 나타내는 복합 형용사

They are moved mostly by electric-powered trucks. Every day, around
flower-filled carts

20 million flowers are traded and shipped to all corners of the world.
수동태 are traded와 (are) shipped가 접속사 and로 연결되어 있음.

Extra Tip You may wonder whether you can buy just a few flowers
'~인지 아닌지'(접속사), 동사 wonder의 목적어가 되는 명사절을 이끌고 있음.

at the market. Sadly, you cannot, but you can see how wholesale
간접의문문으로 동사 see의 목적어 역할을 함.

flower trading works.
'의문사(how)+주어(wholesale flower trading)+동사(works)'의 어순에 주의한다.

---

suggest 시사하다, 암시하다

effective 효과적인, 유효한

house 거처를 제공하다

be busy with ~으로 바쁘다

mostly 대부분

wholesale 도매의

확인문제

● 다음 문장이 본문의 내용과 일치하면 T, 일치하지 <u>않으면</u> F를 쓰시오.

1　About 70% of the Netherlands is situated below sea level. ☐

2　It is surprising that the Netherlands has the largest flower market in the world. ☐

3　The building where the Aalsmeer Flower Market is housed is bigger than 120 soccer fields. ☐

4　The Aalsmeer Flower Market is busy with hundreds of flower-filled carts. ☐

5　Every day, around 20 million flowers are traded and shipped to all corners of the world at the Aalsmeer Flower Market. ☐

6　You can buy only a few flowers at the Aalsmeer Flower Market. ☐

• 우리말을 참고하여 빈칸에 알맞은 말을 쓰시오.

1   Leah's _____ Story

2   _____ _____ Leah.

3   I _____ _____ _____ a travel blog since I was 18.

4   I go places and _____ my experiences _____ my readers.

5   _____ **Markets Around the World**

6   _____ 15, 20**

7   _____ _____ is a good way to learn about the culture of a country.

8   Markets are _____ _____ you can meet people, learn history, and taste local food.

9   I _____ _____ there is any better way _____ _____ another culture.

10   **1 _____ _____, Turkey**

11   Turkey is a country _____ East meets West, so it has a _____ _____ _____ _____.

12   It is _____ _____ large markets _____ the Grand Bazaar.

13   The market _____ _____ in 1455 in Istanbul.

14   Back then, the market had two big buildings, and people _____ _____ like cloth and gold there.

---

1   Leah의 여행 이야기

2   저는 Leah입니다.

3   18세 때부터 여행 블로그를 써 왔습니다.

4   저는 여기저기 다니며 제 경험을 독자들과 공유하고 있습니다.

5   꼭 방문해야 할 세계의 시장들

6   20**년 7월 15일

7   시장 방문은 한 나라의 문화에 대해 배우는 좋은 방법입니다.

8   시장은 사람들을 만나고, 역사를 배우고, 또 지역 음식을 맛볼 수 있는 장소입니다.

9   다른 문화를 발견하는 데에 더 좋은 방법이 있을지 모르겠습니다.

10   1 터키의 Grand Bazaar(그랜드 바자)

11   터키는 동양과 서양이 만나는 나라이고, 그래서 오랜 교역의 전통을 가지고 있습니다.

12   터키는 Grand Bazaar 같은 대형 시장이 생겨나기에 자연스러운 곳입니다.

13   Grand Bazaar는 1455년 이스탄불에 지어졌습니다.

14   그 당시에 이 시장에는 큰 건물이 두 개 있었고, 거기서 사람들은 직물이나 금 같은 물건을 교환했습니다.

15 Today the Grand Bazaar is _____ bigger, and it is the _____ _____ _____ in the world.

16 It has 64 streets and more than 4,000 shops _____ _____ .

17 The market _____ over 250,000 visitors every day.

18 You can buy _____ _____ _____ item there.

19 **Extra Tip** Ask shop owners _____ they carry *nazar boncuğu*, a _____ _____ _____ for good luck.

20 Also, if you want a nice snack, make sure to try *lokum*, a _____ _____ _____ .

21 **2 Damnoen Saduak _____ Market, Thailand**

22 In the past, Thai people _____ _____ on rivers.

23 This was the _____ _____ _____ _____ in Thailand.

24 _____ _____ _____ _____ , many floating markets disappeared.

25 Since the late 1960s, however, some of them _____ _____ and kept the tradition _____ .

26 Today, one of the most popular floating _____ _____ Damnoen Saduak Floating Market.

27 It is always _____ _____ tourists from all over the world.

28 You can buy local foods and traditional gift items _____ _____ _____ .

15	오늘날 Grand Bazaar는 훨씬 크고, 세계에서 가장 큰 지붕이 덮인 시장입니다.
16	64개의 거리와 4,000개 이상의 상점이 한 지붕 아래에 있습니다.
17	그 시장은 매일 25만 명 이상의 방문객을 불러 모읍니다.
18	그곳에서는 상상할 수 있는 거의 모든 물건을 살 수 있습니다.
19	추가 정보 가게 주인에게 행운을 기원하는 터키 전통 상징인 'nazar boncuğu(나자르 본주)'를 파는지 물어보세요.
20	또한, 만약 맛있는 간식을 원한다면, 터키 전통 사탕인 'lokum(로쿰)'을 꼭 드셔 보세요.
21	2 태국의 Damnoen Saduak(담는 사두악) 수상 시장
22	과거에 태국 사람들은 강에서 물건을 교환했습니다.
23	이것이 태국 수상 시장의 시작이었습니다.
24	도로 교통이 개선되면서, 많은 수상 시장이 사라졌습니다.
25	그러나 1960년대 후반부터 일부가 다시 생겨나 전통을 이어가고 있습니다.
26	오늘날, 가장 인기 있는 수상 시장 중 하나는 Damnoen Saduak 수상 시장입니다.
27	그곳은 전 세계에서 온 관광객들로 항상 붐빕니다.
28	배에서 직접 현지 음식과 전통 선물을 살 수 있습니다.

29 **Extra Tip** I _____ _____ you have ever had a meal on water.

30 _____ _____, try noodles like *pad thai*.

31 The sellers will cook them on their boats and pass them to you

_____ _____ _____ _____.

32 **3 Aalsmeer Flower Market,** _____ _____

33 The Netherlands means " _____ _____."

34 _____ the name _____, about 70% of the country sits

_____ _____ _____.

35 _____, the Dutch built up the land, and one effective way to use

it was _____ _____ flowers and sell them.

36 It is, _____, _____ _____ that the country has the largest

flower market in the world: the Aalsmeer Flower Market.

37 The building _____ the market _____ _____ is bigger

than 120 soccer fields.

38 The market is busy with thousands of _____ carts.

39 They are _____ mostly by electric-powered trucks.

40 Every day, _____ _____ _____ flowers are traded and

shipped to all _____ of the world.

41 **Extra Tip** You may wonder _____ you can buy _____

_____ _____ flowers at the market.

42 Sadly, you cannot, but you can see _____ _____

_____ _____.

29 추가 정보 여러분이 물 위에서 식사해 본 적이 있는지 궁금하네요.

30 만약 그렇지 않다면, 'pad thai(팟 타이)' 같은 면 요리를 드셔 보세요.

31 상인들이 배에서 음식을 만들어 긴 낚싯대로 건네줄 겁니다.

32 3 네덜란드 Aalsmeer(알스메이르) 꽃 시장

33 네덜란드는 '저지대'라는 뜻입니다.

34 이름에서 알 수 있듯이, 이 나라의 약 70%가 해수면보다 낮습니다.

35 그래서 네덜란드 사람들은 땅을 지어 올렸고, 그것을 사용하는 효과적인 방법은 꽃을 재배하고 파는 것이었습니다.

36 그러므로 네덜란드에 세계에서 가장 큰 꽃 시장인 Aalsmeer 꽃 시장이 있다는 것은 놀라운 일이 아닙니다.

37 시장이 들어선 건물은 축구장 120개보다 큽니다.

38 시장은 꽃이 가득 든 수천 개의 수레로 분주합니다.

39 수레는 대부분 전동 트럭에 의해 움직입니다.

40 매일, 약 2천만 송이의 꽃이 거래되어 세계 각지로 운송됩니다.

41 추가 정보 시장에서 꽃을 조금 살 수 있는지 궁금할 겁니다.

42 애석하게도 안 되지만, 꽃이 도매로 어떻게 거래되는지를 볼 수 있습니다.

● 우리말을 참고하여 본문을 영작하시오.

1 Leah의 여행 이야기

➡ _____

2 저는 Leah입니다.

➡ _____

3 18세 때부터 여행 블로그를 써 왔습니다.

➡ _____

4 저는 여기저기 다니며 제 경험을 독자들과 공유하고 있습니다.

➡ _____

5 꼭 방문해야 할 세계의 시장들

➡ _____

6 20**년 7월 15일

➡ _____

7 시장 방문은 한 나라의 문화에 대해 배우는 좋은 방법입니다.

➡ _____

8 시장은 사람들을 만나고, 역사를 배우고, 또 지역 음식을 맛볼 수 있는 장소입니다.

➡ _____

9 다른 문화를 발견하는 데에 더 좋은 방법이 있을지 모르겠습니다.

➡ _____

10 1 터키의 Grand Bazaar(그랜드 바자)

➡ _____

11 터키는 동양과 서양이 만나는 나라이고, 그래서 오랜 교역의 전통을 가지고 있습니다.

➡ _____

12 터키는 Grand Bazaar 같은 대형 시장이 생겨나기에 자연스러운 곳입니다.

➡ _____

13 Grand Bazaar는 1455년 이스탄불에 지어졌습니다.

➡ _____

14 그 당시에 이 시장에는 큰 건물이 두 개 있었고, 거기서 사람들은 직물이나 금 같은 물건을
교환했습니다.

➡ _____

15 오늘날 Grand Bazaar는 훨씬 크고, 세계에서 가장 큰 지붕이 덮인 시장입니다.

➡ _____

16 64개의 거리와 4,000개 이상의 상점이 한 지붕 아래에 있습니다.

➡ _____

17 그 시장은 매일 25만 명 이상의 방문객을 불러 모읍니다.

➡ _____

18 그곳에서는 상상할 수 있는 거의 모든 물건을 살 수 있습니다.

➡ _____

19 추가 정보: 가게 주인에게 행운을 기원하는 터키 전통 상징인 'nazar boncuğu(나자르 본주)'를 파는지 물어보세요.

➡ _____

20 또한, 만약 맛있는 간식을 원한다면, 터키 전통 사탕인 'lokum(로쿰)'을 꼭 드셔 보세요.

➡ _____

21 2 태국의 Damnoen Saduak(담는 사두악) 수상 시장

➡ _____

22 과거에 태국 사람들은 강에서 물건을 교환했습니다.

➡ _____

23 이것이 태국 수상 시장의 시작이었습니다.

➡ _____

24 도로 교통이 개선되면서, 많은 수상 시장이 사라졌습니다.

➡ _____

25 그러나 1960년대 후반부터 일부가 다시 생겨나 전통을 이어 가고 있습니다.

➡ _____

26 오늘날, 가장 인기 있는 수상 시장 중 하나는 Damnoen Saduak 수상 시장입니다.

➡ _____

27 그곳은 전 세계에서 온 관광객들로 항상 붐빕니다.

➡ _____

28 배에서 직접 현지 음식과 전통 선물을 살 수 있습니다.

➡ _____

29 추가 정보: 여러분이 물 위에서 식사해 본 적이 있는지 궁금하네요.

➡ _____

30 만약 그렇지 않다면, 'pad thai(팟 타이)' 같은 면 요리를 드셔 보세요.

➡ _____

31 상인들이 배에서 음식을 만들어 긴 낚싯대로 건네줄 겁니다.

➡ _____

32 3 네덜란드 Aalsmeer(알스메이르) 꽃 시장

➡ _____

33 네덜란드는 '저지대'라는 뜻입니다.

➡ _____

34 이름에서 알 수 있듯이, 이 나라의 약 70%가 해수면보다 낮습니다.

➡ _____

35 그래서 네덜란드 사람들은 땅을 지어 올렸고, 그것을 사용하는 효과적인 방법은 꽃을 재배하고 파는 것이었습니다.

➡ _____

_____

36 그러므로 네덜란드에 세계에서 가장 큰 꽃 시장인 Aalsmeer 꽃 시장이 있다는 것은 놀라운 일이 아닙니다.

➡ _____

_____

37 시장이 들어선 건물은 축구장 120개보다 큽니다.

➡ _____

38 시장은 꽃이 가득 든 수천 개의 수레로 분주합니다.

➡ _____

39 수레는 대부분 전동 트럭에 의해 움직입니다.

➡ _____

40 매일, 약 2천만 송이의 꽃이 거래되어 세계 각지로 운송됩니다.

➡ _____

41 추가 정보: 시장에서 꽃을 조금 살 수 있는지 궁금할 겁니다.

➡ _____

42 애석하게도 안 되지만, 꽃이 도매로 어떻게 거래되는지를 볼 수 있습니다.

➡ _____

[01~03] 다음 글을 읽고 물음에 답하시오.

Must-Visit Markets Around the World

July 15, 20**

Visiting markets (A)[is / are] a good way ⓐto learn about the culture of a country. Markets are places where you can meet people, learn history, and taste local food. I wonder (B)[that / whether] there is any better way to discover (C)[another / the other] culture.

01 위 글의 괄호 (A)~(C)에서 문맥이나 어법상 알맞은 낱말을 골라 쓰시오.

➡ (A) _____ (B) _____ (C) _____

02 위 글의 종류로 알맞은 것을 고르시오.

① review   ② travel blog
③ biography   ④ summary
⑤ book report

03 위 글의 밑줄 친 ⓐto learn과 to부정사의 용법이 같은 것을 모두 고르시오.

① It is about time for you to learn English.
② Can you tell me how to learn English?
③ She is old enough to learn ballet.
④ He is not a man to learn from his mistakes.
⑤ English is hard to learn.

[04~06] 다음 글을 읽고 물음에 답하시오.

1 Grand Bazaar, Turkey

Turkey is a country where East meets West,

so it has a long tradition of trade. (①) The market was built in 1455 in Istanbul. (②) Back then, the market had two big buildings, and people traded goods like cloth and gold there. (③)

Today the Grand Bazaar is ⓐmuch bigger, and it is the largest covered market in the world. (④) It has 64 streets and more than 4,000 shops under one roof. (⑤) The market attracts over 250,000 visitors every day. You can buy almost any imaginable item there.

04 위 글의 밑줄 친 ⓐmuch와 바꿔 쓸 수 없는 말을 고르시오.

① still   ② more   ③ even
④ a lot   ⑤ far

05 위 글의 흐름으로 보아, 주어진 문장이 들어가기에 가장 적절한 곳은?

> It is a natural place for large markets like the Grand Bazaar.

①   ②   ③   ④   ⑤

06 According to the passage, which is NOT true?

① Turkey has a long tradition of trade because it is a country in which East meets West.
② The Grand Bazaar was built in 1455 in Istanbul.
③ At that time when it was built, the Grand Bazaar had two big buildings.
④ Today the Grand Bazaar is the largest outdoor market in the world.
⑤ The Grand Bazaar attracts over 250,000 visitors every day.

[07~09] 다음 글을 읽고 물음에 답하시오.

2 Damnoen Saduak Floating Market, Thailand

In the past, Thai people traded goods on rivers. This was the beginning of floating markets in Thailand. With better road transportation, many floating markets disappeared. Since the late 1960s, however, some of (A)them have come back and kept the tradition alive.

Today, one of the most popular floating markets is Damnoen Saduak Floating Market. It is always crowded ___ⓐ___ tourists from all over the world. You can buy local foods and traditional gift items directly ___ⓑ___ boats.

07 위 글의 빈칸 ⓐ와 ⓑ에 들어갈 전치사가 바르게 짝지어진 것은?

	ⓐ	ⓑ			ⓐ	ⓑ
①	at – in		②	with – from
③	at – from		④	by – for
⑤	with – for			

08 다음 빈칸에 위 글의 밑줄 친 (A)them이 가리키는 것을 쓰시오.

➡ the _____ _____ that disappeared

위 글의 주제로 알맞은 것을 고르시오.

① the beginning of floating markets in Thailand

② the disappearance of many floating markets

③ the comeback of some floating markets in Thailand and the revival of the tradition

④ the most famous tourist attraction in Thailand

⑤ how to buy local foods and traditional gift items in Thailand

[10~13] 다음 글을 읽고 물음에 답하시오.

3 Aalsmeer Flower Market, The Netherlands

The Netherlands means "low lands." (A)As the name suggests, about 70% of the country sits below sea level. (①) Thus, the ___ⓐ___ built up the land, and one effective way to use it was to grow flowers and sell them. (②) The building where the market is housed is bigger than 120 soccer fields. (③) The market is busy with thousands of flower-filled carts. (④) They are moved mostly by electric-powered trucks. (⑤) Every day, around 20 million flowers are traded and shipped to all corners of the world.

10 위 글의 빈칸 ⓐ에 d로 시작하는 말을 쓰시오.

➡ _____

11 위 글의 밑줄 친 (A)As와 같은 의미로 쓰인 것을 고르시오.

① As one grows older, one becomes more silent.

② As the door was open, I could see the inside.

③ Her anger grew as she talked.

④ As he is honest, he is trusted by everyone.

⑤ As the proverb says, a little learning is a dangerous thing.

위 글의 흐름으로 보아, 주어진 문장이 들어가기에 가장 적절한 곳은?

> It is, therefore, no surprise that the country has the largest flower market in the world: the Aalsmeer Flower Market.

①   ②   ③   ④   ⑤

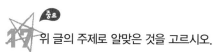

13 위 글의 네덜란드의 사례에 어울리는 속담으로 가장 알맞은 것을 고르시오.

① Prevention is better than cure.
② Haste makes waste.
③ If life gives you a lemon, make lemonade.
④ It never rains but it pours.
⑤ Many hands make light work.

[14~17] 다음 글을 읽고 물음에 답하시오.

1 Grand Bazaar, Turkey

Turkey is a country ⓐ East meets West, so it has a long tradition of trade. ⓑIt is a natural place for large markets like the Grand Bazaar. The market was built in ①1455 in Istanbul. Back then, the market had two big buildings, and people traded goods ②like cloth and gold there.

Today the Grand Bazaar is much bigger, and it is the largest covered market in the world. It has ③64 streets and more than ④4,000 shops under one roof. The market attracts over ⑤250,000 visitors every day. You can buy almost any imaginable item there.

14 위 글의 빈칸 ⓐ에 들어갈 알맞은 말을 모두 고르시오.

① for which   ② where   ③ when
④ which   ⑤ in which

서답형
15 위 글의 밑줄 친 ⓑIt이 가리키는 것을 본문에서 찾아 쓰시오.

➡ _____

16 다음 중 위 글의 밑줄 친 ①~⑤에 대한 설명이 옳지 않은 것을 고르시오.

① fourteen fifty-five로 읽는다.
② such as로 바꿔 쓸 수 있다.
③ sixty-four로 읽는다.
④ four thousands로 읽는다.
⑤ two hundred and fifty thousand로 읽는다.

17 위 글의 주제로 알맞은 것을 고르시오.

① Thanks to its location, Turkey has various cultures.
② People built the Grand Bazaar in Istanbul.
③ The location of Turkey led to the birth of the Grand Bazaar.
④ Today the Grand Bazaar is much bigger than before.
⑤ The Grand Bazaar is an ideal place for shopping.

[18~19] 다음 글을 읽고 물음에 답하시오.

2 Damnoen Saduak Floating Market, Thailand

In the past, Thai people traded goods on rivers. This was the beginning of floating markets in Thailand. With better road transportation, many floating markets disappeared. Since the late 1960s, ⓐ , some of them have come back and kept the tradition alive.

18 위 글의 빈칸 ⓐ에 들어갈 알맞은 말을 고르시오.

① for example   ② in addition
③ however   ④ as a result
⑤ that is

서답형
19 Why did many floating markets disappear? Fill in the blanks with suitable words.

> As the _____ _____ got better, many of them disappeared.

[20~22] 다음 글을 읽고 물음에 답하시오.

2 Damnoen Saduak Floating Market, Thailand
 Today, ⓐ가장 인기 있는 수상 시장 중 하나는 Damnoen Saduak 수상 시장입니다. It is always crowded with tourists from all over the world. You can buy local foods and traditional gift items directly from boats.

Extra Tip I wonder if you ⓑhave ever had a meal on water. If not, try noodles like *pad thai*. The sellers will cook them on their boats and pass them to you with a long fishing pole.

서답형
20 위 글의 밑줄 친 ⓐ의 우리말에 맞게 주어진 어휘를 이용하여 12 단어로 영작하시오.

> floating, Damnoen Saduak Floating Market

➡ _____

_____

21 위 글의 밑줄 친 ⓑ의 현재완료와 용법이 같은 것을 모두 고르시오.

① How many times has she eaten *pad thai*?
② I have just finished reading the book.
③ How long have you studied English?
④ I have never visited New York.
⑤ We have lived in this house for 10 years.

중요
22 Which question CANNOT be answered after reading the passage?

① What is Damnoen Saduak Floating Market?
② When was Damnoen Saduak Floating Market developed?
③ What can you buy at Damnoen Saduak Floating Market?
④ What kind of dish is *pad thai*?
⑤ Can you buy *pad thai* without getting off your boats?

[23~25] 다음 글을 읽고 물음에 답하시오.

3 Aalsmeer Flower Market, The Netherlands
 (A)The building which the market is housed is bigger than 120 soccer fields. The market is busy with thousands of flower-filled carts. They are moved mostly by electric-powered trucks. Every day, (B)약 2천만 송이의 꽃이 거래되어 세계 각지로 운송됩니다.

Extra Tip You may wonder whether you can buy just a few flowers at the market. Sadly, you cannot, but you can see how _____ⓐ_____ flower trading works.

서답형
23 주어진 영영풀이를 참고하여 빈칸 ⓐ에 철자 w로 시작하는 단어를 쓰시오.

> the selling of goods to merchants, usually in large quantities for resale to consumers

➡ _____

서답형
24 위 글의 밑줄 친 (A)에서 어법상 틀린 부분을 찾아 고치시오.

_____ ➡ _____ 또는
_____ ➡ _____

25 위 글의 밑줄 친 (B)의 우리말에 맞게 주어진 어휘를 알맞게 배열하시오.

> shipped / around / the world / and / of / are / 20 million flowers / corners / to / traded / all

➡ _____

_____

[26~28] 다음 글을 읽고 물음에 답하시오.

2 Damnoen Saduak Floating Market, Thailand

(A)Today, one of the most popular floating markets are Damnoen Saduak Floating Market. It is always crowded with tourists ⓐ_____ all over the world. You can buy local foods and traditional gift items directly from boats.

Extra Tip I wonder if you have ever had a meal on water. If not, try noodles like *pad thai*. The sellers will cook (B)them on their boats and pass them to you ⓑ_____ a long fishing pole.

26 위 글의 빈칸 ⓐ와 ⓑ에 들어갈 전치사가 바르게 짝지어진 것은?

     ⓐ   ⓑ   ⓐ   ⓑ
① from – with   ② at – on
③ on – by   ④ from – on
⑤ at – with

27 위 글의 밑줄 친 (A)에서 어법상 틀린 부분을 찾아 고치시오.

_____ ➡ _____

28 위 글의 밑줄 친 (B)them이 가리키는 것을 본문에서 찾아 쓰시오.

➡ _____

[29~30] 다음 글을 읽고 물음에 답하시오.

3 Aalsmeer Flower Market, The Netherlands

The Netherlands means "low lands." As the name suggests, about 70% of the country sits (A)[above / below] sea level. Thus, the Dutch built up the land, and one effective way to use it was to grow flowers and sell them. It is, therefore, no surprise that the country has the largest flower market in the world: the Aalsmeer Flower Market.

The building where the market is housed is bigger than 120 soccer fields. The market is busy with (B)[thousand / thousands] of flower-filled carts. They are moved mostly by electric-powered trucks. Every day, around 20 (C)[million / millions] flowers are traded and shipped to all corners of the world.

29 위 글의 괄호 (A)~(C)에서 문맥이나 어법상 알맞은 낱말을 골라 쓰시오.

➡ (A) _____ (B) _____ (C) _____

30 위 글의 제목으로 알맞은 것을 고르시오.

① The Reason the Netherlands Means "Low Lands"
② How to Utilize Low Lands
③ Could It Be Possible? A Flower Market Bigger than 120 Soccer Fields?
④ The Netherlands Has the Largest Flower Market in the World? No Wonder!
⑤ Thousands of Carts! Don't Worry, They're Electric-powered Trucks!

[01~03] 다음 글을 읽고 물음에 답하시오.

I am Leah. I ___ⓐ___ a travel blog since I was 18. I go places and share my experiences ___ⓑ___ my readers.

Must-Visit Markets Around the World

July 15, 20**

Visiting markets is a good way to learn about the culture of a country. Markets are places where you can meet people, learn history, and taste local food. I wonder whether there is any better way to discover another culture.

01 다음 문장과 같은 뜻이 되도록 위 글의 빈칸 ⓐ에 write를 알맞은 형태로 쓰시오.

I started to write a travel blog when I was 18, and I am still writing it.

➡ _____

02 위 글의 빈칸 ⓑ에 들어갈 알맞은 전치사를 쓰시오.

➡ _____

03 본문의 내용과 일치하도록 다음 빈칸 (A)와 (B)에 알맞은 단어를 쓰시오.

Leah thinks it wouldn't be easy to find any better way to discover another culture than _____ _____ .

[04~06] 다음 글을 읽고 물음에 답하시오.

1 Grand Bazaar, Turkey

Turkey is a country where East meets West, so it has a long tradition of trade. It is a natural place for large markets like the Grand Bazaar. The market was built in 1455 in Istanbul. Back then, the market had two big buildings, and people traded goods like cloth and gold there.

Today the Grand Bazaar is much bigger, and it is the largest covered market in the world. It has 64 streets and ⓐmore than 4,000 shops under one roof. The market attracts over 250,000 visitors every day. You can buy almost any imaginable item there.

04 Why is Turkey a natural place for large markets like the Grand Bazaar? Write two reasons in English beginning with "Because".

➡ (1) _____
   (2) _____

05 위 글의 밑줄 친 ⓐmore than과 바꿔 쓸 수 있는 말을 본문에서 찾아 쓰시오.

➡ _____

06 다음 빈칸 (A)와 (B)에 알맞은 단어를 넣어 처음 지어질 당시의 Grand Bazaar에 대한 소개를 완성하시오.

It was built in the mid 15th century in Istanbul and *consisted of (A)_____ big buildings. People bought, sold, or exchanged (B)_____ such as cloth and gold at the market.

*consist of: ~으로 이루어지다[구성되다]

[07~09] 다음 글을 읽고 물음에 답하시오.

2 Damnoen Saduak Floating Market, Thailand

In the past, Thai people traded goods on rivers. This was the beginning of floating markets in Thailand. With better road transportation, many floating markets (A)[disappeared / were disappeared]. Since the late 1960s, however, some of them have come back and __ⓐ__ the tradition (B)[live / alive].

Today, one of the most popular floating markets is Damnoen Saduak Floating Market. It is always crowded with tourists from all over the world. You can buy local foods and traditional gift items (C)[directly / indirectly] from boats.

07 위 글의 빈칸 ⓐ에 keep을 알맞은 형태로 쓰시오. (한 단어)

➡ _____

08 위 글의 괄호 (A)~(C)에서 문맥이나 어법상 알맞은 낱말을 골라 쓰시오.

➡ (A) _____ (B) _____ (C) _____

09 본문의 내용과 일치하도록 다음 빈칸 (A)와 (B)에 알맞은 단어를 쓰시오.

> The (A)_____ _____ in Thailand began from the tradition that people traded goods (B)_____ _____ and today, one of the most popular floating markets is Damnoen Saduak Floating Market.

[10~11] 다음 글을 읽고 물음에 답하시오.

3 Aalsmeer Flower Market, The Netherlands

The Netherlands means "low lands." As the name suggests, about 70% of the country sits below sea level. Thus, the Dutch built up the land, and one effective way to use it was to grow flowers and sell them. It is, therefore, no surprise that the country has the largest flower market in the world: the Aalsmeer Flower Market.

The building where the market __ⓐ__ is bigger than 120 soccer fields. The market is busy with thousands of flower-filled carts. They are moved mostly by electric-powered trucks. Every day, around 20 million flowers are traded and shipped to all corners of the world.

10 위 글의 빈칸 ⓐ에 house를 알맞은 형태로 쓰시오.

➡ _____

11 Why is it no surprise that the Netherlands has the largest flower market in the world: the Aalsmeer Flower Market? Fill in the blanks (A) and (B) with suitable words.

> Because about 70% of the Netherlands is situated (A)_____ _____ _____, the Dutch built up the land. One effective way to use it was (B)_____ _____ _____ and sell them, which resulted in the largest flower market in the world.

해석

My Speaking Portfolio – Step 2

A: How do you want to travel? I wonder if you want to travel with friends or
<u>if = whether</u>　간접의문문

family.

B: Well, I want to travel with my friends.

......

A: Okay. Do you want to visit museums or markets?

B: I want to visit museums. It's a great way to learn about the local culture.
앞 문장의 내용(= To visit museums)　to부정사의 형용사적 용법

구문해설 · local: 지역의, 현지의

A: 어떻게 여행하는 것을 원하니? 나는 네가 친구들이나 가족들과 여행하는 것을 좋아하는지 궁금해.

B: 음. 나는 내 친구들과 여행하고 싶어.

A: 알겠어. 너는 박물관 또는 시장을 방문하고 싶니?

B: 나는 박물관을 가보고 싶어. 그것은 지역 문화에 대해 배우는 데 좋은 방법이야.

After You Read

This country is a place where East meets West and has a long tradition of
관계부사

trade.

This is a country where trading on boats has a long history.
관계부사
More than two-thirds of the country is below sea level.
부분을 나타내는 말이 주어일 경우 뒤에 나오는 명사의 수에 동사를 일치시킨다.

구문해설 · tradition: 전통 · sea level: 해수면

이 나라는 동양과 서양이 만나는 장소이고, 오랜 교역의 전통을 가지고 있다.

이곳은 배에서 거래하는 오랜 역사가 있는 나라이다.

그 나라의 3분의 2 이상이 해수면보다 낮다.

Wrap Up READING

Every Saturday, I go to Oakville Farmers' Market. That is the place where
선행사가 장소일 때 관계부사 where

I buy food for the coming week. There I find all kinds of fresh vegetables.
= At Oakville Farmers' Market

They are usually picked only a few hours before I buy them. I also find
= All kinds of fresh vegetables that I find there　　= all kinds of fresh vegetables

bread, meat, and home-made jam. Because I can buy the items directly from

the producers, they are usually much cheaper than at other stores. The local
= the items　　= even/still/far/a lot

farmers are always kind and ready to share gardening tips and recipes with
share A with B: A를 B와 공유하다

visitors, too. I love going to the farmers' market.
= to go

구문해설 · pick: (꽃을) 꺾다. (과일 등을) 따다 · directly: 직접적으로 · producer: 생산자
· gardening: 원예 · recipe: 조리법

토요일마다 나는 Oakville 농산물 직거래 시장에 간다. 그곳은 내가 다음 주에 먹을 음식을 사는 곳이다. 그곳에서 나는 온갖 종류의 신선한 채소를 구한다. 채소들은 대개 내가 사기 불과 몇 시간 전에 수확된 것이다. 나는 또한 빵, 고기, 그리고 집에서 만든 잼도 구한다. 물건을 생산자에게서 직접 살 수 있어서 그것들은 대개 다른 가게에서보다 훨씬 저렴하다. 지역 농부들은 항상 친절하고, 원예 정보나 조리법을 방문객들과 공유할 준비가 되어 있다. 나는 농산물 직거래 시장에 가는 것을 좋아한다.

영역별 핵심문제

01 다음 짝지어진 단어의 관계가 같도록 빈칸에 알맞은 말을 쓰시오.

> effective : ineffective = directly : _____

02 다음 영영풀이가 가리키는 것을 고르시오.

> cultural beliefs and customs passed down through generations

① tradition   ② civilization

③ taste   ④ transportation

⑤ cart

03 다음 주어진 문장의 밑줄 친 last와 같은 의미로 쓰인 것은?

> I wonder if there's milk that lasts longer.

① Who wants the last piece of pizza?

② It hardly snowed last winter.

③ I voted Tom in the last election.

④ With his last jump, he won the game.

⑤ While my strength lasts, I'll work for my students.

04 다음 문장에 공통으로 들어갈 말을 고르시오.

> • Did you _____ how your brother was in a bad mood?
> • Prices can be changed without any _____.
> • Did you _____ any changes on her face?

① pick   ② notice   ③ carry

④ discover   ⑤ suggest

05 다음 중 밑줄 친 부분의 뜻풀이가 바르지 않은 것은?

① Most teenagers think youth will last forever. (지속하다, 오래가다)

② Can you discover the secret of his magic trick? (발견하다)

③ In order to save his dog, he tried every means imaginable. (상상할 수 있는)

④ Fruit attracts flies and bugs. (끌어들이다)

⑤ The art museum is housed in an old school. (집)

06 다음 주어진 우리말과 일치하도록 주어진 어구를 알맞게 배열하시오.

(1) 우리는 마을에 두 개의 지역 신문을 갖고 있다.

(have / our / local / we / newspapers / town / two / in)

➡ _____

_____

(2) 박물관은 관광객들로 늘 붐빈다.

(with / is / always / the museum / tourists / crowded)

➡ _____

_____

(3) 교육을 위해 학생들이 소셜 미디어를 사용할 수 있는 약간의 효과적인 방법들이 있다.

(effective / can / use / for / social media / there / education / are / ways / some / students)

➡ _____

_____

07 다음 우리말에 맞게 빈칸에 알맞은 말을 쓰시오.

(1) 공원은 좋은 날씨를 즐기러 나온 사람들로 붐빈다.

➡ The park _____ people who come out to enjoy the good weather.

(2) 나의 오빠는 요즘 구직으로 바쁘다.

➡ My brother _____ his job search these days.

(3) 당근에는 비타민과 미네랄이 풍부하다.

➡ Carrots _____ vitamins and minerals.

Conversation

[08~10] 다음 대화를 읽고 물음에 답하시오.

W: Can I have the bill, please?

M: Here you are. Did you enjoy the meal? ⓐ

W: It was great. I liked the *gondrebap* very much. ⓑ

M: Thanks. It's also good for your health. ⓒ

W: Oh, really? ⓓ

M: Yes. *Gondre* is rich in vitamins A and C. ⓔ

W: Good. _____(A)_____

M: Sure. Do you want me to give you the recipe for *gondrebap*?

W: Yes, that'd be great.

08 위 대화의 ⓐ~ⓔ 중 주어진 문장이 들어가기에 적절한 곳은?

> It also digests well.

① ⓐ　　② ⓑ　　③ ⓒ　　④ ⓓ　　⑤ ⓔ

09 위 대화의 빈칸 (A)에 들어갈 말로 나머지와 의도가 다른 것은?

① I'm curious whether I could buy some *gondre* here.

② Can you tell me if I could buy some *gondre* here?

③ I wonder if I could buy some *gondre* here.

④ I want to know if I could buy some *gondre* here.

⑤ I don't have any doubt that I could buy some *gondre* here.

10 위 대화의 내용과 일치하도록 빈칸을 완성하시오.

> The woman liked the *gondrebap* very much. She heard that it is good for the health, because (A)_____ _____. In addition, she found that (B)_____. So, she decided to buy some *gondre*.

[11~13] 다음 대화를 읽고 물음에 답하시오.

Grandma: Excuse me. Can you help me with this milk?

Brian: Sure. What is it?

Grandma: Read me the date, please.

Brian: Oh, do you want me to tell you the best-before date?

Grandma: Yes, I forgot my glasses.

Brian: Let me see. You should drink it by June 7.

Grandma: That's too soon. I wonder if there's one that lasts longer.

Brian: Wait. I found one. This one is good until June 11.

Grandma: Oh, I'll take that one. Thank you very much.

Brian: You're welcome.

11 What does the grandma want Brian to do for her?

➡ _____

_____

12 Why doesn't the grandma take the first milk?

➡ _____

13 Until when should the grandma drink the milk that she took?

➡ _____

14 다음 대화가 자연스럽게 이어지도록 순서대로 배열하시오.

> M: Welcome to the Tourist Information Office! How may I help you?
> (A) I'm so lucky. Thank you.
> (B) Is there a special place you're looking for?
> (C) Yes. I'd like to try some local food.
> (D) Hi, I wonder if there's a tourist map of the town.
> (E) Then go to Jeongseon Market. It opens every five days, and it's open today.

➡ _____

Grammar

15 다음 문장 중에서 어법상 어색한 문장을 고르시오.

① Markets are places where you can meet people, learn history, and taste local food.
② Do you know the year in which the next Olympic Games take place?
③ I remember the summer when I learned water skiing.
④ This was the way I made *bibimbab*.
⑤ Do you know the reason which she left the party so early?

16 다음 밑줄 친 부분과 바꿔 쓸 수 있는 것은?

> We want to know if she is safe.

① why   ② that   ③ what
④ which   ⑤ whether

17 다음 그림을 보고 주어진 어휘를 활용하여 빈칸을 알맞게 채우시오.

Justin asked her _____.
(with him, hiking, will)

➡ _____

18 두 문장을 관계부사를 사용하여 한 문장으로 썼을 때, 빈칸의 문장을 쓰시오.

(1) May is the month.
   + _____
   → May is the month when I take the mid-term exam.
(2) Is this the store?
   + _____
   → Is this the store where you bought the shoes yesterday?
(3) Tell me the reason.
   + _____
   → Tell me the reason why she was so upset last night.

19 다음 ⓐ~ⓖ 중 어법상 옳은 것을 모두 고르시오.

ⓐ The building when the market is housed is bigger than 120 soccer fields.

ⓑ Do you remember the date where our school festival will take place?

ⓒ Computers have changed the way how people work.

ⓓ This is actually one of the reasons which I am applying to your company.

ⓔ Tell me whether ants lay eggs.

ⓕ He thought deeply if to change jobs.

ⓖ Do you want to know whether your axe is in this pond?

➡ _____

Reading

[20~22] 다음 글을 읽고 물음에 답하시오.

1 Grand Bazaar, Turkey
Extra Tip Ask shop owners ⓐif they ⓑcarry *nazar boncuğu*, a traditional Turkish symbol for good luck. Also, ⓒif you want a nice snack, ⓓ꼭 드셔 보세요 *lokum*, a traditional Turkish candy.

20 아래 〈보기〉에서 위 글의 밑줄 친 ⓐif, ⓒif와 문법적 쓰임이 같은 것을 각각 고르시오.

— 보기 —

① He couldn't tell if she was laughing or crying.

② I can come at once if necessary.

③ Give him this note if you see him.

④ Do you know if he's married?

⑤ You can stay for the weekend if you like.

➡ ⓐ와 같은 것: _____, ⓒ와 같은 것: _____

21 위 글의 밑줄 친 ⓑcarry와 같은 의미로 쓰인 것을 고르시오.

① This elevator cannot carry more than twelve persons.

② I always carry a camera.

③ Newspapers carry weather reports.

④ This shop doesn't carry clothing for men.

⑤ Metals carry heat easily.

22 위 글의 밑줄 친 ⓓ의 우리말에 맞게 주어진 어휘를 이용하여 4 단어로 영작하시오.

make, try

➡ _____

[23~24] 다음 글을 읽고 물음에 답하시오.

JJIMJILBANG Do you want to experience the real Korea? Then try a *jjimjilbang*. It is a place where you can experience a traditional Korean way to relax. It can easily be found in any big city. You can rest on a hot floor or take a nap. Also, you can read a book or chat with friends as you lie on the floor. The best food you can try here is boiled eggs. The place is easy on your wallet because it only costs about 13,000 won. It is usually open 24 hours a day.

23 위 글의 종류로 알맞은 것을 고르시오.

① essay   ② travel brochure

③ manual   ④ book report

⑤ article

24 위 글을 읽고 알 수 없는 것을 고르시오.

① 추천하는 장소   ② 추천 음식

③ 부대시설들   ④ 입장료

⑤ 운영 시간

[25~27] 다음 글을 읽고 물음에 답하시오.

2 Damnoen Saduak Floating Market, Thailand

In the past, ___ⓐ___ people traded goods on rivers. This was the beginning of floating markets in Thailand. ⓑ도로 교통이 개선되면서, 많은 수상 시장이 사라졌습니다. Since the late 1960s, however, some of them have come back and kept the tradition alive.

Today, one of the most popular floating markets is Damnoen Saduak Floating Market. It is always crowded with tourists from all over the world. You can buy local foods and traditional gift items directly from boats.

25 위 글의 빈칸 ⓐ에 Thailand를 알맞은 형태로 쓰시오.

➡ _____

26 위 글의 밑줄 친 ⓑ의 우리말에 맞게 주어진 어휘를 이용하여 8 단어로 영작하시오.

with, road transportation

➡ _____

_____

27 According to the passage, which is NOT true?

① In the past, people traded goods on rivers in Thailand.

② As the road transportation becomes better, many of the floating markets have come back in Thailand.

③ Since the late 1960s, some of the floating markets have kept the tradition of trading goods on rivers alive.

④ Damnoen Saduak Floating Market is always crowded with tourists from all over the world.

⑤ It is possible to buy local foods and traditional gift items directly from boats at Damnoen Saduak Floating Market.

[28~29] 다음 글을 읽고 물음에 답하시오.

3 Aalsmeer Flower Market, The Netherlands

The Netherlands means "low lands." As the name suggests, about 70% of the country sits below sea level. ___ⓐ___, the Dutch built up the land, and one effective way to use it was to grow flowers and sell them. It is, therefore, no surprise that the country has the largest flower market in the world: the Aalsmeer Flower Market.

The building where the market is housed is bigger than 120 soccer fields. The market is busy with thousands of flower-filled carts. They are moved mostly by electric-powered trucks. Every day, around 20 million flowers are traded and shipped to all corners of the world.

28 위 글의 빈칸 ⓐ에 알맞은 것은?

① In other words   ② Thus

③ That is   ④ However

⑤ For example

29 According to the passage, which is NOT true?

① About 70% of the Netherlands is located below sea level.

② One effective way to use the built-up land was to grow flowers and sell them.

③ It is natural that the Netherlands should have the largest flower market in the world.

④ 120 soccer fields are bigger than the building where the market is housed.

⑤ Thousands of flower-filled carts are moved mostly by electric-powered trucks.

[01~03] 다음 대화를 읽고 물음에 답하시오.

M: Welcome to the Tourist Information Office! How may I help you?

W: Hi, I wonder if there's a tourist map of the town.

M: Sure. Is there a special place you're looking for?

W: (A) Yes. I'd like to try some local food.

M: (B) Then go to Jeongseon Market. It opens every five days, and it's open today.

W: (C) I'm so lucky. How can I get there?

M: (D) It takes about 10 minutes.

W: (E) Great. Will you mark the way on the map, please?

M: Sure. Try *gondrebap* when you get there.

출제율 95%

01 위 대화의 (A)~(E) 중 주어진 문장이 들어가기에 적절한 곳은?

> You can walk there.

① (A) ② (B) ③ (C) ④ (D) ⑤ (E)

출제율 90%

02 위 대화에서 남자와 여자의 관계로 적절한 것은?

① doctor – nurse
② attendant – tourist
③ teacher – student
④ librarian – student
⑤ interviewer – reporter

출제율 100%

03 위 대화를 읽고 대답할 수 <u>없는</u> 것은?

① What is the woman looking for at the Tourist Information Office?
② What does the woman want to do?
③ Where does the man recommend to the woman?
④ How long does it take for the woman to get to Jeongseon Market?
⑤ Until what time is Jeongseon Market open?

[04~06] 다음 대화를 읽고 물음에 답하시오.

Grandma: Excuse me. Can you help me with this milk?

Brian: Sure. What is it?

Grandma: Read me the date, please.

Brian: Oh, do you want me to tell you the ____(A)____?

Grandma: Yes, I forgot my glasses.

Brian: Let me see. You should drink it by June 7.

Grandma: That's too soon. I wonder if there's one that (B)lasts longer.

Brian: Wait. I found one. This one is good until June 11.

Grandma: Oh, I'll take that one. Thank you very much.

Brian: You're welcome.

출제율 90%

04 위 대화의 빈칸 (A)에 '유통 기한'을 뜻하는 표현을 2 단어로 쓰시오.

➡ _____

출제율 95%

05 위 대화의 내용과 일치하지 <u>않는</u> 것은?

① 할머니는 Brian에게 도움을 요청하였다.
② 할머니는 안경을 잃어버려서 그것을 계속 찾고 계신다.
③ 할머니는 Brian이 우유의 유통 기한을 읽어주길 원한다.
④ 할머니는 유통 기한이 6월 7일보다 더 긴 게 있는지 궁금해 하신다.
⑤ 할머니는 유통 기한이 6월 11일까지인 우유를 사기로 하셨다.

06 위 대화의 밑줄 친 (B)와 같은 의미로 쓰인 것은?

① Last night, I saw the movie with my friend.

② I caught the last bus home.

③ This is our last bottle of water.

④ She came last in the race.

⑤ The storm lasted three days.

[07~08] 다음 대화를 읽고 물음에 답하시오.

W: Can I have the ⓐbill, please?

M: Here you are. Did you enjoy the meal?

W: It was great. I liked the *gondrebap* very much.

M: Thanks. It's also good for your ⓑhealth.

W: Oh, really?

M: Yes. *Gondre* is rich in vitamins A and C. It also ⓒdigests well.

W: Good. I ⓓwander if I could buy some *gondre* here.

M: Sure. Do you want me to give you the ⓔ recipe for *gondrebap*?

W: Yes, that'd be great.

07 위 대화의 밑줄 친 ⓐ~ⓔ 중 문맥상 어색한 것을 찾아 바르게 고치시오.

08 위 대화를 읽고 대답할 수 없는 것은?

① Where is the woman now?

② What is *gondrebap* good for?

③ Where can the woman buy *gondre*?

④ Who is going to give the recipe for *gondrebap*?

⑤ How much is the woman going to pay for *gondrebap*?

[09~10] 다음 대화를 읽고 물음에 답하시오.

Jane: Dad, look at that cute bag. I wonder how much it is.

Dad: (A)Why don't we go in and check?

Jane: Really? Thanks, Dad.

Dad: I didn't say I will buy it for you. We're just asking the price.

Jane: Of course.

09 위 대화의 밑줄 친 (A)와 바꾸어 쓰기 어색한 것은?

① How about going in and checking?

② I think we can go in and check.

③ It's not fair to go in and check.

④ Let's go in and check.

⑤ What about going in and checking?

10 위 대화의 내용과 일치하지 않는 것은?

① Jane looks at the cute bag.

② Jane wants to know the price of the bag.

③ Jane's dad suggests checking the price of the bag.

④ Jane's dad promises her to buy the bag.

⑤ Jane wants to go into the store with her dad.

11 다음 중 밑줄 친 if의 쓰임이 다른 하나는?

① I'm not sure if you're aware of that.

② I wonder if my robot can choose the best clothes for me.

③ Put your hand up if you know the answer.

④ I asked him if he wanted a watch.

⑤ Please tell me if you're coming to my show or not.

12 다음 그림을 보고 주어진 어휘를 이용하여 빈칸을 알맞게 채우시오. *출제율 95%*

Do you know _____?
(this morning, jog, or not)

➡ _____

13 다음 중 어법상 올바른 문장은? *출제율 100%*

① That's the way how the system works.
② I still remember the evening where we watched the sun go down.
③ The reason when she quit her job is not clear.
④ This is the moment at which the thing begins to move.
⑤ I'm not sure that this will be enough food for the party.

14 다음 두 문장을 관계부사를 이용하여 한 문장으로 쓰시오. *출제율 90%*

(1) • I often go to the gallery.
　 • My mother works at the gallery.
　 ➡ _____
　 　 _____

(2) • May I ask you the reason?
　 • You made that decision for the reason.
　 ➡ _____
　 　 _____

(3) • The pictures were taken on a holiday.
　 • We had a picnic together on the holiday.
　 ➡ _____
　 　 _____

[15~17] 다음 글을 읽고 물음에 답하시오.

1 Grand Bazaar, Turkey

Turkey is a country where East meets West, so it has a long tradition of trade. It is a natural place for large markets like the Grand Bazaar. The market was built in 1455 in Istanbul. Back then, the market had two big buildings, and people traded goods like cloth and gold there.

Today the Grand Bazaar is much bigger, and it is the largest covered market in the world. It has 64 streets and more than 4,000 shops under one roof. The market attracts over 250,000 visitors every day. You can buy almost any imaginable item there.

15 위 글의 제목으로 알맞은 것을 고르시오. *출제율 100%*

① In Turkey, East meets West!
② The Effect of Geographical Feature on History
③ The Culture and Economy of Turkey
④ The Grand Bazaar, a Natural Product of the Location of Turkey
⑤ The Effect of Markets on Tourism

16 What's the difference between the old Grand Bazaar and the modern Grand Bazaar? Fill in the blanks (A) and (B) with suitable words. *출제율 90%*

The number of the buildings has decreased from (A)_____ to one and the size of the market has become (B)_____ than before.

17 위 글을 읽고 예전의 Grand Bazaar에 대해 알 수 없는 것을 고르시오. *출제율 95%*

① 탄생 배경 　　　② 건설 연도
③ 위치 　　　　　④ 취급 품목의 예
⑤ 교역 규모

[18~19] 다음 글을 읽고 물음에 답하시오.

2 Damnoen Saduak Floating Market, Thailand
Today, one of the most popular floating markets is Damnoen Saduak Floating Market. It is always crowded with tourists from all over the world. You can buy local foods and traditional gift items directly from boats.

Extra Tip I wonder if you have ever had a meal on water. ⓐIf not, try noodles like *pad thai*. The sellers will cook them on their boats and pass them to you with a long ⓑfishing pole.

18 위 글의 밑줄 친 ⓐIf not에 생략된 말을 넣어 문장을 다시 쓰시오.

➡ _____

19 위 글의 밑줄 친 ⓑfishing과 문법적 쓰임이 같은 것을 모두 고르시오.

① Please smoke in the smoking room.
② Who is the man fishing over there?
③ He needed a walking stick.
④ She is wearing her dancing shoes.
⑤ I saw him fishing in the river yesterday.

[20~22] 다음 글을 읽고 물음에 답하시오.

3 Aalsmeer Flower Market, The Netherlands
The building where the market is housed is bigger than 120 soccer fields. The market is busy with (A)thousands of flower-filled carts. (B)They are moved mostly by electric-powered trucks. Every day, around 20 million flowers are traded and shipped to all corners of the world.

Extra Tip You may wonder whether you can buy just a few flowers at the market. Sadly, you cannot, but you can see _____ⓐ_____.

20 위 글의 빈칸 ⓐ에 다음 주어진 문장과 같은 의미가 되도록 쓰시오.

| How does wholesale flower trading work? |

➡ _____

21 위 글의 밑줄 친 (A)를 다음과 같이 바꿔 쓸 때 빈칸에 들어갈 알맞은 말을 두 단어로 쓰시오.

➡ thousands of carts _____ _____ flowers

22 위 글의 밑줄 친 (B)They가 가리키는 것을 본문에서 찾아 쓰시오.

➡ _____

[23~24] 다음 글을 읽고 물음에 답하시오.

Every Saturday, I go to Oakville Farmers' Market. That is the place where I buy food for the coming week. There I find all kinds of fresh vegetables. They are usually picked only a few hours before I buy them. I also find bread, meat, and home-made jam. Because I can buy the items directly from the producers, they are usually much cheaper than at other stores. The local farmers are always kind and ready to share gardening tips and recipes with visitors, too. I love going to the farmers' market.

23 다음 중 글쓴이가 Oakville 농산물 직거래 시장에서 구입하는 것이 아닌 것을 고르시오.

① 신선한 채소　　② 빵　　③ 고기
④ 꽃　　⑤ 집에서 만든 잼

24 Why can the writer buy the items at a much cheaper price at Oakville Farmers' Market than at other stores? Answer in English beginning with "Because".

➡ _____

[01~03] 다음 대화를 읽고 물음에 답하시오.

> M: Welcome to the Tourist Information Office! How may I help you?
>
> W: Hi, I wonder if there's a tourist map of the town.
>
> M: Sure. Is there a special place you're looking for?
>
> W: Yes. I'd like to try some local food.
>
> M: Then go to Jeongseon Market. It opens every five days, and it's open today.
>
> W: I'm so lucky. How can I get there?
>
> M: You can walk there. It takes about 10 minutes.
>
> W: Great. Will you mark the way on the map, please?
>
> M: Sure. Try *gondrebap* when you get there.

01 Why does the woman visit the Tourist Information Office?

➡ _____

02 How often does the market open?

➡ _____

03 What would the woman like to do?

➡ _____

04 다음 문장의 빈칸에 알맞은 말을 쓰시오.

(1) This is the park _____ I played basketball with my friends.
  = This is the park _____ _____ I played basketball with my friends.
  = This is the park _____ I played basketball with my friends _____.

(2) 1955 was the year _____ my grandpa was born.

= 1955 was the year _____ _____ my grandpa was born.

= 1955 was the year _____ my grandpa was born _____.

(3) That is the reason _____ he visited the tax office again.

= That is the reason _____ _____ he visited the tax office again.

= That is the reason _____ he visited the tax office _____ again.

05 다음 두 문장을 관계부사나 적절한 접속사를 이용하여 한 문장으로 쓰시오.

(1) • The valley was in the national park.
   • Lots of people came to the national park in summer.

➡ _____
_____

(2) • Do you want to know the reason?
   • Why is he so happy?

➡ _____
_____

(3) • I'm curious.
   • Will he tell the truth?

➡ _____
_____

06 다음 우리말을 주어진 어휘를 이용하여 영작하시오.

(1) 경찰관은 그에게 도둑을 봤는지 묻고 있다.
  (the police officer, the thief, see, asking, 11 단어)

➡ _____
_____

(2) 어린이날은 내가 많은 선물을 받았던 공휴일이다. (presents, Children's Day, the holiday, lots, got, 11 단어)

➡ _____

_____

[07~09] 다음 글을 읽고 물음에 답하시오.

1 Grand Bazaar, Turkey

Today the Grand Bazaar is much bigger, and it is the largest (A)[covering / covered] market in the world. It has 64 streets and more than 4,000 shops under one roof. The market (B)[attacks / attracts] over 250,000 visitors every day. You can buy almost any (C)[imaginable / imaginary] item there.

Extra Tip Ask shop owners if they carry *nazar boncuğu*, a traditional Turkish symbol for good luck. Also, if you want a nice snack, make sure to try *lokum*, a traditional Turkish candy.

07 위 글의 괄호 (A)~(C)에서 문맥이나 어법상 알맞은 낱말을 골라 쓰시오.

➡ (A) _____ (B) _____ (C) _____

08 다음 빈칸 (A)와 (B)에 알맞은 단어를 넣어 *nazar boncuğu* 와 *lokum*에 대한 소개를 완성하시오.

> *Nazar boncuğu* is a (A)_____ _____ for good luck and *lokum* is a (B)_____ _____ _____.

09 다음 빈칸 (A)와 (B)에 알맞은 단어를 넣어 오늘날의 Grand Bazaar에 대한 소개를 완성하시오.

> It is the (A)_____ market with a roof in the world and there are 64 streets and over 4,000 shops (B)_____ _____ _____. More than 250,000 visitors visit it every day.

[10~11] 다음 글을 읽고 물음에 답하시오.

2 Damnoen Saduak Floating Market, Thailand

In the past, Thai people traded goods on rivers. This was the beginning of floating markets in Thailand. With better road transportation, many floating markets disappeared. Since the late 1960s, however, some of them have come back and kept ⓐthe tradition alive.

Today, one of the most popular floating markets is Damnoen Saduak Floating Market. It is always crowded with tourists from all over the world. You can buy local foods and traditional gift items directly from boats.

Extra Tip I wonder if you have ever had a meal on water. If not, try noodles like *pad thai*. The sellers will cook them on their boats and pass them to you with a long fishing pole.

10 위 글의 밑줄 친 ⓐthe tradition이 가리키는 것을 본문에서 찾아 쓰시오.

➡ _____

11 How do the sellers on floating boats pass the food they cook to the customers? Answer in English beginning with "By using".

➡ _____

창의사고력 서술형 문제

01 다음 대화의 내용과 일치하도록 여자의 일기를 완성하시오.

M: Welcome to the Tourist Information Office! How may I help you?

W: Hi, I wonder if there's a tourist map of the town.

M: Sure. Is there a special place you're looking for?

W: Yes. I'd like to try some local food.

M: Then go to Jeongseon Market. It opens every five days, and it's open today.

W: I'm so lucky. How can I get there?

M: You can walk there. It takes about 10 minutes.

W: Great. Will you mark the way on the map, please?

M: Sure. Try *gondrebap* when you get there.

It was my first time to visit Jeongseon. I needed (A)_____ because I liked to try some local food, so I dropped by (B)_____. The officer was so kind that he recommended visiting (C)_____. He said it opens every five days and it was open today. Fortunately, it wasn't far from the office. It took about 10 minutes on (D)_____. I tried *gondrebap* and had wonderful time there.

02 다음 내용을 바탕으로 찜질방을 소개하는 안내문을 쓰시오.

What is the name of the place? Describe the place.
• *Jjimjilbang*: a place where you can experience a traditional Korean way to relax
What can people do there?
• rest on a hot floor or take a nap   • read a book or chat with friends as you lie on the floor
What kind of food can people try there?
• boiled eggs
Are there any extra tips?
• about 13,000 won   • open 24 hours

---

*JJIMJILBANG*__Do you want to experience the real Korea? Then try a *jjimjilbang*. It is a place where you can experience (A)_____. It can easily be found in any big city. You can (B)_____. Also, you can read a book or (C)_____. The best food you can try here is (D)_____. The place is easy on your wallet because it only costs (E)_____. It is usually open (F)_____ a day.

단원별 모의고사

1 다음 문장의 빈칸에 들어갈 말을 〈보기〉에서 골라 알맞게 쓰시오.

> ┌─ 보기 ┐
> be good for / be crowded with / take a nap / make sure to / make an appointment

(1) Please _____ clean up after using these cups.

(2) The hospital _____ patients.

(3) Vegetables _____ your health.

(4) If you don't _____, you may wait to see a doctor for a long time.

(5) Sleepy drivers need to stop along a road to _____.

2 다음 문장의 빈칸에 들어갈 말을 〈보기〉에서 골라 쓰시오.

> ┌─ 보기 ┐
> attract   translate   producers
> pick   coming   suggest

(1) The _____ always listen to the weather forecast.

(2) It will turn colder in the _____ months.

(3) Don't _____ flowers. We should protect nature.

(4) I _____ that you should replace your old computers.

(5) Can you _____ this page for me?

(6) The flowers in the garden _____ bees.

3 다음 대화의 우리말을 주어진 단어를 사용하여 영작하시오.

> A: I'm thirsty.
> B: 제가 물을 좀 가져다드리길 원하세요? (me, get)

➡ _____

4 다음 짝지어진 대화가 어색한 것을 고르시오.

① A: I'm hungry
   B: Do you want me to give you some food?

② A: Could you give me a hand?
   B: How nice! Thank you so much.

③ A: I wonder whether I can make an appointment with him at eleven.
   B: No problem. You can see him anytime after seven.

④ A: My cow is sick. I wonder if you can visit my farm now.
   B: No problem. I can go and see your cow.

⑤ A: Do you want me to give you something to drink, Jake?
   B: Sure. I'd love a milkshake.

5 다음 주어진 단어를 이용하여 영작하시오.

(1) 나는 친구들과 잡담하기 위해 SNS를 사용한다. (chat)
   ➡ _____

(2) 피곤해 보이는구나. 낮잠을 자는 게 어떠니? (why, take)
   ➡ You look tired. _____

(3) 여행과 관련하여 나와 아빠는 몇 가지 공통점을 갖고 있다. (things / in)
   ➡ When it comes to traveling, _____
   _____.

6 다음 대화의 밑줄 친 (A)를 주어진 단어를 사용하여 의미가 통하도록 다시 쓰시오.

> A: My cow is sick. (A)I wonder if you can visit my farm now. (curious)
> B: No problem. I can go and see your cow.

➡ _____

[07~09] 다음 대화를 읽고 물음에 답하시오.

W: Can I have the bill, please?

M: Here you are. Did you enjoy the meal?

W: It was great. I liked the *gondrebap* very much.

M: Thanks. It's also good for your health.

W: Oh, really?

M: Yes. *Gondre* is rich in vitamins A and C. It also digests well.

W: Good. I wonder if I could buy some *gondre* here.

M: Sure. Do you want me to give you the recipe for *gondrebap*?

W: Yes, that'd be great.

07 How did the woman like the *gondrebap*?

➡ _____

08 What does the woman want to buy?

➡ _____

09 What does *gondre* have plentifully?

➡ _____

[10~12] 다음 대화를 읽고 물음에 답하시오.

M: Welcome to the Tourist Information Office! How may I help you?

W: Hi, (A)저는 마을 관광 지도가 있는지 궁금합니다. (the town / wonder / I / there's / of / a tourist map / if)

M: Sure. Is there a special place you're looking for?

W: Yes. I'd like to try some local food.

M: Then go to Jeongseon Market. It opens every five days, and it's open today.

W: I'm so lucky. How can I get there?

M: You can walk there. It takes about 10 minutes.

W: Great. Will you (B)mark the way on the map, please?

M: Sure. Try *gondrebap* when you get there.

10 위 대화의 밑줄 친 (A)의 우리말을 주어진 어구를 모두 배열하여 영작하시오.

➡ _____

11 위 대화의 밑줄 친 (B)와 같은 의미로 쓰인 것은?

① My dog had a black <u>mark</u> on its head.

② I was sad when my teacher gave me a low <u>mark</u>.

③ Can you <u>mark</u> the message after you read it?

④ <u>Mark</u> is a smart and wise student in my class.

⑤ It is considered as a <u>mark</u> of respect.

12 위 대화의 내용과 일치하지 <u>않는</u> 것은?

① 여자는 관광 안내소를 방문하였다.

② 여자는 지역 음식을 먹고 싶어한다.

③ 정선 시장은 매달 5일에 열린다.

④ 정선 시장은 관광 안내소에서 걸어서 약 10분 정도 걸린다.

⑤ 남자는 정선 시장에서 곤드레밥을 먹어 볼 것을 추천하였다.

13 Which is grammatically WRONG?

① I want to know if there are ghosts.

② The question is whether I should go abroad or stay here.

③ Go outside and see if or not it's raining.

④ I wonder if I can find my axe.

⑤ Jack asks the waiter if he can have a milkshake.

14 다음 두 문장을 한 문장으로 바르게 바꿔 쓴 것을 고르시오.

① It is a place. + You can experience a traditional Korean way to relax there.
→ It is a place how you can experience a traditional Korean way to relax.

② I can't forget the week. + I had so many projects to do that week.
→ I can't forget the week where I had so many projects to do.

③ I don't like the way. + She laughs in the way.
→ I don't like the way how she laughs.

④ She refused to tell the reason. + She left her school for the reason.
→ She refused to tell the reason why she left her school.

⑤ My dad doesn't like the restaurant. + The service is very slow at that restaurant.
→ My dad doesn't like the restaurant which the service is very slow.

15 다음 두 문장을 한 문장으로 바꿔 쓸 때 빈칸에 알맞은 말을 쓰시오.

(1) • I am not sure.
 • Is it open on Sundays?
 → I am not sure _____
 _____ .

(2) • I wonder.
 • Is there any better way to discover another culture?
 → I wonder _____
 _____ .

(3) • This is the restaurant.
 • My parents met for the first time.
 → This is the restaurant _____
 _____ .

16 다음 문장에서 어법상 어색한 것을 바르게 고쳐 다시 쓰시오.

(1) It is not certain if they apologize when we meet again.
➡ _____
_____

(2) Can you tell me do they speak Chinese?
➡ _____
_____

(3) Please ask shop owners that they carry *nazar boncuğu*, a traditional Turkish symbol for good luck.
➡ _____
_____

(4) I know a country which people speak Portuguese.
➡ _____
_____

(5) I still remember the evening in when we watched the sun go down.
➡ _____
_____

17 어법상 올바른 문장을 모두 고르시오.

① Seollal is the holiday when I get lots of money.

② I saw my friend at the convenience store which my sister works.

③ May 5 is the day when I go hiking with my family.

④ You may wonder whether you can buy just a few flowers at the market.

⑤ I wonder if or not spiders are insects, too.

⑥ I want to know if my robot does my homework tomorrow.

⑦ The question is whether he will return on time.

[18~21] 다음 글을 읽고 물음에 답하시오.

2 Damnoen Saduak Floating Market, Thailand

In the past, Thai people traded goods on rivers. ⓐThis was the beginning of floating markets in Thailand. (①) With better road transportation, many floating markets disappeared. (②) Since the late 1960s, however, some of them ⓑhave come back and kept the tradition alive. (③)

Today, one of the most popular floating markets is Damnoen Saduak Floating Market. (④) You can buy local foods and traditional gift items directly from boats. (⑤)

18 위 글의 흐름으로 보아, 주어진 문장이 들어가기에 가장 적절한 곳은?

> It is always crowded with tourists from all over the world.

①   ②   ③   ④   ⑤

19 위 글의 밑줄 친 ⓐThis가 가리키는 내용을 우리말로 쓰시오.

➡ _____

20 아래 〈보기〉에서 위 글의 밑줄 친 ⓑhave come과 현재완료의 용법이 다른 것의 개수를 고르시오.

> ┌── 보기 ──┐
> ① Tom has just finished his homework.
> ② I haven't eaten anything since breakfast.
> ③ They have been married for 10 years.
> ④ She has lost her key.
> ⑤ I have learned French for a long time.

① 1개   ② 2개   ③ 3개   ④ 4개   ⑤ 5개

21 What is special about the Damnoen Saduak Floating Market? Fill in the blanks (A) and (B) with suitable words.

> You can not only buy local foods and traditional gift items (A)_____ _____ _____ but also eat noodles like *pad thai* without getting off your (B)_____ at the Damnoen Saduak Floating Market.

[22~24] 다음 글을 읽고 물음에 답하시오.

3 Aalsmeer Flower Market, The Netherlands

(A)[Netherlands / The Netherlands] means "low lands." As the name suggests, about 70% of the country sits below sea level. Thus, the Dutch built up the land, and one effective way to use it was ⓐto grow flowers and sell them. It is, therefore, no surprise that the country has the largest flower market in the world: the Aalsmeer Flower Market.

The building where the market is housed is bigger than 120 soccer fields. The market is busy with thousands of flower-filled carts. They are moved (B)[most / mostly] by electric-powered trucks. Every day, around 20 million flowers are traded and shipped to all corners of the world.

Extra Tip You may wonder whether you can buy just a few flowers at the market. Sadly, you cannot, but you can see how (C)[retail / wholesale] flower trading works.

22 위 글의 괄호 (A)~(C)에서 문맥이나 어법상 알맞은 낱말을 골라 쓰시오.

➡ (A) _____   (B) _____

    (C) _____

23 위 글의 밑줄 친 ⓐto grow와 to부정사의 용법이 다른 것을 <u>모두</u> 고르시오.

① Who is the right person <u>to grow</u> flowers well?

② My hobby is <u>to grow</u> flowers.

③ I was pleased <u>to grow</u> flowers well.

④ It's not easy <u>to grow</u> flowers well.

⑤ I tried <u>to grow</u> flowers in the garden.

24 위 글의 주제로 알맞은 것을 고르시오.

① the difficulty the Dutch had while building up the land

② the reason why the Aalsmeer Flower Market is the largest flower market in the world

③ the success story of changing the geographical weakness into strong point

④ the amazing size of the building where the Aalsmeer Flower Market is housed

⑤ the amount of flowers traded and shipped to all corners of the world at the Aalsmeer Flower Market every day

[25~26] 다음 글을 읽고 물음에 답하시오.

Bukchon Hanok Village

Do you want to experience the real Korea? Then, try Bukchon Hanok Village, (A)[that / which] means north village. It is a place (B)[where / which] you can experience the traditional type of house in Korea. You can rent *hanbok*, the traditional Korean clothing, for a day and take photos at 8 photo spots. It costs about 15,000 won to rent *hanbok* (C)[during / for] 4 hours. Also, you can experience a one-day traditional arts workshop or various cultural events. The best foods you can try here are *mandu* and noodles. People actually live in the neighborhood, so respect their privacy and be careful not to make noise.

25 위 글의 괄호 (A)~(C)에서 문맥이나 어법상 알맞은 낱말을 골라 쓰시오.

➡ (A) _____ (B) _____ (C) _____

26 Which question CANNOT be answered after reading the passage?

① What can you experience in Bukchon Hanok Village?

② How much does it cost to rent *hanbok* for 4 hours?

③ What's the price of experiencing a one-day traditional arts workshop or various cultural events?

④ What are the best foods you can try in Bukchon Hanok Village?

⑤ Do people actually live in the neighborhood?

MEMO

Reading for Fun 2(1)

A Slice of History

Words & Expressions

교과서

Key Words

- **agree** [əgríː] 동 동의하다
- **almost** [ɔ́ːlmoust] 부 거의
- **as** [æz] 접 ~할 때, ~하면서
- **bake** [beik] 동 (음식을) 굽다
- **bread** [bred] 명 빵
- **bring** [briŋ] 동 가지고 오다
- **busy** [bízi] 형 분주한, 바쁜
- **century** [séntʃəri] 명 세기
- **cheap** [tʃiːp] 형 값싼
- **cook** [kuk] 명 요리사
- **delicious** [dilíʃəs] 형 맛있는
- **differ** [dífər] 동 다르다
- **disagree** [dìsəgríː] 동 의견이 다르다
- **everywhere** [évriwɛər] 부 모든 곳에서
- **far** [fɑːr] 형 멀리 떨어진
- **fast-food** [fǽstfùːd] 명 패스트푸드
- **favorite** [féivərit] 형 아주 좋아하는
- **flat** [flæt] 형 납작한, 평평한
- **global** [glóubəl] 형 전 세계적인
- **healthy** [hélθi] 형 건강한
- **however** [hauévər] 부 그러나
- **introduce** [ìntrədjúːs] 동 소개하다
- **learn** [ləːrn] 동 알다, 배우다
- **meat** [miːt] 명 고기
- **move** [muːv] 동 이동하다, 움직이다

- **name** [neim] 동 이름 붙이다
- **national** [nǽʃənl] 형 국가의
- **national flag** 국기
- **onion** [ʌ́njən] 명 양파
- **quickly** [kwíkli] 부 빠르게
- **record** [rékɔːrd] 명 기록
- **restaurant** [réstərənt] 명 식당
- **share** [ʃɛər] 동 공유하다
- **shop** [ʃɑp] 명 상점
- **sick** [sik] 형 아픈
- **since** [sins] 접 ~ 이후로
- **slice** [slais] 명 (얇은) 조각
- **sell** [sel] 동 팔다
- **such** [sʌtʃ] 형 그런, ~와 같은
- **the Greeks** 그리스인들
- **the New World** 신세계
- **the Romans** 로마인들
- **the Stone Age** 석기시대
- **topping** [tápiŋ] 명 고명, 토핑
- **try** [trai] 동 맛보다
- **type** [taip] 명 유형
- **vegetable** [védʒətəbl] 명 채소
- **visit** [vízit] 동 방문하다
- **while** [hwail] 접 ~인 반면에, ~하는 동안에
- **widely** [wáidli] 부 폭넓게

Key Expressions

- **around the world** 전 세계에 걸친
- **at any time** 어느 때이든지
- **at the same time** 동시에
- **be born** 태어나다
- **be used to + 동사원형** ~하기 위하여 사용되다
- **go on to ~** (다음으로) 넘어가다
- **in most parts of** ~의 대부분 지역에서
- **in one form or another** 여러 가지 형태로
- **in time** 이윽고

- **It is believed that ~** ~라고들 믿고 있다
- **near and far** 사방, 천지
- **not ~ until** …까지 ~하지 않다
- **of course** 물론
- **on the street** 거리에서
- **outside of** ~의 바깥쪽에
- **put ~ on** ~에 올려놓다
- **so ~ that** 너무 ~해서 …한
- **topped with** ~로 덮여 있는

Word Power

※ 서로 비슷한 뜻을 가진 어휘

☐ **agree** 동의하다 : **consent** 동의하다

☐ **delicious** 맛있는 : **tasty** 맛있는

☐ **global** 전 세계적인 : **worldwide** 세계적인

☐ **almost** 거의 : **nearly** 거의

☐ **differ** 다르다 : **vary** 다르다

☐ **widely** 폭넓게 : **broadly** 폭넓게

※ 서로 반대의 뜻을 가진 어휘

☐ **agree** 동의하다 ↔ **disagree** 의견이 다르다

☐ **busy** 분주한, 바쁜 ↔ **idle** 한가한

☐ **far** 멀리 떨어진 ↔ **near** 가까운

☐ **healthy** 건강한 ↔ **ill, sick** 아픈, 병이 든

☐ **sell** 팔다 ↔ **buy** 사다

☐ **bring** 가지고 오다 ↔ **take** 가지고 가다

☐ **cheap** 값싼 ↔ **expensive** 값비싼

☐ **favorite** 좋아하는 ↔ **dislikable** 싫어하는

☐ **quickly** 빠르게 ↔ **slowly** 느리게

☐ **widely** 폭넓게 ↔ **narrowly** 협소하게

※ 동사 → 명사

☐ **agree** 동의하다 → **agreement** 동의

☐ **introduce** 소개하다 → **introduction** 소개

☐ **differ** 다르다 → **difference** 차이점

☐ **move** 이동하다 → **movement** 이동, 움직임

※ 명사 → 형용사

☐ **difference** 차이 → **different** 다른

☐ **health** 건강 → **healthy** 건강한

☐ **nation** 국가 → **national** 국가의

☐ **globe** 지구 → **global** 전 세계적인

☐ **introduction** 소개 → **introductive** 소개하는

☐ **type** 유형 → **typical** 전형적인

English Dictionary

☐ **agree** 동의하다
→ to have or express the same opinion
같은 의견을 가지거나 표현하다

☐ **bake** (음식을) 굽다
→ to cook something using dry heat, in an oven
오븐에서 열을 이용하여 음식을 조리하다

☐ **bread** 빵
→ a type of food made from flour and water that is mixed together and then baked
물과 밀가루를 섞어서 구워 만든 음식의 한 종류

☐ **century** 세기
→ a period of 100 years
100년의 기간

☐ **flag** 깃발
→ a piece of cloth with a coloured pattern or picture on it that represents a country or organization
어떤 국가나 조직을 나타내는 무늬나 그림이 있는 천 조각

☐ **global** 전 세계적인
→ affecting or including the whole world
세계 전체에 영향을 주거나 포함하는

☐ **introduce** 소개하다
→ to bring a plan, system, or product into use for the first time
처음으로 어떤 계획, 시스템 혹은 상품을 사용하다

☐ **onion** 양파
→ a round white vegetable with a brown, red, or white skin and many layers
여러 겹으로 되어 있으면서 갈색, 빨간색 또는 흰색의 껍질을 가진 둥글고 하얀 채소

☐ **slice** (얇은) 조각
→ a thin flat piece of food cut from a larger piece
큰 덩어리에서 잘라낸 얇고 납작한 음식의 한 조각

☐ **topping** 고명, 토핑
→ something you put on top of food to make it look nicer or taste better
보기 좋거나 맛을 좋게 하기 위하여 음식의 꼭대기에 올리는 것

A Slice of History

What do you like on your pizza? Though you may disagree on the
<u>What toppings</u>   '~에 대해 의견을 달리하다'
best toppings, you will agree that it is now a global food. It is sold in
= pizza   = pizza
fast-food restaurants or on the street in most parts of the world. How
has pizza become <u>such a favorite food</u> around the world?
such+a+형용사+명사

Since the Stone Age, people <u>have been eating</u> pizza in one form or
'~ 이래로'   현재완료진행형: 과거에서부터 현재까지 계속 이어지는 동작을 나타낸다.
another. Stone Age people baked flat bread on hot rocks. Records show
that the Greeks and the Romans started <u>to put</u> meat and vegetables on
= putting
flat bread. <u>It</u> is believed <u>that</u> the word "pizza" was first used in Italy
가주어   명사절(진주어)을 이끄는 접속사
<u>to name</u> the food over 1,000 years ago.
목적을 나타내는 부사적 용법의 to부정사

However, pizza with tomato toppings was <u>not</u> born <u>until</u> the 16th
'not ~ until ...': '…까지는 ~하지 않다' '…이 되어서야 비로소 ~하다'
century. There were no tomatoes in Italy before Christopher Columbus
and other Europeans brought <u>them</u> from the New World. When <u>they</u>
= tomatoes   = tomatoes
were first introduced to Europe, people thought that tomatoes would
make <u>them</u> sick. In time, people learned that tomatoes were delicious
= people
and healthy.

disagree 일치하지 않다, 의견이 다르다

topping (음식 위에 얹는) 토핑

global 세계적인

the Stone Age 석기시대

flat 납작한, 평평한

record 기록(물)

📎 **확인문제**

● 다음 문장이 본문의 내용과 일치하면 T, 일치하지 <u>않으면</u> F를 쓰시오.

1 Pizza is sold in fast-food restaurants or on the street in most parts of the world. ☐

2 Since the Stone Age, people have been eating pizza in one form. ☐

3 The Greeks and the Romans started to put meat and vegetables on flat bread. ☐

4 It is believed that the word "pizza" was first used in Greece. ☐

5 Pizza with tomato toppings was born only after the 16th century. ☐

6 When tomatoes were first introduced to Europe, people thought that tomatoes were

delicious and healthy. ☐

In the 18th century, Naples was a large city where there were many jobs. Workers from near and far came to the city, and what they needed in their busy lives was food they could eat quickly at any time. Cooks in Naples began to put tomato and other toppings on flat bread and sold slices of pizza on the street. The street food was so cheap and delicious that workers ate it for breakfast, lunch, and dinner. They could buy slices of pizza and eat them as they walked on the street. In 1830, the world's first pizza shop opened in Naples.

In 1889, Queen Margherita of Italy visited Naples and tried pizza. The type of pizza that she loved most had tomato, cheese, and green leaf toppings that showed the three colors on Italy's national flag—red, white, and green. After the queen's visit, pizza went on to become a truly national dish.

Pizza became known outside of Italy in the late 19th century, when many Italians moved to the United States. Italians brought pizza with them, and Americans loved the flat bread topped with meat and vegetables because they could eat bread, meat, and vegetables at the same time. The first pizza restaurant in the United States opened its doors in 1905.

Pizza is now enjoyed almost everywhere. Of course, toppings differ widely from place to place. Koreans love *bulgogi* on their pizza, while Russians like to have fish and onion toppings on their pizza. However, all types of pizza share two things. Each begins with flat bread, and each is a slice of history.

near and far 도처에서, 사방에서

national 국가의

top (다른 것 위에) 얹다

at the same time 동시에

differ 다르다

widely 널리, 크게

확인문제

다음 문장이 본문의 내용과 일치하면 T, 일치하지 <u>않으면</u> F를 쓰시오.

1 Cooks in Naples began to put tomato and other toppings on flat bread and sold slices of pizza on the street. ☐

2 In 1830, the world's first pizza shop opened in Naples. ☐

3 Queen Margherita of Italy visited Naples and cooked pizza in 1889. ☐

4 Pizza was introduced to England by Italian immigrants. ☐

5 In 1905, the first pizza restaurant in the United States opened its doors. ☐

6 Russians like to have meat and onion toppings on their pizza. ☐

• 우리말을 참고하여 빈칸에 알맞은 말을 쓰시오.

1 A _____ of History

2 _____ _____ _____ _____ on your pizza?

3 _____ you may _____ _____ the best toppings, you will agree that it is now a global food.

4 _____ _____ _____ in fast-food restaurants or on the street in most parts of the world.

5 How has pizza become _____ _____ _____ around the world?

6 Since the Stone Age, people _____ _____ _____ pizza in one form or another.

7 Stone Age people baked flat bread _____ _____ _____.

8 _____ _____ that the Greeks and the Romans started to put meat and vegetables on flat bread.

9 _____ _____ _____ that the word "pizza" was first used in Italy _____ _____ the food over 1,000 years ago.

10 However, pizza with tomato toppings _____ _____ _____ _____ the 16th century.

11 There were no tomatoes in Italy _____ Christopher Columbus and other Europeans _____ them _____ the New World.

12 When they were first introduced to Europe, people thought that tomatoes would _____ _____ _____.

13 _____ _____, people learned that tomatoes were delicious and healthy.

14 In the 18th century, Naples was a large city _____ there were many jobs.

15 Workers _____ _____ _____ _____ came to the city, and what they needed in their busy lives was food they could eat quickly _____ _____ _____.

1 한 조각의 역사

2 여러분은 어떤 피자 토핑을 좋아하는가?

3 비록 제일 좋아하는 피자 토핑에 대해 의견이 다를 수 있지만, 피자가 오늘날 세계적인 음식이라는 데에는 모두 동의할 것이다.

4 피자는 세계 대부분 지역의 패스트푸드 식당이나 길거리에서 팔리고 있다.

5 어떻게 해서 피자가 세계적으로 이토록 사랑받는 음식이 되었을까?

6 석기시대부터 사람들은 여러 가지 형태로 피자를 먹어 왔다.

7 석기시대 사람들은 납작한 빵을 뜨거운 돌에 구워 먹었다.

8 기록에 의하면 그리스와 로마 사람들이 납작한 빵에 고기와 채소를 얹기 시작했다.

9 '피자'라는 단어는 이러한 음식을 지칭하기 위해 약 천 년 전에 이탈리아에서 처음 사용되었다고 알려져 있다.

10 하지만 토마토 토핑을 얹은 피자는 16세기까지는 존재하지 않았다.

11 크리스토퍼 콜럼버스와 다른 유럽인들이 신세계에서 가져오기 전까지 이탈리아에는 토마토가 없었다.

12 유럽에 처음 소개되었을 때 사람들은 토마토가 사람들을 아프게 할 거라고 여겼다.

13 시간이 지나며 사람들은 토마토가 맛있고 건강에도 좋다는 것을 알게 되었다.

14 18세기에 나폴리는 다양한 직업이 존재하는 대도시였다.

15 사방에서 노동자들이 이 도시로 모여들었고, 바쁜 생활 중 그들에게 필요했던 것은 언제든지 빨리 먹을 수 있는 음식이었다.

16 Cooks in Naples began to put tomato and other toppings on flat bread and sold _____ _____ _____ on the street.

17 The street food was _____ cheap and delicious _____ workers ate it _____ breakfast, lunch, and dinner.

18 They could buy slices of pizza and eat them _____ they walked _____ _____ _____.

19 In 1830, the _____ _____ _____ _____ opened in Naples.

20 In 1889, Queen Margherita of Italy visited Naples and _____ pizza.

21 The type of pizza _____ _____ _____ had tomato, cheese, and green leaf toppings _____ _____ the three colors _____ Italy's national flag–red, white, and green.

22 After the queen's visit, pizza _____ _____ _____ a truly national dish.

23 Pizza _____ _____ outside of Italy in the late 19th century, when many Italians _____ _____ the United States.

24 Italians _____ _____ _____ _____, and Americans loved the flat bread topped with meat and vegetables because they could eat bread, meat, and vegetables _____ _____ _____.

25 The first pizza restaurant in the United States _____ _____ in 1905.

26 Pizza is now enjoyed _____ _____.

27 Of course, toppings differ widely _____ _____ _____ _____.

28 Koreans love *bulgogi* on their pizza, _____ Russians like to have fish and onion toppings on their pizza.

29 However, all types of pizza _____ _____ _____.

30 Each _____ _____ flat bread, and each is _____ _____ _____.

---

16 나폴리의 요리사들이 납작한 빵에 토마토와 다른 토핑을 얹기 시작해 길거리에서 피자 조각을 팔았다.

17 이 길거리 음식은 무척 저렴하고 맛이 좋아서, 노동자들은 이것을 아침, 점심, 저녁으로 먹었다.

18 그들은 피자 조각을 사서 길을 걸어가며 먹을 수 있었다.

19 1830년에는 세계 최초의 피자 가게가 나폴리에서 문을 열었다.

20 1889년에 이탈리아의 마르게리타 왕비가 나폴리를 방문하여 피자를 맛보았다.

21 그녀가 가장 좋아했던 피자는 이탈리아 국기의 세 가지 색깔인 빨강, 하양, 초록을 나타낸 토마토, 치즈, 녹색 잎 채소 토핑으로 된 것이었다.

22 왕비의 방문 이후로 피자는 진정한 이탈리아의 국가 음식이 되었다.

23 19세기 후반에는 피자가 이탈리아 밖으로 알려지게 되었는데, 이 시기에 많은 이탈리아 사람들이 미국으로 이주를 하였다.

24 이탈리아인들은 피자도 함께 가져갔고, 빵, 고기, 채소를 한꺼번에 먹을 수 있어서 미국인들은 고기와 채소를 얹은 이 납작한 빵을 좋아했다.

25 미국 최초의 피자 가게가 1905년에 문을 열었다.

26 오늘날 피자는 거의 어디에서나 즐길 수 있다.

27 물론, 토핑은 지역에 따라 매우 다양하다.

28 한국인은 불고기를 피자에 얹어 먹기를 좋아하고, 러시아 사람들은 생선과 양파 토핑을 좋아한다.

29 그러나 모든 종류의 피자가 두 가지 사실만큼은 똑같다.

30 모든 피자는 납작한 빵에서 시작하고, 각각은 역사의 한 조각이다.

● 우리말을 참고하여 본문을 영작하시오.

1 한 조각의 역사
➡ _____

2 여러분은 어떤 피자 토핑을 좋아하는가?
➡ _____

3 비록 제일 좋아하는 피자 토핑에 대해 의견이 다를 수 있지만, 피자가 오늘날 세계적인 음식이라는 데에는 모두 동의할 것이다.
➡ _____

4 피자는 세계 대부분 지역의 패스트푸드 식당이나 길거리에서 팔리고 있다.
➡ _____

5 어떻게 해서 피자가 세계적으로 이토록 사랑받는 음식이 되었을까?
➡ _____

6 석기시대부터 사람들은 여러 가지 형태로 피자를 먹어 왔다.
➡ _____

7 석기시대 사람들은 납작한 빵을 뜨거운 돌에 구워 먹었다.
➡ _____

8 기록에 의하면 그리스와 로마 사람들이 납작한 빵에 고기와 채소를 얹기 시작했다.
➡ _____

9 '피자'라는 단어는 이러한 음식을 지칭하기 위해 약 천 년 전에 이탈리아에서 처음 사용되었다고 알려져 있다.
➡ _____

10 하지만 토마토 토핑을 얹은 피자는 16세기까지는 존재하지 않았다.
➡ _____

11 크리스토퍼 콜럼버스와 다른 유럽인들이 신세계에서 가져오기 전까지 이탈리아에는 토마토가 없었다.
➡ _____

12 유럽에 처음 소개되었을 때 사람들은 토마토가 사람들을 아프게 할 거라고 여겼다.
➡ _____

13 시간이 지나며 사람들은 토마토가 맛있고 건강에도 좋다는 것을 알게 되었다.
➡ _____

14 18세기에 나폴리는 다양한 직업이 존재하는 대도시였다.
➡ _____

15 사방에서 노동자들이 이 도시로 모여들었고, 바쁜 생활 중 그들에게 필요했던 것은 언제든지 빨리 먹을 수 있는 음식이었다.
➡ _____
_____

16 나폴리의 요리사들이 납작한 빵에 토마토와 다른 토핑을 얹기 시작해 길거리에서 피자 조각을 팔았다.

➡ _____

17 이 길거리 음식은 무척 저렴하고 맛이 좋아서, 노동자들은 이것을 아침, 점심, 저녁으로 먹었다.

➡ _____

18 그들은 피자 조각을 사서 길을 걸어가며 먹을 수 있었다.

➡ _____

19 1830년에는 세계 최초의 피자 가게가 나폴리에서 문을 열었다.

➡ _____

20 1889년에 이탈리아의 마르게리타 왕비가 나폴리를 방문하여 피자를 맛보았다.

➡ _____

21 그녀가 가장 좋아했던 피자는 이탈리아 국기의 세 가지 색깔인 빨강, 하양, 초록을 나타낸 토마토,
치즈, 녹색 잎 채소 토핑으로 된 것이었다.

➡ _____

22 왕비의 방문 이후로 피자는 진정한 이탈리아의 국가 음식이 되었다.

➡ _____

23 19세기 후반에는 피자가 이탈리아 밖으로 알려지게 되었는데, 이 시기에 많은 이탈리아 사람들이
미국으로 이주를 하였다.

➡ _____

24 이탈리아인들은 피자도 함께 가져갔고, 빵, 고기, 채소를 한꺼번에 먹을 수 있어서 미국인들은
고기와 채소를 얹은 이 납작한 빵을 좋아했다.

➡ _____

25 미국 최초의 피자 가게가 1905년에 문을 열었다.

➡ _____

26 오늘날 피자는 거의 어디에서나 즐길 수 있다.

➡ _____

27 물론, 토핑은 지역에 따라 매우 다양하다.

➡ _____

28 한국인은 불고기를 피자에 얹어 먹기를 좋아하고, 러시아 사람들은 생선과 양파 토핑을 좋아한다.

➡ _____

29 그러나 모든 종류의 피자가 두 가지 사실만큼은 똑같다.

➡ _____

30 모든 피자는 납작한 빵에서 시작하고, 각각은 역사의 한 조각이다.

➡ _____

01 다음 짝지어진 단어의 관계가 같도록 빈칸에 알맞은 말을 쓰시오.

> appear : disappear = agree : _____

02 다음 문장의 빈칸에 들어갈 말을 〈보기〉에서 골라 쓰시오.

┌── 보기 ──┐
at the same time / Stone Age /
near and far / a slice of
└──────────┘

(1) I want to use _____ lemon for my tea.
(2) People in the _____ survived by hunting.
(3) People from _____ came to the singer's last concert.
(4) They left the room _____.

03 다음 우리말에 맞게 빈칸에 알맞은 말을 쓰시오.

(1) 그 여성은 자기 아이가 크고 납작한 빵을 먹고 있는 것을 보았다.
   ➡ The woman saw her child eating a large _____ bread.
(2) 양파는 강한 맛과 냄새를 갖고 있다.
   ➡ An _____ has a strong taste and smell.
(3) 그녀는 자기 남편이 결백하다고 진정으로 믿었다.
   ➡ She _____ believed that her husband was innocent.

04 다음 우리말을 주어진 단어를 이용하여 영작하시오.

(1) 나는 여가 시간에 보통 케이크를 굽는다. (free)
   ➡ _____
(2) 당신은 국기를 그리고 있나요? (draw, national)
   ➡ _____
(3) 우리는 여기저기서 사진을 찍었다. (place)
   ➡ _____

05 다음 두 문장을 한 문장으로 바꿔 쓰시오.

> • People started to eat pizza in the Stone Age.
> • People still are eating pizza.

➡ _____

06 다음 빈칸에 알맞은 말을 쓰시오.

> As the street food was very cheap and delicious, workers ate it for breakfast.
> = The street food was _____ cheap and delicious _____ workers ate it for breakfast

[07~08] 다음 글을 읽고 물음에 답하시오.

> What do you like on your pizza? ⓐAs you may disagree on the best toppings, you will agree that it is now a global food. It is sold in fast-food restaurants or on the street in most parts of the world. How has pizza become ⓑ그토록 좋아하는 음식 around the world?

07 위 글의 밑줄 친 ⓐ에서 흐름상 어색한 부분을 찾아 고치시오.

_____ ➡ _____

08 위 글의 밑줄 친 ⓑ의 우리말에 맞게 주어진 어휘를 알맞게 배열하시오.

favorite / a / food / such

➡ _____

[09~10] 다음 글을 읽고 물음에 답하시오.

However, ⓐpizza with tomato toppings was not born until the 16th century. There were no tomatoes in Italy before Christopher Columbus and other Europeans brought them from the New World. When they were first introduced to Europe, people thought that tomatoes would make them sick. In time, people learned that tomatoes were delicious and healthy.

09 위 글의 밑줄 친 ⓐ를 다음과 같이 바꿔 쓸 때 빈칸에 들어갈 알맞은 말을 두 단어로 쓰시오.

➡ _____ _____ the 16th century was pizza with tomato toppings born

10 In Italy, why was there no pizza with tomato toppings until the 16th century? Answer in Korean.

➡ _____

[11~12] 다음 글을 읽고 물음에 답하시오.

In 1889, Queen Margherita of Italy visited Naples and tried pizza. The type of pizza ___ⓐ___ she loved most had (A)tomato, cheese, and green leaf toppings ___ⓑ___ showed the three colors on Italy's national flag–red, white, and green. After the queen's visit, pizza went on to become a truly national dish.

11 위 글의 빈칸 ⓐ와 ⓑ에 공통으로 들어갈 알맞은 말을 쓰시오.

➡ _____

12 위 글의 밑줄 친 (A)의 토핑이 상징하는 이탈리아 국기의 색을 각각 영어로 쓰시오.

(1) tomato topping이 상징하는 색: _____
(2) cheese topping이 상징하는 색: _____
(3) green leaf topping이 상징하는 색: _____

[13~14] 다음 글을 읽고 물음에 답하시오.

Pizza became known outside of Italy in the late 19th century, when many Italians moved to the United States. Italians brought pizza with them, and Americans loved the flat bread ___ⓐ___ with meat and vegetables because they could eat bread, meat, and vegetables at the same time. The first pizza restaurant in the United States opened its doors in 1905.

Pizza is now enjoyed almost everywhere. Of course, toppings differ widely from place to place. Koreans love *bulgogi* on their pizza, while Russians like to have fish and onion toppings on their pizza. However, all types of pizza share ⓑtwo things. Each begins with flat bread, and each is a slice of history.

13 위 글의 빈칸 ⓐ에 top을 알맞은 형태로 쓰시오.

➡ _____

14 위 글의 밑줄 친 ⓑtwo things가 가리키는 것을 우리말로 쓰시오.

➡ (1) _____
   (2) _____

출제율 100%

01 다음 문장의 빈칸에 들어갈 말을 〈보기〉에서 골라 쓰시오.

┌── 보기 ──
flag flat differ national top
└──

(1) Do you want to _____ your dessert with chocolate and strawberries?

(2) Chuseok is a ___ holiday in Korea.

(3) The two sisters look alike, but they _____ in personality.

(4) The _____ is waving in the breeze.

(5) It is a wide and _____ type of Italian pasta.

출제율 95%

02 다음 영영풀이가 가리키는 것을 고르시오.

to put on the surface of something

① top   ② down
③ left   ④ right
⑤ turn

출제율 90%

03 다음 문장의 빈칸에 공통으로 들어갈 말을 고르시오.

• In old times people believed that the earth was _____.
• The woman is changing a _____ tire.
• There is a house with a _____ roof.

① flat   ② round
③ smooth   ④ sharp
⑤ global

출제율 95%

04 다음 중 밑줄 친 부분의 뜻풀이가 바르지 않은 것은?

① It is widely known that she will be the next president. 널리, 크게
② The school keeps a record of its students dating back 30 years. 기록(물)
③ Trash is one of the global issues. 세계적인
④ What toppings did you put on your ice cream? 최고, 정상
⑤ I'm afraid I have to disagree with you on that issue. 의견이 다르다

출제율 95%

05 다음 주어진 문장의 밑줄 친 record와 같은 의미로 쓰인 것은?

The records show that this movie is one of the popular genres in Korea.

① Did you remember to record the performance in the afternoon?
② The band will record their new album.
③ You should keep a record of your expenses.
④ His speech has been recorded by the tape recorder.
⑤ From now on, we'll record what you say.

출제율 85%

06 다음 우리말과 일치하도록 주어진 단어를 올바르게 배열하시오.

(1) 지금 사람들은 전 세계의 다른 토핑들을 가진 피자를 즐긴다.

(around / the / world / all / with / toppings / pizza / now / enjoy / people / different)

➡ _____
_____

(2) 방문객들이 지역 문화를 즐기기 위해 사방에서 모여들었다.

(near / to / far / came / culture / the / enjoy / from / visitors / and / local)

➡ _____

_____

출제율 90%

7 다음 빈칸에 들어갈 말의 의미가 <u>다른</u> 하나는?

① I doubt _____ he has ever given the matter a thought.

② Try this pizza and see _____ you like it.

③ Only time will tell _____ the treatment has been successful.

④ The judge must decide _____ the DNA evidence is enough.

⑤ Please let me know _____ you cannot come to the party.

출제율 100%

8 다음 중 어법상 <u>어색한</u> 것은?

① Naples was a large city where there were many jobs.

② It was in the days when medical services were rare.

③ You could tell she was foreign by the way how she dressed.

④ May I ask you the reason why you made that decision?

⑤ I always remember the moments when I was at my mother's knees.

출제율 95%

9 다음 우리말을 주어진 어휘를 활용하여 영작하시오.

(1) 그것이 내가 네게 화난 이유이다. (that, angry, the reason)

➡ _____

(2) 수요일은 내가 가장 못생겨 보이는 날이다. (look, ugly, when)

➡ _____

(3) 나는 그녀가 이 시끄러운 곳에서 잘 수 있을지 알고 싶다. (know, this noisy place)

➡ _____

_____

(4) 그는 지난 금요일 이후로 춤 연습을 하지 않고 있다. (since, practice, dance)

➡ _____

_____

(5) 그녀는 너무 배가 고파서 계속 걸을 수 없었다. (feel, keep, to)

➡ _____

(6) 그는 춤을 무척 잘 춰서 1등상을 받았다. (well, win, so)

➡ _____

출제율 95%

10 다음 중 어법상 <u>어색한</u> 것은?

① I was so hungry that I ate all the food.

② She was very kind that everyone likes her.

③ How has pizza become such a favorite food around the world?

④ It was too noisy to talk and too dark to see.

⑤ Dave said, "You are good enough to win a national championship."

출제율 95%

11 다음 빈칸에 알맞은 말을 쓰시오.

> That is the reason _____ she got angry.

➡ _____

12 다음 중 어법상 바르게 쓰인 문장은?

① This is one of the toy cars what are displayed at a toy exhibition.
② She loved the toppings that they showed the three colors on Italy's national flag.
③ She will have to take the things what he gave to her.
④ Is the new position what he is looking for in the company?
⑤ The report showed that I wanted to know.

13 다음 두 문장을 한 문장으로 바꿔 쓰시오. (관계대명사나 that 사용 금지)

(1) • I know a country.
　　• People speak Portuguese in the country.
　　➡ _____
　　_____

(2) • Scientists studied the way.
　　• Those birds could fly so high up in the sky in the way.
　　➡ _____
　　_____

(3) • We all know the reason.
　　• He failed for the reason.
　　➡ _____
　　_____

(4) • Do you remember the moment?
　　• You decided to become a singer at the moment.
　　➡ _____
　　_____

14 다음 빈칸에 들어갈 말이 바르게 짝지어진 것을 고르시오.

| Linda felt _____ nervous _____ she could barely stand on her own two feet. |

① so – that
② that – so
③ very – that
④ cnough – to
⑤ too – to

[15~16] 다음 글을 읽고 물음에 답하시오.

In 1889, Queen Margherita of Italy visited Naples and tried pizza. The type of pizza that she loved most had tomato, cheese, and green leaf toppings that showed the three colors on Italy's national flag — red, white, and green. ⓐAfter the queen's visit, pizza went on to become a truly national dish.

15 위 글의 밑줄 친 ⓐ를 다음과 같이 바꿔 쓸 때 빈칸에 들어갈 알맞은 한 단어를 쓰시오.

➡ Pizza _____ become a truly national dish until the queen's visit.

16 본문의 내용과 일치하도록 다음 빈칸에 알맞은 단어를 쓰시오. (세 단어)

| The type of pizza that Queen Margherita loved most was the pizza with tomato, cheese, and green leaf toppings that showed the three colors on _____ _____ _____ — red, white, and green. |

[17~19] 다음 글을 읽고 물음에 답하시오.

What do you like on your pizza? Though you may disagree on the best toppings, you will agree that it is now a global food. It is sold in fast-food restaurants or on the street in most parts of the world. (A)[How / What] has pizza become such a favorite food around the world?

(B)[For / Since] the Stone Age, people have been eating pizza in one form or another. Stone Age people baked flat bread on hot rocks. Records show that the Greeks and the Romans started to put meat and vegetables on flat bread. It (C)[believes / is believed] that the word "pizza" was first used in Italy @to name the food over 1,000 years ago.

✏ 출제율 95%

17 위 글의 괄호 (A)~(C)에서 어법상 알맞은 낱말을 골라 쓰시오.

➡ (A) _____ (B) _____ (C) _____

✏ 출제율 90%

18 아래 〈보기〉에서 위 글의 밑줄 친 @to name과 to부정사의 용법이 같은 것의 개수를 고르시오.

┌─── 보기 ───
① I don't know how to name the food.
② She was clever enough to name the food.
③ We met yesterday to name the food.
④ It won't be easy to name the food.
⑤ He was eager to name the food.
└────────────

① 1개   ② 2개   ③ 3개   ④ 4개   ⑤ 5개

✏ 출제율 100%

19 According to the passage, which is NOT true?

① People sell pizza in fast-food restaurants or on the street in most parts of the world.

② People have been eating pizza in one form since the Stone Age.

③ In the Stone Age, people baked flat bread on hot rocks.

④ According to the records, it was the Greeks and the Romans that started to put meat and vegetables on flat bread.

⑤ People first used the word "pizza" in Italy over 1,000 years ago.

[20~22] 다음 글을 읽고 물음에 답하시오.

However, @토마토 토핑을 얹은 피자는 16세기까지는 존재하지 않았다. There were no tomatoes in Italy before Christopher Columbus and other Europeans brought them from the New World. When ⓑthey were first introduced to Europe, people thought that tomatoes would make ⓒthem sick. In time, people learned that tomatoes were delicious and healthy.

✏ 출제율 95%

20 위 글의 밑줄 친 @의 우리말에 맞게 주어진 어휘를 이용하여 11 단어로 영작하시오.

┌─────────────────────┐
│ with tomato toppings, not born │
└─────────────────────┘

➡ _____

_____

✏ 출제율 95%

21 위 글의 밑줄 친 ⓑthey와 ⓒthem이 가리키는 것을 각각 본문에서 찾아 쓰시오.

➡ ⓑthey가 가리키는 것: _____,

ⓒthem이 가리키는 것: _____

✏ 출제율 90%

22 본문의 내용과 일치하도록 다음 빈칸에 알맞은 접속사를 쓰시오.

┌─────────────────────┐
│ There were tomatoes in Italy only │
│ _____ Christopher Columbus and │
│ other Europeans brought them from the │
│ New World. │
└─────────────────────┘

[23~25] 다음 글을 읽고 물음에 답하시오.

In the 18th century, Naples was a large city (A)[where / which] there were many jobs. (①) Workers from near and far came to the city, and (B)[that / what] they needed in their busy lives was food they could eat quickly at any time. (②) Cooks in Naples began to put tomato and other toppings on flat bread and sold slices of pizza on the street. (③) The street food was (C)[so / such] cheap and delicious that workers ate it for breakfast, lunch, and dinner. (④) In 1830, the world's first pizza shop opened in Naples. (⑤)

출제율 90%

23 위 글의 괄호 (A)~(C)에서 어법상 알맞은 낱말을 골라 쓰시오.

➡ (A) _____ (B) _____ (C) _____

출제율 95%

24 위 글의 흐름으로 보아, 주어진 문장이 들어가기에 가장 적절한 곳은?

> They could buy slices of pizza and eat them as they walked on the street.

① ② ③ ④ ⑤

출제율 100%

25 위 글의 제목으로 알맞은 것을 고르시오.

① Pizza Becomes a National Dish
② What Do You Know About Pizza?
③ Naples, the Home of Pizza
④ Pizza as a Global Dish
⑤ The Birth of the Word "Pizza"

[26~28] 다음 글을 읽고 물음에 답하시오.

Pizza is now enjoyed almost everywhere. Of course, toppings differ widely from place to place. Koreans love *bulgogi* on their pizza, (A)while Russians like to have fish and onion toppings on their pizza. ___@___, all types of pizza share two things. Each begins with flat bread, and each is a slice of history.

출제율 95%

26 위 글의 빈칸 @에 들어갈 알맞은 말을 고르시오.

① As a result ② However
③ For example ④ Therefore
⑤ In other words

출제율 90%

27 위 글의 밑줄 친 (A)while과 같은 의미로 쓰인 것을 고르시오.

① Strike while the iron is hot.
② While there is life, there is hope.
③ Please wait for a while.
④ While eating, you shouldn't speak.
⑤ The walls are green, while the ceiling is white.

출제율 100%

28 위 글의 주제로 알맞은 것을 고르시오.

① pizza toppings different from place to place
② the difference between the toppings of ancient times and those of today
③ the way pizza became a global dish
④ pizza as a global dish and a slice of history
⑤ the way pizza became known outside of Italy

Lesson 5

Are You into Books?

 의사소통 기능

- 추천 요청하기
  A: Can you recommend some good music?
  B: I recommend you listen to *Happy*.

- 기대 표현하기
  A: You look excited.
  B: Yeah. I'm looking forward to a big curling match this Tuesday.

 언어 형식

- 과거완료
  Jake was late for school because he **had missed** the bus.

- 'It ~ that ...' 강조 구문
  It was Judy **that** lost her wallet on the bus.

Words & Expressions

교과서

Key Words

- achieve[ətʃíːv] 동 이루다, 얻다
- arrest[ərést] 동 체포하다
- arrival[əráivəl] 명 도착
- author[ɔ́ːθər] 명 저자
- borrow[bárou] 동 빌리다
- celebrate[séləbrèit] 동 기념하다, 축하하다
- charge[tʃɑːrdʒ] 명 기소, 혐의
- childhood[tʃáildhùd] 명 어린 시절
- choose[tʃuːz] 동 고르다
- copy[kápi] 명 (책) 한 부 동 베끼다, 복사하다
- decide[disáid] 동 결심하다
- editor[édətər] 명 편집자
- elementary school 초등학교
- express[iksprés] 동 표현하다
- freedom[fríːdəm] 명 자유
- further[fə́ːrðər] 부 더, 더 멀리
- government[gʌ́vərnmənt] 명 정부, 정권
- graduation[grædʒuéiʃən] 명 졸업
- harsh[haːrʃ] 형 가혹한, 혹독한
- hometown[hóumtaun] 명 고향
- independence[ìndipéndəns] 명 독립
- library[láibrèri] 명 도서관
- literary[lítərèri] 형 문학의, 문학적인
- literature[lítərətʃər] 명 문학
- loneliness[lóunlinis] 명 외로움
- longing[lɔ́ːŋiŋ] 명 동경, 갈망
- movement[múːvmənt] 명 운동
- novel[návəl] 명 소설
- particular[pərtíkjulər] 형 특별한, 특정한
- poem[póuəm] 명 (한 편의) 시
- poet[póuit] 명 시인
- poetry[póuitri] 명 (문학 장르) 시
- present[prizént] 동 선사하다, 주다
- publication[pʌbləkéiʃən] 명 출판, 발행
- publish[pʌ́bliʃ] 동 출판하다
- rare[rɛər] 형 희귀한
- recommend[rèkəménd] 동 추천하다
- remain[riméin] 동 남아 있다, 계속 ~하다
- sew[sou] 동 바느질하다
- shine[ʃain] 동 빛나다
- thus[ðʌs] 부 그러므로
- treatment[tríːtmənt] 명 대우, 처리
- wallet[wálit] 명 지갑
- whole[houl] 형 전체의, 모든
- yearbook[jiərbuk] 명 졸업 앨범

Key Expressions

- a surprise ending 뜻밖의 결말
- advise against 반대하는 충고를 하다
- be well known for ~로 유명하다
- by hand 손으로
- check out (도서관에서) 대출하다
- come out 나오다
- give it a try 시도하다
- give up 포기하다
- hang out with ~와 시간을 보내다
- have ~ in mind ~을 염두에 두다
- How about ~? ~하는 것이 어때?
- How would you like ~? ~을 어떻게 하기를 원하니?
- I can't wait! 무척 기대됩니다!
- Let me see. 글쎄, 어디 보자.
- Long time no see. 오랜만이다.
- look forward to ~을 기대하다
- look good on ~에 잘 어울리다
- in a hurry 서둘러
- new arrival 신착 도서, 새로 도착한 것
- put up 세우다, 내걸다
- take a seat 자리에 앉다
- take part in ~에 참가하다
- turn on ~을 켜다
- What brings you here? 무엇 때문에 여기 왔니?
- What's up? 무슨 일 있니?
- You can say that again. 정말 그래., 동의한다.

Word Power

※ 서로 비슷한 뜻을 가진 어휘

□ **achieve** 이루다 : **accomplish** 성취하다

□ **choose** 고르다 : **select** 선택하다

□ **freedom** 자유 : **liberty** 자유

□ **longing** 동경, 갈망 : **aspiration** 열망

□ **thus** 그러므로 : **hence** 그래서

□ **author** 저자 : **writer** 작가

□ **decide** 결심하다 : **determine** 결정하다

□ **loneliness** 외로움 : **solitude** 외로움

□ **rare** 희귀한 : **scarce** 희소한

□ **wallet** 지갑 : **purse** 지갑

※ 서로 반대의 뜻을 가진 어휘

□ **arrival** 도착 ↔ **departure** 출발

□ **dependence** 의존 ↔ **independence** 독립

□ **borrow** 빌리다 ↔ **lend** 빌려주다

□ **rare** 희귀한 ↔ **common** 흔한

※ 동사 → 명사

□ **achieve** 이루다, 얻다 → **achievement** 성취

□ **celebrate** 기념하다 → **celebration** 축하

□ **decide** 결심하다 → **decision** 결심

□ **govern** 지배하다 → **government** 정부, 정권

□ **depend** 의존하다 → **dependence** 의존

□ **arrive** 도착하다 → **arrival** 도착

□ **choose** 고르다 → **choice** 선택

□ **express** 표현하다 → **expression** 표현

□ **graduate** 졸업하다 → **graduation** 졸업

□ **recommend** 추천하다 → **recommendation** 추천

English Dictionary

□ **harsh** 가혹한, 혹독한
→ unpleasant and causing pain to the body or senses
불쾌하고 신체나 감각에 고통을 야기하는

□ **hometown** 고향
→ the town where someone was born and grew up
누군가가 태어나서 자란 마을

□ **independence** 독립
→ the state of not being governed by another country
다른 나라의 지배를 받지 않는 상태

□ **literature** 문학
→ written works which are of artistic value
예술적 가치가 있는 글로 된 작품

□ **loneliness** 외로움
→ a feeling of being unhappy because you are away from other people
다른 사람들로부터 떨어져 있어서 불행한 느낌

□ **longing** 동경, 갈망
→ a strong feeling of wanting something
무언가를 원하는 강한 감정

□ **poem** (한 편의) 시
→ a piece of writing, arranged in patterns of lines and of sounds 행과 운율의 패턴에 따라 배열된 문학 작품

□ **poet** 시인
→ a person who writes poems 시를 쓰는 사람

□ **publication** 출판, 발행
→ the action of making something known to the public
대중들에게 알려지도록 하는 행위

□ **rare** 희귀한
→ not common; unusual 흔치 않은, 진기한

□ **recommend** 추천하다
→ to suggest as being good or worthy
좋거나 가치있는 것으로 제안하다

□ **sew** 바느질하다
→ to make or mend with a needle and thread
바늘과 실로 만들거나 수리하다

□ **whole** 전체의, 모든
→ not divided; all 나누어지지 않은, 전부의

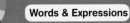
01 다음 짝지어진 단어의 관계가 같도록 빈칸에 알맞은 말을 쓰시오.

> possible : impossible
> = dependence : _____

02 다음 짝지어진 단어의 관계가 나머지와 다른 것은?

① achieve – achievement
② decide – decision
③ publish – publication
④ depend – dependent
⑤ arrive – arrival

03 다음 영영풀이가 가리키는 것을 고르시오.

> a strong feeling of wanting something

① happiness   ② longing
③ loneliness   ④ satisfaction
⑤ harshness

04 다음 중 밑줄 친 부분의 뜻풀이가 바르지 않은 것은?

① I stopped by the library to check out some books. (대출하다)
② What are you looking forward to? (앞으로 나아가다)
③ Why don't you take a seat here? (자리에 앉다)
④ These red pants don't look good on you. (~에게 잘 어울리다)
⑤ Do you have something in mind? (~을 염두에 두다)

05 다음 우리말에 맞게 빈칸에 알맞은 말을 쓰시오.

(1) William Shakespeare는 훌륭한 시인이자 극작가였다.
   ➡ William Shakespeare was a great _____ and playwriter.
(2) 당신이 가장 좋아하는 작가는 누구인가요?
   ➡ Who is your favorite _____?
(3) 그녀의 첫 번째 소설의 출판이 취소되었다.
   ➡ The _____ of her first novel was canceled.
(4) 나의 할아버지는 항상 그의 고향을 그리워하신다.
   ➡ My grandfather always misses his _____.
(5) 불을 켜줄래? 여기 너무 어둡구나.
   ➡ Will you _____ on the light? It's too dark here.

06 다음 주어진 문장의 밑줄 친 express와 다른 의미로 쓰인 것은?

> In class, we learned how to express our opinions clearly.

① I expressed concern about the changes.
② Teenagers often have difficulty expressing themselves.
③ My twins express their feelings in the paintings.
④ I'm going to travel by express.
⑤ Words cannot express how happy I am now.

01 다음 짝지어진 단어의 관계가 같도록 빈칸에 알맞은 말을 쓰시오.

> sell : buy = _____ : lend

02 다음 영영풀이가 가리키는 것을 영어로 쓰시오.

> the town where someone was born and grew up

➡ _____

03 다음 우리말에 맞게 빈칸에 알맞은 어구를 쓰시오.

(1) 그는 한 마디도 없이 서둘러 나갔다. (3 words)
➡ He went out _____ without saying a word.

(2) 그는 손으로 의자를 만들었다. (2 words)
➡ He made a chair _____.

(3) 내 딸은 그녀의 친구들과 시간을 보내는 것을 좋아한다. (3 words)
➡ My daughter likes to _____ her friends.

04 다음 문장의 빈칸에 들어갈 말을 〈보기〉에서 골라 쓰시오.

> ┌─ 보기 ┤
> further / independence / charge / graduation / shine

(1) August 15 is the day when Koreans celebrate their _____ from Japan.

(2) He was arrested on the _____ of robbery.

(3) Stay inside until _____ notice.

(4) The sun will _____ brightly after the rain.

(5) She plans to study abroad after _____.

05 다음 우리말을 주어진 단어를 이용하여 영작하시오.

(1) 홍콩은 1997년에 영국으로부터 독립을 얻어냈다. (gained, the UK)
➡ _____
_____

(2) 나는 나의 소설을 출판하기 전에 나의 사진들을 확인할 필요가 있다. (check, novel)
➡ _____

(3) 숲은 몇몇 희귀한 곤충들과 식물들의 서식지이다. (forest, home)
➡ _____
_____

06 다음 주어진 우리말과 일치하도록 주어진 단어를 모두 배열하여 영작하시오.

(1) 지금 체육관에서 졸업식이 열리고 있다.
(ceremony / being / the graduation / the / gym / now / in / held / is)
➡ _____
_____

(2) 처벌은 가혹하고 불평등했다.
(punishment / harsh / the / was / and / unfair)
➡ _____

(3) 나는 법의 이름으로 당신을 체포합니다.
(you / of / in / I / name / the / the / arrest / law)
➡ _____
_____

Conversation

1 추천 요청하기

> **A** Can you recommend some good music? 좋은 음악 좀 추천해 줄 수 있니?
>
> **B** I recommend you listen to *Happy*. 나는 *Happy*를 들어보라고 추천해.

- 상대방에게 추천을 요청하는 표현은 'recommend(추천하다)'를 사용하여 나타낸다. 상대방에게 요청을 나타낼 때는 can, could, would 등의 조동사를 사용하여 'Can you recommend ~?'(~을 추천해 주실 수 있나요?), 'Could you recommend ~?'(~ 좀 추천해 주시겠습니까?) 등으로 나타낸다.

- 구체적인 내용을 몰라서 상대에게 무엇을 추천할지 물어볼 때는 'What would you recommend?'(무엇을 추천하시겠습니까?), 'Which one would you recommend?'(어느 것을 추천하시겠습니까?) 등으로 나타낸다.

- 상대로부터 추천 요청을 받고 추천을 해 줄 때는 'I recommend ~.'(나는 ~을 추천한다.)라고 한다. recommend는 'recommend+명사', 'recommend -ing', 'recommend (that) 주어(+should)+동사원형 ~'의 형태로 문장을 구성한다.

추천 요청하기

- Can you recommend ~?   ~을 추천해 주시겠어요?
- Could / Would you recommend ~?   ~을 추천해 주시겠습니까?
- What would you recommend?   무엇을 추천하시겠습니까?
- Which one would you recommend?   어느 것을 추천하시겠습니까?

추천하기

- I recommend+명사[동명사] / (that) 주어+(should+)동사원형 ~ 나는 ~을 추천한다.
- How about ~? ~는 어떠니?

핵심 Check

1. 다음 대화의 흐름으로 보아 빈칸에 들어가기에 적절한 것은?

B: Hello, Ms. Seo.

W: Hi, Minjun. Long time no see. What brings you here?

B: I have to write a book report. Can you recommend a good novel to read?

W: _____ There's a new Ken Kuller book, *22nd Street*.

① What do you like?　　　　　　② How about a mystery?
③ Why do you read novels?　　　④ Which one do you like better?
⑤ Can I check it out?

② 기대 표현하기

A You look excited. 너 흥분된 것처럼 보인다.

B Yeah. I'm looking forward to a big curling match this Tuesday.
응, 나는 이번 목요일 큰 컬링 시합을 기대하고 있어.

■ 앞으로 일어날 일이나 하고 싶은 일에 대한 기대를 표현할 때 '~을 기대한다.'라는 의미로 'I'm looking forward to ~.'나 'I look forward to ~.'의 표현을 사용한다. '~을 기대하다'라는 의미의 'look forward to'에서는 to가 전치사이기 때문에 그 뒤에 명사나 동명사가 오는 점에 주의한다. '빨리 ~하고 싶다, ~을 너무 하고 싶다.'라는 뜻으로 'I can't wait for ~.' 'I am dying to ~.' 'I'm expecting to ~.'라고 하기도 한다.

■ 'I can't wait!'(너무 기대된다!/빨리 보고 싶어!)는 원하던 일이 다가오고 있어 빨리하고 싶은 기대감을 나타내는 표현이며, 직역의 의미는 '~하는 것을 기다릴 수 없다'이고, 보통 '당장 ~하고 싶다, 빨리 ~했으면 좋겠다'로 해석한다. to 뒤에는 동사원형을 쓰지만, 뒤에 명사구가 올 경우에는 'I can't wait for+명사(명사구)'의 형태로 쓰기도 한다.

■ '기대하다'라는 의미의 expect를 써서 'I'm expecting to 동사원형 ~'이라고 하거나 '열망하다'라는 의미의 동사 'long'을 사용하여 'I'm longing to+동사원형, I'm longing for+명사'라고 하거나, 형용사 'eager(열망하는)'를 써서 'I'm eager to+동사원형', 'I'm eager for+명사'의 형태로 나타내기도 한다.

기대 표현하기

• I'm looking forward to+명사(구) ~하기를 기대한다.
• I can't wait for+명사 / to+동사원형 빨리 ~했으면 좋겠다.
• I am expecting to+동사원형 ~하기를 기대한다.
• I am longing for+명사 / to+동사원형 ~하기를 열망한다.
• I am eager for+명사 / to+동사원형 ~하기를 기대한다.

핵심 Check

2. 다음 우리말과 일치하도록 빈칸에 알맞은 말을 고르시오.

A: Hi, Sora. You look excited.

B: Yeah. I'm really looking forward to this Tuesday.

A: This Tuesday? What's on Tuesday?

B: There's a big curling match. _____

① How about you?　　② I can't wait!
③ Will you recommend one?　　④ But I don't watch it.
⑤ There're lots of things to see.

Listen – Listen & Answer Dialog 1

Minjun: Hello, Ms. Seo.

Ms. Seo: Hi, Minjun. ❶Long time no see. What brings you here?

Minjun: I have to write a book report. ❷Can you recommend a good novel to read?

Ms. Seo: ❸How about a mystery? There's a new Ken Kuller book, *22nd Street*.

Minjun: Oh, I've heard of ❹him. Can you show me the book?

Ms. Seo: It's in the "❺New Arrivals" area. It's really popular among teens in Great Britain.

Minjun: Thank you for your help. Can I ❻check it out?

Ms. Seo: Sure. You can borrow new books for seven days.

Minjun: Okay.

민준: 안녕하세요, 서 선생님.
서 선생님: 안녕, 민준아. 오랜만이구나. 무슨 일로 여기에 온 거니?
민준: 독후감을 써야 해서요. 읽기에 좋은 소설을 추천해 주시겠어요?
서 선생님: 추리 소설은 어떠니? Ken Kuller의 신간, '22번가'가 있단다.
민준: 아, 그에 관해 들어 본 적이 있어요. 책을 보여 주실 수 있나요?
서 선생님: '신착 도서' 서가에 있단다. 그 책은 영국의 십 대들 사이에서 많은 인기를 끌고 있다.
민준: 도와주셔서 감사합니다. 그 책을 대출할 수 있을까요?
서 선생님: 물론이지. 신간은 7일간 빌릴 수 있어.
민준: 알겠습니다.

❶ Long time no see.: 오랜만이다.　❷ 상대방에게 추천을 요청하는 표현은 'recommend(추천하다)'를 사용하여 나타낸다.
❸ 상대로부터 추천 요청을 받고 추천을 해 줄 때 사용할 수 있는 표현으로 'How about a mystery?' 등을 쓴다.
❹ him은 Ken Kuller를 가리킨다　❺ new arrival: 신착 도서, 새로 도착한 것　❻ check out: (도서관에서) 대출하다

Check(√) True or False

(1) Minjun has to write a book report.　　　　　　　　　　　　T ☐　F ☐

(2) Minjun can borrow new books for a week.　　　　　　　　　T ☐　F ☐

Listen – Listen & Answer Dialog 2

Sora: Hey, Minjun. What are you doing?

Minjun: I'm reading a novel for a book report.

Sora: Let me see. Oh, is this a new book by Ken Kuller?

Minjun: Yeah, I borrowed ❶it this morning. Do you know Ken Kuller?

Sora: Of course. I'm a big fan of his. I've read all of his mystery books.

Minjun: I think he's a great writer. I can't ❷stop reading this book.

Sora: You know what? His novel *Four Eyes* has been made into a movie.

Minjun: Yeah. I saw the movie poster. It ❸looks interesting.

Sora: It'll come out next Thursday. I'm ❹looking forward to seeing it!

Minjun: Maybe we can see the movie together.

소라: 안녕, 민준아. 뭐 하고 있니?
민준: 나는 독후감을 쓰려고 소설을 읽고 있어.
소라: 어디 봐. 아, 이거 Ken Kuller의 신간이지?
민준: 맞아. 오늘 아침에 이걸 대출했어. 너는 Ken Kuller를 알고 있니?
소라: 물론이지. 난 그의 열렬한 팬이야. 그의 추리 소설은 모두 읽었어.
민준: 내 생각에 그는 위대한 작가야. 이 책을 손에서 놓을 수가 없어.
소라: 그거 알아? 그의 소설 '네 개의 눈'이 영화로 만들어졌어.
민준: 맞아. 나도 영화 포스터를 봤어. 재미있어 보이더라.
소라: 영화는 다음 주 목요일에 개봉한대. 그걸 보는 게 기대돼!
민준: 아마 우리 영화를 같이 볼 수 있겠다.

❶ it은 Ken Kuller의 신간을 가리킨다　❷ stop+~ing: ~하는 것을 멈추다, stop+to부정사: ~하기 위해 멈추다
❸ look+형용사: ~하게 보이다　❹ look forward to ~ing: ~을 기대하다 = I can't wait to ~

Check(√) True or False

(3) The movie *Four Eyes* will come out next Thursday.　　　　　T ☐　F ☐

(4) Minjun is going to see the movie with Sora this Thursday.　　T ☐　F ☐

Listen more – Listen and complete

Mike: Good morning, Jiho.

Jiho: Good morning.

Mike: Take a seat, please. ❶How would you like your hair done?

Jiho: Well, I'm taking my pictures for the ❷ yearbook. So I want to look cool.

Mike: When do you take the pictures?

Jiho: This Friday at Dream & Joy Park.

Mike: Sounds good. Do you have a ❸particular style in mind?

Jiho: No. Can you recommend one for me?

Mike: Look at this. ❹How about this style? It'll look good on you.

Jiho: Wow, I like it. ❺I can't wait to see how I'll look in the pictures.

Mike: I'm sure you'll look cool.

❶ How would you like ～?: ～을 어떻게 하기를 원하니?
❷ yearbook: 졸업 앨범
❸ particular: 특정한, 특별한
❹ 추천 요청에 제안하는 표현으로 'I recommend this style.' 또는 'Why don't you try this style?' 등으로 바꾸어 표현할 수 있다.
❺ 기대감을 표현하는 말로 'I'm looking forward to seeing how I'll look in the pictures.'로 바꾸어 표현할 수 있다.

My Speaking Portfolio

Jane: Nice to meet you, Mr. Henry. Is O. Henry your real name?

Mr. Henry: No. My real name is William Sydney Porter.

Jane: Can you tell me ❶where you're from?

Mr. Henry: I'm from the U.S.

Jane: What do you usually write?

Mr. Henry: I'm a short story writer. I have written about 300 short stories.

Jane: Wow! You're great! What is special about your short stories?

Mr. Henry: ❷They're well known for their ❸ surprise endings.

Jane: Can you recommend a popular story with a surprise ending?

Mr. Henry: Sure. I recommend *The Last Leaf*.

Jane: What is ❹it about?

Mr. Henry: ❹It's about a sick girl and an old artist who saves her life.

Jane: Oh, I want to read ❹it. ❺I can't wait.

❶ 간접의문의 어순으로 '의문사+주어+동사' 순서로 이어진다.
❷ be well known for: ～로 유명하다
❸ a surprise ending: 뜻밖의 결말
❹ it은 *The Last Leaf*를 가리킨다.
❺ 기대감을 나타내며 'I'm looking forward to reading it.'으로 바꾸어 표현할 수 있다.

Wrap Up 1

Tony: ❶May I take your order?

Suji: There're so many ❷kinds of hot dogs here. Can you recommend one?

Tony: How about the potato hot dog? It's very popular.

Suji: Okay, I'll have one.

Tony: Try our milkshake, too. It ❸goes well with the potato hot dog.

❶ '주문하시겠어요?'를 뜻하며 'Are you ready to order?' 등으로 바꿔 쓸 수 있다.
❷ kind: 종류
❸ go well with: ～와 잘 어울리다

Wrap Up 2

Emily: You look ❶excited.

James: Yeah. I'm going to the Thunder concert this Friday. I can't wait!

Emily: Who are you going to the concert with?

James: With my mom.

Emily: Does your mother like hip-hop?

James: Yes, ❷she's into hip-hop. ❸She's really looking forward to the concert.

❶ excited: 신이 난
❷ be into ～: ～을 좋아하다
❸ 기대감을 나타내며 'She's longing for the concert.' 등으로 바꿔 쓸 수 있다.

● 다음 우리말과 일치하도록 빈칸에 알맞은 말을 쓰시오.

해석

Listen – Listen & Answer Dialog 1

Minjun: Hello, Ms. Seo.

Ms. Seo: Hi, Minjun. _____ time _____ see. What _____ you here?

Minjun: I have to write _____ _____ _____. Can you _____ a good novel to read?

Ms. Seo: How _____ a mystery? There's a new Ken Kuller book, *22nd Street*.

Minjun: Oh, I've heard of him. Can you _____ _____ the book?

Ms. Seo: It's in the "_____ _____" area. It's really _____ among teens in Great Britain.

Minjun: Thank you for your help. Can I _____ it _____?

Ms. Seo: Sure. You can _____ new books for seven days.

Minjun: Okay.

Listen – Listen & Answer Dialog 2

Sora: Hey, Minjun. What are you doing?

Minjun: I'm reading a _____ for a _____ _____.

Sora: Let _____ _____. Oh, is this a new book by Ken Kuller?

Minjun: Yeah, I _____ it this morning. Do you know Ken Kuller?

Sora: Of course. I'm a _____ of his. I've read _____ of his mystery books.

Minjun: I think he's a great writer. I can't _____ _____ this book.

Sora: You know _____? His novel *Four Eyes* _____ _____ _____ into a movie.

Minjun: Yeah. I saw the movie poster. It looks _____.

Sora: It'll _____ _____ next Thursday. I'm _____ _____ _____ _____ it!

Minjun: Maybe we can see the movie _____.

Listen more – Listen and complete

Mike: Good morning, Jiho.

Jiho: Good morning.

Mike: _____ _____ _____, please. _____ _____ _____ _____ your hair done?

Jiho: Well, I'm taking my pictures for the _____. So I want to look _____.

Mike: When do you _____ the pictures?

Jiho: This Friday at Dream & Joy Park.

Mike: Sounds good. Do you have a _____ style in _____?

Jiho: No. Can you _____ one for me?

Mike: Look at this. How about this style? It'll _____ _____ _____ you.

Jiho: Wow, I like it. I _____ _____ _____ _____ how I'll look in the pictures.

Mike: I'm _____ you'll look cool.

My Speaking Portfolio

Jane: Nice to meet you, Mr. Henry. Is O. Henry your _____ _____?

Mr. Henry: No. My real name is William Sydney Porter.

Jane: Can you tell me _____ _____ _____?

Mr. Henry: I'm from the U.S.

Jane: What do you _____ write?

Mr. Henry: I'm a _____ _____ _____. I have written about 300 short stories.

Jane: Wow! You're great! What is _____ about your short stories?

Mr. Henry: They're _____ _____ _____ their surprise endings.

Jane: Can you _____ a popular story with a _____ _____?

Mr. Henry: Sure. I _____ *The Last Leaf.*

Jane: What is it about?

Mr. Henry: It's about a sick girl and an old artist _____ _____ _____ _____.

Jane: Oh, I want to read it. I _____ _____.

해석

Mike: 안녕, 지호야.

지호: 안녕하세요.

Mike: 자리에 앉으렴. 머리를 어떻게 해 줄까?

지호: 음, 저는 졸업 앨범에 들어갈 사진을 찍을 거예요. 그래서 멋져 보이고 싶어요.

Mike: 언제 사진을 찍니?

지호: 이번 금요일에 Dream & Joy Park에서요.

Mike: 멋지구나. 마음에 둔 특별한 스타일이 있니?

지호: 아니요. 저를 위해 하나 추천해 주시겠어요?

Mike: 이걸 보렴. 이 스타일은 어떠니? 너에게 잘 어울릴 거야.

지호: 와, 마음에 들어요. 제가 사진에서 어떻게 보일지 빨리 보고 싶네요.

Mike: 틀림없이 멋져 보일 거야.

Jane: 만나서 반갑습니다, Henry 씨. O. Henry가 당신의 본명인가요?

Mr. Henry: 아니요. 제 본명은 William Sydney Porter입니다.

Jane: 어디 출신이신지 말씀해 주시겠어요?

Mr. Henry: 저는 미국 출신입니다.

Jane: 주로 무엇을 쓰시나요?

Mr. Henry: 저는 단편 소설 작가입니다. 300여 편의 단편 소설을 썼죠.

Jane: 와! 대단하시네요! 당신의 단편 소설은 무엇이 특별한가요?

Mr. Henry: 그것들은 뜻밖의 결말로 유명합니다.

Jane: 뜻밖의 결말이 있는 유명한 이야기를 하나 추천해 주실 수 있나요?

Mr. Henry: 물론이죠. 저는 '마지막 잎새'를 추천합니다.

Jane: 그것은 무엇에 관한 이야기인가요?

Mr. Henry: 아픈 소녀와 그녀의 목숨을 구하는 늙은 화가의 이야기예요.

Jane: 아, 그것을 읽고 싶네요. 무척 기대됩니다.

[01~02] 다음 대화를 읽고 물음에 답하시오.

Tony: (A)May I take your order?

Suji: There're so many kinds of hot dogs here. Can you recommend one?

Tony: _____ It's very popular.

Suji: Okay, I'll have one.

Tony: Try our milkshake, too. It goes well with the potato hot dog.

01 위 대화의 밑줄 친 (A)와 바꾸어 쓸 수 없는 것은?

① Are you ready to order now?　② Would you like to order?

③ Shall I take your order?　④ Can I get your order?

⑤ Let me confirm your order.

02 위 대화의 빈칸에 들어갈 말로 어색한 것은?

① You don't have to try potato hot dog.

② How about the potato hot dog?

③ I recommend the potato hot dog.

④ Why don't you try the potato hot dog?

⑤ If I were you, I'd try the potato hot dog.

[03~04] 다음 대화를 읽고 물음에 답하시오.

Emily: You look excited.

James: Yeah. I'm going to the Thunder concert this Friday. I can't wait!

Emily: Who are you going to the concert with?

James: With my mom.

Emily: Does your mother like hip-hop?

James: Yes, she's into hip-hop. (A)She's really looking forward to the concert. (wait)

03 위 대화의 밑줄 친 (A)를 같은 의미가 되도록 주어진 단어를 사용하여 다시 쓰시오.

➡ _____

04 Where will James and his mom go this Friday?

➡ _____

[01~03] 다음 대화를 읽고 물음에 답하시오.

Minjun: Hello, Ms. Seo.

Ms. Seo: Hi, Minjun. Long time no see. What brings you here?

Minjun: I have to write a book report. (A)읽기에 좋은 소설을 추천해 주시겠어요?

Ms. Seo: How about a mystery? There's a new Ken Kuller book, *22nd Street*.

Minjun: Oh, I've heard of ⓐhim. Can you show me the book?

Ms. Seo: It's in the "New Arrivals" area. It's really popular among teens in Great Britain.

Minjun: Thank you for your help. Can I check ⓑit out?

Ms. Seo: Sure. You can borrow new books for seven days.

Minjun: Okay.

서답형

01 위 대화의 밑줄 친 (A)의 우리말을 주어진 단어를 모두 배열하여 완성하시오.

(to / you / recommend / good / a / can / read / novel)

➡ _____

서답형

02 위 대화의 밑줄 친 ⓐ와 ⓑ가 각각 가리키는 것을 찾아 쓰시오.

➡ ⓐ _____ ⓑ _____

03 위 대화의 두 사람의 관계로 적절한 것은?

① interview – interviewee
② traveller – flight attendant
③ patient – doctor
④ tourist – guide
⑤ student – librarian

[04~06] 다음 대화를 읽고 물음에 답하시오.

Sora: Hey, Minjun. What are you doing?

Minjun: I'm reading a novel for a book report.

Sora: Let me see. Oh, is this a new book by Ken Kuller?

Minjun: (A) Yeah, I borrowed it this morning. Do you know Ken Kuller?

Sora: (B) I've read all of his mystery books.

Minjun: (C) I think he's a great writer. I can't stop reading this book.

Sora: (D) You know what? His novel Four Eyes has been made into a movie.

Minjun: (E) Yeah. I saw the movie poster. It looks interesting.

Sora: ⓐ그것은 다음 주 목요일에 개봉할 거야. ⓑ I'm looking forward to seeing it!

Minjun: Maybe we can see the movie together.

중요

04 위 대화의 (A)~(E) 중 주어진 문장이 들어가기에 적절한 곳은?

Of course. I'm a big fan of his.

① (A)　② (B)　③ (C)　④ (D)　⑤ (E)

서답형

05 위 대화의 밑줄 친 ⓐ의 우리말을 주어진 단어를 써서 영작하시오. (come)

➡ _____

06 위 대화의 밑줄 친 ⓑ와 바꾸어 쓰기에 어색한 것은?

① I can't wait to see it!
② I'm expecting to see it.
③ I'm longing to see it.
④ I'm eager to see it.
⑤ I'm going to see it.

[07~08] 다음 대화를 읽고 물음에 답하시오.

Mike: Good morning, Jiho.

Jiho: Good morning.

Mike: Take a seat, please. How would you ⓐlike your hair done?

Jiho: Well, I'm taking my pictures for the yearbook. So I want to look ⓑcool.

Mike: When do you take the pictures?

Jiho: This Friday at Dream & Joy Park.

Mike: ⓒSounds good. Do you have a particular style in mind?

Jiho: No. Can you recommend one for me?

Mike: Look at this. How about this style? It'll look good ⓓon you.

Jiho: Wow, I like it. I can't wait ⓔseeing how I'll look in the pictures.

Mike: I'm sure you'll look cool.

서답형

07 위 대화의 밑줄 친 ⓐ~ⓔ 중 어법상 틀린 것을 찾아 바르게 고치시오.

_____ ➡ _____

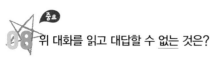
위 대화를 읽고 대답할 수 없는 것은?

① What will Jiho take his pictures for?

② What does Jiho want to do?

③ When is Jiho going to take pictures?

④ Where is Jiho going to take pictures?

⑤ How long should Jiho wait to see his new style?

[09~10] 다음 대화를 읽고 물음에 답하시오.

Jane: Nice to meet you, Mr. Henry. Is O. Henry your real name?

Mr. Henry: No. My real name is William Sydney Porter.

Jane: Can you tell me where (A)[you are / are you] from?

Mr. Henry: I'm from the U.S.

Jane: What do you usually write?

Mr. Henry: I'm a short story writer. I have written about 300 short stories.

Jane: Wow! You're great! What is special about your short stories?

Mr. Henry: They're well (B)[knowing / known] for their surprise endings.

Jane: Can you recommend a popular story with a surprise ending?

Mr. Henry: Sure. I recommend *The Last Leaf*.

Jane: What is it about?

Mr. Henry: It's about a sick girl and an old artist who (C)[save / saves] her life.

Jane: Oh, I want to read it. I can't wait.

09 위 대화의 (A)~(C)에서 알맞은 것을 골라 쓰시오.

➡ (A) _____ (B) _____ (C) _____

10 위 대화의 내용과 일치하지 않는 것은?

① O. Henry의 본명은 William Sydney Porter 이다.

② O. Henry는 미국 출신이다.

③ O. Henry는 단편 소설 작가로 300여 편의 단편 소설을 썼다.

④ O. Henry의 단편 소설은 뜻밖의 결말로 유명하다.

⑤ O. Henry의 '마지막 잎새'를 추천한 이유는 슬픈 결말 때문이다.

[01~02] 다음 대화를 읽고 물음에 답하시오.

Minjun: Hello, Ms. Seo.

Ms. Seo: Hi, Minjun. Long time no see. What brings you here?

Minjun: I have to write a book report. Can you recommend a good novel to read?

Ms. Seo: How about a mystery? There's a new Ken Kuller book, *22nd Street*.

Minjun: Oh, I've heard of him. Can you show me the book?

Ms. Seo: It's in the "New Arrivals" area. It's really popular among teens in Great Britain.

Minjun: Thank you for your help. Can I check it out?

Ms. Seo: Sure. You can borrow new books for seven days.

Minjun: Okay.

01 What does Ms. Seo recommend to Minjun?

➡ _____

02 Where can Minjun find out the book that Ms. Seo recommended?

➡ _____

03 다음 대화를 읽고 대화의 내용과 일치하도록 빈칸을 완성하시오.

Mike: Good morning, Jiho.

Jiho: Good morning.

Mike: Take a seat, please. How would you like your hair done?

Jiho: Well, I'm taking my pictures for the yearbook. So I want to look cool.

Mike: When do you take the pictures?

Jiho: This Friday at Dream & Joy Park.

Mike: Sounds good. Do you have a particular style in mind?

Jiho: No. Can you recommend one for me?

Mike: Look at this. How about this style? It'll look good on you.

Jiho: Wow, I like it. I can't wait to see how I'll look in the pictures.

Mike: I'm sure you'll look cool.

Jiho went to a hairdresser, Mike. Jiho is taking his pictures for (A)_____ this Friday at (B)_____. Jiho didn't have a particular style in mind, so he asked Mike (C)_____ _____. Mike suggested one for him. Jiho was looking forward to (D)_____ _____. Mike was sure that (E)_____.

04 다음 대화가 자연스럽게 이어지도록 순서대로 배열하시오.

Minjun: Do you know Ken Kuller?

Sora: Of course. I'm a big fan of his. I've read all of his mystery books.

(A) You know what? His novel *Four Eyes* has been made into a movie.

(B) Maybe we can see the movie together.

(C) Yeah. I saw the movie poster. It looks interesting.

(D) I think he's a great writer. I can't stop reading this book.

(E) It'll come out next Thursday. I'm looking forward to seeing it!

➡ _____

교과서

Grammar

1 과거완료

> • Jake was late for school because he **had missed** the bus.
> Jake는 버스를 놓쳐서 학교에 지각했다.
>
> • He **had been** wounded in the arm. 그는 팔에 부상을 당했었다.

■ 과거완료는 과거 이전에 일어난 일이 과거의 어느 시점까지 영향을 미칠 때 쓰며, 'had+과거분사'의 형태로 쓴다. 과거완료도 현재완료처럼 완료, 경험, 계속, 결과의 용법이 있다. 또한 과거의 어느 시점에서 그보다 먼저 일어난 일을 나타낼 때도 쓰이며 이것을 보통 '대과거'라고 한다.

- She **had** just **woken** from a deep sleep. 그녀는 막 깊은 잠에서 깨어난 참이었다. 〈완료〉
- She **had** never **ridden** a horse before. 그녀는 전에 말을 타 본 적이 한 번도 없었다. 〈경험〉
- He **had worked** for the family for long. 그는 그 가족들을 위해 오랫동안 일을 했었다. 〈계속〉
- He **had gone** abroad to study more. 그는 공부를 더 하기 위해 유학을 갔다. 〈결과〉
- She remembered everything that **had happened** long before. 그녀는 오래 전에 일어난 일을 모두 기억하고 있었다. 〈대과거〉

■ 한 문장에 두 가지 과거의 일이 나올 때, 두 동작이 거의 동시에 일어났거나 시간차가 거의 없이 연속적으로 일어났을 경우에는 단순과거로 표현한다. 또, 접속사 after나 before는 전후 관계를 분명히 나타내는 표현이므로 과거완료 대신 과거시제를 많이 쓴다.

- The door **opened** and Jo **walked** in. 문이 열리더니 Jo가 걸어 들어왔다. 〈시간차가 거의 없는 연속 동작〉
- I **left** before he **arrived**. 나는 그가 도착하기 전에 떠났다. 〈전후 관계가 명백함〉

핵심 Check

1. 다음 괄호 안에서 알맞은 말을 고르시오.

   (1) They believed the accident (has just occurred / had just occurred).

   (2) Kirk knew that water (had got / got) in and rusted the engine.

   (3) He returned home after he (has met / met) Juliet.

② 'It ~ that ...' 강조 구문

- **It was** Judy **that** lost her wallet on the bus. 버스에서 지갑을 잃어버린 것은 바로 Judy였다.
- **It was** her wallet **that** Judy lost on the bus. 버스에서 Judy가 잃어버린 것은 바로 지갑이었다.

■ 'It + is/was + 강조어(구) + that ...'의 형태로 특정 부분을 강조하여 나타낼 때 사용한다. 강조하고자 하는 부분을 'it is/was'와 'that' 사이에 쓰고, 나머지 부분을 that 뒤에 써서 주어, 목적어인 명사, 부사 (구/절) 등을 강조한다. 'be'동사는 문장의 시제에 맞춰 'is'나 'was'를 사용한다.

- I received a phone call from your mother.
  - → **It was** I **that** received a phone call from your mother. (주어 강조)
  - → **It was** a phone call **that** I received from your mother. (목적어인 명사 강조)
  - → **It was** from your mother **that** I received a phone call. (부사구 강조)

■ 'It ~ that ...' 강조 구문에서 강조하는 대상이 명사일 경우, that 대신에 관계대명사 who[whom](사람일 경우) 또는 which(사물이나 동물일 경우)로 바꿔 쓸 수 있으며, 시간 또는 장소의 부사(구/절)일 경우, when(시간) 또는 where(장소)로 바꿔 쓸 수 있다.

- She bought some bread at the bakery yesterday. 그녀는 어제 그 제과점에서 약간의 빵을 샀다.
  - → **It was** she **that**[**who**] bought some bread at the bakery yesterday.
  - → **It was** some bread **that**[**which**] she bought at the bakery yesterday.
  - → **It was** yesterday **that**[**when**] she bought some bread at the bakery.
  - → **It was** at the bakery **that**[**where**] she bought some bread yesterday.

■ 'It ~ that ...' 강조 구문에서 강조하는 대상이 부사(구/절)일 경우 that 다음에 완전한 절이 나오지만 그 외의 경우에는 불완전한 절이 나오는 것에 유의한다. 또한 강조되는 부분에 보어(형용사)나 동사는 올 수 없다.

- **It was** at the restaurant **that**[**where**] I had dinner with her. 내가 그녀와 저녁을 먹은 곳은 바로 그 식당이었다. (that 다음에 완전한 절)
- It was pretty that she was at that time. (보어(형용사) 강조 ×)
- It was did that I the dishes last night. (동사 강조 ×)

핵심 Check

2. 다음 괄호 안에서 알맞은 말을 고르시오.

(1) (It / That) was in the afternoon that I met Joseph.

(2) It is Molly (that / what) is talking on the phone.

(3) It was Raymond (whom / which) he taught English.

01 다음 빈칸에 들어갈 말로 알맞은 것은?

> John said that he _____ his friend on his way home.

① meet ② meets ③ met
④ has met ⑤ had met

02 다음 괄호 안에서 알맞은 말을 고르시오.

(1) He (already left / had already left) when I returned home.
(2) He told me gloomily that he (was called / had been called) up for army service.
(3) (It / That) was Jane Austen that wrote *Pride and Prejudice* in 1813.
(4) It is you (which / who) are to blame.

03 다음 빈칸에 알맞은 것은?

> However, it was literature _____ he loved most.

① where ② when ③ who
④ that ⑤ what

04 다음 우리말에 맞게 주어진 어휘를 바르게 배열하시오.

(1) 나는 2주 전에 산 배낭을 잃어버렸다.
  (two weeks, the backpack, I, I, bought, lost, had, before, that)
  ➡ _____

(2) 그는 열쇠를 잃어버렸다는 것을 알았다.
  (he, had, the keys, he, realized, lost, that)
  ➡ _____

(3) 모든 사람이 말하고 있는 바로 그 영화이다.
  (everybody, talking, the movie, is, is, it, that, about)
  ➡ _____

01 다음 중 어법상 <u>어색한</u> 것은?

① Ted said that he had never missed a day's work because of illness.

② She strongly insisted that she was not there.

③ Jessica came to the meeting late because she had missed the bus.

④ Ann said her grandmother had lived on the farm.

⑤ When I came back home, I found somebody had broken a cup.

02 다음 중 어법상 <u>어색한</u> 것은?

① It was in 1945 that World War Ⅱ ended.

② It was Ben who sang on the stage.

③ It was told that Mirae me a lie the other day.

④ It was Betty whom he met in the library.

⑤ It was dinner which we had together last Saturday.

03 다음 빈칸에 알맞은 말이 바르게 짝지어진 것은?

> • It was the red shirt _____ she bought online.
> • He said that he _____ his homework the night before.

① that – had finished

② which – has finished

③ that – has finished

④ which – finished

⑤ what – have finished

서답형

04 다음 괄호 안에서 알맞은 말을 고르시오.

(1) It was by far the worst speech that he (has ever made / had ever made).

(2) Linda wore the necklace which her boyfriend (had presented / presented) to her.

(3) Pamela died in 1992 in Detroit, where she (lived / had lived) since 1957.

(4) It was Kate (which / who) lost her wallet in the museum.

(5) It was yesterday (which / when) she lost her smartphone.

(6) It was in the library (which / where) we studied math with Jane.

05 주어진 문장의 <u>틀린</u> 부분을 찾아 올바르게 고친 것을 고르시오.

> He had said that he lived in Korea for 10 years.

① He had said that he lives in Korea for 10 years.

② He had said that he lived in Korea for 10 years.

③ He had said that he had lived in Korea for 10 years.

④ He said that he had lived in Korea for 10 years.

⑤ He said that he has lived in Korea for 10 years.

06 다음 문장의 밑줄 친 부분 중 어법상 어색한 것은?

> He ①wasn't exactly ②a stranger. I ③ have met him ④once ⑤before.

①   ②   ③   ④   ⑤

07 빈칸 (A)와 (B)에 알맞은 말이 바르게 짝지어진 것은?

> It is a number of books on the subject ____(A)____ he ____(B)____ up to now.

	(A)	(B)
①	what	has written
②	if	had written
③	if	wrote
④	that	wrote
⑤	that	has written

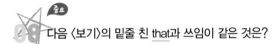

08 다음 〈보기〉의 밑줄 친 that과 쓰임이 같은 것은?

> ┌─ 보기 ─┐
> It was in 1813 that Jane Austen wrote *Pride and Prejudice.*

① I can't walk that far.
② The entire population of one city in China is more than that of three cities in Korea.
③ It was Chaucer that really turned English into a literary language.
④ I heard that you've been abroad.
⑤ Look at that man over there.

[09~10] 다음 문장의 빈칸에 알맞은 말은?

09
> When I came back home, I found somebody _____ the room.

① cleans   ② cleaned
③ had cleaning   ④ had cleaned
⑤ has cleaned

10 중요
> It was my grandfather _____ named me Jongsu.

① that   ② what   ③ when
④ which   ⑤ where

11 다음 우리말을 바르게 영작한 것을 고르시오.

> The Statue of Liberty를 건축한 사람은 바로 Gustave Eiffel이었다.

① It was the Statue of Liberty that Gustave Eiffel built.
② It was Gustave Eiffel that built the Statue of Liberty.
③ It was Gustave Eiffel what built the Statue of Liberty.
④ It was Gustave Eiffel when built the Statue of Liberty.
⑤ It was Gustave Eiffel which built the Statue of Liberty.

서답형
12 다음 문장에서 어법상 어색한 것을 바르게 고쳐 다시 쓰시오.

> Sherill found the box that Adam hid a week before.

➡ _____
_____

서답형

13 다음 두 문장을 한 문장으로 바꿔 쓰고자 한다. 빈칸에 들어갈 알맞은 말을 쓰시오.

> • Son started to play soccer when he was 8 years old.
> • Son played soccer wonderfully at the stadium yesterday.
> = Son played soccer wonderfully at the stadium yesterday as he _____ it since he was 8 years old.

➡ _____

14 다음 중 It ~ that 쓰임이 나머지와 <u>다른</u> 하나는?

① It is in July that we go camping together.
② It is important that Koreans remember the true meaning of the traditional holiday.
③ It was in the restaurant that I had *samgyupsal* with Anne yesterday.
④ It was her umbrella that she lost after enjoying dinner at the restaurant.
⑤ It was yesterday that she asked me to go for a walk.

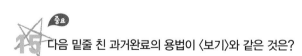 다음 밑줄 친 과거완료의 용법이 <보기>와 같은 것은?

> ┤ 보기 ├
> Linda <u>had been</u> sick in bed for a week.

① The child <u>had</u> just <u>wakened</u>.
② I thought she <u>had</u> never <u>ridden</u> a horse before.
③ How long <u>had</u> you <u>had</u> the symptoms?
④ Mary didn't know he <u>had gone</u> to America.
⑤ She realized that everybody <u>had been</u> listening to the song.

서답형

16 다음 문장에서 어법상 <u>어색한</u> 것을 바르게 고쳐 다시 쓰시오.

(1) I looked at something I had never seen ago.

➡ _____
_____

(2) He had remembered what he read.

➡ _____
_____

(3) It was the lamp who someone broke in the room.

➡ _____
_____

(4) It was when Mike told his wife something which she realized her mistake.

➡ _____
_____

(5) It is the school gym that we play basketball every Saturday.

➡ _____
_____

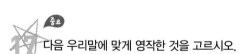 다음 우리말에 맞게 영작한 것을 고르시오.

> 그것은 세상 사람 누구도 본 적이 없는 것이었다.

① It had been something that the world never saw before.
② It had been something that the world had never seen before.
③ It was something that the world has never seen before.
④ It was something that the world had never seen before.
⑤ It was something that the world had never seen ago.

01 시간 흐름에 따른 사건 전개에 맞게 빈칸을 채워 문장을 완성하시오.

> My mom bought a new smartphone for me last month.
> → I lost the smartphone yesterday.
> → I don't have the smartphone now.

➡ I lost the smartphone that my mom _____ last month.

02 다음 우리말에 맞게 주어진 어구를 바르게 배열하시오.

(1) Joanne이 점심으로 먹은 것은 바로 김밥이었다. (Joanne, was, ate, that, *gimbap*, lunch, it, for)

➡ _____

(2) 내가 수영 수업을 받는 날은 바로 토요일이다. (swimming, I, that, it, take, is, a, Saturdays, lesson, on)

➡ _____

(3) 그 경찰관은 Green 씨가 빨간 신호등을 무시하고 운전했다고 말했다. (Mr. Green, the police officer, light, driven, said, had, red, a, through)

➡ _____

(4) 우리는 그 차가 고장 나기 전까지 15년 동안 소유했다. (it, we, car, 15 years, had, broke, had, that, before, for, down)

➡ _____

03 다음 문장에서 어법상 <u>어색한</u> 것을 바르게 고쳐 다시 쓰시오.

(1) He has never studied English before he went to London.

➡ _____

(2) Daniel was never to London until he met Jane.

➡ _____

(3) He took items that he has given to Carolyn and gave them to Dora.

➡ _____

(4) It was her wallet who Judy lost on the bus.

➡ _____

(5) It was a small island that I was born.

➡ _____

(6) It was carefully that he drove his car.

➡ _____

04 그림을 보고, 주어진 어휘를 이용하여 빈칸을 알맞게 채우시오.

(1) Jessica noticed that her brother _____ Plum's toy. (break, already)

(2) _____ that the spider wanted to catch. (it, a ladybug)

05 다음을 when을 이용하여 한 문장으로 연결할 때 빈칸을 알맞게 채우시오. (시제에 유의할 것.)

(1) I came back home. I found one thing. Somebody opened the window.

➡ When I came back home, I found that somebody _____ the window.

(2) Mariel promised to meet Charlotte at the cafe. She went there very late. Charlotte already left the cafe. So, she couldn't meet her.

➡ When Mariel got to the cafe to meet Charlotte, she _____ the cafe.

06 다음 문장을 주어진 단어를 강조하는 문장으로 고쳐 쓰시오. that은 사용하지 말 것.

> My brother bought the cake at the store last night.

(1) My brother

➡ _____

_____

(2) bought

➡ _____

_____

(3) the cake

➡ _____

_____

(4) at the store

➡ _____

_____

(5) last night

➡ _____

_____

07 다음 문장의 밑줄 친 부분을 강조하는 문장으로 바꿔 쓰시오.

(1) I learned how to read and write <u>at the age of six</u>.

➡ _____

_____

(2) <u>My dad</u> gets up earliest in my family.

➡ _____

_____

(3) I eat <u>an egg sandwich</u> when I feel blue.

➡ _____

_____

(4) Did I see <u>Nick</u> at the bookstore?

➡ _____

_____

A Poet Who Loved Stars

In the sky where seasons pass in a hurry
Autumn fills the air.
And ready I stand, without a worry,
To count all the stars there.

......

Memory for one star,
Love for another star,
Loneliness for another star,
Longing for another star,
Poetry for another star,
And, oh, mother, mother for another star.

......

Have you read these lines before? They are part of the poem "Counting Stars at Night" by Yoon Dong-ju. The poem was written a long time ago but still remains one of Korea's favorite poems.

Dong-ju was born in 1917 near Yanbin, China. As a young boy, he loved sports, and he was a soccer player for his school. He also loved sewing so much that he sewed the numbers on all his friends' soccer uniforms. However, it was literature that he loved most. In elementary school he wrote a lot of poems. He even made a literary magazine with his cousin, Song Mong-gyu. In middle school he once borrowed a poetry book by a famous poet of the time, Baek Seok, and copied the whole book by hand. He really wanted to have his own copy of the rare book.

poet 시인
in a hurry 서둘러
loneliness 외로움
longing 동경, 갈망
poetry (문학 장르) 시
poem (한 편의) 시
remain 남아 있다, 계속 ~하다
sew 바느질하다
literature 문학
literary 문학의, 문학적인
copy 베끼다, 복사하다; 복사본, (책) 한 부
whole 전체의, 모든
by hand 손으로, 직접
rare 희귀한

 확인문제

● 다음 문장이 본문의 내용과 일치하면 T, 일치하지 않으면 F를 쓰시오.

1 "Counting Stars at Night" was written a long time ago by Yoon Dong-ju.

2 When he was a young boy, he loved sports, and he was a soccer player for his village.

3 In elementary school he wrote many poems.

4 In middle school he even made a literary magazine with his cousin.

His parents wanted him to be a doctor, but Dong-ju chose to study literature at a college in Seoul. During his college years, he often hung out with other young poets and wrote poetry where he expressed feelings about his hometown and lost country. To celebrate his graduation, he wished to publish 19 of his poems under the title, *Heaven, Wind, Stars, and Poetry*. He made three copies of the book by hand. One was given to his close friend, Jeong Byeong-uk, another was presented to his favorite professor, and the last one was kept for himself. However, his professor advised against his plan because he thought the Japanese government would not allow the publication. Dong-ju followed his advice and gave up the idea.

Dong-ju decided to study further in the country where his father had studied before. So, in 1942, Dong-ju and his cousin began to study in Japan. On July 10 the following year, his cousin was arrested by the Japanese police for taking part in an independence movement. Four days later, Dong-ju was also arrested on the same charges. In 1945, Dong-ju and his cousin died in prison after harsh treatment by the police. It was just a few months later that Korea achieved independence from Japan.

In 1948, Jeong Byeong-uk brought Dong-ju's poems to the poet's brother, and they were finally published. The book was given the title the poet had thought of many years before. His poems are loved by people of all ages, and thus they still shine brightly in our hearts like the stars in the autumn night sky.

hang out with ~와 시간을 보내다
hometown 고향
celebrate 기념하다
graduation 졸업
publish 출판하다
government 정부
publication 출판, 발행
further 더, 더 멀리
arrest 체포하다
take part in ~에 참가하다
independence 독립
charge 기소, 혐의
harsh 가혹한, 혹독한
treatment 대우, 처리
achieve 이루다, 얻다
shine 빛나다

 확인문제

● 다음 문장이 본문의 내용과 일치하면 T, 일치하지 않으면 F를 쓰시오.

1 Dong-ju wrote poetry where he expressed feelings about his hometown and lost country. ☐

2 To celebrate his graduation, Dong-ju published 19 of his poems under the title, *Heaven, Wind, Stars, and Poetry*. ☐

3 In 1943, Dong-ju's cousin was arrested by the Japanese police for taking part in an independence movement. ☐

4 In 1948, Jeong Byeong-uk brought Dong-ju's poems to Dong-ju's parents, and they were finally published. ☐

● 우리말을 참고하여 빈칸에 알맞은 말을 쓰시오.

1 A Poet _____ Loved Stars

2 In the sky _____ seasons pass _____ _____ _____

3 Autumn _____ the air.

4 And ready I stand, _____ _____ _____ ,

5 To _____ all the stars there.

6 _____ for one star,

7 Love for _____ star,

8 _____ for another star,

9 _____ for another star,

10 Poetry _____ another star,

11 And, oh, mother, mother _____ _____ _____ .

12 Have you read _____ _____ before?

13 They are _____ _____ the poem "Counting Stars at Night" _____ Yoon Dong-ju.

14 The poem was written a long time ago but _____ _____ one of Korea's favorite _____ .

15 Dong-ju _____ _____ in 1917 near Yanbin, China.

16 As a young boy, he loved sports, and he was a soccer player _____ _____ .

17 He also loved sewing _____ much _____ he sewed the numbers on all his friends' soccer uniforms.

1	별을 사랑한 시인
2	계절이 지나가는 하늘에는
3	가을로 가득 차 있습니다.
4	나는 아무 걱정도 없이
5	가을 속의 별들을 다 헤일 듯합니다.
6	별 하나에 추억과
7	별 하나에 사랑과
8	별 하나에 쓸쓸함과
9	별 하나에 동경과
10	별 하나에 시와
11	별 하나에 어머니, 어머니,
12	당신은 이 시 구절을 읽어 본 적이 있는가?
13	이것은 윤동주의 시 '별 헤는 밤'의 일부이다.
14	시는 오래 전에 쓰였지만 여전히 한국의 가장 좋아하는 시 중의 하나로 남아 있다.
15	동주는 중국 연변 근처에서 1917년에 태어났다.
16	어린 소년이었을 때 그는 운동을 좋아했고, 학교의 축구 선수였다.
17	그는 또한 바느질하는 것을 무척 좋아해서 친구들의 축구 유니폼에 번호를 바느질해 주기도 했다.

18 However, _____ _____ literature _____ he loved most.

19 In elementary school he wrote _____ _____ _____ _____.

20 He even made _____ _____ _____ with his cousin, Song Mong-gyu.

21 In middle school he once borrowed a poetry book by a famous poet of the time, Baek Seok, and _____ the whole book _____ _____.

22 He really wanted _____ _____ _____ _____ _____ of the rare book.

23 His parents wanted him _____ _____ _____ _____, but Dong-ju chose to study literature at a college in Seoul.

24 During his college years, he often _____ _____ _____ other young poets and wrote poetry _____ he expressed feelings about his hometown and _____ _____.

25 _____ _____ _____ _____, he wished to publish 19 of his poems _____ _____ _____, *Heaven, Wind, Stars, and Poetry.*

26 He made _____ _____ of the book _____ _____.

27 One _____ _____ _____ his close friend, Jeong Byeong-uk, _____ was presented to his favorite professor, and _____ _____ _____ was kept for himself.

28 However, his professor _____ _____ his plan because he thought the Japanese government would not allow the publication.

18 그러나 그가 가장 사랑한 것은 문학이었다.

19 초등학교에 다닐 때 그는 많은 시를 썼다.

20 심지어 사촌 송몽규와 문학잡지를 만들기도 했다.

21 그가 중학교에 다니던 때 한번은 당대의 유명한 시인 백석의 시집을 빌려 와서 책 전체를 필사하기도 했다.

22 그는 정말로 그 희귀한 책을 한 부 갖고 싶었던 것이다.

23 그의 부모는 그가 의사가 되기를 바랐지만 동주는 서울에 있는 대학에서 문학 공부를 하기로 했다.

24 대학 시절에 그는 종종 다른 젊은 시인들과 어울려 다녔고, 고향과 잃어버린 조국에 대한 심정을 표현하는 시를 썼다.

25 졸업을 기념하여 그는 '하늘과 바람과 별과 시'라는 제목으로 자신의 시 19편을 출판하고 싶어 했다.

26 그는 책 세 부를 손으로 만들었다.

27 한 부는 가까운 친구인 정병욱에게 주었고, 또 하나는 그가 가장 좋아하는 교수에게 선물했으며, 마지막 하나는 자신이 보관했다.

28 그러나 그의 교수는 일본 정부가 출판을 허가하지 않으리라 여겨, 그의 계획에 반대하는 충고를 했다.

29 Dong-ju _____ his advice and _____ _____ the idea.

30 Dong-ju decided _____ _____ _____ in the country where his father _____ _____ before.

31 So, in 1942, Dong-ju and his cousin _____ _____ _____ in Japan.

32 On July 10 the following year, his cousin was arrested by the Japanese police _____ _____ _____ _____ an independence movement.

33 Four days later, Dong-ju was also arrested _____ _____ _____ _____.

34 In 1945, Dong-ju and his cousin died in prison _____ _____ _____ by the police.

35 _____ _____ just a few months later _____ Korea achieved independence from Japan.

36 In 1948, Jeong Byeong-uk brought Dong-ju's poems to the poet's brother, and _____ _____ _____ _____.

37 The book _____ _____ the title the poet _____ _____ _____ many years before.

38 His poems _____ _____ _____ people of all ages, and thus they still shine brightly in our hearts _____ the stars in the autumn night sky.

29 동주는 그의 충고를 따랐고 그 생각을 포기했다.

30 동주는 그의 아버지가 예전에 공부했던 나라에서 학업을 이어가기로 했다.

31 그리하여 1942년에 동주와 그의 사촌은 일본에서 공부를 시작했다.

32 다음 해 7월 10일에 그의 사촌은 독립운동에 가담했다는 이유로 일본 경찰에게 체포되었다.

33 나흘 뒤 동주 역시 같은 혐의로 체포되었다.

34 1945년에 동주와 그의 사촌은 경찰의 가혹 행위를 당한 후 감옥에서 사망했다.

35 한국이 일본으로부터 독립을 이룬 것은 그로부터 불과 몇 달 후의 일이었다.

36 1948년에 정병욱이 동주의 시를 시인의 동생에게 가져다주었고, 마침내 그것들은 출판되었다.

37 그 책에는 시인이 수년 전에 생각해 두었던 제목이 붙었다.

38 그의 시는 모든 세대의 사랑을 받고 있고, 따라서 그것들은 가을밤 하늘의 별처럼 우리 가슴 속에 여전히 밝게 빛나고 있다.

우리말을 참고하여 본문을 영작하시오.

1 별을 사랑한 시인
➡ _____

2 계절이 지나가는 하늘에는
➡ _____

3 가을로 가득 차 있습니다.
➡ _____

4 나는 아무 걱정도 없이
➡ _____

5 가을 속의 별들을 다 헤일 듯합니다.
➡ _____

6 별 하나에 추억과
➡ _____

7 별 하나에 사랑과
➡ _____

8 별 하나에 쓸쓸함과
➡ _____

9 별 하나에 동경과
➡ _____

10 별 하나에 시와
➡ _____

11 별 하나에 어머니, 어머니,
➡ _____

12 당신은 이 시 구절을 읽어 본 적이 있는가?
➡ _____

13 이것은 윤동주의 시 '별 헤는 밤'의 일부이다.
➡ _____

14 시는 오래 전에 쓰였지만 여전히 한국의 가장 좋아하는 시 중의 하나로 남아 있다.
➡ _____

15 동주는 중국 연변 근처에서 1917년에 태어났다.
➡ _____

16 ▶ 어린 소년이었을 때 그는 운동을 좋아했고, 학교의 축구 선수였다.

➡ _____

17 ▶ 그는 또한 바느질하는 것을 무척 좋아해서 친구들의 축구 유니폼에 번호를 바느질해 주기도 했다.

➡ _____

18 ▶ 그러나 그가 가장 사랑한 것은 문학이었다.

➡ _____

19 ▶ 초등학교에 다닐 때 그는 많은 시를 썼다.

➡ _____

20 ▶ 심지어 사촌 송몽규와 문학잡지를 만들기도 했다.

➡ _____

21 ▶ 그가 중학교에 다니던 때 한번은 당대의 유명한 시인 백석의 시집을 빌려 와서 책 전체를 필사하기도 했다.

➡ _____

_____

22 ▶ 그는 정말로 그 희귀한 책을 한 부 갖고 싶었던 것이다.

➡ _____

23 ▶ 그의 부모는 그가 의사가 되기를 바랐지만 동주는 서울에 있는 대학에서 문학 공부를 하기로 했다.

➡ _____

24 ▶ 대학 시절에 그는 종종 다른 젊은 시인들과 어울려 다녔고, 고향과 잃어버린 조국에 대한 심정을 표현하는 시를 썼다.

➡ _____

_____

25 ▶ 졸업을 기념하여 그는 '하늘과 바람과 별과 시'라는 제목으로 자신의 시 19편을 출판하고 싶어 했다.

➡ _____

_____

26 ▶ 그는 책 세 부를 손으로 만들었다.

➡ _____

27 ▶ 한 부는 가까운 친구인 정병욱에게 주었고, 또 하나는 그가 가장 좋아하는 교수에게 선물했으며, 마지막 하나는 자신이 보관했다.

➡ _____

_____

28 그러나 그의 교수는 일본 정부가 출판을 허가하지 않으리라 여겨, 그의 계획에 반대하는 충고를 했다.

➡ _____

_____

29 동주는 그의 충고를 따랐고 그 생각을 포기했다.

➡ _____

30 동주는 그의 아버지가 예전에 공부했던 나라에서 학업을 이어 가기로 했다.

➡ _____

31 그리하여 1942년에 동주와 그의 사촌은 일본에서 공부를 시작했다.

➡ _____

32 다음 해 7월 10일에 그의 사촌은 독립운동에 가담했다는 이유로 일본 경찰에게 체포되었다.

➡ _____

_____

33 나흘 뒤 동주 역시 같은 혐의로 체포되었다.

➡ _____

34 1945년에 동주와 그의 사촌은 경찰의 가혹 행위를 당한 후 감옥에서 사망했다.

➡ _____

35 한국이 일본으로부터 독립을 이룬 것은 그로부터 불과 몇 달 후의 일이었다.

➡ _____

36 1948년에 정병욱이 동주의 시를 시인의 동생에게 가져다주었고, 마침내 그것들은 출판되었다.

➡ _____

_____

37 그 책에는 시인이 수년 전에 생각해 두었던 제목이 붙었다.

➡ _____

38 그의 시는 모든 세대의 사랑을 받고 있고, 따라서 그것들은 가을밤 하늘의 별처럼 우리 가슴 속에 여전히 밝게 빛나고 있다.

➡ _____

_____

[01~03] 다음 글을 읽고 물음에 답하시오.

In the sky where seasons pass ⓐ a hurry
Autumn fills the air.

And ready I stand, without a worry,
To count all the stars there.
......
Memory for one star,
Love for another star,
Loneliness for another star,
Longing for another star,
Poetry for another star,
And, oh, mother, mother for another star.
......
(A)Have you read these lines before? They are part of the poem "Counting Stars at Night" ⓑ Yoon Dong-ju. (B)The poem was written a long time ago but still remains one of Korea's favorite poem.

01 위 글의 빈칸 ⓐ와 ⓑ에 들어갈 전치사가 바르게 짝지어진 것은?

ⓐ	ⓑ		ⓐ	ⓑ
① on	– from		② in	– by
③ in	– from		④ on	– to
⑤ for	– by			

중요

02 위 글의 밑줄 친 (A)의 현재완료 용법과 같은 것을 모두 고르시오.

① We have done it several times.
② He hasn't seen her since last night.
③ John hasn't eaten his hamburger yet.
④ He has seen my sister once.
⑤ I have known him for the past 5 years.

서답형

03 위 글의 밑줄 친 (B)에서 어법상 틀린 부분을 찾아 고치시오.

_____ ➡ _____

[04~06] 다음 글을 읽고 물음에 답하시오.

His parents wanted him to be a doctor, but Dong-ju chose to study literature at a college in Seoul. (A)[During / While] his college years, he often hung out with (B)[another / other] young poets and wrote poetry where he expressed feelings about his hometown and lost country. To celebrate his graduation, he wished to publish 19 of his poems (a)'하늘과 바람과 별과 시'라는 제목으로. He made three copies of the book by hand. One was given to his close friend, Jeong Byeong-uk, (C)[another / the other] was presented to his favorite professor, and the last one was kept for himself. However, his professor advised against his plan because he thought the Japanese government would not allow the publication. Dong-ju followed his advice and ⓐ the idea.

04 위 글의 빈칸 ⓐ에 들어갈 알맞은 말을 두 개 고르시오.

① abandoned　　② offered
③ gave up　　④ explained
⑤ suggested

서답형

05 위 글의 괄호 (A)~(C)에서 어법상 알맞은 낱말을 골라 쓰시오.

➡ (A) _____ (B) _____ (C) _____

서답형

06 위 글의 밑줄 친 (a)의 우리말에 맞게 주어진 어휘를 이용하여 8 단어로 영작하시오.

> title, *Heaven, Wind, Stars, and Poetry*

➡ _____

_____

[07~09] 다음 글을 읽고 물음에 답하시오.

Dong-ju was born in 1917 near Yanbin, China. ⓐAs a young boy, he loved sports, and he was a soccer player for his school. He also loved sewing so much that he sewed the numbers on all his friends' soccer uniforms. However, it was literature that he loved most. In elementary school he wrote a lot of poems. He even made a literary magazine with his cousin, Song Mong-gyu. In middle school he once borrowed a poetry book by a famous poet of the time, Baek Seok, and copied the whole book by hand. He really wanted to have his own copy of the rare book.

07 위 글의 밑줄 친 ⓐAs와 같은 의미로 쓰인 것을 고르시오.

① They did as I had asked.
② She may need some help as she's new.
③ As you know, Julia is leaving soon.
④ She sang as she walked.
⑤ She was as beautiful as I had imagined.

서답형

08 본문의 내용과 일치하도록 다음 빈칸 (A)와 (B)에 알맞은 단어를 쓰시오.

> Dong-ju wrote many (A)_____ in elementary school, and even made (B)_____ _____ _____ with his cousin, Song Mong-gyu.

09 Which question CANNOT be answered after reading the passage?

① When was Dong-ju born?
② What sport did Dong-ju love as a young boy?
③ Why did Dong-ju sew the numbers on all his friends' soccer uniforms?
④ When did Dong-ju make a literary magazine with his cousin, Song Mong-gyu?
⑤ What was the title of the poetry book that Dong-ju copied by hand?

[10~12] 다음 글을 읽고 물음에 답하시오.

Dong-ju decided to study further in the country ⓐwhere his father had studied before. So, in 1942, Dong-ju and his cousin began to study in Japan. On July 10 the following year, his cousin was arrested by the Japanese police for taking part in an independence movement. Four days later, Dong-ju was also arrested on the same ⓑcharges. In 1945, Dong-ju and his cousin died in prison after harsh treatment by the police. It was just a few months later that Korea achieved independence from Japan.

서답형

10 위 글의 밑줄 친 ⓐwhere를 두 단어로 바꿔 쓰시오.

➡ _____

11 위 글의 밑줄 친 ⓑcharges와 같은 의미로 쓰인 것을 고르시오.

① The admission charges are free.
② She always charges the battery before use.
③ He denied all charges in court.
④ A prosecutor charges a person with a crime.
⑤ He charges 100 dollars for the repairs.

서답형

12 In July 1943, why were Dong-ju and his cousin arrested by the Japanese police? Fill in the blanks with suitable words. (2 words)

> They were arrested by the Japanese police for _____ _____ an independence movement.

[13~15] 다음 글을 읽고 물음에 답하시오.

Dong-ju was born in 1917 near Yanbin, China. (①) As a young boy, he loved sports, and he was a soccer player for his school. (②) He also loved ___ⓐ___ so much that he sewed the numbers on all his friends' soccer uniforms. (③) In elementary school he wrote a lot of poems. (④) He even made a literary magazine with his cousin, Song Mong-gyu. (⑤) In middle school he once borrowed a poetry book by a famous poet of the time, Baek Seok, and copied the whole book by hand. He really wanted to have his own copy of the rare book.

서답형

13 위 글의 빈칸 ⓐ에 sew를 알맞은 형태로 쓰시오.

➡ _____ 또는 _____

14 위 글의 흐름으로 보아, 주어진 문장이 들어가기에 가장 적절한 곳은?

> However, it was literature that he loved most.

① ② ③ ④ ⑤

중요

15 According to the passage, which is NOT true?

① As a young boy, Dong-ju was a soccer player for his school.

② Dong-ju sewed the numbers on all his friends' soccer uniforms.

③ Dong-ju loved literature more than sewing.

④ In middle school Dong-ju made a literary magazine with his cousin, Song Mong-gyu.

⑤ Dong-ju really wanted to have his own copy of a poetry book by Baek Seok.

[16~18] 다음 글을 읽고 물음에 답하시오.

(A)His parents wanted him to be a doctor, but Dong-ju chose studying literature at a college in Seoul. During his college years, he often hung out with other young poets and wrote poetry where he expressed feelings about his hometown and lost country. To celebrate ①his graduation, he wished to publish 19 of ②his poems under the title, *Heaven, Wind, Stars, and Poetry*. He made three copies of the book by hand. One was given to ③his close friend, Jeong Byeong-uk, another was presented to his favorite professor, and the last one was kept for himself. However, ④his professor advised ___ⓐ___ his plan because he thought the Japanese government would not allow the publication. Dong-ju followed ⑤his advice and gave up the idea.

16 위 글의 빈칸 ⓐ에 들어갈 알맞은 전치사를 고르시오.

① on ② against ③ for
④ to ⑤ over

17 밑줄 친 ①~⑤ 중에서 가리키는 대상이 나머지 넷과 <u>다른</u> 것은?

①   ②   ③   ④   ⑤

서답형

18 위 글의 밑줄 친 (A)에서 어법상 <u>틀린</u> 부분을 찾아 고치시오.

_____ ➡ _____

[19~21] 다음 글을 읽고 물음에 답하시오.

  Dong-ju decided to study further in the country where his father had studied before. (①) So, ⓐin 1942, Dong-ju and his cousin began to study in Japan. (②) ⓑIn July 10 the following year, his cousin was arrested by the Japanese police ⓒfor taking part in an independence movement. (③) In 1945, Dong-ju and his cousin died in prison after harsh treatment ⓓby the police. (④) It was just a few months later that Korea achieved independence ⓔfrom Japan. (⑤)

19 위 글의 흐름으로 보아, ①~⑤ 중 주어진 문장이 들어가기에 가장 적절한 곳은?

> Four days later, Dong-ju was also arrested on the same charges.

①   ②   ③   ④   ⑤

서답형

20 위 글의 밑줄 친 ⓐ~ⓔ에서 전치사의 쓰임이 적절하지 <u>않</u>은 것을 찾아 알맞게 고치시오.

_____ 번 ➡ _____

21 위 글의 주제로 알맞은 것을 고르시오.

① Dong-ju and his father's decision about his studying abroad
② Dong-ju's cousin who also began to study in Japan
③ Dong-ju's cousin's arrest by the Japanese police
④ the harsh treatment by the police in prison
⑤ Dong-ju and his cousin's independence movement and unfortunate death

22 다음 글의 밑줄 친 ⓐ를 'it is ~ that ...강조 구문'으로 고친 것 중 옳지 <u>않은</u> 것을 고르시오.

> ⓐIn 1948, Jeong Byeong-uk brought Dong-ju's poems to the poet's brother, and they were finally published. The book was given the title the poet had thought of many years before. His poems are loved by people of all ages, and thus they still shine brightly in our hearts like the stars in the autumn night sky.

① It was in 1948 that Jeong Byeong-uk brought Dong-ju's poems to the poet's brother.
② It was Jeong Byeong-uk that brought Dong-ju's poems to the poet's brother in 1948.
③ It was brought that Jeong Byeong-uk Dong-ju's poems to the poet's brother in 1948.
④ It was Dong-ju's poems that Jeong Byeong-uk brought to the poet's brother in 1948.
⑤ It was to the poet's brother that Jeong Byeong-uk brought Dong-ju's poems in 1948.

[01~03] 다음 글을 읽고 물음에 답하시오.

In the sky ⓐ_____ seasons pass ⓑin a hurry
Autumn fills the air.

And ready I stand, without a worry,
To count all the stars there.
......

Have you read these lines before? ⓒThey are part of the poem "Counting Stars at Night" by Yoon Dong-ju. The poem was written a long time ago but still remains one of Korea's favorite poems.

01 위 글의 빈칸 ⓐ에 들어갈 알맞은 단어를 쓰시오.

➡ _____

02 위 글의 밑줄 친 ⓑin a hurry와 바꿔 쓸 수 있는 두 단어를 쓰시오.

➡ _____

03 위 글의 밑줄 친 ⓒThey가 가리키는 것을 본문에서 찾아 쓰시오.

➡ _____

[04~06] 다음 글을 읽고 물음에 답하시오.

Dong-ju was born in 1917 near Yanbin, China. As a young boy, he loved sports, and he was a soccer player for his school. He also loved sewing so much that he sewed the numbers on all his friends' soccer uniforms. However, ⓐ그가 가장 사랑한 것은 문학이었다. In elementary school he wrote a lot of (A)[poems / poets]. He even made a (B)[literally / literary] magazine with his cousin, Song Mong-gyu. In middle school he once borrowed a poetry book by a famous poet of the time, Baek Seok, and copied the whole book by hand. He really wanted to have his own copy of the (C)[common / rare] book.

04 위 글의 괄호 (A)~(C)에서 문맥이나 어법상 알맞은 낱말을 골라 쓰시오.

➡ (A) _____ (B) _____ (C) _____

05 위 글의 밑줄 친 ⓐ의 우리말에 맞게 주어진 어휘를 이용하여 7 단어로 영작하시오.

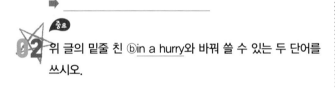

that, most

➡ _____

06 다음 문장에서 위 글의 내용과 다른 부분을 찾아서 고치시오.

In middle school Dong-ju once copied by hand a whole poetry book he had bought, and it was written by Baek Seok, a famous poet of the time. He really wanted to have his own copy of the rare book.

_____ ➡ _____

[07~09] 다음 글을 읽고 물음에 답하시오.

In (A)1948, Jeong Byeong-uk brought Dong-ju's poems to the poet's brother, and they were finally published. The book ⓐ_____ the title the poet had thought of many years before. His poems are loved by people of all ages, and thus (B)they still shine brightly in our hearts like the stars in the autumn night sky.

07 위 글의 빈칸 ⓐ에 give를 알맞은 형태로 쓰시오.

➡ _____

08 위 글의 밑줄 친 (A)1948을 영어로 읽는 법을 쓰시오.

➡ _____

중요

09 위 글의 밑줄 친 (B)they가 가리키는 것을 본문에서 찾아 쓰시오.

➡ _____

[10~11] 다음 글을 읽고 물음에 답하시오.

Dong-ju decided to study ___ⓐ___ in the country where his father had studied before. So, in 1942, Dong-ju and his cousin began to study in Japan. On July 10 the following year, his cousin was arrested by the Japanese police for taking part in an independence movement. Four days later, Dong-ju was also arrested on the same charges. In 1945, Dong-ju and his cousin died in prison after harsh treatment by the police. It was just a few months later that Korea achieved independence from Japan.

10 위 글의 빈칸 ⓐ에 far의 비교급을 쓰시오.

➡ _____

고난이도

11 Why did Dong-ju and his cousin die in prison in 1945? Fill in the blanks with suitable words.

Because there was _____ _____ by the Japanese police.

[12~14] 다음 글을 읽고 물음에 답하시오.

His parents wanted him to be a doctor, but Dong-ju chose to study literature at a college in Seoul. During his college years, he often hung out with other young poets and wrote poetry where he expressed feelings about his hometown and lost country. To celebrate his graduation, he wished to publish 19 of his poems under the title, *Heaven, Wind, Stars, and Poetry*. He made three copies of the book by hand. ⓐOne was given to his close friend, Jeong Byeong-uk, another was presented to his favorite professor, and the last one was kept for himself. However, his professor advised against ⓑhis plan because he thought the Japanese government would not allow the publication. Dong-ju followed his advice and gave up the idea.

중요

12 위 글의 밑줄 친 ⓐ를 능동태로 고치시오.

➡ _____

_____

_____

13 위 글의 밑줄 친 ⓑhis plan이 가리키는 것을 우리말로 쓰시오.

➡ _____

_____

14 본문의 내용과 일치하도록 다음 빈칸 (A)와 (B)에 알맞은 단어를 쓰시오.

Dong-ju majored in (A)_____ at a college in Seoul, though his parents wanted him to be (B)_____ _____.

Communicate: Speak

Tom: Hi, Sora. You look excited.
<u>look+형용사: ~하게 보이다</u>

Sora: Yeah. I'm really <u>looking forward to</u> this Tuesday.
<u>look forward to+명사: ~을 기대한다</u>

Tom: This Tuesday? What's on Tuesday?

Sora: There's a big curling match. I can't wait!

구문해설 • **look forward to**+명사 = **can't wait for**+명사 = **long for**+명사 = **be eager for**+명사:
~을 기대하다

Tom: 안녕, 소라. 너 신나 보여.

Sora: 응. 나는 정말로 이번 주 화요일이 기대돼.

Tom: 이번 주 화요일? 화요일에 무슨 일이 있니?

Sora: 큰 컬링 게임이 있어. 나는 너무 기대돼!

Before You Read

Last week we celebrated August 15 in our class. We put up pictures of people

who <u>had lived</u> through harsh times and tried <u>to achieve</u> independence. Also,
과거보다 앞선 시점(대과거)이므로 과거완료   부정사의 명사적 용법(목적어)

there was a talk <u>on</u> writers who <u>had expressed</u> their longing for freedom in
= about   과거보다 앞선 시점(대과거)이므로 과거완료

literary works.

구문해설 • **celebrate**: 기념하다 • **put up**: 내걸다, 게시하다 • **harsh**: 가혹한, 혹독한
• **independence**: 독립 • **longing**: 동경, 갈망 • **literary**: 문학의, 문학적인

지난주에 우리는 반에서 8월 15일을 기념했습니다. 우리는 가혹한 시대를 살면서 독립을 쟁취하려고 노력한 사람들의 사진을 전시했습니다. 또한, 자유를 향한 동경을 문학 작품에 표현한 작가들에 관한 강연도 있었습니다.

Wrap Up READING

Do you enjoy plays, poems, novels, or cartoons? They are different kinds of

literature, and people <u>differ in</u> which kind they prefer. However, all of them
differ in: ~에 대해 다르다   which kind 이하는 간접의문문으로 전치사 in의 목적어

<u>allow us to go</u> beyond our own small world <u>where</u> we live. When we read
allow+목적어+to부정사: (목적어)가 ~하게 허락하다   where가 이끄는 관계부사절이 앞의 our own small world를 수식

literature, we come across the ideas of great writers who lived long ago. We

can even imagine <u>being</u> someone else or living in a completely different place.
동사 imagine의 목적어로 쓰인 동명사

In short, literature opens up for us new worlds that we <u>have never visited</u>
현재완료 경험 용법

before.

구문해설 • **cartoon**: 만화 • **literature**: 문학 • **beyond**: ~ 저편에[너머]
• **come across**: ~을 우연히 만나다 • **in short**: 요컨대

당신은 희곡, 시, 소설 또는 만화를 즐기는가? 그것들은 다양한 종류의 문학으로, 어떤 종류를 선호하는지는 사람에 따라 다르다. 그러나 그것들은 모두 우리를 우리가 사는 작은 세계 너머로 가게 해 준다. 문학을 읽을 때, 우리는 오래 전에 살았던 위대한 작가들의 생각과 마주치게 된다. 심지어 우리는 다른 누군가가 되거나 완전히 다른 장소에서 사는 상상을 할 수도 있다. 요컨대, 문학은 이전에 가 본 적이 없는 새로운 세계를 우리 앞에 펼쳐 준다.

영역별 핵심문제

01 다음 영영풀이가 가리키는 것을 쓰시오.

> the state of not being governed by another country

➡ _____

02 다음 중 밑줄 친 부분의 뜻풀이가 바르지 <u>않은</u> 것은?

① My friends saw my picture in the <u>yearbook</u>. (졸업 앨범)
② I have nothing <u>particular</u> to do this afternoon. (특별한, 특정한)
③ The <u>poet</u> was in deep thought by the river. (시)
④ My grandfather <u>remained</u> a farmer for the rest of his life. (여전히 ~이었다)
⑤ Did you know how to <u>sew</u>? (바느질하다)

03 다음 문장의 빈칸에 들어갈 말을 〈보기〉에서 골라 쓰시오.

> ┌── 보기 ├──
> rare / loneliness / poem / whole / literature

(1) He showed me the _____ he had written himself.
(2) The _____ wall was painted white.
(3) His hobby is collecting _____ stones.
(4) The greedy man lived in _____.
(5) I liked soccer and sewing, but I loved _____ the most.

04 다음 문장의 빈칸에 공통으로 들어갈 말을 고르시오.

> • Where do I need to check _____ the new arrivals?
> • Several animals come _____ only at night.
> • When I was hanging _____ with my boyfriend, my mother called me.

① out ② on ③ of ④ in ⑤ for

05 다음 주어진 문장의 밑줄 친 present(ed)와 같은 의미로 쓰인 것은?

> The waiter <u>presented</u> the bill to me.

① They wrote the letter after receiving the <u>present</u>.
② What can I get him for a birthday <u>present</u>?
③ The <u>present</u> situation is safe and peaceful.
④ Do you know who the <u>present</u> owner of this house is?
⑤ Last week Mike <u>presented</u> the documents to us.

06 다음 우리말을 주어진 단어를 이용하여 영작하시오.

(1) 강도가 은행 근처에서 체포되었다. (robber)
  ➡ _____
(2) 우리 팀은 혹독한 훈련을 겪었다. (through)
  ➡ _____
(3) 그는 그의 목표를 이루기 위해 최선을 다했다. (tried)
  ➡ _____
(4) 나는 공정한 대우를 원합니다. (fair)
  ➡ _____

07 다음 우리말과 일치하도록 주어진 단어를 모두 배열하여 영작하시오.

(1) 교수님은 설탕 사용에 반대하는 충고를 했다.
(advised / the / of / use / against / sugar / the / professor)

➡ _____

(2) 우리의 졸업을 축하하고 파티를 하자!
(have / and / our / a / party / let's / graduation / celebrate)

➡ _____

_____

(3) 디자이너들과 편집자들은 좋은 책을 만들기 위해 최선을 다한다.
(to / their / make / a / book / editors / designers / good / try / best / and)

➡ _____

_____

Conversation

[08~09] 다음 대화를 읽고 물음에 답하시오.

Sora: Hey, Minjun. What are you doing?

Minjun: I'm reading a novel for a book report.

Sora: Let me see. Oh, is this a new book by Ken Kuller?

Minjun: Yeah, I borrowed it this morning. Do you know Ken Kuller?

Sora: Of course. I'm ⓐa big fan of his. I've read all of his mystery books.

Minjun: I think he's a great writer. I can't stop ⓑreading this book.

Sora: You know what? His novel *Four Eyes* ⓒ has been made into a movie.

Minjun: Yeah. I saw the movie poster. It looks interesting.

Sora: It'll ⓓcome out next Thursday. I'm looking forward ⓔto see it!

Minjun: Maybe we can see the movie together.

08 위 대화의 밑줄 친 ⓐ~ⓔ 중 어법상 틀린 것을 찾아 바르게 고치시오.

➡ _____

09 위 대화의 내용과 일치하지 않는 것은?

① 민준이는 독후감을 위해 소설을 읽고 있다.

② 소라는 Ken Kuller의 열렬한 팬이다.

③ 민준이는 Ken Kuller가 위대한 작가라고 생각한다.

④ Ken Kuller의 신간 소설이 영화로 만들어졌다.

⑤ Ken Kuller의 소설을 바탕으로 만들어진 영화가 다음 주 목요일에 개봉한다.

[10~12] 다음 대화를 읽고 물음에 답하시오.

Minjun: Hello, Ms. Seo.

Ms. Seo: Hi, Minjun. Long time no see. ⓐ무엇 때문에 여기에 왔니?

Minjun: (A) I have to write a book report. Can you recommend a good novel to read?

Ms. Seo: (B) There's a new Ken Kuller book, *22nd Street*.

Minjun: (C) Oh, I've heard of him. Can you show me the book?

Ms. Seo: (D) It's in the "New Arrivals" area. It's really popular among teens in Great Britain.

Minjun: (E) Thank you for your help. Can I check it out?

Ms. Seo: Sure. You can borrow new books for seven days.

Minjun: Okay.

10 위 대화의 (A)~(E) 중 주어진 문장이 들어가기에 적절한 곳은?

How about a mystery?

① (A)　② (B)　③ (C)　④ (D)　⑤ (E)

11 위 대화의 밑줄 친 @의 우리말을 4 단어로 영작하시오.

➡ _____

12 위 대화의 내용과 일치하지 <u>않는</u> 것은?

① 민준이는 독후감을 써야 한다.
② 민준이는 읽기 좋은 소설을 추천 받고 싶다.
③ 서 선생님은 민준이에게 추리소설을 추천하였다.
④ 신착 도서 서가에 Ken Kuller의 책이 있다.
⑤ '22nd Street'은 인기가 많아 지금 대여할 수 없다.

13 다음 대화가 자연스럽게 이어지도록 순서대로 배열하시오.

> Mike: Good morning, Jiho.
> Jiho: Good morning.
> Mike: Take a seat, please. How would you like your hair done?
> Jiho: Well, I'm taking my pictures for the yearbook. So I want to look cool.
> Mike: When do you take the pictures?
> (A) Look at this. How about this style? It'll look good on you.
> (B) This Friday at Dream & Joy Park.
> (C) No. Can you recommend one for me?
> (D) Wow, I like it. I can't wait to see how I'll look in the pictures.
> (E) Sounds good. Do you have a particular style in mind?
> Mike: I'm sure you'll look cool.

➡ _____

14 다음 짝지어진 대화가 <u>어색한</u> 것은?

① A: Can you recommend a gift shop nearby?
  B: Go to Anne's Gifts. There're lots of things to buy.

② A: Will you recommend a fun TV program?
  B: *Pam and Sam* is really fun.

③ A: I'm looking forward to visiting the restaurant by the river.
  B: Me, too. There we can have a nice dinner.

④ A: You look happy. What's up?
  B: I'm looking forward to seeing Ken Kuller's new movie.

⑤ A: I feel a little bored. Can you recommend a good movie?
  B: You can say that again. It's a good movie.

Grammar

15 다음 밑줄 친 부분과 바꿔 쓸 수 있는 것은?

> It was in a small village near Mokpo <u>that</u> I was born.

① what
② which
③ who
④ when
⑤ where

16 다음 문장 중에서 어법상 <u>어색한</u> 문장을 고르시오.

① I was very hungry because I had not eaten anything since then.
② When I came back home, I found somebody had done the dishes.
③ No one told me that the supermarket had closed.
④ He already left when I had returned home.
⑤ Before I came home, my brother washed our dog.

17 다음 ⓐ~ⓖ 중 어법상 옳은 것을 <u>모두</u> 고르시오.

> ⓐ Dong-ju decided to study further in the country where his father had studied before.
>
> ⓑ When he had got to school, the class already began.
>
> ⓒ When Ms. Bae came back home, she found somebody has taken her corn.
>
> ⓓ She could not go into her house because she had lost her key.
>
> ⓔ I think it was on the bus that I lost it.
>
> ⓕ It was Junsu which called me last night.
>
> ⓖ That was Spanish which he learned when he was five.

➡ _____

18 다음 중 어법상 <u>어색한</u> 것을 고르시오. (2개)

① Because she did not have studied hard, she failed the test.

② It was 2014 that my family moved to this city.

③ Sora had never been to Busan before she was 16.

④ It was William Shakespeare who wrote *Romeo and Juliet*.

⑤ It was in 1885 that Vincent van Gogh painted *The Potato Eaters*.

Reading

[19~21] 다음 글을 읽고 물음에 답하시오.

Dong-ju was born in 1917 near Yanbin, China. As a young boy, he loved sports, and he was a soccer player for his school. He also loved sewing so much that he sewed the numbers ____ⓐ____ all his friends' soccer uniforms. However, it was literature that he loved most. In elementary school he wrote a lot of poems. He even made a literary magazine with his cousin, Song Mong-gyu. In middle school he once borrowed a poetry book by a famous poet of the time, Baek Seok, and copied the whole book ____ⓑ____ hand. He really wanted to have his own copy of the rare book.

19 위 글의 빈칸 ⓐ와 ⓑ에 들어갈 전치사가 바르게 짝지어진 것은?

	ⓐ	ⓑ		ⓐ	ⓑ
①	for	in	②	on	at
③	in	by	④	for	at
⑤	on	by			

20 위 글의 주제로 알맞은 것을 고르시오.

① Dong-ju was a poet during the period of Japanese colonial rule.

② Dong-ju loved both sports and sewing.

③ What Dong-ju loved most of all was literature.

④ Copying the whole book by hand was a difficult way to have a poetry book.

⑤ Dong-ju liked Baek Seok's poems, so he copied the whole book by hand.

21 위 글을 읽고 알 수 <u>없는</u> 것을 고르시오.

① Where was Dong-ju born?

② Why did Dong-ju love sports as a young boy?

③ What did Dong-ju sew for his friends?

④ With whom did Dong-ju make a literary magazine in elementary school?

⑤ Whose poetry book did Dong-ju copy by hand in middle school?

[22~24] 다음 글을 읽고 물음에 답하시오.

His parents wanted him to be a doctor, but Dong-ju chose to study literature at a college in Seoul. During his college years, he often hung out with other young poets and wrote poetry ___ⓐ___ he expressed feelings about his hometown and lost country. ⓑTo celebrate his graduation, he wished to publish 19 of his poems under the title, *Heaven, Wind, Stars, and Poetry*. He made three copies of the book by hand. One was given to his close friend, Jeong Byeong-uk, another was presented to his favorite professor, and the last one was kept for himself. However, his professor advised against his plan because he thought the Japanese government would not allow the publication. Dong-ju followed his advice and gave up the idea.

22 위 글의 빈칸 ⓐ에 들어갈 알맞은 말을 고르시오.

① when ② where
③ how ④ which
⑤ why

23 위 글의 밑줄 친 ⓑTo celebrate와 to부정사의 용법이 <u>다른</u> 것을 모두 고르시오.

① It is time <u>to celebrate</u> the start of spring.
② Where did you meet <u>to celebrate</u> his graduation?
③ The purpose of the festival was <u>to celebrate</u> the harvest.
④ A first-birthday party is an event <u>to celebrate</u> the first birthday of a child.
⑤ On Chuseok, they gathered together <u>to celebrate</u> the harvest of the year.

24 According to the passage, which is NOT true?

① Dong-ju's parents hoped that Dong-ju would become a doctor.
② Dong-ju determined to study literature at a college in Seoul.
③ During his college years, Dong-ju often hung around with other young poets.
④ In his poems, Dong-ju expressed feelings about his hometown and lost country.
⑤ To celebrate his graduation, Dong-ju published 19 of his poems under the title, *Heaven, Wind, Stars, and Poetry*.

[25~26] 다음 글을 읽고 물음에 답하시오.

In 1948, Jeong Byeong-uk brought Dong-ju's poems to the poet's brother, and they were (A)<u>finally</u> published. The book was given the title the poet ___ⓐ___ of many years before. His poems are loved by people of all ages, and thus they still shine brightly in our hearts like the stars in the autumn night sky.

25 위 글의 빈칸 ⓐ에 think를 알맞은 형태로 쓰시오.

➡ _____

26 위 글의 밑줄 친 (A)finally와 바꿔 쓸 수 <u>없는</u> 말을 고르시오.

① lastly ② at last
③ in the end ④ eventually
⑤ in the long run

단원별 예상문제

출제율 95%

01 다음 문장의 빈칸에 들어갈 말을 〈보기〉에서 골라 적절한 형태로 쓰시오.

┌─ 보기 ┤

be well known for / take part in / look forward to / give it a try

└──────────────────────────┘

(1) Many people _____ the Polar Bear Swim in Busan every winter.

(2) I'm really _____ my favorite singer's concert.

(3) He _____ cooking skills.

(4) Don't give up! _____ again.

[02~04] 다음 대화를 읽고 물음에 답하시오.

Sora: Hey, Minjun. What are you doing?

Minjun: I'm reading a novel for a book report.

Sora: Let me see. Oh, is this a new book by Ken Kuller?

Minjun: Yeah, I borrowed ⓐit this morning. Do you know Ken Kuller?

Sora: Of course. I'm a big fan of his. I've read all of his mystery books.

Minjun: I think he's a great writer. I can't stop (A)[to read / reading] this book.

Sora: You know what? His novel *Four Eyes* has been (B)[making / made] into a movie.

Minjun: Yeah. I saw the movie poster. ⓑIt looks interesting.

Sora: ⓒIt'll come out next Thursday. I'm looking forward to (C)[see / seeing] ⓓit!

Minjun: Maybe we can see the movie together.

출제율 95%

02 위 대화의 (A)~(C)에 들어갈 말로 바르게 짝지어진 것은?

	(A)	(B)	(C)
①	to read	making	see
②	to read	made	seeing
③	reading	made	see
④	reading	made	seeing
⑤	reading	making	see

출제율 90%

03 위 대화의 밑줄 친 ⓐ~ⓓ 중 나머지 셋과 가리키는 것이 다른 것을 찾아 무엇을 가리키는지 쓰시오.

➡ _____

출제율 100%

04 위 대화를 읽고 대답할 수 없는 것은?

① What is Minjun doing?

② Has Sora read Ken Kuller's books?

③ When did Minjun borrow a new book by Ken Kuller?

④ Who wrote the novel *Four Eyes*?

⑤ When are Minjun and Sora going to see the movie?

[05~07] 다음 대화를 읽고 물음에 답하시오.

Mike: Good morning, Jiho.

Jiho: Good morning.

Mike: Take a seat, please. How would you like your hair done?

Jiho: Well, I'm taking my pictures for the yearbook. So I want to look cool.

Mike: When do you take the pictures?

Jiho: This Friday at Dream & Joy Park.

Mike: Sounds good. Do you have a particular style in mind?

Jiho: No. _____ (A)

Mike: Look at this. How about this style? It'll look good on you.

Jiho: Wow, I like it. I can't wait to see how I'll look in the pictures.

Mike: I'm sure you'll look cool.

05 위 대화의 빈칸 (A)에 들어갈 말을 주어진 단어를 모두 배열하여 영작하시오.

> (you / one / can / me / recommend / for)

➡ _____

06 위 대화에서 지호와 Mike의 관계로 적절한 것은?

① student – teacher

② customer – hairdresser

③ patient – doctor

④ tourist – guide

⑤ employer – employee

07 위 대화의 내용과 일치하지 <u>않는</u> 것은?

① 지호는 졸업 앨범에 들어갈 사진을 찍을 것이다.

② 지호는 이번 금요일에 Dream & Joy Park에서 사진 촬영을 할 것이다.

③ 지호는 졸업 앨범을 위해 마음에 둔 특별한 헤어스타일이 있다.

④ Mike는 지호에게 헤어 스타일 하나를 추천해 주었다.

⑤ 지호는 Mike가 추천한 스타일이 마음에 든다.

[08~11] 다음 대화를 읽고 물음에 답하시오.

Jane: Nice to meet you, Mr. Henry. Is O. Henry your real name?

Mr. Henry: No. My real name is William Sydney Porter.

Jane: Can you tell me where you're from?

Mr. Henry: I'm from the U.S.

Jane: What do you usually write?

Mr. Henry: I'm a short story writer. I have written about 300 short stories.

Jane: Wow! You're great! What is special about your short stories?

Mr. Henry: They're well known for their surprise endings.

Jane: (A)뜻밖의 결말이 있는 인기 있는 이야기를 하나 추천해 주실 수 있나요?

Mr. Henry: Sure. I recommend *The Last Leaf*.

Jane: What is it about?

Mr. Henry: It's about a sick girl and an old artist who saves her life.

Jane: Oh, I want to read it. I can't wait.

08 위 대화의 밑줄 친 (A)의 우리말을 주어진 단어를 모두 배열하여 영작하시오.

> (you / with / a surprise / a popular / ending / story / recommend / can)

➡ _____
_____

09 Why are Mr. Henry's short stories famous?

➡ _____
_____

10 What is *The Last Leaf* about?

➡ _____
_____

11 위 대화를 읽고 다음의 표를 완성하시오.

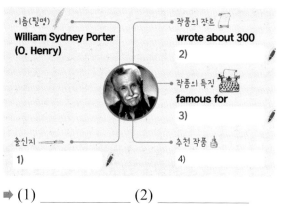

➡ (1) _____ (2) _____

(3) _____ (4) _____

단원별 예상문제 **175**

출제율 90%

12 다음 두 문장을 because를 사용하여 두 사건의 시간차가 드러나도록 한 문장으로 연결하시오.

> • She was not upset.
> • She bought some extra balloons.

➡ _____

_____

출제율 100%

13 다음 중 어법상 어색한 문장은?

① When I got home, the pizza party had already finished.

② It was my mother that named me Boram.

③ I had never seen a kangaroo before I went to Australia.

④ It is the park that Patricia plays badminton every weekend.

⑤ It was a storybook that he bought for his sister.

출제율 95%

14 다음 밑줄 친 부분을 바르게 고쳐 문장을 다시 쓰시오.

(1) He showed me some poems he wrote himself.

➡ _____

_____

(2) When I came back home, I found somebody turned on the TV.

➡ _____

_____

(3) It was the bus which Judy lost her wallet.

➡ _____

_____

(4) It was 1776 what the U.S. gained independence from Great Britain.

➡ _____

_____

출제율 100%

15 다음 빈칸에 들어갈 말을 순서대로 묶은 것은?

> • I'm sorry I lost the book you _____ me.
> • It was at the age of five _____ I learned how to ride a bike.

① had lent – where   ② had lent – when

③ lent – where   ④ lent – what

⑤ lend – that

[16~17] 다음 글을 읽고 물음에 답하시오.

Dong-ju was born in 1917 near Yanbin, China. As a young boy, he loved sports, and he was a soccer player for his school. He also loved sewing so much that he sewed the numbers on all his friends' soccer uniforms. _____ⓐ_____, it was literature ⓑthat he loved most. In elementary school he wrote a lot of poems. He even made a literary magazine with his cousin, Song Mong-gyu. In middle school he once borrowed a poetry book by a famous poet of the time, Baek Seok, and copied the whole book by hand. He really wanted to have his own copy of the rare book.

출제율 90%

16 위 글의 빈칸 ⓐ에 들어갈 알맞은 말을 고르시오.

① However   ② Therefore

③ That is   ④ For example

⑤ As a result

출제율 95%

17 위 글의 밑줄 친 ⓑthat과 문법적 쓰임이 같은 것을 고르시오.

① The trouble is that we are short of money.

② Have you listened to that tape I gave you?

③ I'm glad that you like it.

④ It is you that are to blame.

⑤ The actress hid the fact that she was married.

[18~20] 다음 글을 읽고 물음에 답하시오.

His parents wanted him to be a doctor, but Dong-ju chose to study literature at a college in Seoul. (①) During his college years, he often hung out with other young poets and wrote poetry where he expressed feelings about his hometown and lost country. (②) He made three copies of the book by hand. (③) One was given to his close friend, Jeong Byeong-uk, another was presented to his favorite professor, and the last one was kept ____ⓐ____ himself. (④) However, his professor advised ____ⓑ____ his plan because he thought the Japanese government would not allow the publication. (⑤) Dong-ju followed his advice and gave up the idea.

출제율 90%

18 위 글의 빈칸 ⓐ와 ⓑ에 들어갈 전치사가 바르게 짝지어진 것은?

	ⓐ	ⓑ		ⓐ	ⓑ
①	for	against	②	by	for
③	in	against	④	for	for
⑤	to	on			

출제율 100%

19 위 글의 흐름으로 보아, 주어진 문장이 들어가기에 가장 적절한 곳은?

> To celebrate his graduation, he wished to publish 19 of his poems under the title, *Heaven, Wind, Stars, and Poetry*.

①   ②   ③   ④   ⑤

출제율 100%

20 위 글의 제목으로 알맞은 것을 고르시오.

① His Parents' Desire to Make Dong-ju a Doctor
② A Poet Who Expressed Feelings about Lost Country
③ Dong-ju Made Three Copies of the Book by Hand!
④ Dong-ju and His Close Friend Jeong Byeong-uk
⑤ The Unfulfilled Wish of the Publication of a Poetry Book

[21~22] 다음 글을 읽고 물음에 답하시오.

ⓐDong-ju decided to study further in the country where his father has studied before. So, in 1942, Dong-ju and his cousin began to study in Japan. On July 10 the following year, his cousin was arrested by the Japanese police for ⓑtaking part in an independence movement. Four days later, Dong-ju was also arrested on the same charges. In 1945, Dong-ju and his cousin died in prison after harsh treatment by the police. It was just a few months later that Korea achieved independence from Japan.

출제율 95%

21 위 글의 밑줄 친 ⓐ에서 어법상 틀린 부분을 찾아 고치시오.

_____ ➡ _____

출제율 90%

22 위 글의 밑줄 친 ⓑtaking part in과 바꿔 쓸 수 있는 말을 모두 고르시오.

① attending to
② participating in
③ dealing in
④ joining
⑤ taking into account

[01~03] 다음 대화를 읽고 물음에 답하시오.

Mike: Good morning, Jiho.

Jiho: Good morning.

Mike: Take a seat, please. How would you like your hair done?

Jiho: Well, I'm taking my pictures for the yearbook. So I want to look cool.

Mike: When do you take the pictures?

Jiho: This Friday at Dream & Joy Park.

Mike: Sounds good. Do you have a particular style in mind?

Jiho: No. Can you recommend one for me?

Mike: Look at this. How about this style? It'll look good on you.

Jiho: Wow, I like it. I can't wait to see how I'll look in the pictures.

Mike: I'm sure you'll look cool.

01 Where is Jiho going this Friday?

➡ _____

02 What does Jiho ask Mike to do?

➡ _____

03 For what is Jiho going to take pictures this Friday?

➡ _____

04 다음 문장에서 틀린 것을 고쳐 다시 쓰시오.

(1) The witness admitted that he did not tell the complete truth.

➡ _____
_____

(2) I learned that he was sick since last week.

➡ _____
_____

(3) It was my parents got married in a small restaurant.

➡ _____
_____

(4) It was his endless efforts who moved all the animals' hearts.

➡ _____
_____

05 다음 우리말을 주어진 어휘를 이용하여 영작하시오.

(1) 우리 이모는 London을 여러 번 방문했었기 때문에 그 도시를 아주 잘 알았다. (because, my aunt, so well, visit, 14 단어)

➡ _____
_____

(2) Vincent van Gogh가 1885년에 그린 것은 바로 The Potato Eaters였다. (paint, that, 12 단어)

➡ _____
_____

[06~08] 다음 글을 읽고 물음에 답하시오.

  Dong-ju was born in 1917 near Yanbin, China. As a young boy, he loved sports, and he was a soccer player for his school. He also loved sewing so much that he (A)[sawed / sewed] the numbers on all his friends' soccer uniforms. However, it was literature (B)[that / what] he loved most. In elementary school he wrote a lot of poems. He even made a literary magazine with his cousin, Song Mong-gyu. In middle school he once (C)[borrowed / lent] a poetry book by a famous poet of the time, Baek Seok, and copied the whole book by hand. He really wanted to have his own copy of ⓐthe rare book.

06 위 글의 괄호 (A)~(C)에서 문맥이나 어법상 알맞은 낱말을 골라 쓰시오.

➡ (A) _____ (B) _____ (C) _____

07 위 글의 밑줄 친 ⓐthe rare book이 가리키는 것을 본문에서 찾아 쓰시오.

➡ _____

_____

08 What was the reason why Dong-ju copied Baek Seok's poetry book by hand? Answer in English beginning with "Because".

➡ _____

_____

[09~11] 다음 글을 읽고 물음에 답하시오.

  His parents wanted him to be a doctor, but Dong-ju chose to study literature at a college in Seoul. During his college years, he often (A)[hanged / hung] out with other young poets and wrote poetry where he expressed feelings about his hometown and lost country. To celebrate his graduation, he wished to publish 19 of his poems under the title, *Heaven, Wind, Stars, and Poetry*. He made three copies of the book by hand. One was given to his close friend, Jeong Byeong-uk, another was presented to his favorite professor, and the (B)[last / latest] one was kept for himself. However, ⓐ그의 교수는 일본 정부가 출판을 허가하지 않으리라 여겨, 그의 계획에 반대하는 충고를 했다. Dong-ju (C)[followed / refused] his advice and gave up the idea.

09 위 글의 괄호 (A)~(C)에서 문맥상 알맞은 낱말을 골라 쓰시오.

➡ (A) _____ (B) _____ (C) _____

10 위 글의 밑줄 친 ⓐ의 우리말에 맞게 한 단어를 보충하여, 주어진 어휘를 알맞게 배열하시오.

> the publication / he thought / his plan / because / his professor / would not allow / advised / the Japanese government

➡ _____

_____

_____

11 What did Dong-ju express in his poetry? Answer in English in a full sentence. (9 words)

➡ _____

_____

01 다음 대화를 읽고 대화의 내용과 일치하도록 민준이의 일기를 완성하시오.

Sora: Hey, Minjun. What are you doing?

Minjun: I'm reading a novel for a book report.

Sora: Let me see. Oh, is this a new book by Ken Kuller?

Minjun: Yeah, I borrowed it this morning. Do you know Ken Kuller?

Sora: Of course. I'm a big fan of his. I've read all of his mystery books.

Minjun: I think he's a great writer. I can't stop reading this book.

Sora: You know what? His novel *Four Eyes* has been made into a movie.

Minjun: Yeah. I saw the movie poster. It looks interesting.

Sora: It'll come out next Thursday. I'm looking forward to seeing it!

Minjun: Maybe we can see the movie together.

Mon, Sep 7th, 2020

While reading the new book of Ken Kuller for (A)_____, Sora came to me and talked about Ken Kuller. I found that Sora already knew Ken Kuller and read (B)_____. She told me that his novel *Four Eyes* (C)_____. When I saw the movie poster, it looked (D)_____. Sora was looking forward to seeing it.

02 다음 내용을 바탕으로 시를 쓰시오.

소재 / 주제: animal

아이디어: What do you want to write?

> A cat whose name is Tommy lives with my family.

> Tommy washes his face every morning.

> Tommy has beautiful black eyes and little ears.

> Tommy jumps high to catch a butterfly.

> Tommy likes me very much.

> Tommy always sleeps in my bed.

형식: Which type of poem do you want to write?

A cat lives with my family. His name is (A)_____.

He is clean. He (B)_____ every morning.

He is cute. He has beautiful (C)_____ and little ears.

He is fast. He (D)_____ to catch a butterfly.

Tommy likes me very much. He always sleeps (E)_____.

단원별 모의고사

01 다음 우리말에 맞게 빈칸에 알맞은 말을 쓰시오.

(1) 사람들은 정부 정책에 따라야 한다.
➡ People should follow the _____ policy.

(2) Ms. Gray는 출판 전에 원고를 점검하고 있다.
➡ Ms. Gray is checking her draft before _____.

(3) 나의 언니는 영문학을 전공했다.
➡ My big sister majored in English _____.

(4) 그의 시는 문학잡지에 출판되었다.
➡ His poem was published in a _____ magazine.

[02~04] 다음 대화를 읽고 물음에 답하시오.

Minjun: Hello, Ms. Seo.

Ms. Seo: Hi, Minjun. Long time no see. ⓐ What brings you here?

Minjun: I have to write a book report. Can you recommend a good novel to read?

Ms. Seo: ⓑHow about a mystery? There's a new Ken Kuller book, *22nd Street*.

Minjun: Oh, ⓒI've heard of him. Can you show me the book?

Ms. Seo: It's in the "New Arrivals" area. ⓓ It's really popular among teens in Great Britain.

Minjun: Thank you for your help. ⓔCan I check out it?

Ms. Seo: Sure. You can borrow new books for seven days.

Minjun: Okay.

02 위 대화의 밑줄 친 ⓐ~ⓔ 중 어법상 틀린 것을 찾아 바르게 고치시오.

➡ _____

03 위 대화를 읽고 대답할 수 없는 것은?

① Why does Minjun come to Ms. Seo?
② What should Minjun write?
③ In which area is *22nd Street*?
④ How long can Minjun borrow new books?
⑤ Why is *22nd Street* popular among teens in Great Britain?

04 위 대화의 내용과 일치하도록 민준이의 일기를 완성하시오.

> Mon, August 31st, 2020
> Today, I went to the library to borrow a book. I had to write a book report but I didn't know what to read. I asked Ms. Seo to recommend (A)_____. She introduced (B)_____ _____. I heard that it's really popular (C)_____ in Great Britain. I found it in the (D)_____. I'm looking forward to reading this book.

[05~07] 다음 대화를 읽고 물음에 답하시오.

Sora: Hey, Minjun. What are you doing?

Minjun: I'm reading a novel for a book report.

Sora: Let me see. Oh, is this a new book by Ken Kuller?

Minjun: Yeah, I borrowed it this morning. Do you know Ken Kuller?

Sora: Of course. I'm a big fan of his. I've read all of his mystery books.

Minjun: I think he's a great writer. I can't stop reading this book.

Sora: You know what? His novel *Four Eyes* has been made into a movie.

Minjun: Yeah. I saw the movie poster. It looks interesting.

Sora: It'll come out next Thursday. I'm looking forward to seeing it!

Minjun: Maybe we can see the movie together.

05 When did Minjun borrow the new book by Ken Kuller?

➡ _____

06 Among Ken Kuller's novels, which one has been made into a movie?

➡ _____

07 What does Minjun think about Ken Kuller?

➡ _____

[08~10] 다음 대화를 읽고 물음에 답하시오.

Mike: Good morning, Jiho.

Jiho: Good morning.

Mike: Take a seat, please. How would you like your hair done?

Jiho: Well, I'm taking my pictures for the yearbook. So I want to look cool. ⓐ

Mike: When do you take the pictures?

Jiho: This Friday at Dream & Joy Park. ⓑ

Mike: Sounds good. ⓒ

Jiho: No. Can you recommend one for me?

Mike: Look at this. How about this style? It'll look good on you. ⓓ

Jiho: Wow, I like it. (A)I can't wait to see how I'll look in the pictures. (forward)

Mike: I'm sure you'll look cool. ⓔ

08 위 대화의 ⓐ~ⓔ 중 주어진 문장이 들어가기에 적절한 곳은?

| Do you have a particular style in mind? |

① ⓐ ② ⓑ ③ ⓒ ④ ⓓ ⑤ ⓔ

09 위 대화의 밑줄 친 (A)와 바꾸어 쓸 수 있는 말을 주어진 단어를 이용하여 다시 쓰시오.

➡ _____

_____

10 위 대화가 이루어지는 곳으로 적절한 곳은?

① Post office   ② Airport

③ Hospital   ④ Library

⑤ Hair salon

[11~12] 다음 대화를 읽고 물음에 답하시오.

Jane: Nice to meet you, Mr. Henry. Is O. Henry your real name?

Mr. Henry: No. My real name is William Sydney Porter.

Jane: Can you tell me where you're from?

Mr. Henry: (A) I'm from the U.S.

Jane: What do you usually write?

Mr. Henry: (B) I have written about 300 short stories.

Jane: Wow! You're great! What is special about your short stories?

Mr. Henry: (C) They're well known for their surprise endings.

Jane: Can you recommend a popular story with a surprise ending?

Mr. Henry: (D) Sure. I recommend *The Last Leaf*.

Jane: What is it about?

Mr. Henry: (E) It's about a sick girl and an old artist who saves her life.

Jane: Oh, I want to read it. I can't wait.

11 위 대화의 (A)~(E) 중 주어진 문장이 들어가기에 적절한 곳은?

> I'm a short story writer.

① (A) ② (B) ③ (C) ④ (D) ⑤ (E)

12 위 대화를 읽고 대답할 수 <u>없는</u> 것은?

① What does Mr. Henry do?
② Where is Mr. Henry from?
③ How many short stories has Mr. Henry written?
④ What story does Mr. Henry recommend?
⑤ In *The Last Leaf*, how does an old artist save a sick girl?

13 다음을 같은 뜻이 되도록 빈칸에 알맞은 말을 쓰시오.

(1) I went to the cafe. Alicia went back home and I couldn't meet her.
　= When I went to the cafe, Alicia _____ back home.

(2) Mr. Han said. He fixed the bike the day before. But it was a lie.
　= Mr. Han said he _____ the bike the day before, but it was a lie.

14 Which is grammatically WRONG?

① It was not until yesterday that I noticed it.
② It was last Saturday when we threw a surprise party for Ms. Song.
③ It is the car who James Bond drove in the famous films called 007.
④ It was under the lemon tree where the concert was held.
⑤ It is my father who gets up earliest in my family.

15 다음 주어진 문장의 밑줄 친 부분과 용법이 같은 것은?

> My father regretted that he <u>had washed</u> his car.

① Tricia was not at home. She <u>had gone</u> shopping.
② Melina <u>had played</u> the piano since she was 6.
③ He <u>had failed</u> twice, but he decided to start again
④ I <u>had saved</u> my document before the computer crashed.
⑤ Unknown to me, he <u>had</u> already <u>signed</u> the agreement.

16 다음 문장에서 어법상 어색한 것을 바르게 고쳐 다시 쓰시오.

(1) It was fried chicken that I eat when I feel good.
　➡ _____

(2) It was Mr. Brown saved the child in the river.
　➡ _____

(3) She insisted that she was not there the previous night.
　➡ _____

(4) When the children arrived at the camp, their parents has already started cooking.
　➡ _____

17 다음 중 어법상 옳은 문장을 <u>모두</u> 고르시오.

① Jake was late for school because he had missed the bus.

② The train left when I had arrived at the station.

③ When Ms. Bae came back home, she found somebody had opened the kitchen door.

④ He was an engineer before he became an architect.

⑤ It was Uncle Ben which broke Plum's toy.

⑥ It was just a few months later that Korea achieved independence from Japan.

⑦ It was the drums when he played this year.

[18~20] 다음 글을 읽고 물음에 답하시오.

Dong-ju was born in 1917 near Yanbin, China. As a young boy, he loved sports, and he was a soccer player for his school. (A) <u>그는 또한 바느질하는 것을 무척 좋아해서 친구들의 축구 유니폼에 번호를 바느질해 주기도 했다.</u> However, it was literature that he loved most. In elementary school he wrote a lot of poems. He even made a ___@___ magazine with his cousin, Song Mong-gyu. In middle school he once borrowed a poetry book by a famous poet of the time, Baek Seok, and copied the whole book by hand. He really wanted to have his own copy of the rare book.

18 주어진 영영풀이를 참고하여 빈칸 @에 철자 l로 시작하는 단어를 쓰시오.

concerned with or connected with the writing, study, or appreciation of literature

➡ _____

19 위 글의 밑줄 친 (A)의 우리말에 맞게 한 단어를 보충하여, 주어진 어휘를 알맞게 배열하시오.

on all his friends' soccer uniforms / sewing / he / that / also / sewed / much / the numbers / loved / he

➡ _____

_____

20 본문의 내용과 일치하도록 다음 빈칸에 알맞은 단어를 쓰시오.

Among other things, what Dong-ju loved most was _____.

[21~23] 다음 글을 읽고 물음에 답하시오.

His parents wanted him to be a doctor, but Dong-ju chose to study literature at a college in Seoul. During his college years, he often hung out with other young poets and wrote poetry where he expressed feelings about his hometown and lost country. To celebrate his graduation, he wished to publish 19 of his poems under the title, *Heaven, Wind, Stars, and Poetry*. He made three copies of the book by hand. One was given to his close friend, Jeong Byeong-uk, another was presented to his favorite professor, and the last (A)<u>one</u> was kept for himself. ___@___, his professor advised against his plan because he thought the Japanese government would not allow the publication. Dong-ju followed his advice and gave up the idea.

21 위 글의 빈칸 @에 들어갈 알맞은 말을 고르시오.

① In addition   ② In other words

③ Similarly   ④ Thus

⑤ However

22 위 글의 밑줄 친 (A)one이 가리키는 것을 영어로 쓰시오.

➡ _____

23 Why did Dong-ju's professor advise against Dong-ju's plan? Answer in English beginning with "Because".

➡ _____

_____

[24~25] 다음 글을 읽고 물음에 답하시오.

Dong-ju decided to study further in the country where his father had studied before. So, in 1942, Dong-ju and his cousin began to study in Japan. On July 10 the following year, his cousin was arrested by the Japanese police for ⓐtaking part in an independence movement. Four days later, Dong-ju was also arrested on the same charges. In 1945, Dong-ju and his cousin died in prison after harsh treatment by the police. It was just a few months later that Korea achieved independence from Japan.

24 아래 〈보기〉에서 위 글의 밑줄 친 ⓐtaking과 문법적 쓰임이 같은 것의 개수를 고르시오.

┌─── 보기 ├───
① The man underline{standing} over there is my father.
② He is good at underline{speaking} English.
③ He is underline{taking} part in an independence movement.
④ I watched him underline{playing} baseball.
⑤ His hobby is underline{collecting} stamps.
└────────────

① 1개 ② 2개 ③ 3개 ④ 4개 ⑤ 5개

25 According to the passage, which is NOT true?

① Dong-ju studied further in the country where his father had studied before.
② It was in 1942 that Dong-ju and his cousin began to study in Japan.
③ In 1942, Dong-ju's cousin was arrested by the Japanese police for taking part in an independence movement.
④ Dong-ju was also arrested in 1943.
⑤ Dong-ju and his cousin had died in prison before Korea was liberated from Japan's colonial rule.

[26~27] 다음 글을 읽고 물음에 답하시오.

Do you enjoy plays, poems, novels, or cartoons? They are different kinds of literature, and people differ in which kind they prefer. However, all of (A)them allow us to go beyond our own small world where we live. When we read literature, we come across the ideas of great writers who lived long ago. We can even imagine being someone else or ___ⓐ___ in a completely different place. In short, literature opens up for us new worlds that we have never visited before.

26 위 글의 빈칸 ⓐ에 live를 알맞은 형태로 쓰시오.

➡ _____

27 위 글의 밑줄 친 (A)them이 가리키는 것을 본문에서 찾아 쓰시오.

➡ _____

MEMO

INSIGHT
on the textbook

교과서 파헤치기

※ 다음 영어를 우리말로 쓰시오.

01 artificial _____

02 bother _____

03 cause _____

04 relieved _____

05 gloomy _____

06 friendship _____

07 helpful _____

08 positive _____

09 stressed _____

10 improve _____

11 appearance _____

12 scream _____

13 well-known _____

14 relieve _____

15 argue _____

16 patient _____

17 chemical _____

18 besides _____

19 method _____

20 common _____

21 nervous _____

22 boring _____

23 matter _____

24 scary _____

25 produce _____

26 effect _____

27 focus _____

28 salty _____

29 sleepy _____

30 tidy _____

31 work _____

32 schoolwork _____

33 media _____

34 leave _____

35 used to _____

36 thanks to _____

37 at the same time _____

38 feel low _____

39 according to _____

40 make sense _____

41 deal with _____

42 as long as _____

43 have difficulty -ing _____

※ 다음 우리말을 영어로 쓰시오.

01	매체		22	덜다
02	안심이 되는		23	지루한
03	생산하다		24	짠
04	주장하다		25	깔끔한
05	도움이 되는		26	효과가 있다
06	졸리는		27	우울한
07	그 외에도		28	인공적인
08	집중하다		29	성가시게 하다
09	개선하다		30	원인
10	소리를 지르다		31	긍정적인
11	외모		32	효과
12	문제가 되다, 중요하다		33	학교 공부
13	화학물질		34	우정
14	무서운		35	~에 따르면
15	흔한		36	다른 방식으로
16	남겨두다		37	~하는 한
17	불안한		38	~할 것을 잊어버리다
18	스트레스 받은		39	동시에
19	인내하는		40	~ 대신에
20	방법		41	~을 다루다, 처리하다
21	유명한		42	약속을 어기다
			43	~하곤 했다

※ 다음 영영풀이에 알맞은 단어를 <보기>에서 골라 쓴 후, 우리말 뜻을 쓰시오.

1 _____ : a relationship between friends: _____

2 _____ : a particular way of doing something: _____

3 _____ : known about by a lot of people: _____

4 _____ : not real or not made of natural things: _____

5 _____ : a person, event, or thing that makes something happen: _____

6 _____ : a change that is caused by an event, action, etc.: _____

7 _____ : sad because you think the situation will not improve: _____

8 _____ : to make something better, or to become better: _____

9 _____ : expressing support, agreement, or approval: _____

10 _____ : to disagree with someone in words, often in an angry way: _____

11 _____ : neatly arranged with everything in the right place: _____

12 _____ : happening often; existing in large numbers or in many places:

_____

13 _____ : the way someone or something looks to other people: _____

14 _____ : to make someone feel slightly worried, upset, or concerned: _____

15 _____ : to shout something in a loud, high voice because of fear, anger, etc.:

_____

16 _____ : to give attention, effort, etc. to one particular subject, situation or person

rather than another: _____

보기			
cause	scream	artificial	bother
gloomy	appearance	method	focus
common	well-known	tidy	effect
argue	friendship	positive	improve

※ 다음 우리말과 일치하도록 빈칸에 알맞은 말을 쓰시오.

Listen and Answer – Dialog 1

W: Today, I'd like to _____ to you _____ teen stress. _____ _____ you _____ the most _____? _____ 9,000 teens _____ this question. _____ you can _____, schoolwork was the most _____ _____ of stress. _____ _____ _____ the students said schoolwork _____ them the most. _____ with friends _____ second place _____ 15.3%. _____ came family and _____ about the future. 8.2% of the students said they _____ _____ _____ _____ _____ their _____.

Listen and Answer – Dialog 2

W: _____ are you _____, Oliver?

B: I'm _____ _____ the math test, Mom. _____ stress me out.

W: I understand. I _____ _____ feel that _____, _____.

B: Really? I didn't _____ that.

W: Yeah, but _____ _____ _____ was _____ for me.

B: _____ _____ you _____ that?

W: I _____ _____ when I had an exam, but _____ _____ _____ _____ it made me _____ and _____ _____.

B: I see. Did stress _____ you _____ _____ _____?

W: Yes, it helped _____ my _____.

Listen More – Listen and choose.

B1: Today, let's _____ about the class T-shirt. We _____ _____ _____ on the design.

G: _____ me _____ you some _____ on the screen.

B2: We have to _____ a T-shirt with _____ _____.

B1: _____ _____ you _____ that?

B2: _____ we'll _____ the T-shirt on Sports Day. It's in June.

G: That _____ _____. What _____ this green one?

B2: I like it. The bee on the T-shirt is so _____.

G: And it's not _____.

B1: Yes. I think it's the _____ _____.

W: 오늘, 저는 여러분에게 십 대들의 스트레스에 관해 말씀드리려고 합니다. 여러분에게 가장 많이 스트레스를 주는 것은 무엇인가요? 약 9,000명의 십 대들이 이 질문에 답했습니다. 보시다시피, 학업이 스트레스의 가장 흔한 원인이었습니다. 절반이 넘는 학생들은 학업이 스트레스를 가장 많이 준다고 말했습니다. 친구와의 문제는 15.3%로 2위를 차지했습니다. 다음은 가족, 그리고 장래에 대한 걱정 순이었습니다. 8.2%의 학생들은 외모 때문에 스트레스를 받는다고 말했습니다.

W: 뭐 하고 있니, Oliver?

B: 수학 시험이 있어서 공부하고 있어요, 엄마. 성적이 제게 스트레스를 줘요.

W: 이해한단다. 나도 그렇게 느끼곤 했거든.

B: 정말요? 그러신 줄 몰랐어요.

W: 그래, 하지만 약간의 스트레스는 내게 도움이 되기도 했단다.

B: 왜 그렇게 말씀하세요?

W: 나는 시험이 있을 때 스트레스를 받았지만, 동시에 그 스트레스가 나를 집중하고 더 열심히 노력하게 했거든.

B: 그렇군요. 스트레스가 다른 방식으로 엄마에게 도움이 된 적이 있나요?

W: 그럼, 내 기억력을 높이는 데 도움을 주었단다.

B1: 오늘은 학급 티셔츠에 관해 이야기해 보자. 우리는 디자인을 정해야 해.

G: 화면으로 몇 가지 디자인을 보여 줄게.

B2: 우리는 반팔 티셔츠를 골라야 해.

B1: 무슨 이유로 그렇게 말하는 거야?

B2: 우리가 체육대회 때 티셔츠를 입기 때문이야. 그건 6월에 열려.

G: 그 말이 맞아. 이 초록색 티셔츠는 어때?

B2: 나는 마음에 들어. 티셔츠 위의 벌 그림이 정말 귀엽다.

G: 그리고 비싸지 않아.

B1: 맞아. 그게 제일 좋겠어.

Speak – Talk in groups.

Hi. Today, I'd _____ _____ _____ about Frida Kahlo. She was a Mexican painter. _____ of her _____ _____ _____ is *Viva la Vida*.

안녕하세요. 오늘은 Frida Kahlo에 대하여 이야기하겠습니다. 그녀는 멕시코인 화가입니다. 그녀의 가장 유명한 그림 중 하나는 Viva la Vida입니다.

Speak – Talk in pairs.

A: I want to _____ more time on social media.

B: What _____ you _____ that?

A: I can _____ more friends from _____ _____ _____.

B: That _____ _____.

A: 나는 소셜 미디어에 더 많은 시간을 쓰고 싶어.
B: 왜 그렇게 생각하니?
A: 나는 전 세계로부터 더 많은 친구를 사귈 수 있어.
B: 옳은 말이야.

My Speaking Portfolio Step 3

I'd _____ to talk about some _____ _____ _____ when you get _____. First, it's good to _____ _____ _____. Second, _____ to ten is a great idea. Also, _____ cold water helps. _____, _____ happy _____ can help.

여러분이 화가 났을 때 긴장을 풀 수 있는 방법에 관하여 이야기하겠습니다. 첫째, 심호흡을 하는 것이 좋습니다. 둘째, 열까지 세는 것은 좋은 생각입니다. 또한 차가운 물을 마시는 것도 도움이 됩니다. 마지막으로 행복한 생각을 하는 것이 도움이 됩니다.

Wrap Up – Listening & Speaking 1

W: Hello, teens. I'm Dr. Broccoli. Last time, I _____ about different _____ that _____ _____ for your health. Today, I'd _____ _____ talk about _____ habits. First, try to eat _____. Second, it's important _____ _____ _____ when you're _____.

여: 안녕하세요, 십 대 여러분. 저는 Broccoli 박사입니다. 지난 시간에, 건강에 좋은 다양한 음식에 관해 이야기했죠. 오늘은 건강한 식습관에 관해 이야기하고자 합니다. 먼저, 천천히 먹으려고 노력하세요. 둘째, 배가 부르면 그만 먹는 것이 중요합니다.

Wrap Up – Listening & Speaking 2

G: Why _____ we _____ a sport club?

B: Sounds good. Let's _____ a baseball club.

G: Well, I think a _____ club is a _____ _____.

B: What _____ you _____ that?

G: All _____ _____ is a ball to play basketball.

G: 우리 운동 동아리를 만드는 게 어때?
B: 좋아. 야구 동아리를 만들자.
G: 글쎄, 농구 동아리가 더 좋은 생각인 것 같아.
B: 왜 그렇게 말하는 거야?
G: 농구를 하기 위해 우리에게 필요한 건 농구공뿐이잖아.

※ 다음 우리말에 맞도록 대화를 영어로 쓰시오.

Listen and Answer – Dialog 1

W: _____

_____

_____

_____

_____

Listen and Answer – Dialog 2

W: _____

B: _____

W: _____

B: _____

W: _____

B: _____

W: _____

B: _____

W: _____

Listen More – Listen and choose.

B1: _____

G: _____

B2: _____

B1: _____

B2: _____

G: _____

B2: _____

G: _____

B1: _____

해석

W: 오늘, 저는 여러분에게 십 대들의 스트레스에 관해 말씀드리려고 합니다. 여러분에게 가장 많이 스트레스를 주는 것은 무엇인가요? 약 9,000명의 십 대들이 이 질문에 답했습니다. 보시다시피, 학업이 스트레스의 가장 흔한 원인이었습니다. 절반이 넘는 학생들은 학업이 스트레스를 가장 많이 준다고 말했습니다. 친구들과의 문제는 15.3%로 2위를 차지했습니다. 다음은 가족, 그리고 장래에 대한 걱정 순이었습니다. 8.2%의 학생들은 외모 때문에 스트레스를 받는다고 말했습니다.

W: 뭐 하고 있니, Oliver?
B: 수학 시험이 있어서 공부하고 있어요, 엄마. 성적이 제게 스트레스를 줘요.
W: 이해한단다. 나도 그렇게 느끼곤 했거든.
B: 정말요? 그러신 줄 몰랐어요.
W: 그래, 하지만 약간의 스트레스는 내게 도움이 되기도 했단다.
B: 왜 그렇게 말씀하세요?
W: 나는 시험이 있을 때 스트레스를 받았지만, 동시에 그 스트레스가 나를 집중하고 더 열심히 노력하게 했거든.
B: 그렇군요. 스트레스가 다른 방식으로 엄마에게 도움이 된 적이 있나요?
W: 그럼, 내 기억력을 높이는 데 도움을 주었단다.

B1: 오늘은 학급 티셔츠에 관해 이야기해 보자. 우리는 디자인을 정해야 해.
G: 화면으로 몇 가지 디자인을 보여 줄게.
B2: 우리는 반팔 티셔츠를 골라야 해.
B1: 무슨 이유로 그렇게 말하는 거야?
B2: 우리가 체육대회 때 티셔츠를 입기 때문이야. 그건 6월에 열려.
G: 그 말이 맞아. 이 초록색 티셔츠는 어때?
B2: 나는 마음에 들어. 티셔츠 위의 벌 그림이 정말 귀엽다.
G: 그리고 비싸지 않아.
B1: 맞아. 그게 제일 좋겠어.

Speak – Talk in groups.

_____

_____

안녕하세요. 오늘은 Frida Kahlo에 대하여 이야기하겠습니다. 그녀는 멕시코인 화가입니다. 그녀의 가장 유명한 그림 중 하나는 Viva la Vida입니다.

Speak – Talk in pairs.

A: _____

B: _____

A: _____

B: _____

A: 나는 소셜 미디어에 더 많은 시간을 쓰고 싶어.
B: 왜 그렇게 생각하니?
A: 나는 전 세계로부터 더 많은 친구를 사귈 수 있어.
B: 옳은 말이야.

My Speaking Portfolio Step 3

_____

_____

_____

여러분이 화가 났을 때 긴장을 풀 수 있는 방법에 관하여 이야기하겠습니다. 첫째, 심호흡을 하는 것이 좋습니다. 둘째, 열까지 세는 것은 좋은 생각입니다. 또한 차가운 물을 마시는 것도 도움이 됩니다. 마지막으로 행복한 생각을 하는 것이 도움이 됩니다.

Wrap Up – Listening & Speaking 1

W: _____

_____

_____

여: 안녕하세요, 십 대 여러분. 저는 Broccoli 박사입니다. 지난 시간에, 건강에 좋은 다양한 음식에 관해 이야기했죠. 오늘은 건강한 식습관에 관해 이야기하고자 합니다. 먼저, 천천히 먹으려고 노력하세요. 둘째, 배가 부르면 그만 먹는 것이 중요합니다.

Wrap Up – Listening & Speaking 2

G: _____

B: _____

G: _____

B: _____

G: _____

G: 우리 운동 동아리를 만드는 게 어때?
B: 좋아. 야구 동아리를 만들자.
G: 글쎄, 농구 동아리가 더 좋은 생각인 것 같아.
B: 왜 그렇게 말하는 거야?
G: 농구를 하기 위해 우리에게 필요한 건 농구공뿐이잖아.

※ 다음 우리말과 일치하도록 빈칸에 알맞은 것을 골라 쓰시오.

1 Say _____ to _____
A. Stress   B. Goodbye

2 Some people _____ time _____ friends when they _____
_____.
A. feel   B. with   C. low   D. spend

3 _____ eat special foods to _____ _____.
A. feel   B. others   C. better

4 _____ simply sleep for a _____.
A. while   B. others   C. still

5 _____ do you _____ stress?
A. deal   B. how   C. with

6 _____ are some stories about people who _____
_____.
A. different   B. suggest   C. ways   D. here

Mina (15, Daejeon)

7 Sometimes my friends give me stress _____ _____ bad things about me, _____ promises, or _____ over small things.
A. breaking   B. saying   C. arguing   D. by

8 _____ this _____, I watch _____ movies!
A. happens   B. horror   C. when

9 Good horror movies are _____ scary _____ I scream a _____.
A. that   B. so   C. lot

10 I guess that _____ at the _____ of my _____ helps me _____ better.
A. lungs   B. feel   C. top   D. screaming

11 Also, _____ to scary _____ and sound _____, I can forget about what _____ me.
A. bothers   B. scenes   C. effects   D. thanks

12 I've _____ this _____ for the past several months, and it really _____.
A. method   B. usinig   C. works   D. been

Junho (14, Yeosu)

13 My uncle _____ _____ college two years _____.
A. from   B. ago   C. graduated

14 He lives _____ my family, and he's _____ _____
_____ a job for some time.
A. looking   B. with   C. for   D. been

15 I know that he's _____ _____, but he always tries to be positive by _____ _____.
A. out   B. fishing   C. stressed   D. going

16 He never _____ when he doesn't _____ any _____.
A. catch   B. gets   C. fish   D. upset

17 He says, "_____ I fish, I'm _____ focused _____ I can leave all my worries _____.
A. behind   B. that   C. so   D. while

18 _____, it teaches me to _____."
A. besides   B. patient   C. be

1 스트레스와 이별하라

2 어떤 사람들은 울적할 때 친구들과 시간을 보낸다.

3 다른 사람들은 기분이 좋아지도록 특별한 음식을 먹는다.

4 또 다른 사람들은 그저 잠시 잠을 자기도 한다.

5 여러분은 스트레스를 어떻게 다루는가?

6 여기 다양한 방법을 제안하는 사람들의 이야기가 있다.

미나 (15살, 대전)

7 때때로 내 친구들은 나에 관해 나쁜 말을 하거나, 약속을 어기거나, 혹은 사소한 일을 두고 언쟁을 하며 내게 스트레스를 준다.

8 이럴 때, 나는 공포 영화를 본다!

9 훌륭한 공포 영화는 너무 무서워서 나는 소리를 많이 지르게 된다.

10 있는 힘껏 소리 지르는 것은 내 기분이 나아지는 데 도움이 된다고 생각한다.

11 또한, 무서운 장면과 음향 효과 덕분에 나를 괴롭히는 것들을 잊을 수 있다.

12 나는 지난 몇 달간 이 방법을 써 오고 있는데, 효과가 아주 좋다.

준호 (14살, 여수)

13 우리 삼촌은 2년 전에 대학을 졸업했다.

14 삼촌은 우리 가족과 함께 살고 있고, 얼마 전부터 직장을 구하고 있다.

15 나는 삼촌이 스트레스를 받고 있지만 낚시를 다니며 긍정적으로 지내려고 항상 노력한다는 것을 안다.

16 물고기를 한 마리도 잡지 못했을 때에도 삼촌은 절대 속상해하지 않는다.

17 삼촌은 "낚시하는 동안, 나는 아주 몰입해서 모든 걱정을 잊을 수 있어.

18 게다가 낚시는 나에게 인내를 가르쳐 준단다."라고 말한다

19 I'm _____ that _____ _____ one thing helps us _____ about something else.

    A. forget   B. on   C. sure   D. focusing

Dobin (16, Seoul)

20 My sister, a _____ student in high school, has a wonderful _____ to stay _____ _____ stress.

    A. free   B. second-year   C. from   D. way

21 She feels a lot of stress from schoolwork, but my mother _____ to _____ the situation _____ a good _____.

    A. seems   B. reason   C. for   D. like

22 It is _____ cleaning is my sister's _____ _____ to make life _____!

    A. because   B. way   C. number-one   D. better

23 When she's _____ stressed _____ her life _____, she cleans her room.

    A. gloomy   B. that   C. so   D. looks

24 She says, "_____ I clean my room, I _____ _____ I'm also _____ stress.

    A. relieving   B. as   C. like   D. feel

25 _____ my room looks _____, my life _____ _____."

    A. tidy   B. when   C. brighter   D. looks

Yulia (14, Ansan)

26 _____ me _____ you _____ my mother does about her stress.

    A. tell   B. what   C. let

27 She feels _____ by all the _____ she _____ to do at _____ and at home.

    A. has   B. stressed   C. work   D. things

28 When she's _____ _____, she _____ "Me Time" on her _____.

    A. writes   B. under   C. calendar   D. stress

29 This means she _____ some time _____ for _____.

    A. herself   B. takes   C. out

30 She _____ a book, _____ a movie, or _____ with her friends.

    A. watches   B. reads   C. talks

31 She says, "It doesn't really _____ what I do, _____ _____ _____ it's something I like.

    A. as   B. matter   C. as   D. long

32 I've _____ _____ 'Me Time' _____ my calendar for two months, and I feel _____ better."

    A. writing   B. much   C. on   D. been

33 _____ _____ will _____ _____ you?

    A. work   B. methods   C. which   D. for

34 _____ some of these ideas _____, and find your best _____ to say goodbye to _____.

    A. way   B. yourself   C. stress   D. try

19 한 가지 일에 집중하는 것이 다른 무언가를 잊는 데 도움이 된다고 나는 확신한다.

도빈 (16살, 서울)

20 고등학교 2학년인 우리 누나에게는 스트레스에서 벗어나는 훌륭한 방법이 있다.

21 누나가 학업 때문에 많은 스트레스를 받지만, 그럴 만한 이유로 우리 어머니는 그 상황을 좋아하시는 것 같다.

22 그것은 바로, 청소가 누나의 삶을 향상하는 최고의 방법이기 때문이다.

23 스트레스를 너무 많이 받아서 인생이 우울해 보일 때, 누나는 방을 청소한다.

24 누나는 "방을 청소하면서 스트레스도 해소되는 것 같아.

25 내 방이 깔끔해 보이면 내 삶도 더 밝아 보여."라고 말한다.

Yulia (14살, 안산)

26 우리 어머니께서 스트레스를 어떻게 다루시는지 소개하려고 한다.

27 어머니는 직장과 집에서 해야 하는 온갖 일로 인해 스트레스를 받으신다.

28 스트레스를 받을 때면 어머니는 달력에 '나만의 시간'이라고 적으신다.

29 이것은 어머니 자신을 위해 잠깐 시간을 낸다는 의미이다.

30 어머니는 책을 읽거나, 영화를 보거나, 친구들과 이야기를 나누신다.

31 어머니는 "내가 좋아하는 것이라면, 무엇을 하는지는 별로 중요하지 않아.

32 나는 두 달째 달력에 '나만의 시간'을 적어 왔고, 기분이 훨씬 좋아졌어."라고 말씀하신다.

33 어떤 방법이 여러분에게 효과가 있을까?

34 이 아이디어 중 몇 개를 직접 해 보고, 스트레스와 이별하는 자신만의 최고의 방법을 찾아라.

※ 다음 우리말과 일치하도록 빈칸에 알맞은 말을 쓰시오.

1 _____ _____ to Stress

2 Some people _____ _____ _____ friends when they _____ _____.

3 _____ eat special foods _____ _____ _____.

4 _____ _____ simply sleep _____ _____ _____.

5 How do you _____ _____ stress?

6 Here are some stories about people who _____ _____ _____.

Mina (15, Daejeon)

7 Sometimes my friends give me stress by _____ bad things about me, _____ promises, or _____ _____ small things.

8 _____ _____ _____, I watch horror movies!

9 Good horror movies are _____ scary _____ I scream a lot.

10 I guess that screaming _____ _____ _____ _____ me _____ better.

11 Also, _____ _____ scary _____ and sound _____, I can forget about _____ _____ _____.

12 _____ _____ this method for the past _____ _____, and it really _____.

Junho (14, Yeosu)

13 My uncle _____ _____ college two years _____.

14 He lives with my family, and _____ _____ _____ _____ a job for some time.

15 I know that _____ _____ _____, but he _____ to be positive _____ _____ _____.

16 He never _____ _____ when he doesn't catch any fish.

17 He says, "While I fish, I'm _____ focused _____ I _____ all my _____ _____.

18 _____, it teaches me _____ _____ _____."

19 I'm sure that _____ _____ one thing helps us _____ about _____ _____ .

Dobin (16, Seoul)

20 My sister, a _____ student in high school, has a wonderful way _____ _____ _____ stress.

21 She feels a lot of stress from schoolwork, but my mother _____ _____ _____ the situation _____ _____ _____ .

22 It is because cleaning is my sister's _____ _____ _____ life better!

23 When she's _____ stressed _____ her life _____ _____ , she cleans her room.

24 She says, "_____ I clean my room, I _____ _____ I'm also _____ stress.

25 When my room _____ _____ , my life _____ _____ ."

Yulia (14, Ansan)

26 _____ me tell you _____ my mother does about her stress.

27 She feels stressed by _____ _____ _____ _____ _____ _____ _____ and at home.

28 When _____ _____ _____ , she writes "Me Time" on her calendar.

29 This means she _____ _____ _____ _____ for herself.

30 She _____ a book, _____ a movie, or _____ with her friends.

31 She says, "It doesn't really _____ _____ I do, _____ _____ _____ it's something I like.

32 _____ _____ _____ 'Me Time' on my calendar for two months, and I _____ _____ _____ ."

33 _____ methods will _____ _____ _____ ?

34 Try some of these ideas yourself, and find your best way _____ _____ _____ _____ _____ .

19 한 가지 일에 집중하는 것이 다른 무언가를 잊는 데 도움이 된다고 나는 확신한다.

도빈 (16살, 서울)

20 고등학교 2학년인 우리 누나에게는 스트레스에서 벗어나는 훌륭한 방법이 있다.

21 누나가 학업 때문에 많은 스트레스를 받지만, 그럴 만한 이유로 우리 어머니는 그 상황을 좋아하시는 것 같다.

22 그것은 바로, 청소가 누나의 삶을 향상하는 최고의 방법이기 때문이다.

23 스트레스를 너무 많이 받아서 인생이 우울해 보일 때, 누나는 방을 청소한다.

24 누나는 "방을 청소하면서 스트레스도 해소되는 것 같아.

25 내 방이 깔끔해 보이면 내 삶도 더 밝아 보여."라고 말한다.

Yulia (14살, 안산)

26 우리 어머니께서 스트레스를 어떻게 다루시는지 소개하려고 한다.

27 어머니는 직장과 집에서 해야 하는 온갖 일로 인해 스트레스를 받으신다.

28 스트레스를 받을 때면 어머니는 달력에 '나만의 시간'이라고 적으신다.

29 이것은 어머니 자신을 위해 잠깐 시간을 낸다는 의미이다.

30 어머니는 책을 읽거나, 영화를 보거나, 친구들과 이야기를 나누신다.

31 어머니는 "내가 좋아하는 것이라면, 무엇을 하는지는 별로 중요하지 않아.

32 나는 두 달째 달력에 '나만의 시간'을 적어 왔고, 기분이 훨씬 좋아졌어."라고 말씀하신다.

33 어떤 방법이 여러분에게 효과가 있을까?

34 이 아이디어 중 몇 개를 직접 해 보고, 스트레스와 이별하는 자신만의 최고의 방법을 찾아라.

※ 다음 문장을 우리말로 쓰시오.

1   Say Goodbye to Stress

➡ _____

2   Some people spend time with friends when they feel low.

➡ _____

3   Others eat special foods to feel better.

➡ _____

4   Still others simply sleep for a while.

➡ _____

5   How do you deal with stress?

➡ _____

6   Here are some stories about people who suggest different ways.

➡ _____

미나 (15살, 대전) Mina (15, Daejeon)

7   Sometimes my friends give me stress by saying bad things about me, breaking promises, or arguing over small things.

➡ _____

8   When this happens, I watch horror movies!

➡ _____

9   Good horror movies are so scary that I scream a lot.

➡ _____

10   I guess that screaming at the top of my lungs helps me feel better.

➡ _____

11   Also, thanks to scary scenes and sound effects, I can forget about what bothers me.

➡ _____

12   I've been using this method for the past several months, and it really works.

➡ _____

준호 (14살, 여수) Junho (14, Yeosu)

13   My uncle graduated from college two years ago.

➡ _____

14   He lives with my family, and he's been looking for a job for some time.

➡ _____

15   I know that he's stressed out, but he always tries to be positive by going fishing.

➡ _____

16   He never gets upset when he doesn't catch any fish.

➡ _____

17 He says, "While I fish, I'm so focused that I can leave all my worries behind.
➡ _____

18 Besides, it teaches me to be patient."
➡ _____

19 I'm sure that focusing on one thing helps us forget about something else.
➡ _____

도빈 (16살, 서울) Dobin (16, Seoul)

20 My sister, a second-year student in high school, has a wonderful way to stay free from stress.
➡ _____

21 She feels a lot of stress from schoolwork, but my mother seems to like the situation for a good reason.
➡ _____

22 It is because cleaning is my sister's number-one way to make life better!
➡ _____

23 When she's so stressed that her life looks gloomy, she cleans her room.
➡ _____

24 She says, "As I clean my room, I feel like I'm also relieving stress.
➡ _____

25 When my room looks tidy, my life looks brighter."
➡ _____

Yulia (14살, 안산) Yulia (14, Ansan)

26 Let me tell you what my mother does about her stress.
➡ _____

27 She feels stressed by all the things she has to do at work and at home.
➡ _____

28 When she's under stress, she writes "Me Time" on her calendar.
➡ _____

29 This means she takes some time out for herself.
➡ _____

30 She reads a book, watches a movie, or talks with her friends.
➡ _____

31 She says, "It doesn't really matter what I do, as long as it's something I like.
➡ _____

32 I've been writing 'Me Time' on my calendar for two months, and I feel much better."
➡ _____

33 Which methods will work for you?
➡ _____

34 Try some of these ideas yourself, and find your best way to say goodbye to stress.
➡ _____

※ 다음 괄호 안의 단어들을 우리말에 맞도록 바르게 배열하시오.

1 (to / Say / Stress / Goodbye)
➡ _____

2 (people / some / time / spend / friends / with / they / when / low. / feel)
➡ _____

3 (eat / others / foods / special / feel / better. / to)
➡ _____

4 (others / still / sleep / simply / for / while. / a)
➡ _____

5 (do / how / you / with / stress? / deal)
➡ _____

6 (are / here / stories / some / people / about / suggest / who / ways. / different)
➡ _____

Mina (15, Daejeon)

7 (my / sometimes / friends / me / give / stress / saying / by / things / bad / me, / about / promises, / breaking / or / over / arguing / things. / small)
➡ _____

8 (this / when / happens, / watch / I / movies! / horror)
➡ _____

9 (horror / good / are / movies / scary / so / I / that / a / scream / lot.)
➡ _____

10 (guess / I / screaming / that / the / at / of / top / lungs / my / me / helps / better. / feel)
➡ _____

11 (thanks / also, / scary / to / scenes / and / effects, / sound / can / I / forget / what / about / me / bothers)
➡ _____

12 (been / I've / this / using / method / the / for / several / past / months, / and / really / it / works.)
➡ _____

Junho (14, Yeosu)

13 (uncle / my / from / graduated / college / ago. / years / two)
➡ _____

14 (lives / he / my / with / family, / he's / and / looking / been / for / job / a / for / time. / some)
➡ _____

15 (know / I / that / stressed / he's / out, / but / always / he / to / tries / be / positive / going / by / fishing.)
➡ _____

16 (never / he / upset / gets / he / when / catch / doesn't / fish. / any)
➡ _____

17 (says, / he / I / "while / fish, / so / I'm / that / focused / can / I / leave / all / worries / my / behind.)
➡ _____

18 (it / besides, / teaches / to / me / patient." / be)
➡ _____

1 스트레스와 이별하라

2 어떤 사람들은 울적할 때 친구들과 시간을 보낸다.

3 다른 사람들은 기분이 좋아지도록 특별한 음식을 먹는다.

4 또 다른 사람들은 그저 잠시 잠을 자기도 한다.

5 여러분은 스트레스를 어떻게 다루는가?

6 여기 다양한 방법을 제안하는 사람들의 이야기가 있다.

미나 (15살, 대전)

7 때때로 내 친구들은 나에 관해 나쁜 말을 하거나, 약속을 어기거나, 혹은 사소한 일을 두고 언쟁을 하며 내게 스트레스를 준다.

8 이럴 때, 나는 공포 영화를 본다!

9 훌륭한 공포 영화는 너무 무서워서 나는 소리를 많이 지르게 된다.

10 있는 힘껏 소리 지르는 것은 내 기분이 나아지는 데 도움이 된다고 생각한다.

11 또한, 무서운 장면과 음향 효과 덕분에 나를 괴롭히는 것들을 잊을 수 있다.

12 나는 지난 몇 달간 이 방법을 써 오고 있는데, 효과가 아주 좋다.

준호 (14살, 여수)

13 우리 삼촌은 2년 전에 대학을 졸업했다.

14 삼촌은 우리 가족과 함께 살고 있고, 얼마 전부터 직장을 구하고 있다.

15 나는 삼촌이 스트레스를 받고 있지만 낚시를 다니며 긍정적으로 지내려고 항상 노력한다는 것을 안다.

16 물고기를 한 마리도 잡지 못했을 때에도 삼촌은 절대 속상해하지 않는다.

17 삼촌은 "낚시하는 동안, 나는 아주 몰입해서 모든 걱정을 잊을 수 있어.

18 게다가 낚시는 나에게 인내를 가르쳐 준단다."라고 말한다

19 (sure / I'm / focusing / that / one / on / helps / thing / forget / us / something / about / else.)

➡ _____

Dobin (16, Seoul)

20 (sister, / my / second-year / a / in / student / school, / high / a / has / wonderful / to / way / free / stay / stress. / from)

➡ _____

21 (feels / she / lot / a / of / from / stress / schoolwork, / my / but / mother / to / seems / like / to / the / situation / for / good / a / reason.)

➡ _____

22 (is / it / cleaning / because / my / is / sister's / way / number-one / make / to / better! / life)

➡ _____

23 (she's / when / stressed / so / that / life / her / gloomy, / looks / cleans / she / room. / her)

➡ _____

24 (says, / she / "as / clean / I / room, / my / feel / I / like / I'm / releiving / stress. / also)

➡ _____

25 (my / when / room / tidy, / looks / life / my / brighter." / looks)

➡ _____

Yulia (14, Ansan)

26 (me / let / you / tell / what / mother / my / about / does / stress. / her)

➡ _____

27 (feels / she / by / stressed / all / things / the / has / she / to / at / do / work / and / home. / at)

➡ _____

28 (she's / when / stress, / under / writes / she / Time" / "Me / her / on / calender.)

➡ _____

29 (means / this / takes / she / time / some / for / out / herself.)

➡ _____

30 (reads / she / book, / a / watches / movie, / a / talks / or / her / with / friends.)

➡ _____

31 (says / she / "it / really / doesn't / what / matter / do, / I / long / as / it's / as / something / like. / I)

➡ _____

32 (been / I've / writing / Time' / 'Me / my / on / calender / two / for / months, / I / and / much / feel / better.")

➡ _____

33 (methods / which / work / will / you? / for)

➡ _____

34 (some / try / these / of / yourself, / ideas / and / your / find / way / best / say / to / goodbye / stress. / to)

➡ _____

19 한 가지 일에 집중하는 것이 다른 무언가를 잊는 데 도움이 된다고 나는 확신한다.

도빈 (16살, 서울)

20 고등학교 2학년인 우리 누나에게는 스트레스에서 벗어나는 훌륭한 방법이 있다.

21 누나가 학업 때문에 많은 스트레스를 받지만, 그럴 만한 이유로 우리 어머니는 그 상황을 좋아하시는 것 같다.

22 그것은 바로, 청소가 누나의 삶을 향상하는 최고의 방법이기 때문이다.

23 스트레스를 너무 많이 받아서 인생이 우울해 보일 때, 누나는 방을 청소한다.

24 누나는 "방을 청소하면서 스트레스도 해소되는 것 같아.

25 내 방이 깔끔해 보이면 내 삶이 더 밝아 보여."라고 말한다.

Yulia (14살, 안산)

26 우리 어머니께서 스트레스를 어떻게 다루시는지 소개하려고 한다.

27 어머니는 직장과 집에서 해야 하는 온갖 일로 인해 스트레스를 받으신다.

28 스트레스를 받을 때면 어머니는 달력에 '나만의 시간'이라고 적으신다.

29 이것은 어머니 자신을 위해 잠깐 시간을 낸다는 의미이다.

30 어머니는 책을 읽거나, 영화를 보거나, 친구들과 이야기를 나누신다.

31 어머니는 "내가 좋아하는 것이라면, 무엇을 하는지는 별로 중요하지 않아.

32 나는 두 달째 달력에 '나만의 시간'을 적어 왔고, 기분이 훨씬 좋아졌어."라고 말씀하신다.

33 어떤 방법이 여러분에게 효과가 있을까?

34 이 아이디어 중 몇 개를 직접 해 보고, 스트레스와 이별하는 자신만의 최고의 방법을 찾아라.

※ 다음 우리말을 영어로 쓰시오.

1 스트레스와 이별하라

➡ _____

2 어떤 사람들은 울적할 때 친구들과 시간을 보낸다.

➡ _____

3 다른 사람들은 기분이 좋아지도록 특별한 음식을 먹는다.

➡ _____

4 또 다른 사람들은 그저 잠시 잠을 자기도 한다.

➡ _____

5 여러분은 스트레스를 어떻게 다루는가?

➡ _____

6 여기 다양한 방법을 제안하는 사람들의 이야기가 있다.

➡ _____

미나 (15살, 대전) Mina (15, Daejeon)

7 때때로 내 친구들은 나에 관해 나쁜 말을 하거나, 약속을 어기거나, 혹은 사소한 일을 두고 언쟁을 하며 내게 스트레스를 준다.

➡ _____

_____

8 이럴 때, 나는 공포 영화를 본다!

➡ _____

9 훌륭한 공포 영화는 너무 무서워서 나는 소리를 많이 지르게 된다.

➡ _____

10 있는 힘껏 소리 지르는 것은 내 기분이 나아지는 데 도움이 된다고 생각한다.

➡ _____

11 또한, 무서운 장면과 음향 효과 덕분에 나를 괴롭히는 것들을 잊을 수 있다.

➡ _____

12 나는 지난 몇 달간 이 방법을 써 오고 있는데, 효과가 아주 좋다.

➡ _____

준호 (14살, 여수) Junho (14, Yeosu)

13 우리 삼촌은 2년 전에 대학을 졸업했다.

➡ _____

14 삼촌은 우리 가족과 함께 살고 있고, 얼마 전부터 직장을 구하고 있다.

➡ _____

15 나는 삼촌이 스트레스를 받고 있지만 낚시를 다니며 긍정적으로 지내려고 항상 노력한다는 것을 안다.

➡ _____

16 물고기를 한 마리도 잡지 못했을 때에도 삼촌은 절대 속상해 하지 않는다.

➡ _____

17 삼촌은 "낚시하는 동안, 나는 아주 몰입해서 모든 걱정을 잊을 수 있어.
➡ _____

18 게다가 낚시는 나에게 인내를 가르쳐 준단다."라고 말한다.
➡ _____

19 한 가지 일에 집중하는 것이 다른 무언가를 잊는 데 도움이 된다고 나는 확신한다.
➡ _____

도빈 (16살, 서울) Dobin (16, Seoul)

20 고등학교 2학년인 우리 누나에게는 스트레스에서 벗어나는 훌륭한 방법이 있다.
➡ _____

21 누나가 학업 때문에 많은 스트레스를 받지만, 그럴 만한 이유로 우리 어머니는 그 상황을 좋아하시는 것 같다.
➡ _____

22 그것은 바로, 청소가 누나의 삶을 향상하는 최고의 방법이기 때문이다.
➡ _____

23 스트레스를 너무 많이 받아서 인생이 우울해 보일 때, 누나는 방을 청소한다.
➡ _____

24 누나는 "방을 청소하면서 스트레스도 해소되는 것 같아.
➡ _____

25 내 방이 깔끔해 보이면 내 삶도 더 밝아 보여."라고 말한다.
➡ _____

Yulia (14살, 안산) Yulia (14, Ansan)

26 우리 어머니께서 스트레스를 어떻게 다루시는지 소개하려고 한다.
➡ _____

27 어머니는 직장과 집에서 해야 하는 온갖 일로 인해 스트레스를 받으신다.
➡ _____

28 스트레스를 받을 때면 어머니는 달력에 '나만의 시간'이라고 적으신다.
➡ _____

29 이것은 어머니 자신을 위해 잠깐 시간을 낸다는 의미이다.
➡ _____

30 어머니는 책을 읽거나, 영화를 보거나, 친구들과 이야기를 나누신다.
➡ _____

31 어머니는 "내가 좋아하는 것이라면, 무엇을 하는지는 별로 중요하지 않아.
➡ _____

32 나는 두 달째 달력에 '나만의 시간'을 적어 왔고, 기분이 훨씬 좋아졌어."라고 말씀하신다.
➡ _____

33 어떤 방법이 여러분에게 효과가 있을까?
➡ _____

34 이 아이디어 중 몇 개를 직접 해 보고, 스트레스와 이별하는 자신만의 최고의 방법을 찾아라.
➡ _____

※ 다음 우리말과 일치하도록 빈칸에 알맞은 말을 쓰시오.

Words in Action

1. Tests _____ me _____. Grades give _____ _____ _____.

2. _____ _____, smile more. Worry _____ _____.

3. I work hard. I have _____ _____ _____ _____ _____.

4. I need a _____. I will _____ _____ _____.

5. I _____ just _____ _____ fish. I want _____ _____ some more.

1. 시험은 나를 지치게 해. 성적은 나에게 더 많은 스트레스를 준다.
2. 걱정은 줄이고 더 많이 웃어라. 걱정은 전혀 도움이 되지 않아.
3. 나는 열심히 일한다. 나는 할 일이 많다.
4. 나는 기분 전환이 필요하다. 나는 헤어스타일을 바꿀 것이다.
5. 나는 겨우 물고기 몇 마리를 잡았다. 나는 몇 마리 더 낚고 싶다.

Speak – Get ready.

1. I want to _____ more/_____ _____ on social media.

2. _____ _____ a team _____ _____ difficult/_____.

3. I like _____/playing sports _____.

4. _____ a _____ _____ as a teen can be good/_____.

1. 나는 소셜미디어에 더 많은/적은 시간을 보내기를 원한다.
2. 팀을 이루어 일하는 것은 어려울 수 있다/도움이 될 수 있다.
3. 나는 스포츠 보는 것을/하는 것을 더 좋아한다.
4. 십대일 때 아르바이트를 하는 것은 좋다/나쁘다.

Wrap Up - Reading

1. Are you _____ or _____ _____?

2. Then here is _____ _____ _____ for you.

3. _____ _____ simple _____ can _____ you!

4. First, go _____ and get _____ _____ sunlight.

5. _____ _____ scientists, this helps _____ a special chemical _____ _____ _____, and the chemical _____ _____ _____ happy!

6. _____ _____ _____ _____ _____ _____ is exercise.

7. This helps _____ _____ _____ _____ of the "_____ _____."

8. _____ these _____ _____ the next time you _____ _____.

9. _____ _____ _____ in _____ of a screen, go outdoors and _____ _____ in the sun!

1. 스트레스를 받았거나 기분이 우울한가?
2. 그렇다면 여기 당신에게 좋은 소식이 있다.
3. 간단한 몇 가지 절차가 도움이 될 것이다!
4. 첫째, 밖에 나가서 충분한 양의 햇볕을 쬐라.
5. 과학자들에 따르면 이것이 뇌 속에 특별한 화학물질을 만드는 데 도움을 주고, 이 화학물질은 당신을 행복하게 만든다고 한다!
6. 당신이 할 수 있는 또 다른 일은 운동이다.
7. 이것은 훨씬 더 많은 '행복 화학물질'을 만드는 데 도움을 준다.
8. 다음에 당신이 우울하다면 이 간단한 조언을 시도해 보라.
9. 화면 앞에 앉아 있는 대신, 밖에 나가 태양 아래에서 뛰어 다녀라!

※ 다음 우리말을 영어로 쓰시오.

Words in Action

1. 시험은 나를 지치게 해. 성적은 나에게 더 많은 스트레스를 준다.
➡ _____

2. 걱정은 줄이고 더 많이 웃어라. 걱정은 전혀 도움이 되지 않아.
➡ _____

3. 나는 열심히 일한다. 나는 할 일이 많다.
➡ _____

4. 나는 기분 전환이 필요하다. 나는 헤어스타일을 바꿀 것이다.
➡ _____

5. 나는 겨우 물고기 몇 마리를 잡았다. 나는 몇 마리 더 낚고 싶다.
➡ _____

Speak – Get ready.

1. 나는 소셜미디어에 더 많은/적은 시간을 보내기를 원한다.
➡ _____

2. 팀을 이루어 일하는 것은 어려울 수 있다/도움이 될 수 있다.
➡ _____

3. 나는 스포츠 보는 것을/하는 것을 더 좋아한다.
➡ _____

4. 십대일 때 아르바이트를 하는 것은 좋다/나쁘다.
➡ _____

Wrap Up - Reading

1. 스트레스를 받았거나 기분이 우울한가?
➡ _____

2. 그렇다면, 여기 당신에게 좋은 소식이 있다.
➡ _____

3. 간단한 몇 가지 절차가 도움이 될 것이다!
➡ _____

4. 첫째, 밖에 나가서 충분한 양의 햇볕을 쐬라.
➡ _____

5. 과학자들에 따르면 이것이 뇌 속에 특별한 화학물질을 만드는 데 도움을 주고, 이 화학물질은 당신을 행복하게 만든다고 한다.
➡ _____
_____

6. 당신이 할 수 있는 또 다른 일은 운동이다.
➡ _____

7. 이것은 훨씬 더 많은 "행복 화학물질"을 만드는 데 도움을 준다.
➡ _____

8. 다음에 당신이 우울하다면 이 간단한 조언을 시도해 보라.
➡ _____

9. 화면 앞에 앉아 있는 대신, 밖에 나가 태양 아래에서 뛰어 다녀라!
➡ _____

※ 다음 영어를 우리말로 쓰시오.

01	alive
02	popular
03	relax
04	directly
05	present
06	effective
07	gardening
08	whether
09	producer
10	electric-powered
11	wholesale
12	imaginable
13	digest
14	recipe
15	architect
16	translate
17	bill
18	insect
19	last
20	ship
21	attract

22	transportation
23	local
24	environment
25	mostly
26	suggest
27	discover
28	notice
29	float
30	therefore
31	disappear
32	trade
33	way
34	work
35	chat with
36	take a nap
37	be crowded with
38	have ~ in common
39	be good for
40	make an appointment
41	be rich in
42	best-before date
43	make sure to

※ 다음 우리말을 영어로 쓰시오.

01 번역하다	
02 상상할 수 있는	
03 지속하다, 오래가다	
04 살아 있는	
05 뜨다	
06 건축가	
07 ~인지 아닌지	
08 곤충	
09 끌어들이다, 끌어당기다	
10 운반하다	
11 운송, 교통	
12 계산서	
13 사라지다	
14 도매의	
15 지붕이 덮인	
16 작동하다, 효과가 있다	
17 제안하다	
18 발견하다, 알아내다	
19 그러므로, 따라서	
20 효과적인, 실질적인	
21 환경	

22 현지의, 지역의	
23 천연의, 자연스러운	
24 주로, 대부분	
25 경험	
26 무역	
27 원예	
28 주목하다	
29 운송하다, 실어 나르다	
30 곧장, 바로, 직접적으로	
31 조리법	
32 쉬다	
33 소화하다	
34 선물	
35 낮잠을 자다	
36 ~이 풍부하다	
37 ~와 잡담하다	
38 ~로 붐비다, 꽉 차다	
39 약속하다	
40 ~에 유익하다	
41 반드시 ~하다	
42 ~한 공통점이 있다	
43 유효 기한, 유통 기한	

※ 다음 영영풀이에 알맞은 단어를 <보기>에서 골라 쓴 후, 우리말 뜻을 쓰시오.

1 _____ : to find out: _____

2 _____ : to see no longer: _____

3 _____ : a person who designs buildings: _____

4 _____ : a set of instructions for making food: _____

5 _____ : possible to think of in your mind: _____

6 _____ : a person who is traveling for pleasure: _____

7 _____ : without stopping; with nothing in between: _____

8 _____ : cultural beliefs and customs passed down through generations: _____

9 _____ : the activity or process of buying, selling, or exchanging goods or services: _____

10 _____ : the action of selling things in large amounts and at low prices: _____

11 _____ : to send people or things somewhere by ship, truck, and so on: _____

12 _____ : the market which buys and sells things directly on a boat: _____

13 _____ : a small animal that has six legs and a body formed of three parts and that may have wings: _____

14 _____ : something that you give to someone especially as a way of showing affection or thanks: _____

15 _____ : to make someone interested in something and cause them to come to it: _____

16 _____ : a system for carrying people or goods from one place to another using vehicles, roads, etc.: _____

보기

attract	wholesale	directly	tradition
trade	ship	disappear	architect
present	transportation	tourist	imaginable
floating market	insect	discover	recipe

※ 다음 우리말과 일치하도록 빈칸에 알맞은 말을 쓰시오.

Listen – Listen & Answer Dialog 1

M: _____ _____ the Tourist Information Office! _____ may I _____ you?

W: Hi, I _____ there's a _____ _____ of the town.

M: Sure. _____ _____ a special place you're _____ _____?

W: Yes. I'd _____ _____ _____ some _____ food.

M: Then go to Jeongseon Market. It _____ every _____ _____, and it's _____ today.

W: I'm so _____. _____ _____ _____ _____ _____?

M: You _____ _____ there. It _____ _____ 10 _____.

W: Great. Will you _____ the _____ on the map, please?

M: Sure. _____ gondrebap _____ you _____ there.

Listen – Listen & Answer Dialog 2

W: Can I _____ the _____, please?

M: _____ you are. Did you enjoy the _____?

W: It was great. I liked the *gondrebap* very much.

M: Thanks. It's also _____ _____ _____ _____.

W: Oh, really?

M: Yes. *Gondre* _____ _____ _____ vitamins A and C. It also _____ well.

W: Good. I _____ _____ I could buy some *gondre* here.

M: Sure. Do you _____ _____ _____ _____ you the _____ _____ *gondrebap*?

W: Yes, that'd _____ _____.

Listen More – Listen and complete

W: _____ me. Can you _____ _____ _____ this _____?

B: Sure. What is it?

W: _____ _____ the _____, please.

B: Oh, do you _____ _____ _____ _____ you _____ _____ _____?

W: Yes, I _____ my _____.

B: _____ me _____. You should drink it _____ June 7.

남: 관광 안내소에 오신 것을 환영합니다! 무엇을 도와드릴까요?

여: 안녕하세요. 저는 마을 관광 지도가 있는지 궁금합니다.

남: 물론이죠. 특별히 찾으시는 곳이 있나요?

여: 네. 이 지역 음식을 먹어 보고 싶어요.

남: 그렇다면 정선 시장에 가 보세요. 시장이 5일마다 열리는데, 오늘 열렸네요.

여: 제가 정말 운이 좋군요. 그곳에 어떻게 가나요?

남: 거기까지 걸어갈 수 있어요. 10분 정도 걸려요.

여: 잘됐군요. 지도에 길을 표시해 주시겠어요?

남: 물론이죠. 거기에 가면 곤드레밥을 드셔 보세요.

여: 계산서 좀 주시겠어요?

남: 여기 있습니다. 식사는 맛있게 하셨나요?

여: 아주 훌륭했어요. 저는 곤드레밥이 정말 좋았어요.

남: 고맙습니다. 그것은 건강에도 좋답니다.

여: 오, 정말요?

남: 네. 곤드레는 비타민 A와 C가 풍부합니다. 그리고 소화도 잘돼요.

여: 그렇군요. 여기서 곤드레를 좀 살 수 있을까요?

남: 물론이죠. 제가 곤드레밥 조리법을 드릴까요?

여: 네, 그러면 정말 좋겠어요.

여: 미안하지만, 이 우유 (사는 것) 좀 도와주겠니?

남: 그럼요. 뭔데요?

여: 날짜를 좀 읽어 주렴.

남: 아, 유통 기한을 말씀드리길 원하세요?

여: 그래, 내가 안경을 두고 왔단다.

남: 잠깐만요. 6월 7일까지 드셔야 해요.

W: That's too soon. _____ _____ _____ there's one that

_____ _____.

B: Wait. I _____ one. This _____ is good _____ _____

_____.

W: Oh, I'll take that _____. Thank you very much.

B: You're _____.

여: 그건 너무 짧네. 기한이 더 긴 게 있
는지 궁금하구나.
남: 잠깐만요. 하나 찾았어요. 이것은 6
월 11일까지 드실 수 있어요.
여: 오, 그걸로 사야겠다. 정말 고맙구
나.
남: 천만에요.

Speak – Talk in pairs. 1

A: _____ me. I _____ if there's a bank _____ _____.

B: I'm sorry, _____ we _____ _____ _____ _____ here.

A: That's _____ _____. Thanks.

A: 실례합니다. 이 근처에 은행이 있는
지 궁금합니다.
B: 미안하지만 이 근처에는 없어요.
A: 괜찮아요. 고맙습니다.

Speak – Talk in pairs. 2

A: What's _____, Grandpa?

B: I'm _____.

A: Do you _____ _____ _____ play *baduk* _____ you?

B: That'd _____ _____. Thank you.

A: 무슨 일이세요, 할아버지?
B: 지루하구나.
A: 제가 함께 바둑을 두길 원하세요?
B: 그러면 좋겠구나. 고맙구나.

Wrap Up 1

G: I _____ _____.

B: I'll make *ramyeon* for you.

G: _____ nice!

B: Do you _____ me _____ _____ an egg?

G: That'd be great.

여: 나 배고파.
남: 내가 널 위해 라면을 끓여 줄게.
여: 좋아!
남: 달걀을 넣길 원하니?
여: 그러면 정말 좋겠어.

Wrap Up 2

G: Dad, _____ _____ that cute bag. _____ _____ _____ _____

_____ _____.

M: _____ _____ we _____ _____ and _____?

G: Really? Thanks, Dad.

M: I _____ _____ I will _____ _____ _____ _____.

We're just _____ the _____.

G: Of _____.

여: 아빠, 저 귀여운 가방을 보세요. 얼
마인지 궁금해요.
남: 들어가서 확인해 보는 게 어떻겠니?
여: 정말요? 고마워요, 아빠.
남: 사 주겠다고는 말하지 않았단다. 그
냥 가격만 물어보는 거야.
여: 물론이죠.

※ 다음 우리말에 맞도록 대화를 영어로 쓰시오.

Listen – Listen & Answer Dialog 1

M: _____

W: _____

M: _____

W: _____

M: _____

W: _____

M: _____

W: _____

M: _____

Listen – Listen & Answer Dialog 2

W: _____

M: _____

W: _____

M: _____

W: _____

M: _____

W: _____

M: _____

W: _____

Listen More – Listen and complete

W: _____

B: _____

W: _____

B: _____

W: _____

B: _____

 해석

남: 관광 안내소에 오신 것을 환영합니다! 무엇을 도와드릴까요?

여: 안녕하세요, 저는 마을 관광 지도가 있는지 궁금합니다.

남: 물론이죠. 특별히 찾으시는 곳이 있나요?

여: 네. 이 지역 음식을 먹어 보고 싶어요.

남: 그렇다면 정선 시장에 가 보세요. 시장이 5일마다 열리는데, 오늘 열렸네요.

여: 제가 정말 운이 좋군요. 그곳에 어떻게 가나요?

남: 거기까지 걸어갈 수 있어요. 10분 정도 걸려요.

여: 잘됐군요. 지도에 길을 표시해 주시겠어요?

남: 물론이죠. 거기에 가면 곤드레밥을 드셔 보세요.

여: 계산서 좀 주시겠어요?

남: 여기 있습니다. 식사는 맛있게 하셨나요?

여: 아주 훌륭했어요. 저는 곤드레밥이 정말 좋았어요.

남: 고맙습니다. 그것은 건강에도 좋답니다.

여: 오, 정말이요?

남: 네. 곤드레는 비타민 A와 C가 풍부합니다. 그리고 소화도 잘돼요.

여: 그렇군요. 여기서 곤드레를 좀 살 수 있을까요?

남: 물론이죠. 제가 곤드레밥 조리법을 드릴까요?

여: 네, 그러면 정말 좋겠어요.

여: 미안하지만, 이 우유 (사는 것) 좀 도와주겠니?

남: 그럼요. 뭔데요?

여: 날짜를 좀 읽어 주렴.

남: 아, 유통 기한을 말씀드리길 원하세요?

여: 그래, 내가 안경을 두고 왔단다.

남: 잠깐만요. 6월 7일까지 드셔야 해요.

W: _____

B: _____

W: _____

B: _____

여: 그건 너무 짧네. 기한이 더 긴 게 있는지 궁금하구나.

남: 잠깐만요. 하나 찾았어요. 이것은 6월 11일까지 드실 수 있어요.

여: 오, 그걸로 사야겠다. 정말 고맙구나.

남: 천만에요.

Speak – Talk in pairs. 1

A: _____

B: _____

A: _____

A: 실례합니다. 이 근처에 은행이 있는지 궁금합니다.

B: 미안하지만 이 근처에는 없어요.

A: 괜찮아요. 고맙습니다.

Speak – Talk in pairs. 2

A: _____

B: _____

A: _____

B: _____

A: 무슨 일이세요, 할아버지?

B: 지루하구나.

A: 제가 함께 바둑을 두길 원하세요?

B: 그러면 좋겠구나. 고맙구나.

Wrap Up 1

G: _____

B: _____

G: _____

B: _____

G: _____

여: 나 배고파.

남: 내가 널 위해 라면을 끓여 줄게.

여: 좋아!

남: 달걀을 넣길 원하니?

여: 그러면 정말 좋겠어.

Wrap Up 2

G: _____

M: _____

G: _____

M: _____

G: _____

여: 아빠, 저 귀여운 가방을 보세요. 얼마인지 궁금해요.

남: 들어가서 확인해 보는 게 어떻겠니?

여: 정말요? 고마워요, 아빠.

남: 사 주겠다고는 말하지 않았단다. 그냥 가격만 물어보는 거야.

여: 물론이죠.

※ 다음 우리말과 일치하도록 빈칸에 알맞은 것을 골라 쓰시오.

1 Leah's _____ _____
A. Travel   B. Story

2 _____ _____ Leah.
A. am   B. I

3 I _____ _____ _____ a travel blog _____ I was 18.
A. since   B. writing   C. been   D. have

4 I go _____ and _____ my _____ _____ my readers.
A. with   B. places   C. experiences   D. share

5 _____ Markets _____ the World
A. Around   B. Must-Visit

6 _____ _____ , 20**
A. 15   B. July

7 _____ markets is a good _____ to learn about the _____ of a _____ .
A. culture   B. visiting   C. country   D. way

8 Markets are _____ _____ you can meet people, learn history, and _____ _____ food.
A. where   B. taste   C. places   D. local

9 I _____ _____ there is any better _____ to discover _____ culture.
A. whether   B. another   C. wonder   D. way

10 1 _____ Bazaar, _____
A. Turkey   B. Grand

11 Turkey is a country _____ East meets West, so it has a _____ _____ of _____ .
A. trade   B. where   C. tradition   D. long

12 It is a _____ _____ for large _____ _____ the Grand Bazaar.
A. like   B. natural   C. markets   D. place

13 The market _____ _____ in 1455 _____ Istanbul.
A. built   B. was   C. in

14 _____ then, the market had two big buildings, and people _____ _____ like _____ and gold there.
A. traded   B. back   C. cloth   D. goods

---

1 Leah의 여행 이야기

2 저는 Leah입니다.

3 18세 때부터 여행 블로그를 써 왔습니다.

4 저는 여기저기 다니며 제 경험을 독자들과 공유하고 있습니다.

5 꼭 방문해야 할 세계의 시장들

6 20**년 7월 15일

7 시장 방문은 한 나라의 문화에 대해 배우는 좋은 방법입니다.

8 시장은 사람들을 만나고, 역사를 배우고, 또 지역 음식을 맛볼 수 있는 장소입니다.

9 다른 문화를 발견하는 데에 더 좋은 방법이 있을지 모르겠습니다.

10 1 터키의 Grand Bazaar(그랜드 바자)

11 터키는 동양과 서양이 만나는 나라이고, 그래서 오랜 교역의 전통을 가지고 있습니다.

12 터키는 Grand Bazaar 같은 대형 시장이 생겨나기에 자연스러운 곳입니다.

13 Grand Bazaar는 1455년 이스탄불에 지어졌습니다.

14 그 당시에 이 시장에는 큰 건물이 두 개 있었고, 거기서 사람들은 직물이나 금 같은 물건을 교환했습니다.

15 Today the Grand Bazaar is _____ bigger, and it is the _____ _____ _____ in the world.

    A. covered   B. much   C. largest   D. market

16 It has 64 _____ and more than 4,000 _____ _____ one _____.

    A. roof   B. streets   C. under   D. shops

17 The market _____ _____ 250,000 visitors _____ day.

    A. every   B. over   C. attracts

18 You can buy _____ any _____ _____ there.

    A. imaginable   B. almost   C. item

19 **Extra Tip** Ask shop _____ if they _____ *nazar boncuğu*, a _____ Turkish symbol for good _____.

    A. traditional   B. owners   C. carry   D. luck

20 Also, if you want a nice snack, _____ _____ to _____ *lokum*, a _____ Turkish candy.

    A. sure   B. try   C. traditional   D. make

21 **2 Damnoen Saduak** _____ _____ , _____

    A. Market   B. Floating   C. Thailand

22 In the _____, Thai people _____ goods _____ rivers.

    A. on   B. past   C. traded

23 This was the _____ of _____ _____ in Thailand.

    A. floating   B. beginning   C. markets

24 _____ better road _____ , many _____ markets _____.

    A. disappeared   B. transportation   C. floating   D. with

25 _____ the late 1960s, _____ , some of them have come _____ and kept the tradition _____.

    A. alive   B. however   C. back   D. since

26 Today, _____ of the _____ _____ floating _____ is Damnoen Saduak Floating Market.

    A. popular   B. most   C. one   D. markets

27 It is always _____ _____ tourists _____ all the world.

    A. from   B. crowded   C. over   D. with

28 You can buy _____ foods and _____ gift _____ directly from _____.

    A. items   B. local   C. boats   D. traditional

---

15 오늘날 Grand Bazaar는 훨씬 크고, 세계에서 가장 큰 지붕이 덮인 시장입니다.

16 64개의 거리와 4,000개 이상의 상점이 한 지붕 아래에 있습니다.

17 그 시장은 매일 25만 명 이상의 방문객을 불러 모읍니다.

18 그곳에서는 상상할 수 있는 거의 모든 물건을 살 수 있습니다.

19 추가 정보 가게 주인에게 행운을 기원하는 터키 전통 상징인 'nazar boncuğu(나자르 본주)'를 파는지 물어보세요.

20 또한, 만약 맛있는 간식을 원한다면, 터키 전통 사탕인 'lokum(로쿰)'을 꼭 드셔 보세요.

21 2 태국의 Damnoen Saduak(담는 사두악) 수상 시장

22 과거에 태국 사람들은 강에서 물건을 교환했습니다.

23 이것이 태국 수상 시장의 시작이었습니다.

24 도로 교통이 개선되면서, 많은 수상 시장이 사라졌습니다.

25 그러나 1960년대 후반부터 일부가 다시 생겨나 전통을 이어가고 있습니다.

26 오늘날, 가장 인기 있는 수상 시장 중 하나는 Damnoen Saduak 수상 시장입니다.

27 그곳은 전 세계에서 온 관광객들로 항상 붐빕니다.

28 배에서 직접 현지 음식과 전통 선물을 살 수 있습니다.

29 **Extra Tip** I _____ if you have ever _____ a _____ on water.

A. meal   B. wonder   C. had

30 _____ not, _____ noodles _____ *pad thai.*

A. try   B. like   C. if

31 The sellers will _____ them on their boats and _____ them to you _____ a long fishing _____ .

A. with   B. cook   C. pole   D. pass

32 **3 Aalsmeer** _____ _____ , The _____

A. Netherlands   B. Market   C. Flower

33 The Netherlands _____ " _____ _____ ."

A. lands   B. means   C. low

34 _____ the name _____ , about 70% of the country sits _____ sea _____ .

A. suggests   B. level   C. as   D. below

35 Thus, the Dutch _____ _____ the land, and one _____ way to use it was to _____ flowers and sell them.

A. effective   B. built   C. grow   D. up

36 It is, _____ , no _____ _____ the country has the _____ flower market in the world: the Aalsmeer Flower Market.

A. surprise   B. largest   C. therefore   D. that

37 The building _____ the market is _____ is _____ _____ 120 soccer fields.

A. housed   B. than   C. bigger   D. where

38 The market is _____ _____ thousands of _____ carts.

A. with   B. flower-filled   C. busy

39 They are _____ _____ _____ electric-powered trucks.

A. mostly   B. moved   C. by

40 Every day, _____ 20 million flowers are _____ and _____ to all _____ of the world.

A. corners   B. traded   C. around   D. shipped

41 **Extra Tip** You may _____ you can _____ just a _____ flowers at the market.

A. few   B. wonder   C. buy   D. whether

42 Sadly, you cannot, but you can see _____ _____ flower _____ _____ .

A. wholesale   B. works   C. how   D. trading

---

29 추가 정보 여러분이 물 위에서 식사해 본 적이 있는지 궁금하네요.

30 만약 그렇지 않다면, 'pad thai(팟 타이)' 같은 면 요리를 드셔 보세요.

31 상인들이 배에서 음식을 만들어 긴 낚싯대로 건네줄 겁니다.

32 3 네덜란드 Aalsmeer(알스메이르) 꽃 시장

33 네덜란드는 '저지대'라는 뜻입니다.

34 이름에서 알 수 있듯이, 이 나라의 약 70%가 해수면보다 낮습니다.

35 그래서 네덜란드 사람들은 땅을 지어 올렸고, 그것을 사용하는 효과적인 방법은 꽃을 재배하고 파는 것이었습니다.

36 그러므로 네덜란드에 세계에서 가장 큰 꽃 시장인 Aalsmeer 꽃 시장이 있다는 것은 놀라운 일이 아닙니다.

37 시장이 들어선 건물은 축구장 120개보다 큽니다.

38 시장은 꽃이 가득 든 수천 개의 수레로 분주합니다.

39 수레는 대부분 전동 트럭에 의해 움직입니다.

40 매일, 약 2천만 송이의 꽃이 거래되어 세계 각지로 운송됩니다.

41 추가 정보 시장에서 꽃을 조금 살 수 있는지 궁금할 겁니다.

42 애석하게도 안 되지만, 꽃이 도매로 어떻게 거래되는지를 볼 수 있습니다.

※ 다음 우리말과 일치하도록 빈칸에 알맞은 것을 골라 쓰시오.

1 Leah's _____ _____

2 _____ _____ Leah.

3 I _____ _____ _____ a travel blog _____ I was 18.

4 I go places and _____ _____ _____ _____ my readers.

5 _____ Markets _____ the World

6 _____ 15, 20**

7 _____ _____ is a _____ _____ _____ _____ about the culture of a country.

8 Markets are _____ _____ you can meet people, learn history, and _____ _____ _____ .

9 I _____ _____ there is any better way _____ _____ _____ _____ .

10 1 _____ _____ , Turkey

11 Turkey is a country _____ East meets West, _____ it has a _____ _____ _____ _____ _____ .

12 It is _____ _____ _____ _____ large markets _____ the Grand Bazaar.

13 The market _____ _____ _____ 1455 in Istanbul.

14 Back then, the market had two big buildings, and people _____ _____ _____ _____ and _____ there.

1 Leah의 여행 이야기

2 저는 Leah입니다.

3 18세 때부터 여행 블로그를 써 왔습니다.

4 저는 여기저기 다니며 제 경험을 독자들과 공유하고 있습니다.

5 꼭 방문해야 할 세계의 시장들

6 20**년 7월 15일

7 시장 방문은 한 나라의 문화에 대해 배우는 좋은 방법입니다.

8 시장은 사람들을 만나고, 역사를 배우고, 또 지역 음식을 맛볼 수 있는 장소입니다.

9 다른 문화를 발견하는 데에 더 좋은 방법이 있을지 모르겠습니다.

10 1 터키의 Grand Bazaar(그랜드 바자)

11 터키는 동양과 서양이 만나는 나라이고, 그래서 오랜 교역의 전통을 가지고 있습니다.

12 터키는 Grand Bazaar 같은 대형 시장이 생겨나기에 자연스러운 곳입니다.

13 Grand Bazaar는 1455년 이스탄불에 지어졌습니다.

14 그 당시에 이 시장에는 큰 건물이 두 개 있었고, 거기서 사람들은 직물이나 금 같은 물건을 교환했습니다.

15 Today the Grand Bazaar is _____ _____ , and it is the _____ _____ _____ in the world.

16 It has 64 streets and _____ _____ 4,000 shops _____ _____ _____ .

17 The market _____ _____ 250,000 visitors every day.

18 You can buy _____ _____ _____ _____ there.

19 **Extra Tip** Ask shop owners _____ they carry *nazar boncuğu*, a _____ _____ _____ for _____ _____ .

20 Also, if you want a nice snack, _____ _____ _____ try *lokum*, a _____ _____ _____ .

21 **2 Damnoen Saduak _____ Market, _____**

22 In the past, Thai people _____ _____ _____ rivers.

23 This was the _____ _____ _____ _____ in Thailand.

24 _____ _____ _____ _____ , many _____ _____ _____ .

25 _____ the late 1960s, however, some of them _____ _____ _____ and _____ the tradition _____ .

26 Today, one of _____ _____ _____ floating _____ _____ Damnoen Saduak Floating Market.

27 It is always _____ _____ _____ from all over the world.

28 You can buy local foods and _____ _____ items _____ _____ .

| 15 | 오늘날 Grand Bazaar는 훨씬 크고, 세계에서 가장 큰 지붕이 덮인 시장입니다.

| 16 | 64개의 거리와 4,000개 이상의 상점이 한 지붕 아래에 있습니다.

| 17 | 그 시장은 매일 25만 명 이상의 방문객을 불러 모읍니다.

| 18 | 그곳에서는 상상할 수 있는 거의 모든 물건을 살 수 있습니다.

| 19 | 추가 정보 가게 주인에게 행운을 기원하는 터키 전통 상징인 'nazar boncuğu(나자르 본주)'를 파는지 물어보세요.

| 20 | 또한, 만약 맛있는 간식을 원한다면, 터키 전통 사탕인 'lokum(로쿰)'을 꼭 드셔 보세요.

| 21 | 2 태국의 Damnoen Saduak(담는 사두악) 수상 시장

| 22 | 과거에 태국 사람들은 강에서 물건을 교환했습니다.

| 23 | 이것이 태국 수상 시장의 시작이었습니다.

| 24 | 도로 교통이 개선되면서, 많은 수상 시장이 사라졌습니다.

| 25 | 그러나 1960년대 후반부터 일부가 다시 생겨나 전통을 이어가고 있습니다.

| 26 | 오늘날, 가장 인기 있는 수상 시장 중 하나는 Damnoen Saduak 수상 시장입니다.

| 27 | 그곳은 전 세계에서 온 관광객들로 항상 붐빕니다.

| 28 | 배에서 직접 현지 음식과 전통 선물을 살 수 있습니다.

29 **Extra Tip** I _____ _____ you _____ ever _____ a meal on water.

30 _____ _____, try noodles _____ *pad thai*.

31 The sellers will cook them on their boats and pass them to you _____ _____ _____ _____ _____.

32 **3 Aalsmeer Flower Market,** _____

33 The Netherlands _____ "_____ _____."

34 _____ the name _____, _____ 70% of the country sits _____ _____ _____.

35 _____, the Dutch _____ _____ the land, and one _____ _____ to use it was _____ _____ flowers and sell them.

36 It is, _____, _____ _____ that the country has _____ _____ _____ _____ in the world: the Aalsmeer Flower Market.

37 The building _____ the market _____ _____ is _____ _____ 120 soccer fields.

38 The market is _____ _____ _____ thousands of _____ carts.

39 They are _____ _____ _____ electric-powered trucks.

40 Every day, _____ _____ _____ flowers are _____ and _____ to all _____ of the world.

41 **Extra Tip** You may wonder _____ you can buy _____ _____ _____ flowers at the market.

42 Sadly, you cannot, but you can see _____ _____ _____.

29 추가 정보 여러분이 물 위에서 식사해 본 적이 있는지 궁금하네요.

30 만약 그렇지 않다면, 'pad thai(팟 타이)' 같은 면 요리를 드셔 보세요.

31 상인들이 배에서 음식을 만들어 긴 낚싯대로 건네줄 겁니다.

32 3 네덜란드 Aalsmeer(알스메이르) 꽃 시장

33 네덜란드는 '저지대'라는 뜻입니다.

34 이름에서 알 수 있듯이, 이 나라의 약 70%가 해수면보다 낮습니다.

35 그래서 네덜란드 사람들은 땅을 지어 올렸고, 그것을 사용하는 효과적인 방법은 꽃을 재배하고 파는 것이었습니다.

36 그러므로 네덜란드에 세계에서 가장 큰 꽃 시장인 Aalsmeer 꽃 시장이 있다는 것은 놀라운 일이 아닙니다.

37 시장이 들어선 건물은 축구장 120개보다 큽니다.

38 시장은 꽃이 가득 든 수천 개의 수레로 분주합니다.

39 수레는 대부분 전동 트럭에 의해 움직입니다.

40 매일, 약 2천만 송이의 꽃이 거래되어 세계 각지로 운송됩니다.

41 추가 정보 시장에서 꽃을 조금 살 수 있는지 궁금할 겁니다.

42 애석하게도 안 되지만, 꽃이 도매로 어떻게 거래되는지를 볼 수 있습니다.

※ 다음 문장을 우리말로 쓰시오.

1 Leah's Travel Story

➡ _____

2 I am Leah.

➡ _____

3 I have been writing a travel blog since I was 18.

➡ _____

4 I go places and share my experiences with my readers.

➡ _____

5 Must-Visit Markets Around the World

➡ _____

6 July 15, 20**

➡ _____

7 Visiting markets is a good way to learn about the culture of a country.

➡ _____

8 Markets are places where you can meet people, learn history, and taste local food.

➡ _____

9 I wonder whether there is any better way to discover another culture.

➡ _____

10 1 Grand Bazaar, Turkey

➡ _____

11 Turkey is a country where East meets West, so it has a long tradition of trade.

➡ _____

12 It is a natural place for large markets like the Grand Bazaar.

➡ _____

13 The market was built in 1455 in Istanbul.

➡ _____

14 Back then, the market had two big buildings, and people traded goods like cloth and gold there.

➡ _____

15 Today the Grand Bazaar is much bigger, and it is the largest covered market in the world.

➡ _____

16 It has 64 streets and more than 4,000 shops under one roof.

➡ _____

17 The market attracts over 250,000 visitors every day.

➡ _____

18 You can buy almost any imaginable item there.

➡ _____

19 Extra Tip: Ask shop owners if they carry nazar boncuğu, a traditional Turkish symbol for good luck.

➡ _____

20 Also, if you want a nice snack, make sure to try lokum, a traditional Turkish candy.

➡ _____

21 2 Damnoen Saduak Floating Market, Thailand

➡ _____

22 In the past, Thai people traded goods on rivers.

➡ _____

23 This was the beginning of floating markets in Thailand.

➡ _____

24 With better road transportation, many floating markets disappeared.

➡ _____

25 Since the late 1960s, however, some of them have come back and kept the tradition alive.

➡ _____

26 Today, one of the most popular floating markets is Damnoen Saduak Floating Market.

➡ _____

27 It is always crowded with tourists from all over the world.

➡ _____

28 You can buy local foods and traditional gift items directly from boats.

➡ _____

29 Extra Tip: I wonder if you have ever had a meal on water.

➡ _____

30 If not, try noodles like *pad thai*.

➡ _____

31 The sellers will cook them on their boats and pass them to you with a long fishing pole.

➡ _____

32 3 Aalsmeer Flower Market, The Netherlands

➡ _____

33 The Netherlands means "low lands."

➡ _____

34 As the name suggests, about 70% of the country sits below sea level.

➡ _____

35 Thus, the Dutch built up the land, and one effective way to use it was to grow flowers and sell them.

➡ _____

36 It is, therefore, no surprise that the country has the largest flower market in the world: the Aalsmeer Flower Market.

➡ _____

37 The building where the market is housed is bigger than 120 soccer fields.

➡ _____

38 The market is busy with thousands of flower-filled carts.

➡ _____

39 They are moved mostly by electric-powered trucks.

➡ _____

40 Every day, around 20 million flowers are traded and shipped to all corners of the world.

➡ _____

41 Extra Tip: You may wonder whether you can buy just a few flowers at the market.

➡ _____

42 Sadly, you cannot, but you can see how wholesale flower trading works.

➡ _____

※ 다음 괄호 안의 단어들을 우리말에 맞도록 바르게 배열하시오.

1 (Travel / Leah's / Story)
➡ _____

2 (Leah. / am / I)
➡ _____

3 (have / I / writing / been / travel / a / blog / I / since / 18. / was)
➡ _____

4 (go / I / and / places / my / share / expreriences / my / with / readers.)
➡ _____

5 (Markets / Must-Visit / the / World / Around)
➡ _____

6 (20** / 15, / July)
➡ _____

7 (markets / visiting / a / is / good / to / way / about / learn / culture / the / a / of / country.)
➡ _____

8 (are / markets / where / places / can / you / people, / meet / history, / learn / taste / and / food. / local)
➡ _____

9 (wonder / I / there / whether / is / better / any / to / way / discover / culture. / another)
➡ _____

10 (Grand / 1 / Turkey / Bazaar)
➡ _____

11 (is / Turkey / a / where / country / meets / East / West, / it / so / a / has / tradition / long / trade. / of)
➡ _____

12 (is / it / natural / a / for / place / markets / large / the / like / Bazaar. / Grand)
➡ _____

13 (market / the / built / was / 1455 / in / Istanbul. / in)
➡ _____

14 (then, / back / market / the / two / had / buildings / big / and / traded / people / like / goods / cloth / gold / and / there.)
➡ _____
_____

1 Leah의 여행 이야기

2 저는 Leah입니다.

3 18세 때부터 여행 블로그를 써 왔습니다.

4 저는 여기저기 다니며 제 경험을 독자들과 공유하고 있습니다.

5 꼭 방문해야 할 세계의 시장들

6 20**년 7월 15일

7 시장 방문은 한 나라의 문화에 대해 배우는 좋은 방법입니다.

8 시장은 사람들을 만나고, 역사를 배우고, 또 지역 음식을 맛볼 수 있는 장소입니다.

9 다른 문화를 발견하는 데에 더 좋은 방법이 있을지 모르겠습니다.

10 1 터키의 Grand Bazaar(그랜드 바자)

11 터키는 동양과 서양이 만나는 나라이고, 그래서 오랜 교역의 전통을 가지고 있습니다.

12 터키는 Grand Bazaar 같은 대형 시장이 생겨나기에 자연스러운 곳입니다.

13 Grand Bazaar는 1455년 이스탄불에 지어졌습니다.

14 그 당시에 이 시장에는 큰 건물이 두 개 있었고, 거기서 사람들은 직물이나 금 같은 물건을 교환했습니다.

15 (the / today / Grand / is / Bazaar / bigger, / much / it / and / is / largest / the / market / covered / the / world. / in)

➡ _____

_____

16 (has / it / streets / 64 / and / than / more / shops / 4,000 / one / roof. / under)

➡ _____

17 (market / the / over / attracts / visitors / 250,000 / day. / every)

➡ _____

18 (can / you / almost / buy / imaginable / any / there. / item)

➡ _____

19 (Tip / Extra // shop / ask / if / owners / carry / they *boncuğu*, / *nazar* / a / Turkish / traditional / for / luck. / symbol / good)

➡ _____

_____

20 (if / also, / you / want / nice / a / snack, / sure / make / try / to *lokum*, / a / Turkish / candy. / traditional)

➡ _____

_____

21 (2 / Saduak / Damnoen / Market, / Floating / Thailand)

➡ _____

22 (the / in / past, / people / Thai / goods / traded / rivers. / on)

➡ _____

23 (was / this / beginning / the / floating / of / in / markets / Thailand.)

➡ _____

24 (better / with / transportation, / road / floating / many / disappeared. / markets)

➡ _____

25 (the / since / 1960s, / late / some / however, / them / of / come / have / back / and / the / kept / alive. / tradition)

➡ _____

_____

26 (one / today, / of / most / the / floating / popular / is / markets / Saduak / Damnoen / Market. / Floating)

➡ _____

_____

27 (is / it / crowded / always / tourists / with / all / from / the / over / world.)

➡ _____

28 (can / you / local / buy / foods / and / gift / traditional / directly / items / boats. / from)

➡ _____

15 오늘날 Grand Bazaar는 훨씬 크고, 세계에서 가장 큰 지붕이 덮인 시장입니다.

16 64개의 거리와 4,000개 이상의 상점이 한 지붕 아래에 있습니다.

17 그 시장은 매일 25만 명 이상의 방문객을 불러 모읍니다.

18 그곳에서는 상상할 수 있는 거의 모든 물건을 살 수 있습니다.

19 추가 정보 가게 주인에게 행운을 기원하는 터키 전통 상징인 'nazar boncuğu(나자르 본주)'를 파는지 물어보세요.

20 또한, 만약 맛있는 간식을 원한다면, 터키 전통 사탕인 'lokum(로쿰)'을 꼭 드셔 보세요.

21 2 태국의 Damnoen Saduak(담는 사두악) 수상 시장

22 과거에 태국 사람들은 강에서 물건을 교환했습니다.

23 이것이 태국 수상 시장의 시작이었습니다.

24 도로 교통이 개선되면서, 많은 수상 시장이 사라졌습니다.

25 그러나 1960년대 후반부터 일부가 다시 생겨나 전통을 이어가고 있습니다.

26 오늘날, 가장 인기 있는 수상 시장 중 하나는 Damnoen Saduak 수상 시장입니다.

27 그곳은 전 세계에서 온 관광객들로 항상 붐빕니다.

28 배에서 직접 현지 음식과 전통 선물을 살 수 있습니다.

29 (Tip / Extra // wonder / I / you / if / ever / have / had / meal / a / water. / on)

➡ _____

30 (not, / if / noodles / try / *pad* / like / *thai*.)

➡ _____

31 (sellers / the / cook / will / them / their / on / boats / and / them / pass / you / to / a / with / long / pole. / fishing)

➡ _____

_____

32 (3 / Flower / Aalsmeer / Market, / Netherlands / The)

➡ _____

33 (Netherlands / The / means / lands." / "low)

➡ _____

34 (the / as / suggests / name / 70% / about / the / of / sits / country / sea / below / level.)

➡ _____

35 (the / thus, / built / Dutch / the / up / land, / one / and / way / effective / use / to / it / to / was / flowers / grow / and / them. / sell)

➡ _____

36 (is, / it / therefore, / surprise / no / the / that / country / the / has / flower / largest / in / market / the / world: / the / Flower / Aalsmeer / Market.)

➡ _____

37 (building / the / the / where / market / housed / is / bigger / is / 120 / than / fields. / soccer)

➡ _____

38 (market / the / busy / is / thousands / with / flower-filled / of / carts.)

➡ _____

39 (are / they / mostly / moved / electric-powered / by / trucks.)

➡ _____

40 (day, / every / 20 / around / flowers / million / traded / are / and / to / shipped / all / corners / the / of / world.)

➡ _____

_____

41 (Tip / Extra // you / wonder / may / you / whether / can / just / buy / few / a / flowers / the / at / market.)

➡ _____

_____

42 (you / sadly, / cannot, / you / but / see / can / wholesale / how / trading / flower / works.)

➡ _____

_____

---

29 추가 정보 여러분이 물 위에서 식사해 본 적이 있는지 궁금하네요.

30 만약 그렇지 않다면, 'pad thai(팟 타이)' 같은 면 요리를 드셔 보세요.

31 상인들이 배에서 음식을 만들어 긴 낚싯대로 건네줄 겁니다.

32 3 네덜란드 Aalsmeer(알스메이르) 꽃 시장

33 네덜란드는 '저지대'라는 뜻입니다.

34 이름에서 알 수 있듯이, 이 나라의 약 70%가 해수면보다 낮습니다.

35 그래서 네덜란드 사람들은 땅을 지어 올렸고, 그것을 사용하는 효과적인 방법은 꽃을 재배하고 파는 것이었습니다.

36 그러므로 네덜란드에 세계에서 가장 큰 꽃 시장인 Aalsmeer 꽃 시장이 있다는 것은 놀라운 일이 아닙니다.

37 시장이 들어선 건물은 축구장 120개보다 큽니다.

38 시장은 꽃이 가득 든 수천 개의 수레로 분주합니다.

39 수레는 대부분 전동 트럭에 의해 움직입니다.

40 매일, 약 2천만 송이의 꽃이 거래되어 세계 각지로 운송됩니다.

41 추가 정보 시장에서 꽃을 조금 살 수 있는지 궁금할 겁니다.

42 애석하게도 안 되지만, 꽃이 도매로 어떻게 거래되는지를 볼 수 있습니다.

※ 다음 우리말을 영어로 쓰시오.

1 Leah의 여행 이야기

➡ _____

2 저는 Leah입니다.

➡ _____

3 18세 때부터 여행 블로그를 써 왔습니다.

➡ _____

4 저는 여기저기 다니며 제 경험을 독자들과 공유하고 있습니다.

➡ _____

5 꼭 방문해야 할 세계의 시장들

➡ _____

6 20**년 7월 15일

➡ _____

7 시장 방문은 한 나라의 문화에 대해 배우는 좋은 방법입니다.

➡ _____

8 시장은 사람들을 만나고, 역사를 배우고, 또 지역 음식을 맛볼 수 있는 장소입니다.

➡ _____

9 다른 문화를 발견하는 데에 더 좋은 방법이 있을지 모르겠습니다.

➡ _____

10 1 터키의 Grand Bazaar(그랜드 바자)

➡ _____

11 터키는 동양과 서양이 만나는 나라이고, 그래서 오랜 교역의 전통을 가지고 있습니다.

➡ _____

12 터키는 Grand Bazaar 같은 대형 시장이 생겨나기에 자연스러운 곳입니다.

➡ _____

13 Grand Bazaar는 1455년 이스탄불에 지어졌습니다.

➡ _____

14 그 당시에 이 시장에는 큰 건물이 두 개 있었고, 거기서 사람들은 직물이나 금 같은 물건을 교환했습니다.

➡ _____

15 오늘날 Grand Bazaar는 훨씬 크고, 세계에서 가장 큰 지붕이 덮인 시장입니다.

➡ _____

16 64개의 거리와 4,000개 이상의 상점이 한 지붕 아래에 있습니다.

➡ _____

17 그 시장은 매일 25만 명 이상의 방문객을 불러 모읍니다.

➡ _____

18 그곳에서는 상상할 수 있는 거의 모든 물건을 살 수 있습니다.

➡ _____

19 추가 정보: 가게 주인에게 행운을 기원하는 터키 전통 상징인 'nazar boncuğu(나자르 본주)'를 파는지 물어보세요.

➡ _____

20 또한, 만약 맛있는 간식을 원한다면, 터키 전통 사탕인 'lokum(로쿰)'을 꼭 드셔 보세요.

➡ _____

21 2 태국의 Damnoen Saduak(담는 사두악) 수상 시장

➡ _____

22 과거에 태국 사람들은 강에서 물건을 교환했습니다.

➡ _____

23 이것이 태국 수상 시장의 시작이었습니다.

➡ _____

24 도로 교통이 개선되면서, 많은 수상 시장이 사라졌습니다.

➡ _____

25 그러나 1960년대 후반부터 일부가 다시 생겨나 전통을 이어 가고 있습니다.

➡ _____

26 오늘날, 가장 인기 있는 수상 시장 중 하나는 Damnoen Saduak 수상 시장입니다.

➡ _____

27 그곳은 전 세계에서 온 관광객들로 항상 붐빕니다.

➡ _____

28 배에서 직접 현지 음식과 전통 선물을 살 수 있습니다.

➡ _____

29 추가 정보: 여러분이 물 위에서 식사해 본 적이 있는지 궁금하네요.

➡ _____

30 만약 그렇지 않다면, 'pad thai(팟 타이)' 같은 면 요리를 드셔 보세요.

➡ _____

31 상인들이 배에서 음식을 만들어 긴 낚싯대로 건네줄 겁니다.

➡ _____

32 3 네덜란드 Aalsmeer(알스메이르) 꽃 시장

➡ _____

33 네덜란드는 '저지대'라는 뜻입니다.

➡ _____

34 이름에서 알 수 있듯이, 이 나라의 약 70%가 해수면보다 낮습니다.

➡ _____

35 그래서 네덜란드 사람들은 땅을 지어 올렸고, 그것을 사용하는 효과적인 방법은 꽃을 재배하고 파는 것이었습니다.

➡ _____

_____

36 그러므로 네덜란드에 세계에서 가장 큰 꽃 시장인 Aalsmeer 꽃 시장이 있다는 것은 놀라운 일이 아닙니다.

➡ _____

_____

37 시장이 들어선 건물은 축구장 120개보다 큽니다.

➡ _____

38 시장은 꽃이 가득 든 수천 개의 수레로 분주합니다.

➡ _____

39 수레는 대부분 전동 트럭에 의해 움직입니다.

➡ _____

40 매일, 약 2천만 송이의 꽃이 거래되어 세계 각지로 운송됩니다.

➡ _____

41 추가 정보: 시장에서 꽃을 조금 살 수 있는지 궁금할 겁니다.

➡ _____

42 애석하게도 안 되지만, 꽃이 도매로 어떻게 거래되는지를 볼 수 있습니다.

➡ _____

※ 다음 우리말과 일치하도록 빈칸에 알맞은 말을 쓰시오.

My Speaking Portfolio - Step 2

1. A: _____ do you _____ _____ _____? I _____ _____
   you want to travel _____ _____ or _____.
2. B: Well, I _____ _____ _____ _____ my friends.
   ......
3. A: Okay. Do you want _____ _____ _____ or _____?
4. B: I want to visit museums. _____ a great way _____ _____
   _____ the _____ _____.

1. A: 어떻게 여행하는 것을 원하니? 나는 네가 친구들이나 가족들과 여행하는 것을 좋아하는지 궁금해.
2. B: 음, 나는 내 친구들과 여행하고 싶어.
......
3. A: 알겠어. 너는 박물관 또는 시장을 방문하고 싶니?
4. B: 나는 박물관을 가보고 싶어. 그것은 지역 문화에 대해 배우는 데 좋은 방법이야.

After You Read

1. This country is a _____ _____ _____ _____ _____
   and has a _____ _____ _____ _____ _____.
2. This is a _____ _____ _____ _____ _____ has a _____
   _____.
3. _____ _____ _____ of the country _____ _____ _____
   _____.

1. 이 나라는 동양과 서양이 만나는 장소이고, 오랜 교역의 전통을 가지고 있다.
2. 이곳은 배에서 거래하는 오랜 역사가 있는 나라이다.
3. 그 나라의 3분의 2 이상이 해수면보다 낮다.

Wrap Up READING

1. _____ _____, I _____ _____ Oakville Farmers' Market.
2. That is _____ _____ _____ _____ I buy food for the _____
   _____.
3. There I find _____ _____ _____ _____ _____ _____.
4. They _____ _____ _____ only _____ _____ _____
   before I buy them.
5. I _____ _____ bread, _____, and _____ jam.
6. _____ I can buy _____ _____ _____ _____ the producers,
   they are usually _____ _____ _____ _____ _____ _____.
7. The _____ _____ are always kind and _____ _____ _____
   gardening tips and _____ _____ visitors, too.
8. I _____ _____ _____ the _____ _____.

1. 토요일마다 나는 Oakville 농산물 직거래 시장에 간다.
2. 그곳은 내가 다음 주에 먹을 음식을 사는 곳이다.
3. 그곳에서 나는 온갖 종류의 신선한 채소를 구한다.
4. 채소들은 대개 내가 사기 불과 몇 시간 전에 수확된 것이다.
5. 나는 또한 빵, 고기, 그리고 집에서 만든 잼도 구한다.
6. 물건을 생산자에게서 직접 살 수 있어서 그것들은 대개 다른 가게에서보다 훨씬 저렴하다.
7. 지역 농부들은 항상 친절하고, 원예 정보나 조리법을 방문객들과 공유할 준비가 되어 있다.
8. 나는 농산물 직거래 시장에 가는 것을 좋아한다.

※ 다음 우리말을 영어로 쓰시오.

My Speaking Portfolio - Step 2

1. A: 어떻게 여행하는 것을 원하니? 나는 네가 친구들이나 가족들과 여행하는 것을 좋아하는지 궁금해.
   ➡ _____

2. B: 음, 나는 내 친구들과 여행하고 싶어.
   ➡ _____

......

3. A: 알겠어. 너는 박물관 또는 시장을 방문하고 싶니?
   ➡ _____

4. B: 나는 박물관을 가보고 싶어. 그것은 지역 문화에 대해 배우는 데 좋은 방법이야.
   ➡ _____

After You Read

1. 이 나라는 동양과 서양이 만나는 장소이고, 오랜 교역의 전통을 가지고 있다.
   ➡ _____

2. 이곳은 배에서 거래하는 오랜 역사가 있는 나라이다.
   ➡ _____

3. 그 나라의 3분의 2 이상이 해수면보다 낮다.
   ➡ _____

Wrap Up READING

1. 토요일마다 나는 Oakville 농산물 직거래 시장에 간다.
   ➡ _____

2. 그곳은 내가 다음 주에 먹을 음식을 사는 곳이다.
   ➡ _____

3. 그곳에서 나는 온갖 종류의 신선한 채소를 구한다.
   ➡ _____

4. 채소들은 대개 내가 사기 불과 몇 시간 전에 수확된 것이다.
   ➡ _____

5. 나는 또한 빵, 고기, 그리고 집에서 만든 잼도 구한다.
   ➡ _____

6. 물건을 생산자에게서 직접 살 수 있어서 그것들은 대개 다른 가게에서보다 훨씬 저렴하다.
   ➡ _____

7. 지역 농부들은 항상 친절하고, 원예 정보나 조리법을 방문객들과 공유할 준비가 되어 있다.
   ➡ _____

8. 나는 농산물 직거래 시장에 가는 것을 좋아한다.
   ➡ _____

※ 다음 영어를 우리말로 쓰시오.

01	onion	
02	widely	
03	sick	
04	cheap	
05	delicious	
06	century	
07	everywhere	
08	sell	
09	healthy	
10	differ	
11	slice	
12	however	
13	flat	
14	introduce	
15	learn	
16	disagree	
17	share	
18	far	
19	bring	
20	meat	
21	almost	

22	national flag	
23	topping	
24	the New World	
25	record	
26	national	
27	favorite	
28	global	
29	since	
30	type	
31	such	
32	busy	
33	the Stone Age	
34	vegetable	
35	outside of	
36	in time	
37	topped with	
38	at the same time	
39	put ~ on	
40	in one form or another	
41	at any time	
42	be used to+동사원형	
43	It is believed that ~	

※ 다음 우리말을 영어로 쓰시오.

01 분주한, 바쁜

02 세기

03 맛보다

04 유형

05 거의

06 ~인 반면에,
   ~하는 동안에

07 ~할 때, ~하면서

08 ~ 이후로

09 맛있는

10 국기

11 양파

12 공유하다

13 다르다

14 폭넓게

15 고기

16 상점

17 멀리 떨어진

18 납작한, 평평한

19 전 세계적인

20 그러나

21 이름 붙이다

22 가지고 오다

23 팔다

24 값싼

25 국가의

26 의견이 다르다

27 건강한

28 모든 곳에서

29 기록

30 이동하다

31 (얇은) 조각

32 그런, ~와 같은

33 고명, 토핑

34 소개하다

35 이윽고

36 어느 때이든지

37 ~로 덮여 있는

38 너무 ~해서 …한

39 (다음으로) 넘어가다

40 동시에

41 ~하기 위하여 사용되다

42 전 세계에 걸친

43 ~라고들 믿고 있다

※ 다음 영영풀이에 알맞은 단어를 <보기>에서 골라 쓴 후, 우리말 뜻을 쓰시오.

1 _____ : where you buy something: _____

2 _____ : to have or express the same opinion: _____

3 _____ : a period of 100 years: _____

4 _____ : affecting or including the whole world: _____

5 _____ : to cook something using dry heat, in an oven: _____

6 _____ : costing little money or less money than you expected: _____

7 _____ : a thin flat piece of food cut from a larger piece: _____

8 _____ : to bring a plan, system, or product into use for the first time: _____

9 _____ : a round white vegetable with a brown, red, or white skin and many
layers: _____

10 _____ : something you put on top of food to make it look nicer or taste better:
_____

11 _____ : a type of food made from flour and water that is mixed together and then
baked: _____

12 _____ : a piece of cloth with a coloured pattern or picture on it that represents a
country or organization: _____

보기

century	agree	shop	global
bread	topping	slice	flag
cheap	bake	onion	introduce

※ 다음 우리말과 일치하도록 빈칸에 알맞은 것을 골라 쓰시오.

1 A _____ of _____

    A. History   B. Slice

2 _____ do you _____ on _____ pizza?

    A. like   B. what   C. your

3 _____ you may _____ _____ the best toppings, you will agree that it is now a _____ food.

    A. global   B. disagree   C. on   D. though

4 It is _____ in fast-food restaurants or on the _____ in _____ _____ of the world.

    A. parts   B. sold   C. most   D. street

5 How has pizza _____ _____ a _____ food _____ the world?

    A. favorite   B. become   C. around   D. such

6 _____ the Stone Age, people have been _____ pizza in one _____ or _____.

    A. form   B. since   C. another   D. eating

7 Stone Age people _____ _____ bread on _____ _____.

    A. flat   B. rocks   C. baked   D. hot

8 Records _____ that the Greeks and the Romans started to _____ _____ and vegetables _____ flat bread.

    A. put   B. on   C. show   D. meat

9 It is _____ that the word "pizza" was first _____ in Italy to _____ the food _____ 1,000 years ago.

    A. over   B. believed   C. name   D. used

10 However, pizza _____ tomato toppings was not _____ _____ the 16th _____.

    A. until   B. with   C. century   D. born

11 There were no tomatoes in Italy _____ Christopher Columbus and _____ Europeans _____ them _____ the New World.

    A. other   B. from   C. brought   D. before

---

1 한 조각의 역사

2 여러분은 어떤 피자 토핑을 좋아하는가?

3 비록 제일 좋아하는 피자 토핑에 대해 의견이 다를 수 있지만, 피자가 오늘날 세계적인 음식이라는 데에는 모두 동의할 것이다.

4 피자는 세계 대부분 지역의 패스트푸드 식당이나 길거리에서 팔리고 있다.

5 어떻게 해서 피자가 세계적으로 이토록 사랑받는 음식이 되었을까?

6 석기시대부터 사람들은 여러 가지 형태로 피자를 먹어 왔다.

7 석기시대 사람들은 납작한 빵을 뜨거운 돌에 구워 먹었다.

8 기록에 의하면 그리스와 로마 사람들이 납작한 빵에 고기와 채소를 얹기 시작했다.

9 '피자'라는 단어는 이러한 음식을 지칭하기 위해 약 천 년 전에 이탈리아에서 처음 사용되었다고 알려져 있다.

10 하지만 토마토 토핑을 얹은 피자는 16세기까지는 존재하지 않았다.

11 크리스토퍼 콜럼버스와 다른 유럽인들이 신세계에서 가져오기 전까지 이탈리아에는 토마토가 없었다.

12 When they were first _____ to Europe, people _____ that tomatoes would _____ them _____.

A. thought   B. sick   C. make   D. introduced

13 _____ time, people _____ that tomatoes were _____ and _____.

A. learned   B. healthy   C. delicious   D. in

14 In the 18th _____, Naples was a _____ city _____ there were many _____.

A. where   B. century   C. large   D. jobs

15 Workers from _____ and _____ came to the city, and what they needed in their busy _____ was food they could eat quickly at any _____.

A. lives   B. time   C. far   D. near

16 Cooks in Naples began to put tomato and _____ toppings on _____ bread and _____ _____ of pizza on the street.

A. flat   B. slices   C. other   D. sold

17 The _____ food was so _____ and _____ that _____ ate it for breakfast, lunch, and dinner.

A. workers   B. cheap   C. delicious   D. street

18 They could buy _____ _____ pizza and eat them _____ they walked _____ the street.

A. as   B. of   C. on   D. slices

19 In 1830, the _____ _____ pizza _____ _____ in Naples.

A. shop   B. world's   C. opened   D. first

20 _____ 1889, Queen Margherita _____ Italy _____ Naples and _____ pizza.

A. visited   B. tried   C. in   D. of

21 The _____ of pizza that she loved most had tomato, cheese, and green _____ toppings that showed the three _____ on Italy's national _____—red, white, and green.

A. leaf   B. type   C. flag   D. colors

12 유럽에 처음 소개되었을 때 사람들은 토마토가 사람들을 아프게 할 거라고 여겼다.

13 시간이 지나며 사람들은 토마토가 맛있고 건강에도 좋다는 것을 알게 되었다.

14 18세기에 나폴리는 다양한 직업이 존재하는 대도시였다.

15 사방에서 노동자들이 이 도시로 모여들었고, 바쁜 생활 중 그들에게 필요했던 것은 언제든지 빨리 먹을 수 있는 음식이었다.

16 나폴리의 요리사들이 납작한 빵에 토마토와 다른 토핑을 얹기 시작해 길거리에서 피자 조각을 팔았다.

17 이 길거리 음식은 무척 저렴하고 맛이 좋아서, 노동자들은 이것을 아침, 점심, 저녁으로 먹었다.

18 그들은 피자 조각을 사서 길을 걸어가며 먹을 수 있었다.

19 1830년에는 세계 최초의 피자 가게가 나폴리에서 문을 열었다.

20 1889년에 이탈리아의 마르게리타 왕비가 나폴리를 방문하여 피자를 맛보았다.

21 그녀가 가장 좋아했던 피자는 이탈리아 국기의 세 가지 색깔인 빨강, 하양, 초록을 나타낸 토마토, 치즈, 녹색 잎 채소 토핑으로 된 것이었다.

22 After the queen's _____ , pizza went _____ to _____ a truly national _____ .

A. on   B. dish   C. become   D. visit

23 Pizza _____ _____ outside of Italy in the _____ 19th century, when many Italians _____ to the United States.

A. moved   B. known   C. late   D. became

24 Italians _____ pizza with them, and Americans loved the flat bread topped _____ meat and vegetables _____ they could eat bread, meat, and vegetables at the _____ time.

A. with   B. same   C. brought   D. because

25 The _____ pizza restaurant in the United States _____ _____ _____ in 1905.

A. opened   B. first   C. doors   D. its

26 Pizza is now _____ _____ _____ .

A. almost   B. enjoyed   C. everywhere

27 Of _____ , toppings _____ widely _____ place _____ place.

A. from   B. differ   C. course   D. to

28 Koreans love *bulgogi* on their pizza, _____ Russians like to _____ fish and _____ toppings _____ their pizza.

A. have   B. on   C. while   D. onion

29 _____ , all _____ _____ pizza _____ two things.

A. share   B. types   C. however   D. of

30 _____ begins _____ _____ bread, and each is a _____ of history.

A. slice   B. with   C. each   D. flat

22 왕비의 방문 이후로 피자는 진정한 이탈리아의 국가 음식이 되었다.

23 19세기 후빈에는 피자가 이탈리아 밖으로 알려지게 되었는데, 이 시기에 많은 이탈리아 사람들이 미국으로 이주를 하였다.

24 이탈리아인들은 피자도 함께 가져갔고, 빵, 고기, 채소를 한꺼번에 먹을 수 있어서 미국인들은 고기와 채소를 얹은 이 납작한 빵을 좋아했다.

25 미국 최초의 피자 가게가 1905년에 문을 열었다.

26 오늘날 피자는 거의 어디에서나 즐길 수 있다.

27 물론, 토핑은 지역에 따라 매우 다양하다.

28 한국인은 불고기를 피자에 얹어 먹기를 좋아하고, 러시아 사람들은 생선과 양파 토핑을 좋아한다.

29 그러나 모든 종류의 피자가 두 가지 사실만큼은 똑같다.

30 모든 피자는 납작한 빵에서 시작하고, 각각은 역사의 한 조각이다.

※ 다음 우리말과 일치하도록 빈칸에 알맞은 것을 골라 쓰시오.

1 A _____ _____ _____

2 _____ _____ _____ _____ on your pizza?

3 _____ you may _____ _____ the best toppings, you will agree that it is now a _____ _____.

4 _____ _____ _____ in fast-food restaurants or on the street _____ _____ _____ of the _____.

5 How _____ pizza _____ _____ _____ _____ _____ around the world?

6 _____ the Stone Age, people _____ _____ _____ pizza in one form or _____.

7 Stone Age people baked flat bread _____ _____ _____.

8 _____ _____ that the Greeks and the Romans started _____ _____ meat and vegetables _____ flat bread.

9 _____ _____ _____ that the word "pizza" was first used in Italy _____ _____ the food _____ 1,000 years ago.

10 _____, pizza with tomato toppings _____ _____ _____ the 16th century.

11 There were no tomatoes in Italy _____ Christopher Columbus and other Europeans _____ them _____ the New World.

12 When they _____ first _____ to Europe, people thought that tomatoes would _____ _____ _____.

13 _____ _____, people learned that tomatoes were _____ and _____.

14 _____ the 18th _____, Naples was a large city _____ there were many jobs.

15 Workers _____ _____ _____ _____ came to the city, and what they needed in their _____ _____ was food they could eat quickly _____ _____ _____.

1 한 조각의 역사

2 여러분은 어떤 피자 토핑을 좋아하는가?

3 비록 제일 좋아하는 피자 토핑에 대해 의견이 다를 수 있지만, 피자가 오늘날 세계적인 음식이라는 데에는 모두 동의할 것이다.

4 피자는 세계 대부분 지역의 패스트푸드 식당이나 길거리에서 팔리고 있다.

5 어떻게 해서 피자가 세계적으로 이토록 사랑받는 음식이 되었을까?

6 석기시대부터 사람들은 여러 가지 형태로 피자를 먹어 왔다.

7 석기시대 사람들은 납작한 빵을 뜨거운 돌에 구워 먹었다.

8 기록에 의하면 그리스와 로마 사람들이 납작한 빵에 고기와 채소를 얹기 시작했다.

9 '피자'라는 단어는 이러한 음식을 지칭하기 위해 약 천 년 전에 이탈리아에서 처음 사용되었다고 알려져 있다.

10 하지만 토마토 토핑을 얹은 피자는 16세기까지는 존재하지 않았다.

11 크리스토퍼 콜럼버스와 다른 유럽인들이 신세계에서 가져오기 전까지 이탈리아에는 토마토가 없었다.

12 유럽에 처음 소개되었을 때 사람들은 토마토가 사람들을 아프게 할 거라고 여겼다.

13 시간이 지나며 사람들은 토마토가 맛있고 건강에도 좋다는 것을 알게 되었다.

14 18세기에 나폴리는 다양한 직업이 존재하는 대도시였다.

15 사방에서 노동자들이 이 도시로 모여들었고, 바쁜 생활 중 그들에게 필요했던 것은 언제든지 빨리 먹을 수 있는 음식이었다.

16 Cooks in Naples began to _____ tomato and other toppings _____ flat bread and sold _____ _____ _____ on the street.

17 The street food was _____ _____ and _____ _____ workers ate it _____ breakfast, lunch, and dinner.

18 They could buy _____ _____ pizza and eat them _____ they walked _____ _____ _____.

19 In 1830, the _____ _____ _____ _____ opened in Naples.

20 In 1889, Queen Margherita of Italy visited Naples and _____ pizza.

21 The type of pizza _____ _____ _____ _____ had tomato, cheese, and green leaf toppings _____ _____ the three colors _____ Italy's national flag–red, white, and green.

22 After the queen's visit, pizza _____ _____ _____ _____ a truly _____ _____.

23 Pizza _____ _____ _____ _____ Italy in the late 19th century, when many Italians _____ _____ the United States.

24 Italians _____ _____ _____ _____, and Americans loved the flat bread _____ _____ meat and vegetables because they could eat bread, meat, and vegetables _____ _____ _____.

25 The first pizza restaurant in the United States _____ _____ _____ 1905.

26 Pizza is now enjoyed _____ _____.

27 _____ _____, toppings _____ widely _____ _____ _____.

28 Koreans love *bulgogi* on their pizza, _____ Russians like to have fish and _____ _____ on their pizza.

29 However, all types of pizza _____ _____ _____.

30 Each _____ _____ flat bread, and each is _____ _____ _____ _____.

16 나폴리의 요리사들이 납작한 빵에 토마토와 다른 토핑을 얹기 시작해 길거리에서 피자 조각을 팔았다.

17 이 길거리 음식은 무척 저렴하고 맛이 좋아서, 노동자들은 이것을 아침, 점심, 저녁으로 먹었다.

18 그들은 피자 조각을 사서 길을 걸어가며 먹을 수 있었다.

19 1830년에는 세계 최초의 피자 가게가 나폴리에서 문을 열었다.

20 1889년에 이탈리아의 마르게리타 왕비가 나폴리를 방문하여 피자를 맛보았다.

21 그녀가 가장 좋아했던 피자는 이탈리아 국기의 세 가지 색깔인 빨강, 하양, 초록을 나타낸 토마토, 치즈, 녹색 잎 채소 토핑으로 된 것이었다.

22 왕비의 방문 이후로 피자는 진정한 이탈리아의 국가 음식이 되었다.

23 19세기 후반에는 피자가 이탈리아 밖으로 알려지게 되었는데, 이 시기에 많은 이탈리아 사람들이 미국으로 이주를 하였다.

24 이탈리아인들은 피자도 함께 가져갔고, 빵, 고기, 채소를 한꺼번에 먹을 수 있어서 미국인들은 고기와 채소를 얹은 이 납작한 빵을 좋아했다.

25 미국 최초의 피자 가게가 1905년에 문을 열었다.

26 오늘날 피자는 거의 어디에서나 즐길 수 있다.

27 물론, 토핑은 지역에 따라 매우 다양하다.

28 한국인은 불고기를 피자에 얹어 먹기를 좋아하고, 러시아 사람들은 생선과 양파 토핑을 좋아한다.

29 그러나 모든 종류의 피자가 두 가지 사실만큼은 똑같다.

30 모든 피자는 납작한 빵에서 시작하고, 각각은 역사의 한 조각이다.

※ 다음 문장을 우리말로 쓰시오.

1 A Slice of History

➡ _____

2 What do you like on your pizza?

➡ _____

3 Though you may disagree on the best toppings, you will agree that it is now a global food.

➡ _____

_____

4 It is sold in fast-food restaurants or on the street in most parts of the world.

➡ _____

5 How has pizza become such a favorite food around the world?

➡ _____

6 Since the Stone Age, people have been eating pizza in one form or another.

➡ _____

7 Stone Age people baked flat bread on hot rocks.

➡ _____

8 Records show that the Greeks and the Romans started to put meat and vegetables on flat bread.

➡ _____

9 It is believed that the word "pizza" was first used in Italy to name the food over 1,000 years ago.

➡ _____

10 However, pizza with tomato toppings was not born until the 16th century.

➡ _____

11 There were no tomatoes in Italy before Christopher Columbus and other Europeans brought them from the New World.

➡ _____

12 When they were first introduced to Europe, people thought that tomatoes would make them sick.

➡ _____

13 In time, people learned that tomatoes were delicious and healthy.

➡ _____

14 In the 18th century, Naples was a large city where there were many jobs.

➡ _____

15 Workers from near and far came to the city, and what they needed in their busy lives was food they could eat quickly at any time.

➡ _____

16 Cooks in Naples began to put tomato and other toppings on flat bread and sold slices of pizza on the street.

➡ _____

17 The street food was so cheap and delicious that workers ate it for breakfast, lunch, and dinner.

➡ _____

18 They could buy slices of pizza and eat them as they walked on the street.

➡ _____

19 In 1830, the world's first pizza shop opened in Naples.

➡ _____

20 In 1889, Queen Margherita of Italy visited Naples and tried pizza.

➡ _____

21 The type of pizza that she loved most had tomato, cheese, and green leaf toppings that showed the three colors on Italy's national flag—red, white, and green.

➡ _____

_____

22 After the queen's visit, pizza went on to become a truly national dish.

➡ _____

23 Pizza became known outside of Italy in the late 19th century, when many Italians moved to the United States.

➡ _____

24 Italians brought pizza with them, and Americans loved the flat bread topped with meat and vegetables because they could eat bread, meat, and vegetables at the same time.

➡ _____

25 The first pizza restaurant in the United States opened its doors in 1905.

➡ _____

26 Pizza is now enjoyed almost everywhere.

➡ _____

27 Of course, toppings differ widely from place to place.

➡ _____

28 Koreans love *bulgogi* on their pizza, while Russians like to have fish and onion toppings on their pizza.

➡ _____

29 However, all types of pizza share two things.

➡ _____

30 Each begins with flat bread, and each is a slice of history.

➡ _____

※ 다음 괄호 안의 단어들을 우리말에 맞도록 바르게 배열하시오.

1 (Slice / A / History / of)
➡ _____

2 (do / what / like / you / on / pizza? / your)
➡ _____

3 (you / though / disagree / may / the / on / best / toppings, / will / you / that / agree / is / it / a / now / food. / global)
➡ _____
_____

4 (is / it / in / sold / fast-food / or / restaurants / on / street / the / most / in / of / parts / world. / the)
➡ _____
_____

5 (has / how / become / pizza / a / such / food / favorite / around / world? / the)
➡ _____
_____

6 (the / since / Age, / Stone / have / people / eating / been / in / pizza / form / one / another. / or)
➡ _____
_____

7 (Age / Stone / baked / people / bread / flat / on / rocks. / hot)
➡ _____

8 (show / records / the / that / and / Greeks / the / started / Romans / put / to / meat / and / vegetables / flat / on / bread.)
➡ _____
_____

9 (is / it / believed / the / that / word / was / "pizza" / first / in / used / Italy / name / to / food / the / 1,000 / over / ago. / years)
➡ _____
_____

10 (pizza / however, / tomato / with / was / toppings / born / not / until / 16th / the / century.)
➡ _____
_____

11 (were / there / tomatoes / no / Italy / in / before / Colombus / Christopher / and / Europeans / other / brought / from / them / New / the / World.)
➡ _____
_____

1 한 조각의 역사

2 여러분은 어떤 피자 토핑을 좋아하는가?

3 비록 제일 좋아하는 피자 토핑에 대해 의견이 다를 수 있지만, 피자가 오늘날 세계적인 음식이라는 데에는 모두 동의할 것이다.

4 피자는 세계 대부분 지역의 패스트푸드 식당이나 길거리에서 팔리고 있다.

5 어떻게 해서 피자가 세계적으로 이토록 사랑받는 음식이 되었을까?

6 석기시대부터 사람들은 여러 가지 형태로 피자를 먹어 왔다.

7 석기시대 사람들은 납작한 빵을 뜨거운 돌에 구워 먹었다.

8 기록에 의하면 그리스와 로마 사람들이 납작한 빵에 고기와 채소를 얹기 시작했다.

9 '피자'라는 단어는 이러한 음식을 지칭하기 위해 약 천 년 전에 이탈리아에서 처음 사용되었다고 알려져 있다.

10 하지만 토마토 토핑을 얹은 피자는 16세기까지는 존재하지 않았다.

11 크리스토퍼 콜럼버스와 다른 유럽인들이 신세계에서 가져오기 전까지 이탈리아에는 토마토가 없었다.

12 (they / when / first / were / to / introduced / Europe, / thought / people / tomatoes / that / make / would / sick. / them)

➡ _____

_____

13 (time, / in / learned / people / tomatoes / that / delicious / were / healthy. / and)

➡ _____

14 (the / in / century, / 18th / was / Naples / a / city / large / there / where / were / jobs. / many)

➡ _____

15 (from / workers / near / and / came / far / the / to / city, / what / and / needed / they / in / busy / their / lives / food / was / could / they / quickly / eat / any / time. / at)

➡ _____

_____

16 (in / cooks / began / Naples / put / to / tomato / and / toppings / other / flat / on / bread / and / slices / sold / pizza / of / the / on / street.)

➡ _____

_____

17 (street / the / was / food / cheap / so / and / that / delicious / workers / it / ate / breakfast, / for / and / lunch, / dinner.)

➡ _____

_____

18 (could / they / slices / buy / pizza / of / and / them / eat / as / walked / they / the / on / street.)

➡ _____

19 (1830, / in / world's / the / pizza / first / opened / shop / Naples. / in)

➡ _____

20 (1889, / in / Margherita / Queen / Italy / of / Naples / visited / and / pizza. / tried)

➡ _____

21 (type / the / pizza / of / she / that / most / loved / tomato, / had / and / cheese, / green / toppings / leaf / showed / that / three / the / on / colors / national / Italy's / flag / – / white, / red, / green. / and)

➡ _____

_____

_____

12 유럽에 처음 소개되었을 때 사람들은 토마토가 사람들을 아프게 할 거라고 여겼다.

13 시간이 지나며 사람들은 토마토가 맛있고 건강에도 좋다는 것을 알게 되었다.

14 18세기에 나폴리는 다양한 직업이 존재하는 대도시였다.

15 사방에서 노동자들이 이 도시로 모여들었고, 바쁜 생활 중 그들에게 필요했던 것은 언제든지 빨리 먹을 수 있는 음식이었다.

16 나폴리의 요리사들이 납작한 빵에 토마토와 다른 토핑을 얹기 시작해 길거리에서 피자 조각을 팔았다.

17 이 길거리 음식은 무척 저렴하고 맛이 좋아서, 노동자들은 이것을 아침, 점심, 저녁으로 먹었다.

18 그들은 피자 조각을 사서 길을 걸어가며 먹을 수 있었다.

19 1830년에는 세계 최초의 피자 가게가 나폴리에서 문을 열었다.

20 1889년에 이탈리아의 마르게리타 왕비가 나폴리를 방문하여 피자를 맛보았다.

21 그녀가 가장 좋아했던 피자는 이탈리아 국기의 세 가지 색깔인 빨강, 하양, 초록을 나타낸 토마토, 치즈, 녹색 잎 채소 토핑으로 된 것이었다.

22 (the / after / visit, / queen's / went / pizza / to / on / become / truly / a / dish. / national)

➡ _____

23 (became / pizza / outside / known / Italy / of / the / in / late / century, / 19th / many / when / moved / Italians / to / United / the / States.)

➡ _____

24 (brought / Italians / with / pizza / them, / Americans / and / loved / flat / the / bread / with / topped / meat / and / because / vegetables / could / they / eat / bread, / and / meat, / vegetables / the / at / time. / same)

➡ _____
_____

25 (fist / the / restaurant / pizza / the / in / States / United / its / opened / doors / 1905. / in)

➡ _____

26 (is / pizza / enjoyed / now / everywhere. / almost)

➡ _____

27 (couese, / of / differ / toppings / from / widely / place / place. / to)

➡ _____

28 (love / Koreans / *bulgogi* / their / on /. pizza, / Russians / while / to / like / fish / have / onion / and / on / toppings / pizza. / their)

➡ _____
_____

29 (all / however, / of / types / share / pizza / things. / two)

➡ _____

30 (begins / each / flat / with / bread, / each / and / a / is / slice / history. / of)

➡ _____

22 왕비의 방문 이후로 피자는 진정한 이탈리아의 국가 음식이 되었다.

23 19세기 후반에는 피자가 이탈리아 밖으로 알려지게 되었는데, 이 시기에 많은 이탈리아 사람들이 미국으로 이주를 하였다.

24 이탈리아인들은 피자도 함께 가져갔고, 빵, 고기, 채소를 한꺼번에 먹을 수 있어서 미국인들은 고기와 채소를 얹은 이 납작한 빵을 좋아했다.

25 미국 최초의 피자 가게가 1905년에 문을 열었다.

26 오늘날 피자는 거의 어디에서나 즐길 수 있다.

27 물론, 토핑은 지역에 따라 매우 다양하다.

28 한국인은 불고기를 피자에 얹어 먹기를 좋아하고, 러시아 사람들은 생선과 양파 토핑을 좋아한다.

29 그러나 모든 종류의 피자가 두 가지 사실만큼은 똑같다.

30 모든 피자는 납작한 빵에서 시작하고, 각각은 역사의 한 조각이다.

※ 다음 우리말을 영어로 쓰시오.

1 한 조각의 역사

➡ _____

2 여러분은 어떤 피자 토핑을 좋아하는가?

➡ _____

3 비록 제일 좋아하는 피자 토핑에 대해 의견이 다를 수 있지만, 피자가 오늘날 세계적인 음식이라는 데에는 모두 동의할 것이다.

➡ _____

4 피자는 세계 대부분 지역의 패스트푸드 식당이나 길거리에서 팔리고 있다.

➡ _____

5 어떻게 해서 피자가 세계적으로 이토록 사랑받는 음식이 되었을까?

➡ _____

6 석기시대부터 사람들은 여러 가지 형태로 피자를 먹어 왔다.

➡ _____

7 석기시대 사람들은 납작한 빵을 뜨거운 돌에 구워 먹었다.

➡ _____

8 기록에 의하면 그리스와 로마 사람들이 납작한 빵에 고기와 채소를 얹기 시작했다.

➡ _____

9 '피자'라는 단어는 이러한 음식을 지칭하기 위해 약 천 년 전에 이탈리아에서 처음 사용되었다고 알려져 있다.

➡ _____

10 하지만 토마토 토핑을 얹은 피자는 16세기까지는 존재하지 않았다.

➡ _____

11 크리스토퍼 콜럼버스와 다른 유럽인들이 신세계에서 가져오기 전까지 이탈리아에는 토마토가 없었다.

➡ _____

12 유럽에 처음 소개되었을 때 사람들은 토마토가 사람들을 아프게 할 거라고 여겼다.

➡ _____

13 시간이 지나며 사람들은 토마토가 맛있고 건강에도 좋다는 것을 알게 되었다.

➡ _____

14 18세기에 나폴리는 다양한 직업이 존재하는 대도시였다.

➡ _____

15 사방에서 노동자들이 이 도시로 모여들었고, 바쁜 생활 중 그들에게 필요했던 것은 언제든지 빨리 먹을 수 있는 음식이었다.

➡ _____

_____

16 나폴리의 요리사들이 납작한 빵에 토마토와 다른 토핑을 얹기 시작해 길거리에서 피자 조각을 팔았다.

➡ _____

_____

17 이 길거리 음식은 무척 저렴하고 맛이 좋아서, 노동자들은 이것을 아침, 점심, 저녁으로 먹었다.

➡ _____

18 그들은 피자 조각을 사서 길을 걸어가며 먹을 수 있었다.

➡ _____

19 1830년에는 세계 최초의 피자 가게가 나폴리에서 문을 열었다.

➡ _____

20 1889년에 이탈리아의 마르게리타 왕비가 나폴리를 방문하여 피자를 맛보았다.

➡ _____

21 그녀가 가장 좋아했던 피자는 이탈리아 국기의 세 가지 색깔인 빨강, 하양, 초록을 나타낸 토마토, 치즈, 녹색 잎 채소 토핑으로 된 것이었다.

➡ _____

_____

22 왕비의 방문 이후로 피자는 진정한 이탈리아의 국가 음식이 되었다.

➡ _____

23 19세기 후반에는 피자가 이탈리아 밖으로 알려지게 되었는데, 이 시기에 많은 이탈리아 사람들이 미국으로 이주를 하였다.

➡ _____

_____

24 이탈리아인들은 피자도 함께 가져갔고, 빵, 고기, 채소를 한꺼번에 먹을 수 있어서 미국인들은 고기와 채소를 얹은 이 납작한 빵을 좋아했다.

➡ _____

_____

25 미국 최초의 피자 가게가 1905년에 문을 열었다.

➡ _____

26 오늘날 피자는 거의 어디에서나 즐길 수 있다.

➡ _____

27 물론, 토핑은 지역에 따라 매우 다양하다.

➡ _____

28 한국인은 불고기를 피자에 얹어 먹기를 좋아하고, 러시아 사람들은 생선과 양파 토핑을 좋아한다.

➡ _____

29 그러나 모든 종류의 피자가 두 가지 사실만큼은 똑같다.

➡ _____

30 모든 피자는 납작한 빵에서 시작하고, 각각은 역사의 한 조각이다.

➡ _____

※ 다음 영어를 우리말로 쓰시오.

01 arrival	_____	22 whole	_____
02 poet	_____	23 harsh	_____
03 literature	_____	24 remain	_____
04 copy	_____	25 sew	_____
05 particular	_____	26 poem	_____
06 charge	_____	27 treatment	_____
07 literary	_____	28 wallet	_____
08 express	_____	29 present	_____
09 loneliness	_____	30 publication	_____
10 childhood	_____	31 independence	_____
11 freedom	_____	32 longing	_____
12 publish	_____	33 author	_____
13 rare	_____	34 editor	_____
14 further	_____	35 give up	_____
15 library	_____	36 in a hurry	_____
16 government	_____	37 check out	_____
17 achieve	_____	38 be well known for	_____
18 graduation	_____	39 hang out with	_____
19 movement	_____	40 take part in	_____
20 poetry	_____	41 have ~ in mind	_____
21 celebrate	_____	42 look good on	_____
		43 give it a try	_____

※ 다음 우리말을 영어로 쓰시오.

01 가혹한, 혹독한 _____

02 전체의, 모든 _____

03 체포하다 _____

04 외로움 _____

05 도착 _____

06 독립 _____

07 기소, 혐의 _____

08 (한 편의) 시 _____

09 문학의, 문학적인 _____

10 졸업 _____

11 편집자 _____

12 졸업 앨범 _____

13 선사하다, 주다 _____

14 이루다, 얻다 _____

15 빌리다 _____

16 기념하다, 축하하다 _____

17 동경, 갈망 _____

18 운동 _____

19 자유 _____

20 희귀한 _____

21 남아 있다, 계속 ~하다 _____

22 더, 더 멀리 _____

23 정부, 정권 _____

24 저자 _____

25 (문학 장르) 시 _____

26 출판하다 _____

27 바느질하다 _____

28 문학 _____

29 출판, 발행 _____

30 대우, 처리 _____

31 어린 시절 _____

32 표현하다 _____

33 시인 _____

34 추천하다 _____

35 포기하다 _____

36 세우다, 내걸다 _____

37 ~에 참가하다 _____

38 서둘러 _____

39 ~에 잘 어울리다 _____

40 ~을 염두에 두다 _____

41 시도하다 _____

42 ~을 기대하다 _____

43 ~와 시간을 보내다 _____

※ 다음 영영풀이에 알맞은 단어를 <보기>에서 골라 쓴 후, 우리말 뜻을 쓰시오.

1 _____ : not divided; all: _____

2 _____ : not common; unusual: _____

3 _____ : a person who writes poems: _____

4 _____ : the receiving of an academic degree: _____

5 _____ : written works which are of artistic value: _____

6 _____ : a strong feeling of wanting something: _____

7 _____ : to suggest as being good or worthy: _____

8 _____ : the town where someone was born and grew up: _____

9 _____ : the state of not being governed by another country: _____

10 _____ : to make or mend with needle and thread: _____

11 _____ : unpleasant and causing pain to the body or senses: _____

12 _____ : a feeling of being unhappy because you are away from other people:

_____

13 _____ : a piece of writing, arranged in patterns of lines and of sounds:

_____

14 _____ : the action of making something known to the public: _____

15 _____ : a person who prepares a book to be published, for example by checking

and correcting the text, making improvements, etc.: _____

16 _____ : to do something special or enjoyable for an important event, occasion,

holiday, etc.: _____

보기			
sew	independence	literature	poet
editor	celebrate	rare	longing
loneliness	recommend	harsh	hometown
poem	publication	whole	graduation

※ 다음 우리말과 일치하도록 빈칸에 알맞은 말을 쓰시오.

Listen - Listen & Answer Dialog 1

Minjun: Hello, Ms. Seo.

Ms. Seo: Hi, Minjun. _____ time _____ see. What _____ you here?

Minjun: I _____ _____ write _____ _____ _____. Can you _____ a good novel _____ _____?

Ms. Seo: How _____ a mystery? There's a new Ken Kuller book, *22nd Street.*

Minjun: Oh, I've _____ _____ him. Can you _____ _____ the book?

Ms. Seo: It's in the "_____ _____" area. It's really _____ _____ teens in Great Britain.

Minjun: Thank you for your help. Can I _____ it _____?

Ms. Seo: Sure. You can _____ new books _____ _____ _____.

Minjun: Okay.

민준: 안녕하세요, 서 선생님.
서 선생님: 안녕, 민준아. 오랜만이구나. 무슨 일로 여기에 온 거니?
민준: 독후감을 써야 해서요. 읽기에 좋은 소설을 추천해 주시겠어요?
서 선생님: 추리 소설은 어떠니? Ken Kuller의 신간, '22번가'가 있단다.
민준: 아, 그에 관해 들어 본 적이 있어요. 책을 보여 주실 수 있나요?
서 선생님: '신착 도서' 서가에 있단다. 그 책은 영국의 십 대들 사이에서 많은 인기를 끌고 있어.
민준: 도와주셔서 감사합니다. 그 책을 대출할 수 있을까요?
서 선생님: 물론이지. 신간은 7일간 빌릴 수 있어.
민준: 알겠습니다.

Listen - Listen & Answer Dialog 2

Sora: Hey, Minjun. What _____ you _____?

Minjun: I'm reading a _____ for a _____ _____.

Sora: Let _____ _____. Oh, is this a new book by Ken Kuller?

Minjun: Yeah, I _____ it this morning. Do you know Ken Kuller?

Sora: Of _____. I'm a _____ _____ of his. I've read _____ of his _____ _____.

Minjun: I think he's a great _____. I can't _____ _____ this book.

Sora: You know _____? His novel *Four Eyes* _____ _____ _____ _____ a movie.

Minjun: Yeah. I saw the movie poster. It _____ _____.

Sora: It'll _____ _____ next Thursday. I'm _____ _____ _____ _____ it!

Minjun: Maybe we can see the movie _____.

소라: 안녕, 민준아. 뭐 하고 있니?
민준: 나는 독후감을 쓰려고 소설을 읽고 있어.
소라: 어디 봐. 아, 이거 Ken Kuller의 신간이지?
민준: 맞아, 오늘 아침에 이걸 대출했어. 너는 Ken Kuller를 알고 있니?
소라: 물론이지. 난 그의 열렬한 팬이야. 그의 추리 소설은 모두 읽었어.
민준: 내 생각에 그는 위대한 작가야. 이 책을 손에서 놓을 수가 없어.
소라: 그거 알아? 그의 소설 '네 개의 눈'이 영화로 만들어졌어.
민준: 맞아. 나도 영화 포스터를 봤어. 재미있어 보이더라.
소라: 영화는 다음 주 목요일에 개봉한대. 그걸 보는 게 기대돼!
민준: 아마 우리 영화를 같이 볼 수 있겠다.

Listen more - Listen and complete

Mike: Good morning, Jiho.

Jiho: Good morning.

Mike: _____ _____ _____, please. _____ _____ _____ _____ your hair done?

Jiho: Well, I'm _____ my pictures for the _____. So I want to look _____.

Mike: When do you _____ the pictures?

Jiho: This Friday at Dream & Joy Park.

Mike: Sounds good. Do you have a _____ style in _____?

Jiho: No. Can you _____ one for me?

Mike: _____ _____ this. How about this style? It'll _____ _____ _____ you.

Jiho: Wow, I like it. I _____ _____ _____ _____ how I'll look in the pictures.

Mike: I'm _____ you'll _____ _____.

Mike: 안녕, 지호야.

지호: 안녕하세요.

Mike: 자리에 앉으렴. 머리를 어떻게 해 줄까?

지호: 음, 저는 졸업 앨범에 들어갈 사진을 찍을 거예요. 그래서 멋져 보이고 싶어요.

Mike: 언제 사진을 찍니?

지호: 이번 금요일에 Dream & Joy Park에서요.

Mike: 멋지구나. 마음에 둔 특별한 스타일이 있니?

지호: 아니요. 저를 위해 하나 추천해 주시겠어요?

Mike: 이걸 보렴. 이 스타일은 어떠니? 너에게 잘 어울릴 거야.

지호: 와, 마음에 들어요. 제가 사진에서 어떻게 보일지 빨리 보고 싶네요.

Mike: 틀림없이 멋져 보일 거야.

My Speaking Portfolio

Jane: Nice _____ _____ you, Mr. Henry. Is O. Henry your _____ _____?

Mr. Henry: No. My real name is William Sydney Porter.

Jane: Can you tell me _____ _____ _____?

Mr. Henry: I'm _____ the U.S.

Jane: What do you _____ _____?

Mr. Henry: I'm a _____ _____ _____. I _____ _____ about 300 short stories.

Jane: Wow! You're great! What is _____ about your short stories?

Mr. Henry: They're _____ _____ _____ their _____ _____.

Jane: Can you _____ a popular story _____ a _____ _____?

Mr. Henry: Sure. I _____ *The Last Leaf.*

Jane: What is it _____?

Mr. Henry: It's about a sick girl and an old artist _____ _____ _____ _____.

Jane: Oh, I want to read it. I _____ _____.

Jane: 만나서 반갑습니다, Henry 씨. O. Henry가 당신의 본명인가요?

Mr. Henry: 아니요. 제 본명은 William Sydney Porter입니다.

Jane: 어디 출신이신지 말씀해 주시겠어요?

Mr. Henry: 저는 미국 출신입니다.

Jane: 주로 무엇을 쓰시나요?

Mr. Henry: 저는 단편 소설 작가입니다. 300여 편의 단편 소설을 썼죠.

Jane: 와! 대단하시네요! 당신의 단편 소설은 무엇이 특별한가요?

Mr. Henry: 그것들은 뜻밖의 결말로 유명합니다.

Jane: 뜻밖의 결말이 있는 유명한 이야기를 하나 추천해 주실 수 있나요?

Mr. Henry: 물론이죠. 저는 '마지막 잎새'를 추천합니다.

Jane: 그것은 무엇에 관한 이야기인가요?

Mr. Henry: 아픈 소녀와 그녀의 목숨을 구하는 늙은 화가의 이야기예요.

Jane: 아, 그것을 읽고 싶네요. 무척 기대됩니다.

※ 다음 우리말에 맞도록 대화를 영어로 쓰시오.

Listen - Listen & Answer Dialog 1

Minjun: _____

Ms. Seo: _____

Minjun: _____

Ms. Seo: _____

Minjun: _____

Ms. Seo: _____

_____

Minjun: _____

Ms. Seo: _____

Minjun: _____

민준: 안녕하세요, 서 선생님.

서 선생님: 안녕, 민준아. 오랜만이구나. 무슨 일로 여기에 온 거니?

민준: 독후감을 써야 해서요. 읽기에 좋은 소설을 추천해 주시겠어요?

서 선생님: 추리 소설은 어떠니? Ken Kuller의 신간, '22번가'가 있단다.

민준: 아, 그에 관해 들어 본 적이 있어요. 책을 보여 주실 수 있나요?

서 선생님: '신착 도서' 서가에 있단다. 그 책은 영국의 십 대들 사이에서 많은 인기를 끌고 있어.

민준: 도와주셔서 감사합니다. 그 책을 대출할 수 있을까요?

서 선생님: 물론이지. 신간은 7일간 빌릴 수 있어.

민준: 알겠습니다.

Listen - Listen & Answer Dialog 2

Sora: _____

Minjun: _____

Sora: _____

Minjun: _____

Sora: _____

Minjun: _____

Sora: _____

Minjun: _____

Sora: _____

Minjun: _____

소라: 안녕, 민준아. 뭐 하고 있니?

민준: 나는 독후감을 쓰려고 소설을 읽고 있어.

소라: 어디 봐. 아, 이거 Ken Kuller의 신간이지?

민준: 맞아, 오늘 아침에 이걸 대출했어. 너는 Ken Kuller를 알고 있니?

소라: 물론이지. 난 그의 열렬한 팬이야. 그의 추리 소설은 모두 읽었어.

민준: 내 생각에 그는 위대한 작가야. 이 책을 손에서 놓을 수가 없어.

소라: 그거 알아? 그의 소설 '네 개의 눈'이 영화로 만들어졌어.

민준: 맞아. 나도 영화 포스터를 봤어. 재미있어 보이더라.

소라: 영화는 다음 주 목요일에 개봉한대. 그걸 보는 게 기대돼!

민준: 아마 우리 영화를 같이 볼 수 있겠다.

Listen more - Listen and complete

Mike: _____

Jiho: _____

Mike: _____

Jiho: _____

Mike: _____

Jiho: _____

Mike: _____

Jiho: _____

Mike: _____

Jiho: _____

Mike: _____

Mike: 안녕, 지호야.

지호: 안녕하세요.

Mike: 자리에 앉으렴. 머리를 어떻게 해 줄까?

지호: 음, 저는 졸업 앨범에 들어갈 사진을 찍을 거예요. 그래서 멋져 보이고 싶어요.

Mike: 언제 사진을 찍니?

지호: 이번 금요일에 Dream & Joy Park에서요.

Mike: 멋지구나. 마음에 둔 특별한 스타일이 있니?

지호: 아니요. 저를 위해 하나 추천해 주시겠어요?

Mike: 이걸 보렴. 이 스타일은 어떠니? 너에게 잘 어울릴 거야.

지호: 와, 마음에 들어요. 제가 사진에서 어떻게 보일지 빨리 보고 싶네요.

Mike: 틀림없이 멋져 보일 거야.

My Speaking Portfolio

Jane: _____

Mr. Henry: _____

Jane: _____

Mr. Henry: _____

Jane: _____

Mr. Henry: _____

Jane: _____

Mr. Henry: _____

Jane: _____

Mr. Henry: _____

Jane: _____

Mr. Henry: _____

Jane: _____

Jane: 만나서 반갑습니다, Henry 씨. O. Henry가 당신의 본명인가요?

Mr. Henry: 아니요. 제 본명은 William Sydney Porter입니다.

Jane: 어디 출신이신지 말씀해 주시겠어요?

Mr. Henry: 저는 미국 출신입니다.

Jane: 주로 무엇을 쓰시나요?

Mr. Henry: 저는 단편 소설 작가입니다. 300여 편의 단편 소설을 썼죠.

Jane: 와! 대단하시네요! 당신의 단편 소설은 무엇이 특별한가요?

Mr. Henry: 그것들은 뜻밖의 결말로 유명합니다.

Jane: 뜻밖의 결말이 있는 유명한 이야기를 하나 추천해 주실 수 있나요?

Mr. Henry: 물론이죠. 저는 '마지막 잎새'를 추천합니다.

Jane: 그것은 무엇에 관한 이야기인가요?

Mr. Henry: 아픈 소녀와 그녀의 목숨을 구하는 늙은 화가의 이야기예요.

Jane: 아, 그것을 읽고 싶네요. 무척 기대됩니다.

※ 다음 우리말과 일치하도록 빈칸에 알맞은 것을 골라 쓰시오.

1 A _____ _____ _____ Stars
A. Loved   B. Poet   C. Who

2 In the sky _____ seasons pass _____ _____ _____
A. hurry   B. where   C. a   D. in

3 _____ _____ the _____.
A. fills   B. autumn   C. air

4 And _____ I _____, _____ a _____,
A. without   B. ready   C. worry   D. stand

5 _____ _____ all the _____ there.
A. stars   B. count   C. to

6 _____ for _____ star,
A. one   B. memory

7 _____ for _____ star,
A. another   B. love

8 _____ for _____ star,
A. another   B. loneliness

9 _____ for _____ star,
A.another   B. longing

10 _____ _____ another _____,
A. poetry   B. star   C. for

11 And, oh, mother, mother _____ _____ _____.
A. another   B. for   C. star

12 _____ you _____ these _____ before?
A. lines   B. read   C. have

13 They are _____ _____ the _____ "Counting Stars at Night" _____ Yoon Dong-ju.
A. by   B. of   C. poem   D. part

14 The poem was _____ a long time ago but _____ _____ one of Korea's favorite _____.
A. remains   B. poems   C. written   D. still

15 Dong-ju _____ _____ _____ 1917 _____ Yanbin, China.
A. near   B. born   C. in   D. was

16 _____ a young boy, he loved sports, and he was a soccer player _____ his _____.
A. for   B. as   C. school

17 He also loved _____ _____ much _____ he _____ the numbers on all his friends' soccer uniforms.
A. that   B. sewed   C. so   D. sewing

1 별을 사랑한 시인

2 계절이 지나가는 하늘에는

3 가을로 가득 차 있습니다.

4 나는 아무 걱정도 없이

5 가을 속의 별들을 다 헤일 듯합니다.

6 별 하나에 추억과

7 별 하나에 사랑과

8 별 하나에 쓸쓸함과

9 별 하나에 동경과

10 별 하나에 시와

11 별 하나에 어머니, 어머니,

12 당신은 이 시 구절을 읽어 본 적이 있는가?

13 이것은 윤동주의 시 '별 헤는 밤'의 일부이다.

14 시는 오래 전에 쓰였지만 여전히 한국의 가장 좋아하는 시 중의 하나로 남아 있다.

15 동주는 중국 연변 근처에서 1917년에 태어났다.

16 어린 소년이었을 때 그는 운동을 좋아했고, 학교의 축구 선수였다.

17 그는 또한 바느질하는 것을 무척 좋아해서 친구들의 축구 유니폼에 번호를 바느질해 주기도 했다.

18 However, _____ _____ literature _____ he loved _____.

A. most   B. that   C. was   D. it

19 In elementary school he _____ a _____ of _____.

A. poems   B. lot   C. wrote

20 He even made a _____ _____ _____ his _____, Song Mong-gyu.

A. cousin   B. literary   C. with   D. magazine

21 In middle school he once _____ a _____ book by a famous poet of the time, Baek Seok, and _____ the _____ book by hand.

A. copied   B. borrowed   C. whole   D. poetry

22 He really wanted to _____ his _____ _____ of the _____ book.

A. rare   B. own   C. have   D. copy

23 His parents wanted him to be a _____, but Dong-ju _____ to study _____ at a _____ in Seoul.

A. literature   B. college   C. chose   D. doctor

24 During his college years, he often _____ _____ with other young poets and wrote poetry where he _____ feelings about his hometown and _____ country.

A. expressed   B. hung   C. lost   D. out

25 To _____ his _____, he wished to _____ 19 of his poems _____ the title, *Heaven, Wind, Stars, and Poetry*.

A. publish   B. celebrate   C. under   D. graduation

26 He made _____ _____ of the book _____ _____.

A. by   B. copies   C. three   D. hand

27 One was _____ to his close friend, Jeong Byeong-uk, _____ was _____ to his favorite professor, and the last one was _____ for himself.

A. another   B. kept   C. given   D. presented

28 However, his professor _____ _____ his plan _____ he thought the Japanese government would not allow the _____.

A. against   B. publication   C. advised   D. because

18 그러나 그가 가장 사랑한 것은 문학이었다.

19 초등학교에 다닐 때 그는 많은 시를 썼다.

20 심지어 사촌 송몽규와 문학잡지를 만들기도 했다.

21 그가 중학교에 다니던 때 한번은 당대의 유명한 시인 백석의 시집을 빌려 와서 책 전체를 필사하기도 했다.

22 그는 정말로 그 희귀한 책을 한 부 갖고 싶었던 것이다.

23 그의 부모는 그가 의사가 되기를 바랐지만 동주는 서울에 있는 대학에서 문학 공부를 하기로 했다.

24 대학 시절에 그는 종종 다른 젊은 시인들과 어울려 다녔고, 고향과 잃어버린 조국에 대한 심정을 표현하는 시를 썼다.

25 졸업을 기념하여 그는 '하늘과 바람과 별과 시'라는 제목으로 자신의 시 19편을 출판하고 싶어 했다.

26 그는 책 세 부를 손으로 만들었다.

27 한 부는 가까운 친구인 정병욱에게 주었고, 또 하나는 그가 가장 좋아하는 교수에게 선물했으며, 마지막 하나는 자신이 보관했다.

28 그러나 그의 교수는 일본 정부가 출판을 허가하지 않으리라 여겨, 그의 계획에 반대하는 충고를 했다.

29 Dong-ju _____ his _____ and _____ _____ the idea.

    A. up   B. followed   C. gave   D. advice

30 Dong-ju decided to _____ _____ in the country where his father _____ _____ before.

    A. further   B. studied   C. study   D. had

31 So, _____ 1942, Dong-ju and his cousin _____ _____ _____ in Japan.

    A. study   B. in   C. to   D. began

32 On July 10 the _____ year, his cousin was _____ by the Japanese police for talking _____ in an _____ movement.

    A. part   B. arrested   C. following   D. independence

33 Four days _____, Dong-ju was also _____ on the _____.

    A. same   B. later   C. charges   D. arrested

34 In 1945, Dong-ju and his cousin died in _____ _____ _____ _____ by the police.

    A. prison   B. treatment   C. harsh   D. after

35 _____ was just a _____ months later _____ Korea _____ independence from Japan.

    A. achieved   B. it   C. that   D. few

36 In 1948, Jeong Byeong-uk _____ Dong-ju's poems to the _____ brother, and they were _____ _____.

    A. finally   B. brought   C. poet's   D. published

37 The book _____ _____ the title the poet _____ _____ of many years before.

    A. thought   B. given   C. had   D. was

38 His poems are loved by people of all _____, and thus they still shine _____ in our _____ _____ the stars in the autumn night sky.

    A. hearts   B. ages   C. brightly   D. like

---

29 동주는 그의 충고를 따랐고 그 생각을 포기했다.

30 동주는 그의 아버지가 예전에 공부했던 나라에서 학업을 이어 가기로 했다.

31 그리하여 1942년에 동주와 그의 사촌은 일본에서 공부를 시작했다.

32 다음 해 7월 10일에 그의 사촌은 독립운동에 가담했다는 이유로 일본 경찰에게 체포되었다.

33 나흘 뒤 동주 역시 같은 혐의로 체포되었다.

34 1945년에 동주와 그의 사촌은 경찰의 가혹 행위를 당한 후 감옥에서 사망했다.

35 한국이 일본으로부터 독립을 이룬 것은 그로부터 불과 몇 달 후의 일이었다.

36 1948년에 정병욱이 동주의 시를 시인의 동생에게 가져다주었고, 마침내 그것들은 출판되었다.

37 그 책에는 시인이 수년 전에 생각해 두었던 제목이 붙었다.

38 그의 시는 모든 세대의 사랑을 받고 있고, 따라서 그것들은 가을밤 하늘의 별처럼 우리 가슴 속에 여전히 밝게 빛나고 있다.

※ 다음 우리말과 일치하도록 빈칸에 알맞은 것을 골라 쓰시오.

1 A _____ _____ Loved Stars

2 In the sky _____ seasons pass _____ _____ _____

3 Autumn _____ the air.

4 And ready I stand, _____ _____ _____,

5 To _____ all the stars there.

6 _____ for one star,

7 Love for _____ star,

8 _____ for another star,

9 _____ for another star,

10 _____ _____ another star,

11 And, oh, mother, mother _____ _____ _____.

12 _____ you _____ _____ _____ before?

13 They are _____ _____ the poem "Counting Stars at Night" _____ Yoon Dong-ju.

14 The poem _____ _____ a long time ago but _____ _____ one of Korea's favorite _____.

15 Dong-ju _____ _____ _____ 1917 near Yanbin, China.

16 _____ a young boy, he loved sports, and he was a soccer player _____ _____ _____.

17 He also loved _____ _____ much _____ he _____ the numbers on all his friends' soccer uniforms.

1 별을 사랑한 시인

2 계절이 지나가는 하늘에는

3 가을로 가득 차 있습니다.

4 나는 아무 걱정도 없이

5 가을 속의 별들을 다 헤일 듯합니다.

6 별 하나에 추억과

7 별 하나에 사랑과

8 별 하나에 쓸쓸함과

9 별 하나에 동경과

10 별 하나에 시와

11 별 하나에 어머니, 어머니,

12 당신은 이 시 구절을 읽어 본 적이 있는가?

13 이것은 윤동주의 시 '별 헤는 밤'의 일부이다.

14 시는 오래 전에 쓰였지만 여전히 한국의 가장 좋아하는 시 중의 하나로 남아 있다.

15 동주는 중국 연변 근처에서 1917년에 태어났다.

16 어린 소년이었을 때 그는 운동을 좋아했고, 학교의 축구 선수였다.

17 그는 또한 바느질하는 것을 무척 좋아해서 친구들의 축구 유니폼에 번호를 바느질해 주기도 했다.

18 However, _____ _____ literature _____ he loved _____ .

19 In elementary school he _____ _____ _____ _____
_____ .

20 He even made _____ _____ _____ _____ _____ his cousin, Song Mong-gyu.

21 In middle school he once _____ a poetry book by a famous poet of the time, Baek Seok, and _____ the whole book _____
_____ .

22 He really wanted _____ _____ _____ _____ _____ of the _____ _____ .

23 His parents wanted him _____ _____ _____ _____ , but Dong-ju _____ _____ _____ _____ at a college in Seoul.

24 _____ his college years, he often _____ _____
_____ _____ _____ and wrote poetry _____ he _____
_____ about his hometown and _____ _____ .

25 _____ _____ _____ _____ _____ , he wished to _____ 19 of his poems _____ _____ _____ , *Heaven, Wind, Stars, and Poetry*.

26 He made _____ _____ of the book _____ _____ .

27 One _____ _____ _____ his close friend, Jeong Byeong-uk, _____ was presented to his favorite professor, and _____ _____ was kept _____ _____ .

28 However, his professor _____ _____ his plan _____ he thought the Japanese government would not _____ the _____ .

18 그러나 그가 가장 사랑한 것은 문학이었다.

19 초등학교에 다닐 때 그는 많은 시를 썼다.

20 심지어 사촌 송몽규와 문학잡지를 만들기도 했다.

21 그가 중학교에 다니던 때 한번은 당대의 유명한 시인 백석의 시집을 빌려 와서 책 전체를 필사하기도 했다.

22 그는 정말로 그 희귀한 책을 한 부 갖고 싶었던 것이다.

23 그의 부모는 그가 의사가 되기를 바랐지만 동주는 서울에 있는 대학에서 문학 공부를 하기로 했다.

24 대학 시절에 그는 종종 다른 젊은 시인들과 어울려 다녔고, 고향과 잃어버린 조국에 대한 심정을 표현하는 시를 썼다.

25 졸업을 기념하여 그는 '하늘과 바람과 별과 시'라는 제목으로 자신의 시 19편을 출판하고 싶어 했다.

26 그는 책 세 부를 손으로 만들었다.

27 한 부는 가까운 친구인 정병욱에게 주었고, 또 하나는 그가 가장 좋아하는 교수에게 선물했으며, 마지막 하나는 자신이 보관했다.

28 그러나 그의 교수는 일본 정부가 출판을 허가하지 않으리라 여겨, 그의 계획에 반대하는 충고를 했다.

29 Dong-ju _____ his advice and _____ _____ the idea.

30 Dong-ju _____ _____ _____ _____ in the country where his father _____ _____ _____.

31 So, in 1942, Dong-ju and his cousin _____ _____ _____ in Japan.

32 On July 10 the _____ _____, his cousin was arrested by the Japanese police _____ _____ _____ _____ an _____ _____.

33 Four days _____, Dong-ju was also _____ _____ _____ _____ _____ _____.

34 In 1945, Dong-ju and his cousin died in prison _____ _____ _____ _____ _____ _____.

35 _____ _____ just a few months later _____ Korea _____ _____ from Japan.

36 In 1948, Jeong Byeong-uk _____ Dong-ju's poems _____ the poet's brother, and _____ _____ _____ _____.

37 The book _____ _____ the title the poet _____ _____ _____ many years _____.

38 His poems _____ _____ _____ people of all ages, and thus they still _____ _____ in our hearts _____ the stars in the autumn night sky.

---

29 동주는 그의 충고를 따랐고 그 생각을 포기했다.

30 동주는 그의 아버지가 예전에 공부했던 나라에서 학업을 이어 가기로 했다.

31 그리하여 1942년에 동주와 그의 사촌은 일본에서 공부를 시작했다.

32 다음 해 7월 10일에 그의 사촌은 독립운동에 가담했다는 이유로 일본 경찰에게 체포되었다.

33 나흘 뒤 동주 역시 같은 혐의로 체포되었다.

34 1945년에 동주와 그의 사촌은 경찰의 가혹 행위를 당한 후 감옥에서 사망했다.

35 한국이 일본으로부터 독립을 이룬 것은 그로부터 불과 몇 달 후의 일이었다.

36 1948년에 정병욱이 동주의 시를 시인의 동생에게 가져다주었고, 마침내 그것들은 출판되었다.

37 그 책에는 시인이 수년 전에 생각해 두었던 제목이 붙었다.

38 그의 시는 모든 세대의 사랑을 받고 있고, 따라서 그것들은 가을밤 하늘의 별처럼 우리 가슴 속에 여전히 밝게 빛나고 있다.

※ 다음 문장을 우리말로 쓰시오.

1 A Poet Who Loved Stars

➡ _____

2 In the sky where seasons pass in a hurry

➡ _____

3 Autumn fills the air.

➡ _____

4 And ready I stand, without a worry,

➡ _____

5 To count all the stars there.

➡ _____

6 Memory for one star,

➡ _____

7 Love for another star,

➡ _____

8 Loneliness for another star,

➡ _____

9 Longing for another star,

➡ _____

10 Poetry for another star,

➡ _____

11 And, oh, mother, mother for another star.

➡ _____

12 Have you read these lines before?

➡ _____

13 They are part of the poem "Counting Stars at Night" by Yoon Dong-ju.

➡ _____

14 The poem was written a long time ago but still remains one of Korea's favorite poems.

➡ _____

15 Dong-ju was born in 1917 near Yanbin, China.

➡ _____

16 As a young boy, he loved sports, and he was a soccer player for his school.

➡ _____

17 He also loved sewing so much that he sewed the numbers on all his friends' soccer uniforms.

➡ _____

18 However, it was literature that he loved most.

➡ _____

19 In elementary school he wrote a lot of poems.

➡ _____

20 He even made a literary magazine with his cousin, Song Mong-gyu.

➡ _____

21 In middle school he once borrowed a poetry book by a famous poet of the time, Baek Seok, and copied the whole book by hand.

➡ _____

22 He really wanted to have his own copy of the rare book.

➡ _____

23 His parents wanted him to be a doctor, but Dong-ju chose to study literature at a college in Seoul.

➡ _____

24 During his college years, he often hung out with other young poets and wrote poetry where he expressed feelings about his hometown and lost country.

➡ _____

25 To celebrate his graduation, he wished to publish 19 of his poems under the title, *Heaven, Wind, Stars, and Poetry*.

➡ _____

26 He made three copies of the book by hand.

➡ _____

27 One was given to his close friend, Jeong Byeong-uk, another was presented to his favorite professor, and the last one was kept for himself.

➡ _____

_____

28 However, his professor advised against his plan because he thought the Japanese government would not allow the publication.

➡ _____

29 Dong-ju followed his advice and gave up the idea.

➡ _____

30 Dong-ju decided to study further in the country where his father had studied before.

➡ _____

31 So, in 1942, Dong-ju and his cousin began to study in Japan.

➡ _____

32 On July 10 the following year, his cousin was arrested by the Japanese police for taking part in an independence movement.

➡ _____

33 Four days later, Dong-ju was also arrested on the same charges.

➡ _____

34 In 1945, Dong-ju and his cousin died in prison after harsh treatment by the police.

➡ _____

35 It was just a few months later that Korea achieved independence from Japan.

➡ _____

36 In 1948, Jeong Byeong-uk brought Dong-ju's poems to the poet's brother, and they were finally published.

➡ _____

37 The book was given the title the poet had thought of many years before.

➡ _____

38 His poems are loved by people of all ages, and thus they still shine brightly in our hearts like the stars in the autumn night sky.

➡ _____

_____

※ 다음 괄호 안의 단어들을 우리말에 맞도록 바르게 배열하시오.

1 (Poet / A / Loved / Who / Stars)
➡ _____

2 (the / in / where / sky / pass / seasons / a / in / hurry)
➡ _____

3 (fills / autumn / air. / the)
➡ _____

4 (ready / and / stand, / I / a / without / worry,)
➡ _____

5 (count / to / the / all / there. / stars)
➡ _____

6 (for / memory / star, / one)
➡ _____

7 (for / love / star, / another)
➡ _____

8 (for / loneliness / star, / another)
➡ _____

9 (for / longing / star, / another)
➡ _____

10 (for / poetry / star, / another)
➡ _____

11 (oh, / and, / mother / mother, / another / for / star.)
➡ _____

12 (you / have / these / read / before? / lines)
➡ _____

13 (are / they / of / part / poem / the / Stars / "Counting / Night" / at / Yoon / by / Dong-ju.)
➡ _____

14 (poem / the / written / was / long / a / time / but / ago / remains / still / of / one / favorite / Korea's / poems.)
➡ _____
_____

15 (was / Dong-ju / in / born / near / 1917 / China. / Yanbin,)
➡ _____

16 (a / as / boy, / young / loved / he / sports, / he / and / a / was / player / soccer / his / school. / for)
➡ _____

17 (also / he / sewing / loved / much / so / he / that / the / sewed / numbers / all / on / friends' / his / uniforms. / soccer)
➡ _____
_____

1 별을 사랑한 시인

2 계절이 지나가는 하늘에는

3 가을로 가득 차 있습니다.

4 나는 아무 걱정도 없이

5 가을 속의 별들을 다 헤일 듯합니다.

6 별 하나에 추억과

7 별 하나에 사랑과

8 별 하나에 쓸쓸함과

9 별 하나에 동경과

10 별 하나에 시와

11 별 하나에 어머니, 어머니,

12 당신은 이 시 구절을 읽어 본 적이 있는가?

13 이것은 윤동주의 시 '별 헤는 밤'의 일부이다.

14 시는 오래 전에 쓰였지만 여전히 한국의 가장 좋아하는 시 중의 하나로 남아 있다.

15 동주는 중국 연변 근처에서 1917년에 태어났다.

16 어린 소년이었을 때 그는 운동을 좋아했고, 학교의 축구 선수였다.

17 그는 또한 바느질하는 것을 무척 좋아해서 친구들의 축구 유니폼에 번호를 바느질해 주기도 했다.

18 (it / however, / was / that / literature / loved / he / most.)

➡ _____

19 (elementary / in / school / wrote / he / lot / a / poems. / of)

➡ _____

20 (even / he / a / made / magazine / literary / his / with / cousin, / Mong-gyu. / Song)

➡ _____

21 (middle / in / he / school / borrowed / once / poetry / a / by / book / famous / a / of / poet / time, / the / Seok, / Baek / and / the / copied / book / whole / hand. / by)

➡ _____

_____

22 (really / he / to / wanted / have / own / his / of / copy / the / book. / rare)

➡ _____

23 (parents / his / him / wanted / be / to / doctor, / a / but / chose / Dong-ju / study / to / at / literature / college / a / Seoul. / in)

➡ _____

_____

24 (his / during / years, / college / often / he / out / hung / other / with / poets / young / and / poetry / wrote / he / where / feelings / expressed / his / about / hometown / and / country. / lost)

➡ _____

_____

25 (celebrate / to / graduation, / his / wished / he / publish / to / of / 19 / poems / his / the / under / title, / *Wind, / Heaven, / and / Stars, / Poetry.*)

➡ _____

_____

26 (made / he / copies / three / the / of / book / hand. / by)

➡ _____

27 (was / one / given / his / to / friend, / close / Byeong-uk, / Jeong / was / another / to / presented / his / professor, / favorite / and / last / the / was / one / for / kept / himself.)

➡ _____

_____

28 (his / however, / professor / against / advised / plan / his / he / because / the / thought / Japanese / would / government / allow / not / publication. / the)

➡ _____

_____

18 그러나 그가 가장 사랑한 것은 문학이었다.

19 초등학교에 다닐 때 그는 많은 시를 썼다.

20 심지어 사촌 송몽규와 문학잡지를 만들기도 했다.

21 그가 중학교에 다니던 때 한번은 당대의 유명한 시인 백석의 시집을 빌려 와서 책 전체를 필사하기도 했다.

22 그는 정말로 그 희귀한 책을 한 부 갖고 싶었던 것이다.

23 그의 부모는 그가 의사가 되기를 바랐지만 동주는 서울에 있는 대학에서 문학 공부를 하기로 했다.

24 대학 시절에 그는 종종 다른 젊은 시인들과 어울려 다녔고, 고향과 잃어버린 조국에 대한 심정을 표현하는 시를 썼다.

25 졸업을 기념하여 그는 '하늘과 바람과 별과 시'라는 제목으로 자신의 시 19편을 출판하고 싶어 했다.

26 그는 책 세 부를 손으로 만들었다.

27 한 부는 가까운 친구인 정병욱에게 주었고, 또 하나는 그가 가장 좋아하는 교수에게 선물했으며, 마지막 하나는 자신이 보관했다.

28 그러나 그의 교수는 일본 정부가 출판을 허가하지 않으리라 여겨, 그의 계획에 반대하는 충고를 했다.

29 (followed / Dong-ju / advice / his / and / up / gave / idea. / the)

➡ _____

30 (decided / Dong-ju / study / to / in / further / the / country / his / where / father / studied / before. / had)

➡ _____

31 (in / so, / 1942, / Dong-ju / his / and / cousin / to / began / in / study / Japan.)

➡ _____

32 (July / on / the / 10 / year, / following / cousin / his / arrested / was / the / by / police / Japanese / for / part / taking / an / in / movement. / independence)

➡ _____

_____

33 (days / four / later, / was / Dong-ju / arrested / also / the / on / charges. / same)

➡ _____

34 (1945, / in / and / Dong-ju / cousin / his / in / died / prison / harsh / after / by / treatment / police. / the)

➡ _____

_____

35 (was / it / a / just / months / few / that / later / achieved / Korea / from / independence / Japan.)

➡ _____

36 (1948, / in / Byeong-uk / Jeong / brought / poems / Dong-ju's / to / poet's / the / and / brother, / were / they / published. / finally)

➡ _____

_____

37 (book / the / given / was / title / the / poet / the / thought / had / many / of / before. / years)

➡ _____

38 (poems / his / loved / are / people / by / ages, / all / of / and / thus / still / they / brightly / shine / our / in / like / hearts / the / in / stars / the / night / autumn / sky.)

➡ _____

_____

29 동주는 그의 충고를 따랐고 그 생각을 포기했다.

30 동주는 그의 아버지가 예전에 공부했던 나라에서 학업을 이어 가기로 했다.

31 그리하여 1942년에 동주와 그의 사촌은 일본에서 공부를 시작했다.

32 다음 해 7월 10일에 그의 사촌은 독립운동에 가담했다는 이유로 일본 경찰에게 체포되었다.

33 나흘 뒤 동주 역시 같은 혐의로 체포되었다.

34 1945년에 동주와 그의 사촌은 경찰의 가혹 행위를 당한 후 감옥에서 사망했다.

35 한국이 일본으로부터 독립을 이룬 것은 그로부터 불과 몇 달 후의 일이었다.

36 1948년에 정병욱이 동주의 시를 시인의 동생에게 가져다주었고, 마침내 그것들은 출판되었다.

37 그 책에는 시인이 수년 전에 생각해 두었던 제목이 붙었다.

38 그의 시는 모든 세대의 사랑을 받고 있고, 따라서 그것들은 가을밤 하늘의 별처럼 우리 가슴 속에 여전히 밝게 빛나고 있다.

Step5

※ 다음 우리말을 영어로 쓰시오.

1 별을 사랑한 시인

➡ _____

2 계절이 지나가는 하늘에는

➡ _____

3 가을로 가득 차 있습니다.

➡ _____

4 나는 아무 걱정도 없이

➡ _____

5 가을 속의 별들을 다 헤일 듯합니다.

➡ _____

6 별 하나에 추억과

➡ _____

7 별 하나에 사랑과

➡ _____

8 별 하나에 쓸쓸함과

➡ _____

9 별 하나에 동경과

➡ _____

10 별 하나에 시와

➡ _____

11 별 하나에 어머니, 어머니,

➡ _____

12 당신은 이 시 구절을 읽어 본 적이 있는가?

➡ _____

13 이것은 윤동주의 시 '별 헤는 밤'의 일부이다.

➡ _____

14 시는 오래 전에 쓰였지만 여전히 한국의 가장 좋아하는 시 중의 하나로 남아 있다.

➡ _____

15 동주는 중국 연변 근처에서 1917년에 태어났다.

➡ _____

16 어린 소년이었을 때 그는 운동을 좋아했고, 학교의 축구 선수였다.

➡ _____

17 그는 또한 바느질하는 것을 무척 좋아해서 친구들의 축구 유니폼에 번호를 바느질해 주기도 했다.

➡ _____

18 그러나 그가 가장 사랑한 것은 문학이었다.

➡ _____

19 초등학교에 다닐 때 그는 많은 시를 썼다.

➡ _____

20 심지어 사촌 송몽규와 문학잡지를 만들기도 했다.

➡ _____

21 그가 중학교에 다니던 때 한번은 당대의 유명한 시인 백석의 시집을 빌려 와서 책 전체를 필사
하기도 했다.

➡ _____

22 그는 정말로 그 희귀한 책을 한 부 갖고 싶었던 것이다.

➡ _____

23 그의 부모는 그가 의사가 되기를 바랐지만 동주는 서울에 있는 대학에서 문학 공부를 하기로 했다.

➡ _____

24 대학 시절에 그는 종종 다른 젊은 시인들과 어울려 다녔고, 고향과 잃어버린 조국에 대한 심정을
표현하는 시를 썼다.

➡ _____

_____

25 졸업을 기념하여 그는 '하늘과 바람과 별과 시'라는 제목으로 자신의 시 19편을 출판하고 싶어
했다.

➡ _____

_____

26 그는 책 세 부를 손으로 만들었다.

➡ _____

27 한 부는 가까운 친구인 정병욱에게 주었고, 또 하나는 그가 가장 좋아하는 교수에게 선물했으며,
마지막 하나는 자신이 보관했다.

➡ _____

_____

28 그러나 그의 교수는 일본 정부가 출판을 허가하지 않으리라 여겨, 그의 계획에 반대하는 충고를 했다.

➡ _____

_____

29 동주는 그의 충고를 따랐고 그 생각을 포기했다.

➡ _____

30 동주는 그의 아버지가 예전에 공부했던 나라에서 학업을 이어 가기로 했다.

➡ _____

31 그리하여 1942년에 동주와 그의 사촌은 일본에서 공부를 시작했다.

➡ _____

32 다음 해 7월 10일에 그의 사촌은 독립운동에 가담했다는 이유로 일본 경찰에게 체포되었다.

➡ _____

_____

33 나흘 뒤 동주 역시 같은 혐의로 체포되었다.

➡ _____

34 1945년에 동주와 그의 사촌은 경찰의 가혹 행위를 당한 후 감옥에서 사망했다.

➡ _____

35 한국이 일본으로부터 독립을 이룬 것은 그로부터 불과 몇 달 후의 일이었다.

➡ _____

36 1948년에 정병욱이 동주의 시를 시인의 동생에게 가져다주었고, 마침내 그것들은 출판되었다.

➡ _____

_____

37 그 책에는 시인이 수년 전에 생각해 두었던 제목이 붙었다.

➡ _____

38 그의 시는 모든 세대의 사랑을 받고 있고, 따라서 그것들은 가을밤 하늘의 별처럼 우리 가슴 속에 여전히 밝게 빛나고 있다.

➡ _____

_____

※ 다음 우리말과 일치하도록 빈칸에 알맞은 말을 쓰시오.

Communicate: Speak

1. Tom: Hi, Sora. You _____ _____.
2. Sora: Yeah. I'm really _____ _____ _____ this Tuesday.
3. Tom: This Tuesday? What's _____ Tuesday?
4. Sora: There's a big _____ _____. I _____ _____!

1. Tom: 안녕, 소라. 너 신나 보여.
2. Sora: 응. 나는 정말로 이번 주 화요일이 기대돼.
3. Tom: 이번 주 화요일? 화요일에 무슨 일이 있니?
4. Sora: 큰 컬링 게임이 있어. 나는 너무 기대돼!

Before You Read

1. _____ _____ we _____ August 15 in our class.
2. We _____ _____ pictures of people who _____ _____ through _____ _____ and _____ _____ _____ independence.
3. Also, there was a talk on _____ who _____ _____ their _____ _____ _____ in _____ _____.

1. 지난주에 우리는 반에서 8월 15일을 기념했습니다.
2. 우리는 가혹한 시대를 살면서 독립을 쟁취하려고 노력한 사람들의 사진을 전시했습니다.
3. 또한, 자유를 향한 동경을 문학 작품에 표현한 작가들에 관한 강연도 있었습니다.

Wrap Up READING

1. Do you enjoy plays, _____, novels, or _____?
2. They are _____ _____ _____ literature, and people _____ _____ _____ _____ _____.
3. However, all of them _____ _____ _____ _____ our own small world _____ _____ _____.
4. When we read literature, we _____ _____ the ideas of great _____ _____ _____ long ago.
5. We can even imagine _____ someone else or _____ in a _____ _____ _____.
6. _____ _____, literature opens up for us new worlds that we _____ _____ _____ before.

1. 당신은 희곡, 시, 소설 또는 만화를 즐기는가?
2. 그것들은 다양한 종류의 문학으로, 어떤 종류를 선호하는지는 사람에 따라 다르다.
3. 그러나 그것들은 모두 우리를 우리가 사는 작은 세계 너머로 가게 해 준다.
4. 문학을 읽을 때, 우리는 오래 전에 살았던 위대한 작가들의 생각과 마주치게 된다.
5. 심지어 우리는 다른 누군가가 되거나 완전히 다른 장소에서 사는 상상을 할 수도 있다.
6. 요컨대, 문학은 이전에 가 본 적이 없는 새로운 세계를 우리 앞에 펼쳐 준다.

※ 다음 우리말을 영어로 쓰시오.

Communicate: Speak

1. Tom: 안녕, 소라. 너 신나 보여.

➡ _____

2. Sora: 응. 나는 정말로 이번 주 화요일이 기대돼.

➡ _____

3. Tom: 이번 주 화요일? 화요일에 무슨 일이 있니?

➡ _____

4. Sora: 큰 컬링 게임이 있어. 나는 너무 기대돼!

➡ _____

Before You Read

1. 지난주에 우리는 반에서 8월 15일을 기념했습니다.

➡ _____

2. 우리는 가혹한 시대를 살면서 독립을 쟁취하려고 노력한 사람들의 사진을 전시했습니다.

➡ _____

3. 또한, 자유를 향한 동경을 문학 작품에 표현한 작가들에 관한 강연도 있었습니다.

➡ _____

Wrap Up READING

1. 당신은 희곡, 시, 소설 또는 만화를 즐기는가?

➡ _____

2. 그것들은 다양한 종류의 문학으로, 어떤 종류를 선호하는지는 사람에 따라 다르다.

➡ _____

3. 그러나 그것들은 모두 우리를 우리가 사는 작은 세계 너머로 가게 해 준다.

➡ _____

4. 문학을 읽을 때, 우리는 오래 전에 살았던 위대한 작가들의 생각과 마주치게 된다.

➡ _____

5. 심지어 우리는 다른 누군가가 되거나 완전히 다른 장소에서 사는 상상을 할 수도 있다.

➡ _____

6. 요컨대, 문학은 이전에 가 본 적이 없는 새로운 세계를 우리 앞에 펼쳐 준다.

➡ _____

MEMO

MEMO

적중100

정답 및 해설

천재 | 이재영

중 **3**

적중100

영어 기출 문제집

적중100

1학기

정답 및 해설

천재 | 이재영

중 3

Be Positive, Be Happy

시험대비 실력평가   p.08

01 (a)rtificial   02 (n)ervous   03 ①   04 ⑤

05 ⑤   06 ①   07 ②

01 주어진 단어는 반의어 관계이다. cause 원인 effect 결과 artificial 인공적인 natural 자연적인

02 주어진 단어는 반의어 관계이다. patient 참을성이 있는 impatient 조바심을 내는 nervous 불안한 calm 차분한

03 '종종 화를 내면서 말로 다른 사람과 의견을 달리하다'는 '주장하다'에 해당한다.

04 'used to+동사원형'에서 used to는 조동사로 '~하곤 했다'의 의미이다.

05 인공조명 불빛으로 인해서 생기는 문제는 밤에 잠을 자는 것과 관련된 문제이다.

06 put on: ~을 입다 deal with:~을 다루다

07 ① bother 성가시게 하다 ② nothing/something ③ scary 무서운 ④ spend 보내다, 쓰다 ⑤ gloomy 우울한

서술형 시험대비   p.09

01 out   02 (c)ommon   03 stressed

04 (1) decide   (2) artificial   (3) sleepy

05 (a)rtificial   06 with

07 (1) relax   (2) deep   (3) counting   (4) drinking
      (5) happy

01 stress out 지치게 하다 take some time out 잠시 동안 시간을 내다

02 "드문, 희귀한"이라는 뜻의 "rare"와 의미상 반대가 되는 단어는 "common 흔한"이다.

03 '스트레스를 주다'에 해당하는 동사의 과거분사 형용사를 써서 '스트레스를 받은'이라는 의미가 되도록 해야 한다.

05 '진짜처럼 보이도록 만들어졌지만 진짜가 아니거나 자연적인 것으로 만들어지지 않은'은 '인공적인'에 해당하는 의미이다.

06 deal with 처리하다, 해결하다 spend time with ~와 시간을 보내다

07 (1) 기분이 상했을 때 긴장을 가라앉히는 방법 (2) 깊은 숨을 쉬다 (3) 열까지 세기 (4) 차가운 물 마시기 (5) 행복한 생각하기'의 의미가 자연스럽다.

Conversation

핵심 Check   p.10~11

1 (1) talk   (2) let's, Because, sense

2 (A) out   (B) used   (C) What   (D) focus

02 (A) 스트레스로 지치게 하다 = stress out (B) ~하곤 했 다. ~했었다 = used to (C) ~에 집중하다 = focus, concentrate

교과서 대화문 익히기

Check(√) True or False   p.12

1 T   2 T   3 T   4 F

교과서 확인학습   p.14~15

Listen and Answer – Dialog 1

talk, about, What, feel, stressed, About, answered, As, see, common cause, Over, stresses, Problems, took , with, Next, worries, get stressed, appearance

Listen and Answer – Dialog 2

What / studying for, Grades / used to, way / know / stress, helpful / What / got stressed, at, focus / help / improve

Listen More – Listen and choose.

talk, decide / Let, designs / choose, short / say / Because, wear / makes sense, about / cute / expensive

Speak – Talk in groups.

talk, One, well-known

Speak – Talk in pairs.

spend / makes / make / makes

My Speaking Portfolio Step 3

like, relax, upset, take deep, counting, drinking, Lastly

Wrap Up – Listening & Speaking 1

talked, foods, are good, like to, healthy eating, slowly, eating

Wrap Up – Listening & Speaking 2

don't, make / make / basketball / say / we need

시험대비 기본평가   p.16

01 ④   02 ②   03 ②   04 ③

01 주제를 소개할 때는 'I'd like to talk about ~'라고 한다.

02 이유를 물어보는 말로 'What makes you say that?'이라고 한다.

03 talk about: ~에 대하여 말하다

04 ③ 'different foods that are good for your health.'는 지난번 소개한 주제이기 때문에 지금부터 소개할 내용은 아니다.

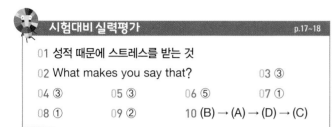

시험대비 실력평가   p.17~18

01 성적 때문에 스트레스를 받는 것

02 What makes you say that?   03 ③

04 ③   05 ③   06 ⑤   07 ①

08 ①   09 ②   10 (B) → (A) → (D) → (C)

01 that way는 앞 문장의 내용을 받는다.

02 "What makes you ~?"는 이유를 묻는 표현이다.

03 약간의 스트레스가 도움이 된다는 엄마의 말에 왜 그런지를 묻는 것으로 보아 Oliver는 그 사실을 모르고 있었다.

04 ③ 스트레스의 가장 흔한 원인은 학교 공부이다.

05 소셜 미디어에 시간을 많이 쓰겠다는 생각을 소개하고 (C) 거기에 대하여 이유를 물어보고, (A) 그 이유에 대한 질문에 대답하는 순서가 자연스러운 배열이다.

06 내용의 흐름상 동의하는 내용이 적절하다. ①~④는 동의하는 의미이고, ⑤는 동의하지 않을 때 쓰는 말이다.

07 소녀가 스포츠 클럽을 만들자는 제안에 대하여 소년은 야구 클럽을 만들고 싶어 하지만, 소녀는 농구가 더 낫다고 서로 다른 의견을 말하고 있다.

08 시험을 앞두고 수학 공부를 할 때 느낄 수 있는 스트레스에 대한 이야기가 적절하다.

09 'Did stress help you in other ways?'를 보면 스트레스가 도움이 되었다는 설명에 이어 또 다른 도움이 된 사실에 대한 설명이라는 것을 파악할 수 있다.

10 (B) 화면에 보여준 티셔츠 중에서 자신이 좋아하는 것을 고른다. (A) 거기에 대하여 이유를 묻는 질문을 하고, 그 뒤에는 그 대답이 이어진다. (D) 또 다른 것에 대한 제안을 하고 그것을 들은 B2는 거기에 대해서 긍정적인 대답을 한다. (C) 앞에 선택된 것에 대한 긍정적인 언급에 이어 또 다른 긍정적인 면에 대한 언급이 이어진다.

서술형 시험대비   p.19

01 What makes you feel the most stressed?

02 Next came family and worries about the future.

03 schoolwork

04 Oliver의 어머니도 스트레스를 느꼈다는 것   05 at

06 it's good to take deep breaths

01 의문대명사 what을 주어로 시작한다.

02 부사 Next로 시작하면 문장은 "부사+동사+주어"의 순서가 되도록 한다.

03 'As you can see, schoolwork was the most common cause of stress.'를 보면 십대의 가장 큰 스트레스 원인은 schoolwork이라는 것을 알 수 있다.

05 at the same time: 동시에

06 심호흡을 하다 = take deep breaths

교과서
Grammar

핵심 Check   p.20~21

1 (1) looking   (2) writing   (3) living

2 (1) have been waiting   (2) has been reading

3 (1) so   (2) such

4 (1) so cold that we didn't

(2) so expensive that he didn't

(3) so strong that they stopped

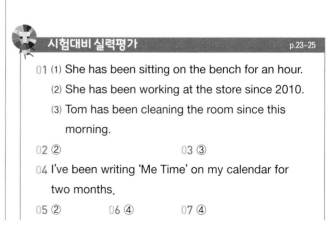

시험대비 기본평가   p.22

01 ⑤   02 ⑤

03 has been teaching English at this middle school for 20 years

04 so, that   05 ①

01 태어난 이후로 현재까지 살았고 지금도 살고 있다는 의미로 현재완료진행이 되어서 'have been living'이 되어야 한다.

02 ⑤ that절에서 eat의 목적어가 필요하다. eat → eat them

04 문맥상 'so ~ that' 구문이 되도록 한다.

05 동사 was의 보어로 형용사가 들어가야 한다.

시험대비 실력평가   p.23~25

01 (1) She has been sitting on the bench for an hour.

(2) She has been working at the store since 2010.

(3) Tom has been cleaning the room since this morning.

02 ②   03 ③

04 I've been writing 'Me Time' on my calendar for two months.

05 ②   06 ④   07 ④

08 (1) She was so tired that she went to bed early.

    (2) The cake looked so delicious that he decided to buy it.

    (3) The story was so interesting that he read it in a day.

09 that   10 ③   11 ①

12 (1) been (2) cleaning (3) so (4) so   13 ③

14 ②   15 ①   16 ①   17 ⑤

18 has been watching

---

01 (1) She has been teaching English at this school for 10 years.

    (2) It has been raining since last night.

    (3) He drove the car so fast that his father told him to drive slowly. .

02 a high mountain

03 (1) Has Mike been doing

    (2) Jack hasn't been playing

04 (1) talking   (2) been

05 has been playing tennis for two hours

06 so rich

07 She is so kind[nice] that everybody likes her.

08 Ann and I have been studying Chinese since last week.

09 (1) so tired   (2) heavy that

    (3) that they wanted more

10 has been using

11 Some people spend time with friends when they feel low.

12 (1) She is so hungry that she can't swim any more.

    (2) The car was so old that it couldn't run fast.

    (3) It was so cold that he put on his coat.

---

01 과거에 시작하여 현재에도 계속하고 있는 행위는 현재완료진행으로 나타내고, 형태는 'have/has been –ing'이다.

02 ② 과거형 수동태이므로 was가 들어가야 한다. 나머지는 모두 been이 들어간다.

03 현재완료진행의 동사 형태는 'have/has been –ing'이다.

04 'I've'에 이어지는 것은 과거분사이고 과거분사 been에 이어질 수 있는 것은 –ing 형태인 writing이다. writing의 목적어는 'Me Time'이고 거기에 이어서 장소와 시간의 부사구가 따라온다.

05 ⓒ 'It was such fine that we went outside.'는 'It was so fine that we went outside.'가 되어야 한다. ⓔ 'She has been living here for 5 years.'가 되어야 한다.

06 ④의 that은 관계대명사이고 나머지는 모두 부사절을 유도하는 접속사이다.

07 ④ 문장의 주어는 부정사나 동명사가 되어야 하기 때문에 Drinking이 되어야 한다.

08 '매우 ~해서 …하다'의 의미를 나타낼 때는 'so ~that' 구문을 이용한다. so와 that 사이에 형용사나 부사를 쓴다.

09 '너무 ~해서 …하다'는 내용을 'so ~ that' 구문으로 나타낸 표현이어서 빈칸에는 that이 들어간다.

10 '한 시간 동안 ~하고 있다'는 'have/has been –ing'의 형태로 현재완료진행형을 사용한다. was → has

11 ① so 뒤에는 형용사나 부사를 쓴다. 'a+형용사+명사' 앞에는 such를 쓴다.

12 (1), (2) 현재완료진행 시제는 'have/has been –ing' 형태가 되어야 하고 (3), (4)는 'so 형용사 that'의 구문이다.

13 ③ 현재완료시제와 함께 사용하는 시간의 표현에서 기간을 나타내어 '~ 동안'이라고 할 때는 전치사 for를 사용한다.

14 '너무 고통스러워 ~할 수 없었다'는 'so painful that ~ couldn't …'이다.

15 ① 현재완료 시제에서 '~ 동안'은 전치사 for, '~ 이래로'는 since를 사용하여 나타낸다.

16 '너무 ~해서 ~할 수 없다'는 'so+형용사/부사+that ~'이나 'such a+형용사+명사+that ~'의 형태로 나타낸다.

17 ⑤ 현재완료는 과거의 시간 표시와 함께 쓸 수 없다.

18 5시간 전부터 텔레비전을 보기 시작해서 지금도 보고 있으므로 현재완료진행형을 써서 나타낸다.

01 전부터 지금까지 하고 있는 일은 현재완료진행 시제로 나타내고, '너무 ~해서 …하다.'는 'so ~ that' 구문으로 나타낸다.

02 '너무 ~해서 ~할 수 없다'는 'such a+형용사+명사+that ~'의 형태로 나타낼 수 있다.

03 (1) 현재완료진행형(have[has] been -ing)의 의문문은 'Have+주어+been –ing ~?'의 어순이다. (2) 현재완료진행형의 부정문은 'have[has] not been -ing'이다.

04 (1), (2) 현재완료진행 시제는 'have[has] been –ing'이다.

05 두 시간 전부터 현재까지 테니스를 치고 있다는 내용의 현재완료진행형(has been playing)을 사용한다.

06 "so ~ that 주어 can" 너무 ~해서 …할 수 있다

07 '매우 ~해서 …하다'는 so ~ that 구문을 이용한다.

08 지난주부터 현재까지 공부하고 있다는 내용은 과거부터 현재까지의 진행을 포함하는 현재완료진행형(have been studying)을 사용한다.

09 '너무 ~해서 …하다'의 의미는 'so 형용사/부사 that'의 구문으로 나타낸다.

10 두 시간 전부터 현재까지 컴퓨터를 사용하고 있다는 내용의 현재완료진행형(has been using)을 사용한다.

11 Some people에 이어지는 동사 spend를 쓰고 종속절은 접속사 when으로 이어지도록 한다.

12 "너무 ~해서 …하다."의 의미로 "so 형용사/부사 that ~"의 구문으로 바꾼다.

Reading

p.28

확인문제

1 T 2 F 3 T 4 F

확인문제

p.29

1 T 2 F 3 F 4 T 5 T 6 F

교과서 확인학습 A

p.30~31

01 Goodbye
02 feel low
03 Others, to feel better
04 Still others
05 deal with
06 suggest different ways
07 saying, breaking, arguing
08 When this happens
09 so, that
10 at the top of my lungs
11 thanks to, what bothers me
12 I've been using, works
13 graduated from
14 he's been looking for
15 he's stressed out, by going fishing
16 gets upset
17 so, that, can leave, behind
18 Besides, to be
19 focusing on, forget
20 second-year, free from
21 seems to like, for a good reason
22 number-one way
23 so, that
24 feel like, relieving
25 looks tidy, looks brighter
26 what
27 all the things she has to do
28 she's under stress
29 takes some time out
30 reads, watches, talks
31 matter, as long as
32 I've been writing
33 work for you
34 to say goodbye to stress

교과서 확인학습 B

p.32~33

1 Say Goodbye to Stress
2 Some people spend time with friends when they feel low.
3 Others eat special foods to feel better.
4 Still others simply sleep for a while.
5 How do you deal with stress?

6 Here are some stories about people who suggest different ways.
7 Sometimes my friends give me stress by saying bad things about me, breaking promises, or arguing over small things.
8 When this happens, I watch horror movies!
9 Good horror movies are so scary that I scream a lot.
10 I guess that screaming at the top of my lungs helps me feel better.
11 Also, thanks to scary scenes and sound effects, I can forget about what bothers me.
12 I've been using this method for the past several months, and it really works.
13 My uncle graduated from college two years ago.
14 He lives with my family, and he's been looking for a job for some time.
15 I know that he's stressed out, but he always tries to be positive by going fishing.
16 He never gets upset when he doesn't catch any fish.
17 He says, "While I fish, I'm so focused that I can leave all my worries behind.
18 Besides, it teaches me to be patient."
19 I'm sure that focusing on one thing helps us forget about something else.
20 My sister, a second-year student in high school, has a wonderful way to stay free from stress.
21 She feels a lot of stress from schoolwork, but my mother seems to like the situation for a good reason.
22 It is because cleaning is my sister's number-one way to make life better!
23 When she's so stressed that her life looks gloomy, she cleans her room.
24 She says, "As I clean my room, I feel like I'm also relieving stress.
25 When my room looks tidy, my life looks brighter."
26 Let me tell you what my mother does about her stress.
27 She feels stressed by all the things she has to do at work and at home.
28 When she's under stress, she writes "Me Time" on her calendar.
29 This means she takes some time out for herself.
30 She reads a book, watches a movie, or talks with her friends.

31 She says, "It doesn't really matter what I do, as long as it's something I like.

32 I've been writing 'Me Time' on my calendar for two months, and I feel much better."

33 Which methods will work for you?

34 Try some of these ideas yourself, and find your best way to say goodbye to stress.

시험대비 실력평가
p.34~37

01 ⑤   02 ②   03 ③   04 ②

05 ③   06 ②, ⑤   07 tidy

08 she cleans her room

09 (A) because   (B) looks   (C) relieving

10 ③   11 what I do   12 ②   13 ④

14 ①   15 screaming at the top of my lungs

16 ③, ④   17 ③   18 fishing   19 ②

20 (A) a job   (B) going fishing   (C) gets upset

21 ④   22 ①, ③

23 (A) cleans her room   (B) make life better

24 ③, ⑤   25 hello → goodbye

01 ⑤는 현재분사, 나머지는 동명사

02 ⓐ와 ② 효과가 있다, ① 일하다, ③ (문학·예술 따위의) 작품, ④ 토목공사, ⑤ (기계장치 등이) 작동되다

03 ③ too ~ to: 너무 ~해서 …할 수 없다, Good horror movies are scary enough to make Mina scream a lot. 으로 고치는 것이 적절하다.

04 ⓐ graduate from: ~을 졸업하다, ⓑ focus on: ~에 집중하다, 초점을 맞추다

05 ③ 낙관적인, 낙천적인, 준호의 삼촌은 스트레스를 받고 있지만 낚시를 다니며 긍정적으로 지내려고 항상 노력한다고 했으므로, '낙천적인' 성격이라고 할 수 있다. ① 수동적인, 소극적인, ② 짜증난[안달하는], ④ 후한, 관대한, ⑤ 부정적인

06 (A)와 ②, ⑤: 계속 용법, ①, ④: 경험 용법, ③ 완료 용법

07 정돈되고, 조직적인 방식으로 배열된, tidy: 깔끔한, 잘 정돈된

08 '그녀가 방을 청소하는 것'을 가리킨다.

09 (A) 뒤에 '이유'를 설명하는 말이 이어지므로 because가 적절하다. why 뒤에는 앞에서 말하고 있는 내용의 '결과'에 해당하는 말이 이어진다. (B) 뒤에 형용사가 나오므로 looks가 적절하다. look+형용사, look like+명사: ~처럼 보이다, (C) 스트레스도 해소되는 것 같다고 해야 하므로 relieving이 적절하다. relieve: (불쾌감·고통 등을) 없애[덜어] 주다

10 ⓑ와 ③: ~할 때, ① …와 같이; …대로, ② …와 같은 정도로 (as ... as ~에서, 앞의 as는 지시부사, 뒤의 as는 접속사), ④

[이유] …이기 때문에, ⑤ …으로서(전치사)

11 ⓐ '내가 무엇을 하는지는' ⓑ '내가 하는 것'

12 이 글은 '스트레스를 다루는 Yulia의 엄마의 방법'에 관한 글이므로, 제목으로는 ②번이 적절하다.

13 ④ 'Yulia의 어머니가 얼마나 자주 "Me Time"을 가지는지' 는 대답할 수 없다. ① By all the things she has to do at work and at home. ② She writes "Me Time" on her calendar. ③ It means she takes some time out for herself. ⑤ For two months.

14 주어진 문장의 this에 주목한다. ①번 앞 문장의 내용을 받고 있으므로 ①번이 적절하다.

15 scream at the top of one's lungs: 있는 힘껏 소리를 지르다

16 ⓑ와 ③, ④: 관계대명사, ① 의문형용사, ②, ⑤ 의문대명사, ② be in debt: 빚이 있다

17 이 글은 '스트레스를 다루는 방법'에 관한 글이므로, 주제로는 ③번이 적절하다. ④ benefit: 이익, 혜택

18 go -ing: ~하러 가다

19 빈칸 앞 문장들에서 '물고기를 한 마리도 잡지 못했을 때에도 삼촌은 절대 속상해 하지 않는다.'고 하면서, '낚시하는 동안, 나는 아주 몰입해서 모든 걱정을 잊을 수 있어.'라고 했고, 빈칸 뒤의 문장에서 낚시는 나에게 인내를 가르쳐 준다.'고 했으므로, 주로 무엇에 대한 또 다른 이유나 주장을 제시할 때 쓰이는 Besides(게다가)가 적절하다. teach+목적어+to부정사: ~하는 법을 가르치다 ① 대신에, ⑤ 그에 반해서, 그와 대조적으로

20 준호의 삼촌은 얼마 전부터 '직장'을 구하고 있다. 그는 스트레스를 받고 있지만 '낚시를 다니며' 긍정적으로 지내려고 항상 노력하고, 물고기를 한 마리도 잡지 못했을 때에도 삼촌은 절대 '속상해 하지' 않는다.

21 ⓐ와 ②: 형용사적 용법, ①, ⑤: 부사적 용법, ③, ④: 명사적 용법

22 뒤에 셀 수 없는 명사가 나오므로, many와 a number of는 바꿔 쓸 수 없다. a lot of와 lots of는 수와 양이 많은 경우에 다 쓸 수 있다.

23 청소가 도빈이 누나의 '삶을 향상하는' 최고의 방법이라서, 스트레스를 너무 많이 받아서 인생이 우울해 보일 때 그녀가 '방을 청소하기' 때문이다.

24 ⓐ와 ③, ⑤: (원하는) 효과가 나다[있다], (계획 따위가) 잘 되어 가다, ① (해야 할) 일(명사), ② (기계나 장치 등을) 작동시키다, ④ 직장(명사)

25 '스트레스와 이별하는 방법'이라고 해야 하므로, hello를 goodbye로 고쳐야 한다. say hello to: ~에게 안부를 전하다, say goodbye to: ~에게 작별인사를 하다

01 ⓐ saying   ⓑ breaking   ⓒ arguing

02 Good horror movies are so scary that I scream a lot.

03 (A) horror movies   (B) her lungs

04 (A) for   (B) positive   (C) so

05 being → to be

06 no difficulty → difficulty   07 what

08 so long as   09 two months, writing

10 without

11 도빈이의 누나가 학업 때문에 많은 스트레스를 받는 상황

12 (A) schoolwork   (B) cleaning her room

13 (A) tell   (B) under   (C) herself

14 자신을 위해 잠깐 시간을 내는 것

15 even, still, far, a lot 중에서 두 개를 쓰면 된다.

01 전치사 by 다음에 동명사를 쓰는 것이 적절하다.

02 so+형용사/부사+that절: 너무 ~해서 …하다

03 미나는 스트레스를 느낄 때 '공포영화'를 보면서 '있는 힘껏' 소리를 지른다.

04 (A) '얼마 동안'이라고 해야 하므로 for가 적절하다. for: ~ 동안, since: ~ 이후로, (B) '긍정적'으로 지내려고 한다고 해야 하므로 positive가 적절하다. positive: 긍정적인, negative: 부정적인, (C) 뒤에 명사는 없고 형용사만 나오므로 so가 적절하다. so+형용사/부사+that절: 너무 ~해서 …하다, such+a+형용사+명사+that절

05 teach+목적어+to부정사: ~에게 …하기를 가르치다

06 '준호의 삼촌은 얼마 전부터 직장을 구하고 있다'고 했으므로, 일자리를 찾는 데 어려움을 '겪고 있다'로 고치는 것이 적절하다. have difficulty ~ing: ~하는 데 어려움을 겪다

07 ⓐ에는 관계대명사 what, ⓑ에는 의문대명사 what이 적절하다.

08 as long as = so long as: ~이기만[하기만] 하면

09 '두 달째 달력에 '나만의 시간'을 적어 왔다'는 것은 '두 달' 전에 달력에 '나만의 시간'을 쓰기 시작해서 지금도 여전히 '쓰고 있는 중'이라는 뜻이다.

10 free from = without: ~이 없는

11 바로 앞의 내용을 가리킨다.

12 (A) 도빈이 누나의 스트레스의 원인: 학교 공부, (B) 스트레스를 해소하는 도빈이 누나의 방법: 그녀의 방을 청소하는 것

13 (A) '사역동사 let+목적어+동사원형'을 써야 하므로 tell이 적절하다. (B) '스트레스를 받고 있다'고 해야 하므로 under가 적절하다. be under stress: 스트레스를 받고 있다, (C) 주어와 목적어가 같을 때는 재귀대명사를 써야 하므로 herself가 적절

14 뒤 문장(This means she takes some time out for herself.)의 내용을 쓰면 된다.

15 much는 비교급을 강조하는 말이며, '훨씬'으로 해석한다.

01 ①   02 (a)rtificial   03 ②   04 ①

05 ②   06 ①   07 (m)akes   08 ③

09 ②   10 ①   11 help   12 ④

13 I guess that screaming at the top of my lungs helps me feel better.

14 tell you what my mother does about her stress

15 ①   16 ④   17 ①   18 ②

19 (1) Little → A little   (2) improving → (to) improve

20 ②   21 ③   22 ⑤

23 ⓐ Some   ⓑ Still   ⓒ who[that]   24 ①, ④

25 What → How   26 ②

27 focusing on one thing helps us forget about something else

28 ③   29 ①

30 When my room looks tidy, my life looks brighter

31 ⓐ Mouth   ⓑ Nose   32 ①

01 '다른 사람에게 보여지는 방식'은 '겉모습, 외모'라는 뜻이다.

02 주어진 단어는 반의의 관계이다. agree 동의하다 disagree 동의하지 않다 artificial 인공적인 natural 자연적인

03 소셜 미디어에 시간을 많이 보내는 이유는 친구를 사귈 수 있다는 장점 때문이다.

04 'cheerless'는 '활기 없는'이라는 뜻으로 gloomy에 해당한다.

05 (B) 상대의 말에 다른 의견을 제시하고 (A) 이에 대한 이유를 묻고 (C) 거기에 대하여 설명하는 순서가 자연스럽다.

06 ① "I'd like to talk about some good ways to relax when you get upset."를 통해서 여기서 소개하는 것은 화를 푸는 방법이라는 것을 알 수 있다.

07 'make sense'는 '의미가 통하다, 말이 되다'의 뜻으로 상대의 말에 동의하는 의미이다.

08 ⓒ 짧은 소매가 좋다는 것으로 보아 여름에 입을 것이라고 생각할 수 있다.

09 시험 공부를 하면서 스트레스를 받는 것으로 보아 성적이 스트레스의 원인이라는 것을 알 수 있다.

10 ① '무엇 때문에 그렇게 말하나요?'는 '무엇 때문에 그렇게 생각하나요?'로 바꿀 수 있다.

11 대답을 통해서 스트레스가 주는 유익함에 대한 질문임을 알 수 있다.

12 '너무 ~해서 …하다'의 의미를 나타내는 'so ~ that …'의 구문이다.

13 '있는 힘껏 소리를 지르는 것이 기분 좋게 느끼도록 도와준다고 생각해'의 의미로 'I guess'를 주절로 하고 종속절의 주어는 'screaming at the top of my lungs'가 되도록 한다.

14 'Let me'에 이어지는 동사원형 tell을 쓰고 직접목적어는 what이 이끄는 명사절이 되도록 한다.

15 ⓓ 명백한 과거를 나타내는 'when she was a child'는 현재완료진행형과 함께 쓸 수 없다.

16 '~ 이후로'의 의미일 때는 since를 쓴다.

17 ① '너무 ~해서 …하다'는 'so 형용사/부사 that ~'의 구문으로 나타낸다.

18 '너무 ~해서 …하다'는 'so 형용사/부사 that ~'의 구문으로 나타낸다.

19 (1) 문맥상 '약간의'라는 긍정의 의미가 되어야 한다. (2) 동사 help의 목적어는 to부정사나 원형부정사이다.

20 ② 부사 Next로 시작하는 문장은 주어와 동사를 도치하도록 한다.

21 ③ makes의 주어가 되어야 하므로 why 대신 what이 와야 한다.

22 '그녀는 아주 정직해서 거짓말을 할 수 없었다.'의 의미인데, ⑤ '그녀는 거짓말을 했지만 '아주 정직했다'라는 뜻이다.

23 Some, Others, Still others: 몇몇은, 다른 사람들은, 또 다른 사람들은, ⓒ 관계대명사 who[that]가 적절하다.

24 (A)와 ①, ④는 부사적 용법, ② 형용사적 용법, ③, ⑤는 명사적 용법

25 What 뒤에 완전한 문장이 이어지므로, What을 부사인 How로 고치는 것이 적절하다.

26 '여기에 다른 방법을 제안하는 사람들에 대한 몇 가지 이야기들이 있다.'고 했으므로, ②번이 적절하다.

27 on을 보충하면 된다. focus on: ~에 집중하다, 초점을 맞추다

28 준호의 삼촌은 스트레스를 받고 있지만 낚시를 다니며 '긍정적'으로 지내려고 항상 노력한다고 했으므로, '부정적인' 태도를 가지고 있다고 한 ③번이 옳지 않다.

29 free from: ~이 없는

30 look+형용사: ~하게 보이다

31 ⓐ '약간의 차를 마셔라.'라고 했으므로, Mouth가 적절하다.
ⓑ '신선한 꽃 냄새를 맡아라.'라고 했으므로, Nose가 적절하다.

32 ① 야외에 있을 때는 '하늘'을 보라고 했다.

단원별 예상문제
p.46~49

01 (b)oring 　 02 ① 　 03 ④ 　 04 ②
05 ② 　 06 ⑤ 　 07 (m)essy 　 08 ①

---

09 ① 　 10 (1) free (2) reason (3) gloomy
11 ① 　 12 ② 　 13 ⑤ 　 14 ④
15 ⑤ 　 16 ③ 　 17 ③
18 친구들이 미나에 관해 나쁜 말을 하거나, 약속을 어기거나, 혹은 사소한 일을 두고 언쟁을 하며 미나에게 스트레스를 주는 것
19 using 　 20 ① scary scenes ② sound effects
21 (A) graduated from (B) upset (C) patient
22 ①, ② 　 23 her → herself
24 important
25 (A) all the things she has to do (B) Me Time
26 ②
27 (A) going outdoors and getting plenty of sunlight
(B) Exercise

01 주어진 단어는 동의어 관계이다. boring 지루한 dull 지루한

02 '사람이 약간 걱정되거나 속상하게 만들다'는 '성가시게 하다, 괴롭히다'의 의미이다.

03 decide on: ~을 결정하다 thanks to: ~ 덕택에

04 ① graduated 졸업했다 ② '그가 지쳤다'의 의미로 stressed가 들어가는 것이 적절하다. ③ positive 긍정적인 ④ focused 집중한 ⑤ forget 잊어버리다

05 공포영화를 설명할 수 있는 단어는 ② 'scary 무서운'이다.

06 '있는 힘껏'이라는 뜻으로 'at the top of my lungs'가 되어야 한다.

07 주어진 단어는 반의어 관계이다. cause 원인 effect 결과 tidy 깔끔한 messy 어질러진

08 ① 여기에 사용된 grade는 '성적'이라는 뜻이다.

09 '화내지 않고 어려움을 받아들이거나 긴 시간 차분하게 기다릴 수 있는'은 'patient 인내하는'에 해당하는 의미이다.

10 (1) '~가 없는'의 뜻으로 'free from'이 적절하다. (2) ~한 이유로 = for a ~ reason (3) 우울한, 침울한 = gloomy

11 ② 소년은 스포츠 클럽 만드는 것에 동의한다. ③ 소녀는 농구 클럽을 원한다. ④ 소녀는 야구 클럽을 만들고자 하는 소년과 의견이 다르다. ⑤ 소녀가 야구를 좋아하는지는 알 수 없다.

12 with: ~이 있는, ~을 가지고 있는

13 내용상 앞에서 선택한 것에 대한 장점이 언급되어 있는 것이 적절하다.

14 대화의 내용으로 보아 그들은 티셔츠를 여름에 입을 것이다.

15 현재완료진행시제는 'have/has been –ing'가 되어야 한다.

16 ③ 현재완료진행시제와 함께 사용하는 시간 표현에서 '~동안'은 전치사 for를 쓴다.

17 ⓒ that절에서 buy의 목적어인 it(= the bag)이 필요하다. ⓓ '너무 ~해서 …하다'는 'so 형용사 that'이다. ⓔ since this morning과 함께 쓰는 문장은 현재완료나 현재완료진행시제를 쓴다.

18 앞 문장의 내용을 가리킨다.

19 과거에 시작한 행동을 지금까지 계속하는 것을 강조할 때에는 현재완료진행형(have been -ing)으로 나타낸다.

20 공포영화의 '무서운 장면들'과 '음향 효과' 덕분에 그녀를 괴롭히는 것들을 잊을 수 있다.

21 (A) 대학을 '졸업했다'고 해야 하므로 graduated from이 적절하다. graduate from: ~을 졸업하다, (B) 물고기를 한 마리도 잡지 못했을 때에도 삼촌은 '속상해 하지' 않는다.고 해야 하므로 upset이 적절하다. relaxed: 느긋한, 여유 있는, (C) 낚시는 나에게 '인내'를 가르쳐 준다고 해야 하므로 patient가 적절하다. impatient: 짜증난, 참을성 없는

22 ⓐ와 ③, ④, ⑤: 게다가, 더욱이, ① 그러므로, ② In addition to 뒤에는 목적어가 와야 한다. ⓐ의 경우, In addition과는 바꿔 쓸 수 있다.

23 for 뒤의 목적어가 주어 자신이므로 재귀대명사 herself를 써야 한다.

24 matter = be important: 중요하다

25 (A) Yulia의 어머니의 스트레스의 원인: 직장과 집에서 해야 하는 온갖 일, (B) 스트레스를 해소하는 Yulia의 어머니의 방법: "나만의 시간"을 가지는 것

26 화면 앞에 앉아 있는 '대신' 밖에 나가 태양 아래에서 뛰어다녀라고 해야 하므로 ②번이 적절하다. Instead of: ~ 대신에, ①, ⑤: 게다가, ③ ~에 덧붙여, ④ ~에도 불구하고

27 (A)는 '밖에 나가서 충분한 양의 햇볕을 쬐는 것', (B)는 '운동'을 가리킨다.

서술형 실전문제 p.50~51

01 (r)eason 02 (w)orried 03 (e)ffect
04 stressed 05 helpful 06 makes
07 무엇이 여러분이 가장 스트레스를 느끼도록 만드는가?
08 appearance
09 My mother has been cooking dinner since 6:00.
10 so, that 11 ⓐ so ⓑ that
12 (A) happens (B) helps (C) what
13 this method 14 ago, is, looking
15 enough to 16 (A) fishing (B) positive

01 주어진 단어는 동의어 관계이다. bother 성가시게 하다 – disturb 방해하다 cause 원인 – reason 이유

02 주어진 단어는 반의어 관계이다. cheap 싼 expensive 비싼 – relieved 안심이 되는 worried 걱정되는

03 '어떤 사건이나 행동에 의해서 초래된 변화'는 '결과, 영향'이라는 뜻이다.

04 that way는 '그렇게'의 뜻으로 stressed를 받는다.

05 was의 보어가 되는 형용사로 고친다.

---

06 이유를 물어보는 말로 'What makes you say that?'이 되어야 한다.

07 this question은 앞 문장을 받는다.

08 appear의 명사형으로 고친다.

09 6시 이후부터 현재까지 요리를 하고 있다는 내용의 현재완료진행형(has been cooking)시제를 사용한다.

10 '너무 ~해서 …하다'의 의미로 'so ~ that ...'이 되어야 한다.

11 so+형용사/부사+that절: 너무 ~해서 …하다

12 (A) happen은 자동사로서 수동태로 쓸 수 없으므로 happens가 적절하다. (B) 주어가 동명사 screaming이므로 helps가 적절하다. (C) 뒤에 불완전한 절이 이어지고 선행사가 없으므로 관계대명사 what이 적절하다.

13 '이 방법'을 가리킨다.

14 준호의 삼촌이 '얼마 전부터 직장을 구하고 있다'는 것은 얼마 '전에' 직장을 구하기 시작해서 지금도 여전히 '구하고 있는 중'이라는 뜻이다.

15 so ~ that S can ... = ~ enough to 동사원형

16 준호의 삼촌은 낚시를 하러 다니는 덕분에, 직장을 구하는 데 어려움을 겪고 있어도 긍정적인 태도를 가지고 있다.

창의사고력 서술형 문제 p.52

|모범답안|

01 working, change, fish stresses, worry

02 have been living in this city / I have been living in this city since I was ten. I have been hanging out with my best friend since I was ten. I have been learning English since I was ten. I have been playing the guitar since I was ten. I have been using this computer since I was ten.

03 (A) Eye (B) Mouth (C) Hand (D) Nose
   (E) Ear

단원별 모의고사 p.53~56

01 ② 02 ④ 03 ⑤ 04 ②
05 stress → stressed 06 ② 07 ③
08 My father has been repairing his car since this morning.
09 ① 10 so hot that
11 (1) like to talk about some good ways to relax when you get upset
   (2) fish, I'm so focused that I can leave all my worries behind

9

12 ①　　13 ③　　14 keeping → breaking
15 the thing which[that]　　16 ①, ④　　17 fishing
18 from　　19 ②　　20 This → It
21 ①　　22 ②

에, 가주어 It으로 고쳐야 한다.

21 ⓑ와 ④: 계속 용법, ① 경험 용법, ② 결과 용법, ③, ⑤: 완료 용법

22 ② Yulia의 어머니 직업이 무엇인지는 위 글에서 알 수 없다.

01 주어진 단어는 동의어 관계이다. tidy 깔끔한 neat 깨끗한 – scream 소리를 지르다 shout 소리치다

02 '더 좋게 만들다 또는 더 좋아지다'의 의미는 improve이다.

03 patient 참을성이 있는 impatient 조바심이 나는

04 (B) 상대의 말에 이유를 묻고 (A) 그 질문에 대한 이유를 설명하고 (C) 거기에 대하여 동의하는 순서가 자연스럽다.

05 ⑤ '스트레스를 받다'는 'get stressed'로 'get+과거분사'의 형태로 수동의 의미를 나타낸다.

06 'Let me show you some designs on the screen'을 보면 티셔츠 디자인을 화면을 보고 결정할 것이라는 것을 알 수 있다.

07 ③ 'such a+형용사+명사'의 순서가 된다.

08 오늘 아침 이후부터 지금까지 차를 수리하고 있다는 뜻으로 현재완료진행형(has been repairing)을 사용한다.

09 현재완료진행시제와 함께 쓰인 시간 표현에서 '~ 동안'의 의미일 때 전치사 for를 쓴다.

10 '너무 ~하기 때문에 …하다'는 so ~ that ...'으로 바꾸어 쓸 수 있다.

11 (1) ~하고 싶다 = would like to ~ ~하는 좋은 몇 가지 방법 = some good ways to ~ (2) 낚시하는 동안 = While I fish

12 ① 현재완료진행과 함께 쓰인 시간 표현에서 '~ 동안'이라는 의미일 때는 전치사 for로 나타낸다.

13 ⓑ, ⓔ '너무 ~해서 …하다'는 'so ~ that ...'이다. ⓕ 현재완료진행시제는 /have/has been –ing' 형태이다.

14 친구들이 약속을 어김으로써 미나에게 스트레스를 준다고 해야 하므로, keeping을 breaking으로 고쳐야 한다. keep promises: 약속을 지키다, break promises: 약속을 어기다

15 동사가 bothers이므로 선행사를 단수인 the thing으로 쓰는 것이 적절하다.

16 ⓐ와 ①, ④: …하고 있는 동안에(접속사), ② 동안, 시간(명사), ③, ⑤: [주절 뒤에서 반대·비교·대조를 나타내어] 그런데, 한편(으로는)

17 '낚시'를 가리킨다.

18 ⓐ free from: ~이 없는, ⓑ from schoolwork: 학업 때문에

19 도빈이의 어머니는 그 상황을 좋아하는 것 같다고 했다.

20 진주어에 해당하는 간접의문문 what I do를 받은 것이기 때문

Opening a Window to the World

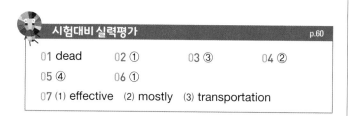

시험대비 실력평가
p.60

01 dead	02 ①	03 ③	04 ②
05 ④	06 ①		

07 (1) effective (2) mostly (3) transportation

01 주어진 관계는 반의어 관계이다. alive: 살아 있는, dead: 죽은

02 '대량으로 그리고 낮은 가격으로 물건을 판매하는 행위'를 가리키는 말은 wholesale(도매의)이다.

03 ③번 문장에서 rich는 '풍부한'을 의미한다.

04 house는 명사로는 '집'을 의미하지만 동사로 '살 곳을 주다, 거처를 제공하다'라는 의미를 갖는다.

05 ④번을 제외한 나머지는 모두 명사와 형용사와의 관계를 나타낸다. advent: 출현, 도래, adventure: 모험

06 주어진 문장에서 covered는 '지붕이 덮인'을 뜻하며 이와 같은 의미로 쓰인 것은 ①번이다. ②, ④: '다루다', ③, ⑤: '(비용을) 감당하다' tuition fee: 학비

서술형 시험대비
p.61

01 subtract　02 floating market

03 (1) selective (2) inventive (3) magical
(4) impressive (5) personal (6) collective
(7) emotional (8) seasonal

04 (1) lasts for two and a half hours
(2) what time the store is going to close
(3) you must use a covered truck

05 (1) best-before date (2) all corners of the world
(3) digest (4) discover (5) natural

06 tourist, discover, transportation, last, local

01 주어진 관계는 반의어 관계이다. add: 더하다, subtract: 빼다

02 '보트 위에서 물건을 직접 사고파는 시장'을 가리키는 말은 floating market(수상 시장)이다.

04 last: 지속되다, covered: 지붕이 덮인, protect: 보호하다

05 digest: 소화시키다, discover: 발견하다, cancer: 암, natural: 자연의

06 local: 지역의, transportation: 교통, last: 지속되다, tourist: 관광객, discover: 발견하다

Conversation

핵심 Check
p.62~63

1 I wonder if there's a tourist map of the town
2 you help me with this milk /
do you want me to tell you the best-before date

01 '~가 있는지 궁금하다.'는 'I wonder if there is ~.'이다.

02 도움을 요청하는 표현은 'Can you help me with ~?'이고 도움을 제안하는 표현은 'Do you want me to ~?'이다.

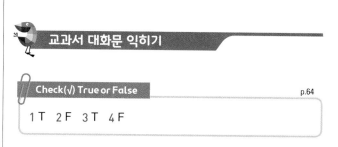

교과서 대화문 익히기

Check(√) True or False
p.64

1 T　2 F　3 T　4 F

교과서 확인학습
p.66~67

Listen – Listen & Answer Dialog 1

Welcome to, help / if, tourist map / Is there, looking for / like to try, local / five days, open / lucky, How can I get there / takes about, minutes / mark / Try, when, get

Listen – Listen & Answer Dialog 2

bill / Here, meal / good for / rich, digests / wonder if / to give, recipe

Listen More – Listen and complete

help me with, milk / Read / the best-before date / glasses / Let, see, by / I wonder if, lasts longer / one, until June 11 / one / welcome

Speak – Talk in pairs. 1

Excuse, wonder, around here / but, don't have one / all right

Speak – Talk in pairs. 2

wrong / bored / want me to, with / be great

Wrap Up 1

hungry / How / want, to, add

Wrap Up 2

look at, I wonder how much it is / Why don't, go in, check / buy it for you, asking, price / course

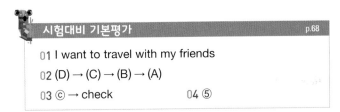

시험대비 기본평가 p.68

01 I want to travel with my friends

02 (D) → (C) → (B) → (A)

03 ⓒ → check   04 ⑤

02 (D) 배고픔을 설명 → (C) 제안 → (B) 고마움 표현 → (A) 질문

03 go와 병렬 구조이므로 check가 알맞다.

04 위 대화에서 귀여운 가방이 얼마인지 알 수 없다.

시험대비 실력평가 p.69~70

01 Will you mark the way on the map   02 tourist

03 ①, ③   04 bill   05 ⑤   06 ②

07 ⑤   08 ⑤

09 I wonder how much it is.

10 Let's go in and check.

11 They are going to ask the price of the cute bag.

12 (C) → (B) → (D) → (A) → (E)

02 '즐거움을 위해 여행하는 사람'을 가리키는 말은 tourist(여행자, 여행객)이다.

03 밑줄 친 (a)는 궁금한 점을 나타내고 있으므로 이와 바꾸어 쓸 수 있는 표현은 ①, ③번이다.

04 '상품이나 서비스에 대해 누군가에게 얼마만큼의 빚을 졌는지 보여주는 서류'를 뜻하는 것은 bill(계산서)이다.

05 여자가 어디에서 곤드레를 구매할 수 있는지 알고 싶어 한다는 설명은 대화의 내용과 일치하지 않는다.

06 주어진 문장은 유통 기한을 설명하고 있으므로 ⓑ번이 적절하다.

07 우유를 구매하는 과정에서 이루어지는 대화이므로 식료품점인 것을 알 수 있다.

08 위 대화에서 오늘 날짜는 알 수 없다.

09 간접의문문 어순으로 '의문사+주어+동사' 순서로 이어져야 한다.

10 (B)는 제안을 나타내고 있다.

11 Jane과 아빠는 가방 가격을 물어보려고 한다.

12 (C) 계산서 건네주기 및 식사에 대한 질문 → (B) 식사에 대한 만족 표현 → (D) 감사 표현 및 곤드레에 대한 설명 → (A) 놀라움 표현 → (E) 곤드레에 대한 추가 설명

서술형 시험대비 p.71

01 I wonder if there's a bank around here.

02 박물관은 현지 문화를 배우기에 좋은 장소이므로 Brian은 박물관을 방문하고 싶어 한다.

03 I wonder if there's one that lasts longer.

04 (A) my glasses   (B) the best-before date
    (C) lasts longer   (D) June 11

05 (D) → (E) → (C) → (B) → (A)

01 I wonder if: ~인지 궁금하다

04 오늘 나는 식료품점에 나의 안경을 가져가지 않았다. 너무 작아서 유통 기한을 읽기가 어려웠다. 나는 소년에게 그것을 읽어달라고 부탁했다. 나는 첫 번째로 집었던 우유는 사지 않았다. 왜냐하면 유통 기한이 너무 짧았기 때문이다. 운이 좋게도 소년은 유통 기한이 좀 더 긴 우유를 찾았다. 나는 내가 6월 11일까지 마실 수 있을 것으로 생각한다. 나는 그에게 감사했다.

05 (D) 궁금한 점 묻기 → (E) 제안 → (C) 감사 표현 → (B) 확인 → (A) 대답

교과서
Grammar

핵심 Check p.72~73

1 (1) when (2) where (3) why

2 (1) if[whether] (2) if[whether] (3) whether

시험대비 기본평가 p.74

01 ①

02 (1) where (2) when (3) if (4) whether 03 ④

04 (1) Tell me the reason why you were late.

   (2) He asked whether he could help.

   (3) Can you find out if he is available now?

01 선행사가 'the day'이므로 when을 써야 한다.

02 (1) 선행사가 'the library'이므로 where가 적절하다. (2) 선행사가 'The day'이므로 when이 적절하다. (3) '그녀가 장미를 좋아한다는 것을 궁금해 한다'는 말은 어색하다. 사실의 여부를 확인하거나 불확실함을 나타내는 if가 적절하다. (4) 바로 뒤에 'or not'이 이어지고 있으므로 whether가 적절하다.

03 Tell의 직접목적어가 나와야 하는데 '~인지 (아닌지)'라는 의미로 명사절을 이끄는 접속사 if가 적절하다.

04 (1) 선행사가 'the reason'이므로 관계부사 why를 이용한다. (2) '~인지 (아닌지)'라는 의미의 접속사로 어떠한 사실의 여부를 확인하거나 불확실함을 나타낼 때 쓰이는 whether를 이용한다. (3) '~인지 (아닌지)'라는 의미의 접속사 if를 이용한다.

01 ②   02 ④   03 ①

04 (1) where   (2) why   (3) where   (4) whether   (5) if

    (6) whether

05 ⑤   06 ③   07 ④   08 ⑤

09 where   10 ②   11 ①

12 (1) the time 또는 when   (2) the reason 또는 why

13 ④

14 (1) Sandra wonders if it will be fine tomorrow.

    (2) Whether he stays or goes doesn't matter that much.

    (3) That is the place where I buy food for the coming week.

    (4) The reason why he did it is complicated.

    (5) The way it was done was the best they could do at the time.

15 ⑤   16 ②, ③

17 Will you tell me if[whether] I still have a place in your heart?

01 선행사가 'the reason'이므로 관계부사 why가 적절하다.

02 '~인지 (아닌지)'라는 의미의 접속사 if[whether]를 쓰는 것이 적절하다. I asked her if[whether] she wanted to marry me, but she wouldn't answer.

03 첫 번째 빈칸에는 '~인지 (아닌지)'라는 의미의 접속사 if나 whether가 적절하다. 두 번째 빈칸에는 선행사가 the day이므로 관계부사 when이 적절하다.

04 (1) 선행사가 'the place'이므로 where가 적절하다. (2) 선행사가 'the reason'이므로 why가 적절하다. (3) 선행사인 'the restaurant' 다음에 나오는 절이 완전하므로 where가 적절하다. (4) 내용상 '~인지 (아닌지)'라는 의미의 접속사 whether가 적절하다. (5) 내용상 '~인지 (아닌지)'라는 의미의 접속사 if가 적절하다. (6) 뒤에 or not이 바로 이어서 나오고 있으므로 whether가 적절하다.

05 관계부사 how는 선행사 'the way'와 함께 쓸 수 없으므로 'the way'나 how만 써야 하며, 'the way in which'나 'the way that'으로 쓸 수 있다.

06 (A) 내용상 '~인지 (아닌지)'라는 의미가 자연스러우므로 if나 whether가 적절하고, (B) 바로 뒤에 or not이 나오므로 whether가 적절하다.

07 선행사가 'the house'이므로 when을 where로 고쳐야 한다.

08 동사의 목적어로 쓰인 명사절을 이끄는 접속사 if는 whether로 바꿔 쓸 수 있다.

09 'a country'를 선행사로 하는 관계부사 where가 적절하다.

10 시간을 선행사로 하는 관계부사를 고른다. ①, ⑤ 의문사 ③, ④ 접속사

11 '~인지 (아닌지)'라는 의미의 명사절을 이끄는 if나 whether가

적절하며 if는 바로 뒤에 or not을 붙여 쓰지 않는다. It이 가주어이고 whether절이 진주어인 구문이다.

12 선행사가 'the time', 'the place', 'the reason'처럼 일반적인 뜻을 나타낼 때 선행사나 관계부사를 생략할 수 있다.

13 '~인지 (아닌지)'라는 의미의 명사절을 이끄는 if는 바로 뒤에 'or not'을 붙여 쓰지 않는다.

14 (1) if가 wonders의 목적어로 쓰인 명사절을 이끌고 있는데 명사절에서는 미래시제를 현재시제로 쓸 수 없으므로 is를 will be로 고치는 것이 적절하다. (2) if가 이끄는 명사절이 주어 역할을 할 수 없으므로 Whether로 고치는 것이 적절하다. (3) 'coming week'이라고 나오고 있고 'the place'가 선행사이므로 when을 where로 고치는 것이 적절하다. (4) 'The reason'이 선행사이고 which 다음의 절이 완전하므로 which를 why로 고치거나 전치사 for를 which 앞이나 관계사절의 끝에 써 주어야 한다. why를 생략해도 좋다. (5) 'The way how'는 쓸 수 없으므로 how를 생략하거나 that이나 'in which'로 고쳐야 한다.

15 선행사가 'the beach'이므로 관계부사 where를 쓰거나 'to which'로 쓰는 것이 적절하다. We will never go back to the beach. + We went to the beach last year.

16 ② if는 전치사의 목적어로 쓰인 명사절을 이끌지 못한다. ③ 선행사가 'a place'이고 뒤의 절이 완전하므로 which를 where로 고치거나 at을 which 앞이나 관계사절의 끝에 써야 한다.

17 if[whether] 뒤에 오는 절은 의문사가 없는 간접의문문으로 'if[whether]+주어+동사'의 어순으로 쓴다.

01 (1) March 14 is the day when people around the world celebrate Pi Day.

    (2) School is the place where I learn, eat, and have fun with my friends.

    (3) Tell me the reason why you were late.

    (4) This is how he killed the big bear.

02 (1) Please let me know if the movie is fun.

    (2) Ask him if it is true.

    (3) I'm not sure if I can do this.

03 (1) I'm not sure if I can pass the exam.

    (2) Whether it will rain soon is important to farmers.

    (3) Penguin Snack is the place where students in my school like to go.

    (4) Don't forget the time when you should leave for the train.

04 (1) If → Whether   (2) if → whether   (3) if → whether

05 (1) if[whether] he can help her with that milk

    (2) how he would like his hair done

06 (1) I'm not sure if[whether] I should tell you the news.

(2) I don't know if[whether] he'll get better.

(3) Turkey is a country where East meets West.

07 (1) This is the bakery where Uncle Ben buys bread every Saturday. /
This is the bakery at which Uncle Ben buys bread every Saturday.

(2) The way he acts makes me mad. /
How he acts makes me mad. /
The way that he acts makes me mad.

08 (1) I am just considering whether to go or not.

(2) Please let me know if you'll be late tonight.

(3) The way (in which) he worked has left much to be desired.

(4) This is the hospital where I was born.

---

01 (1) 'the day'를 선행사로 하고 관계부사 when을 이용한다.
(2) 'the place'를 선행사로 하고 관계부사 where를 이용한다.
(3) 'the reason'을 선행사로 하고 관계부사 why를 이용한다.
(4) the way how로 쓰면 안 된다. how나 the way 중 어느 하나를 생략해야 한다.

02 '~인지 (아닌지)'라는 의미의 접속사로 쓰이는 if를 이용한다. if 뒤에 오는 절은 의문사가 없는 간접의문문으로 'if+주어+동사'의 어순으로 쓴다.

03 (1) if가 명사절을 이끌도록 한다. (2) Whether가 주어인 명사절을 이끌도록 한다. 주어로 쓰이므로 If를 쓸 수 없음에 유의한다. (3) 선행사가 'the place'이므로 관계부사 where를 쓴다. (4) 선행사가 'the time'이므로 관계부사 when을 이용한다.

04 (1) 문두에서 주어를 이끄는 역할을 하고 있으므로 If를 Whether로 고치는 것이 적절하다. (2) 바로 뒤에 or not이 나오고 있으므로 if를 whether로 고치는 것이 적절하다. (3) whether 다음에 to부정사를 쓸 수 있지만 if는 쓸 수 없다.

05 (1) 명사절을 이끄는 if나 whether를 이용한다. (2) 의문사 how가 있으므로 if나 whether가 아닌 의문사를 이용한다.

06 (1), (2) 명사절을 이끄는 if나 whether를 이용하여 두 문장을 연결한다. (3) 'a country'를 선행사로 하고 관계부사 where를 이용하여 두 문장을 연결한다.

07 (1) 선행사가 '장소'를 나타낼 때 관계부사는 where를 쓰며 여기서 where는 'at which'로 바꿔 쓸 수 있다. at을 관계절 끝에 쓸 수도 있다. (2) 선행사가 '방법'을 나타낼 때 관계부사는 how를 쓰며 이때 how와 함께 the way를 쓰지 않는다는 것을 주의한다. the way나 how 또는 the way that이나 the way in which를 쓴다.

08 (1) whether 다음에 to부정사를 쓸 수 있지만 if는 to부정사와 함께 쓰이지 않는다. (2) if가 이끄는 절이 명사절이므로 미래는 미래시제로 나타내야 한다. (3) The way와 how를 함께 쓰지

않는다. (4) 뒤에 완전한 절이 이어지므로 which를 where로 고치는 것이 적절하다. (which 앞에 in을 넣어도 됨.)

확인문제   p.80

1 T   2 F   3 T   4 F   5 T   6 F

확인문제   p.81

1 T   2 F   3 T   4 F   5 T   6 F

확인문제   p.82

1 T   2 F   3 T   4 F   5 T   6 F

 **교과서 확인학습 A**   p.83~85

01 Travel   02 I am

03 have been writing   04 share, with

05 Must-Visit   06 July

07 Visiting markets   08 places where

09 wonder whether, to discover

10 Grand Bazaar

11 where, long tradition of trade

12 a natural place for, like   13 was built

14 traded goods

15 much, largest covered market

16 under one roof   17 attracts

18 almost any imaginable

19 if, traditional Turkish symbol

20 traditional Turkish candy   21 Floating

22 traded goods

23 beginning of floating markets

24 With better road transportation

25 have come back, alive   26 markets is

27 crowded with   28 directly from boats

29 wonder if   30 If not

31 with a long fishing pole   32 The Netherlands

33 low lands

34 As, suggests, below sea level

35 Thus, to grow

36 therefore, no surprise   37 where, is housed

38 flower-filled   39 moved

40 around 20 million, corners   41 whether, just a few

42 how wholesale flower trading works

1 Leah's Travel Story

2 I am Leah.

3 I have been writing a travel blog since I was 18.

4 I go places and share my experiences with my readers.

5 Must-Visit Markets Around the World

6 July 15, 20**

7 Visiting markets is a good way to learn about the culture of a country.

8 Markets are places where you can meet people, learn history, and taste local food.

9 I wonder whether there is any better way to discover another culture.

10 1 Grand Bazaar, Turkey

11 Turkey is a country where East meets West, so it has a long tradition of trade.

12 It is a natural place for large markets like the Grand Bazaar.

13 The market was built in 1455 in Istanbul.

14 Back then, the market had two big buildings, and people traded goods like cloth and gold there.

15 Today the Grand Bazaar is much bigger, and it is the largest covered market in the world.

16 It has 64 streets and more than 4,000 shops under one roof.

17 The market attracts over 250,000 visitors every day.

18 You can buy almost any imaginable item there.

19 Extra Tip: Ask shop owners if they carry nazar boncuğu, a traditional Turkish symbol for good luck.

20 Also, if you want a nice snack, make sure to try lokum, a traditional Turkish candy.

21 2 Damnoen Saduak Floating Market, Thailand

22 In the past, Thai people traded goods on rivers.

23 This was the beginning of floating markets in Thailand.

24 With better road transportation, many floating markets disappeared.

25 Since the late 1960s, however, some of them have come back and kept the tradition alive.

26 Today, one of the most popular floating markets is Damnoen Saduak Floating Market.

27 It is always crowded with tourists from all over the world.

28 You can buy local foods and traditional gift items directly from boats.

29 Extra Tip: I wonder if you have ever had a meal on water.

30 If not, try noodles like pad thai.

31 The sellers will cook them on their boats and pass them to you with a long fishing pole.

32 3 Aalsmeer Flower Market, The Netherlands

33 The Netherlands means "low lands."

34 As the name suggests, about 70% of the country sits below sea level.

35 Thus, the Dutch built up the land, and one effective way to use it was to grow flowers and sell them.

36 It is, therefore, no surprise that the country has the largest flower market in the world: the Aalsmeer Flower Market.

37 The building where the market is housed is bigger than 120 soccer fields.

38 The market is busy with thousands of flower-filled carts.

39 They are moved mostly by electric-powered trucks.

40 Every day, around 20 million flowers are traded and shipped to all corners of the world.

41 Extra Tip: You may wonder whether you can buy just a few flowers at the market.

42 Sadly, you cannot, but you can see how wholesale flower trading works.

01 (A) is   (B) whether   (C) another   02 ②

03 ①, ④   04 ②   05 ①   06 ④

07 ②   08 floating markets   09 ③

10 Dutch   11 ⑤   12 ②   13 ③

14 ②, ⑤   15 Turkey   16 ④   17 ③

18 ③   19 road transportation

20 one of the most popular floating markets is Damnoen Saduak Floating Market.

21 ①, ④   22 ②   23 wholesale

24 which → where나 in which / housed → housed in

25 around 20 million flowers are traded and shipped to all corners of the world

26 ①   27 are → is   28 noodles like pad thai

29 (A) below   (B) thousands   (C) million

30 ④

01 (A) 주어가 동명사 Visiting이므로 단수 취급하여 is가 적절하다. (B) '~인지 아닌지' 모르겠다고 해야 하므로 whether가

15

적절하다. that: 의미적으로 확정된 사건이나 사실, 의견을 말할 때 쓴다. (C) '더 좋은 방법'이라고 해야 하므로 another가 적절하다. another: 또 하나(의), 다른, the other: 둘 중 다른 하나

02 위 글은 '여행 블로그'이다. ① (책·연극·영화 등에 대한) 논평[비평], 감상문, ③ 전기, ④ 요약, 개요, ⑤ 독후감

03 ⓐ와 ①, ④: 형용사적 용법, ②: 명사적 용법, ③, ⑤: 부사적 용법

04 비교급 강조: much, even, still, far, a lot(훨씬)

05 ①번 다음 문장의 The market에 주목한다. 주어진 문장의 the Grand Bazaar를 받고 있으므로 ①번이 적절하다.

06 Grand Bazaar는 노천 시장이 아니라, 세계에서 가장 큰 '지붕이 덮인' 시장이다. outdoor market: 노천 시장

07 ⓐ be crowded with: ~로 붐비다, ⓑ directly from boats: 배에서 직접

08 '사라진 수상 시장들'을 가리킨다.

09 이 글은 '도로 교통이 개선되면서 사라졌던 많은 수상 시장이 1960년대 후반부터 일부가 다시 생겨나 전통을 이어 가고 있다'는 내용의 글이므로, 주제로는 ③번 '태국 수상 시장의 복귀와 전통의 재유행'이 적절하다. revival: 부흥, 재유행, ④ tourist attraction: 관광 명소

10 the Dutch: 네덜란드 사람들

11 (A)와 ⑤: ~하듯이, ①, ③: [비례] ~함에 따라, ~할수록, ②, ④: [이유·원인] ~이므로, ~이기 때문에

12 주어진 문장의 therefore에 주목한다. ②번 앞 문장의 결과에 해당하는 내용을 연결하고 있으므로 ②번이 적절하다.

13 '네덜란드는 국가의 약 70%가 해수면보다 낮기 때문에 네덜란드 사람들은 땅을 지어 올렸고 그것을 사용하는 효과적인 방법으로 꽃을 재배하여 팔았으며, 세계에서 가장 큰 꽃 시장인 Aalsmeer 꽃 시장이 네덜란드에 있다'고 했으므로, 어울리는 속담으로는 '삶이 그대에게 레몬을 준다면, 레모네이드로 만들어라.(살면서 힘든 일이 있다고 해도 그것을 기회로 만들어라)', ① 예방이 치료보다 낫다. ② 급할수록 돌아가라, 급히 먹는 밥이 체한다, ④ 안 좋은 일은 겹쳐서 일어나기 마련이다[불운은 한꺼번에 닥친다], ⑤ 백지장도 맞들면 낫다.

14 'Turkey is a country.'와 'East meets West in the country.'를 합친 문장이므로, 빈칸에는 in which나 where가 적절하다.

15 '터키'를 가리킨다.

16 4,000: four thousand로 읽는다.

17 이 글은 '터키가 동양과 서양이 만나는 나라이고 오랜 교역의 전통을 가지고 있어서 Grand Bazaar 같은 대형 시장이 생겨나기에 자연스러운 곳'이라는 내용의 글이므로, 주제로는 ③번 '터키의 위치가 Grand Bazaar의 탄생을 이끌었다'가 적절하다. ⑤ ideal: 이상적인

18 앞에 나오는 내용과 상반되는 내용이 뒤에 이어지므로

however가 가장 적절하다. ② 게다가, 더욱이, ④ 그 결과, ⑤ 즉[말하자면]

19 '도로 교통'이 개선되면서, 많은 수상 시장이 사라졌다.

20 one of the 복수 명사: ~ 중의 하나

21 ⓑ와 ①, ④: 경험 용법, ② 완료 용법, ③, ⑤: 계속 용법

22 Damnoen Saduak 수상 시장이 언제 형성되었는지는 대답할 수 없다. ① It is one of the most popular floating markets. ③ Local foods and traditional gift items. ④ It is a noodle dish. ⑤ Yes.

23 wholesale: 도매의, 상인들에게 물건을 파는 것, 주로 소비자에게 되팔도록 다량으로

24 which 뒤의 the market is housed가 완전한 문장이므로 관계대명사 which를 관계부사 where 또는 in which로 고치거나, housed 뒤에 전치사 in을 첨가하는 것이 적절하다.

25 around: 약, are traded and shipped: 거래되어 운송된다n 30%'로 고치는 것이 적절하다. ③ three-fifths: 5분의 3

26 ⓐ from: ~에서 온, ⓑ with: ~로, ~을 써서[이용하여]

27 주어가 'one'이기 때문에, 동사를 is로 고치는 것이 적절하다

28 'pad thai와 같은 면 요리'를 가리킨다.

29 (A) 네덜란드는 '저지대'라는 뜻이기 때문에 이 나라의 약 70%가 해수면보다 '낮다'고 하는 것이 적절하므로 below가 적절하다. (B) thousands of: 수천의, thousand 앞에 특정한 수가 나오지 않는 경우에 사용 (two 등과 같이 숫자와 함께 thousand를 쓸 때에는 thousand 끝에 s를 붙이지 않음), (C) two, several 등과 함께 million을 쓸 때에는 million 끝에 s를 붙이지 않으므로 million이 적절하다.

30 이 글은 '네덜란드는 국가의 약 70%가 해수면보다 낮기 때문에 네덜란드 사람들은 땅을 지어 올렸고 그것을 사용하는 효과적인 방법으로 꽃을 재배하여 팔았으며, 세계에서 가장 큰 꽃 시장인 Aalsmeer 꽃 시장이 네덜란드에 있다'는 내용의 글이므로, 제목으로는 ④번 '네덜란드에 세계에서 가장 큰 꽃 시장이 있다고? 놀랄 일이 아니야!'가 적절하다. ② utilize: 활용[이용]하다

🦉 서술형 시험대비   p.94~95

01 have been writing   02 with

03 visiting markets

04 (1) Because Turkey[it] is a country where East meets West.

    (2) Because Turkey[it] has a long tradition of trade.

05 over   06 (A) two (B) goods   07 kept

08 (A) disappeared (B) alive (C) directly

09 (A) floating markets (B) on rivers

10 is housed

11 (A) below sea level (B) to grow flowers

01 18세 때에 여행 블로그를 쓰기 시작해서 지금도 쓰고 있는 것이 므로 '현재완료진행시제'로 쓰는 것이 적절하다.

02 share A with B: A를 B와 함께 쓰다, 공유하다

03 Leah는 '시장 방문'이 한 나라의 문화에 대해 배우는 좋은 방법이고 다른 문화를 발견하는 데에 더 좋은 방법이 있을지 모르겠다고 했으므로, 다른 문화를 발견하기에 '시장 방문'보다 더 좋은 방법을 찾는 것이 쉽지 않을 것이라고 생각한다고 하는 것이 적절하다.

04 터키는 동양과 서양이 만나는 나라이고, 그래서 오랜 교역의 전통을 가지고 있기 때문이다.

05 more than = over: ~ 이상

06 그것은 15세기 중엽에 이스탄불에 지어졌고 큰 건물 '두' 개로 이루어져 있었다. 그 시장에서 사람들은 직물이나 금 같은 '물건'을 사거나 팔거나 교환했다..

07 한 단어로 쓰라고 했으므로 have를 생략하고 kept로 써서 have come back과 병렬을 이루도록 하는 것이 적절하다.

08 (A) disappear는 수동태로 쓸 수 없으므로 disappeared가 적절하다. (B) live는 서술적 용법으로 쓸 수 없으므로 alive가 적절하다. (C) 배에서 '직접' 살 수 있다고 해야 하므로 directly가 적절하다. indirectly: 간접적으로

09 태국 '수상 시장'은 태국 사람들이 '강에서' 물건을 교환했던 전통으로부터 시작했고 오늘날, 가장 인기 있는 수상 시장 중 하나는 Damnoen Saduak 수상 시장이다.

10 '시장이 들어선 건물'이라고 해야 하므로 수동태로 쓰는 것이 적절하다.

11 네덜란드의 약 70%가 '해수면보다 낮아서' 네덜란드 사람들은 땅을 지어 올렸다. 그것을 사용하는 효과적인 방법은 '꽃을 재배하고' 파는 것이었고, 그것이 세계에서 가장 큰 꽃 시장의 결과를 가져왔다.

영역별 핵심문제
p.97~101

01 indirectly
02 ①
03 ⑤
04 ②
05 ⑤
06 (1) We have two local newspapers in our town.
  (2) The museum is always crowded with tourists.
  (3) There are some effective ways students can use social media for education.
07 (1) is crowed with (2) is busy with (3) are rich in
08 ⑤
09 ⑤
10 (A) gondre is rich in vitamins A and C
  (B) it also digests well
11 She wants him to tell her the best-before date of the milk.
12 Because she wants the milk that lasts longer.
13 She should drink it until June 11.

14 (D) → (B) → (C) → (E) → (A)
15 ⑤
16 ⑤
17 if[whether] she would go hiking with him
18 (1) I take the mid-term exam in the month.
  (2) You bought the shoes at the store yesterday.
  (3) She was so upset for the reason last night.
19 ⓔ, ⓖ
20 ①, ④ / ②, ③, ⑤
21 ④
22 make sure to try
23 ②
24 ③
25 Thai
26 With better road transportation, many floating markets disappeared.
27 ②
28 ②
29 ④

01 주어진 관계는 반의어 관계이다. directly 곧장, 직접적으로 – indirectly 간접적으로

02 세대에 걸쳐 전해지는 문화적 신념과 관습을 가리키는 말은 tradition(전통)이다.

03 주어진 문장의 last는 '지속하다'라는 의미로 쓰였으며 이와 같은 의미를 나타내는 것은 ⑤번이다. 나머지는 모두 '마지막의' 또는 '지난'의 의미를 나타낸다. election: 선거

04 notice는 동사로는 '알아차리다', 명사로는 '공지'를 뜻한다.

05 ⑤번 문장에서 house는 '거처를 제공하다'라는 의미로 쓰였다.

06 be crowded with: ~로 붐비다, effective: 효과적인, education: 교육

07 be crowded with: ~로 붐비다, 꽉 차다, be busy with: ~으로 바쁘다, be rich in: ~이 풍부하다

08 주어진 문장은 곤드레밥의 장점을 설명하고 있으므로 ⓔ번이 적절하다.

09 ⑤번을 제외한 나머지는 모두 궁금함을 표현하는 표현이다.

10 여자는 곤드레밥이 매우 마음에 들었다. 그녀는 곤드레가 비타민 A와 C가 풍부하여 건강에 좋다는 것을 알았다. 또한 곤드레는 소화가 잘 된다는 것을 알았다. 그래서 그녀는 약간의 곤드레를 사기로 결정했다.

11 할머니는 Brian이 그녀에게 우유의 유통 기한을 말해주길 원하신다.

12 할머니는 유통 기한이 더 긴 우유를 원하시므로 첫 번째 우유를 선택하지 않으셨다.

13 할머니는 우유를 6월 11일까지 마셔야 한다.

14 (D) 인사 및 궁금한 점 묻기 → (B) 특별한 장소를 찾고 있는지 질문 → (C) 대답 → (E) 장소 추천 → (A) 감사 표현

15 뒤에 나오는 절이 완전하므로 which를 why나 'for which'로 고쳐야 한다.

16 동사의 목적어로 쓰인 명사절을 이끄는 접속사 if는 whether로 바꿔 쓸 수 있다.

17 명사절을 이끄는 접속사 if나 whether를 이용하고 주절이 과거 시제이므로 will을 would로 써야 하는 것에 유의한다.

18 (1) when = in the month (2) where = at the store (3)

17

why = for the reason

19 ⓐ when → where ⓑ where → when ⓒ the way how → the way 또는 how 또는 the way that 또는 the way in which ⓓ which → why ⓕ if → whether

20 ⓐ와 ①, ④: [간접의문문을 이끌어 ~인지 (아닌지) (whether)], ⓒ와 ②, ③, ⑤: [가정·조건을 나타내어] 만약 ~이라면

21 ⓑ와 ④: (가게에서 물품을) 팔다, ① 나르다, 운반하다, ② 휴대하다, 지니다, ③ (신문·TV가) (기사를) 싣다, ⑤ 운반하다, 전하다

22 make sure to: 반드시 (~하도록) 하다[(~을) 확실히 하다]

23 위 글은 '여행 안내서'이다. brochure: (안내·광고용) 책자, ① 수필, ③ (특히 기계 등을 사면 따라 나오는) 설명서, ④ 독후감, ⑤ (신문·잡지의) 글, 기사

24 찜질방의 '부대시설들'은 알 수 없다. ① 찜질방, ② 삶은 달걀, ④ 13,000원, ⑤ 24시간

25 Thai people: 태국 사람들

26 With better road transportation: 도로 교통이 개선되면서

27 도로 교통이 개선되면서, 많은 수상 시장이 '사라졌다.'

28 앞의 내용의 결과가 나오고 있으므로 Thus가 가장 적절하다. ② 그러므로, ① 다시 말해서

29 ④ 시장이 들어선 건물이 축구장 120개보다 크다.

단원별 예상문제
p.102~105

01 ④	02 ②	03 ⑤
04 best-before date	05 ②	06 ⑤
07 ⓓ → wonder	08 ⑤	09 ③
10 ④	11 ③	

12 if[whether] he jogged this morning or not

13 ④

14 (1) I often go to the gallery where my mother works.
　(2) May I ask you the reason why you made that decision?
　(3) The pictures were taken on a holiday when we had a picnic together.

15 ④　　　16 (A) two　(B) bigger　　17 ⑤

18 If you haven't had a meal on water

19 ①, ③, ④

20 how wholesale flower trading works

21 filled[full] with[of]

22 Thousands of flower-filled carts　　23 ④

24 Because the writer can buy the items directly from the producers.

---

01 주어진 문장은 어떻게 갈 수 있는지에 대한 대답으로 적절하므로 (D)가 알맞다.

02 위 대화를 통해 안내원과 관광객의 대화라는 것을 알 수 있다.

03 위 대화를 통해 몇 시까지 정선 시장이 여는지는 알 수 없다.

05 할머니는 안경을 두고 오셨다.

06 (B)는 '지속하다'라는 동사로 쓰였으며 이와 같은 의미를 나타내는 것은 ⑤번이다. 나머지는 '마지막의'를 나타낸다.

07 wonder: 궁금해 하다, wander: 돌아다니다

08 여자가 곤드레밥에 얼마를 지불할지는 대화를 통해 알 수 없다.

09 ③번을 제외한 나머지는 모두 제안하는 표현이다.

10 Jane's dad는 Jane에게 가방을 사주겠다고 약속하지는 않았다.

11 ③번은 '만약 ~한다면'의 의미로 부사절을 이끄는 접속사로 쓰였지만 나머지는 모두 '~인지 아닌지'라는 의미로 명사절을 이끄는 접속사로 쓰였다.

12 명사절을 이끄는 접속사 if나 whether를 이용한다.

13 ① That's the way[how] the system works. ② I still remember the evening when we watched the sun go down. ③ The reason why she quit her job is not clear. ⑤ I'm not sure whether this will be enough food for the party.

14 (1) 'the gallery'를 선행사로 하여 관계부사 where를 쓴다. (2) 'the reason'을 선행사로 하여 관계부사 why를 쓴다. (3) 'a holiday'를 선행사로 하여 관계부사 when을 쓴다.

15 이 글은 '터키가 동양과 서양이 만나는 나라이고 오랜 교역의 전통을 가지고 있어서 Grand Bazaar 같은 대형 시장이 생겨나기에 자연스러운 곳'이라는 내용의 글이므로, 제목으로는 ④번 'Grand Bazaar, 터키의 위치의 자연스러운 산물'이 적절하다. ② feature: 특색, 특징

16 건물의 개수가 '2개'에서 1개로 줄었고, 건물의 규모가 예전보다 더 '커졌다.'

17 '교역 규모'는 알 수 없다. ① 터키는 동양과 서양이 만나는 나라이고 오랜 교역의 전통을 가지고 있어서 Grand Bazaar 같은 대형 시장이 생겨나기에 자연스러운 곳이었다. ② 1455년, ③ 터키의 이스탄불, ④ 직물이나 금

18 If not은 '여러분이 물 위에서 식사해 본 적이 없다면'의 뜻이다.

19 ⓑ와 ①, ③, ④: 동명사, ②, ⑤: 현재분사

20 간접의문문 순서인 '의문사(how)+주어(wholesale flower trading)+동사(works)'의 순서로 쓰는 것이 적절하다.

21 filled with = full of

22 '꽃이 가득 든 수천 개의 수레'를 가리킨다.

23 글쓴이가 '꽃'을 구입한다는 내용은 언급되어 있지 않다.

24 물건을 생산자에게서 직접 살 수 있기 때문이다.

01 She needs a tourist map of the town.

02 It opens every five days.

03 She'd like to try some local food.

04 (1) where / in[at] which / which, in[at]

   (2) when / in which / which, in

   (3) why / for which / which, for

05 (1) The valley was in the national park where lots of people came in summer.

   (2) Do you want to know the reason why he is so happy?

   (3) I'm curious if[whether] he'll tell the truth.

06 (1) The police officer is asking him if[whether] he saw the thief.

   (2) Children's Day is the holiday when I got lots of presents.

07 (A) covered   (B) attracts   (C) imaginable

08 (A) traditional Turkish symbol

   (B) traditional Turkish candy

09 (A) largest   (B) under one roof

10 In the past, Thai people traded goods on rivers.

11 By using a long fishing pole.

---

01 여자는 마을 관광 지도가 필요하여 관광 안내소에 방문하였다.

02 시장은 5일마다 열린다.

03 여자는 지역 음식을 먹어 보고 싶어한다.

04 관계부사는 '전치사+관계대명사(which)'로 바꿔 쓸 수 있으며, which를 쓸 때는 전치사를 which 바로 앞에 쓰거나 관계사절의 끝에 쓴다. (1) 'the park'가 선행사이므로 관계부사 where가 적절하다. where = in[at] which (2) 'the year'가 선행사이므로 관계부사 when이 적절하다. year에는 전치사 in을 쓰므로 when = in which (3) 'the reason'이 선행사이므로 관계부사 why가 적절하다. why = for which

05 (1) 'the national park'를 선행사로 하여 관계부사 where를 쓴다. (2) 'the reason'을 선행사로 하여 관계부사 why를 쓴다. (3) '~인지 (아닌지)'라는 의미의 명사절을 이끄는 접속사 if[whether]를 이용한다.

06 (1) '~인지 (아닌지)'라는 의미의 명사절을 이끄는 접속사 if[whether]를 이용한다. (2) 'the holiday'를 선행사로 하여 관계부사 when을 쓴다.

07 (A) '지붕이 덮인' 시장이라고 해야 하므로 covered가 적절하다. (B) 방문객을 '불러 모은다'고 해야 하므로 attracts가 적절하다. attack: 공격하다, attract: 끌어들이다, (C) '상상할 수 있는' 거의 모든 물건이라고 해야 하므로 imaginable이 적절하다. imaginable: 상상[생각]할 수 있는, imaginary: 상상에만 존재하는, 가상적인

08 *nazar boncuğu*는 행운을 기원하는 '터키의 전통 상징'이고,

*lokum*은 '터키의 전통 사탕'이다.

09 그곳은 세계에서 '가장 큰' 지붕이 덮인 시장이고 64개의 거리와 4,000개 이상의 상점이 '한 지붕 아래에' 있다. 매일 25만 명 이상의 방문객이 그곳을 방문한다.

10 '강에서 무역하던 전통'을 가리킨다.

11 '긴 낚싯대를 사용하여' 건네준다.

|모범답안|

01 (A) a tourist map of the town

   (B) the Tourist Information Office

   (C) Jeongseon Market   (D) foot

02 (A) a traditional Korean way to relax

   (B) rest on a hot floor or take a nap

   (C) chat with friends as you lie on the floor

   (D) boiled eggs   (E) about 13,000 won

   (F) 24 hours

01 (1) make sure to   (2) is crowded with

   (3) are good for   (4) make an appointment

   (5) take a nap

02 (1) producers   (2) coming   (3) pick   (4) suggest

   (5) translate   (6) attract

03 Do you want me to get you some water?

04 ②

05 (1) I use SNS to chat with my friends.

   (2) Why don't you take a nap?

   (3) my father and I have some things in common

06 I'm curious if you can visit my farm now.

07 She liked it very much.

08 She wants to buy some *gondre*.

09 It has vitamins A and C plentifully.

10 I wonder if there's a tourist map of the town.

11 ③   12 ③   13 ③   14 ④

15 (1) if[whether] it is open on Sundays

   (2) if[whether] there is any better way to discover another culture

   (3) where my parents met for the first time

16 (1) It is not certain if they will apologize when we meet again.

   (2) Can you tell me if[whether] they speak Chinese?

   (3) Please ask shop owners if[whether] they carry *nazar boncuğu*, a traditional Turkish symbol for good luck.

⑷ I know a country where people speak
Portuguese.

⑸ I still remember the evening when we watched
the sun go down.

17 ①, ③, ④, ⑦   **18** ④

19 과거에 태국 사람들이 강에서 물건을 교환한 것   **20** ②

21 (A) directly from boats   (B) boats

22 (A) The Netherlands   (B) mostly   (C) wholesale

23 ①, ③   **24** ③

25 (A) which   (B) where   (C) for   **26** ③

---

01 be good for: ~에 유익하다, be crowded with: ~으로 붐비다, take a nap: 낮잠을 자다, make sure to: 반드시 ~하다, make an appointment: 약속하다.

02 attract: 끌어들이다, translate: 번역하다, producer: 생산자, pick: 뽑다, coming: 다가오는, suggest: 제안하다

04 도움을 요청하는 말에 감사함을 표하는 것은 어색하다..

05 chat with:~와 잡담하다, take a nap: 낮잠을 자다, have in common: 공통점을 갖다

07 여자는 곤드레밥을 매우 좋아했다.

08 여자는 약간의 곤드레를 사고 싶어한다.

09 곤드레는 비타민 A와 C를 풍부하게 갖고 있다.

11 (B) mark는 동사로 '표시하다'를 뜻하며 이와 같은 의미로 쓰인 것은 ③번이다. ①번은 '점', ②번은 '점수, 등급', ④번은 남자 이름, ⑤번은 '표시'를 뜻한다.

12 정선 시장은 5일마다 열린다.

13 if는 'if or not'의 형태로 쓰이지 않으므로 if만 쓰거나 or not을 '~ or not.'의 형태로 문장의 뒷부분에 써야 한다.

14 ① how → where ② where → when ③ the way how → the way 또는 how ⑤ which → where

15 (1), (2) 의문사가 없는 간접의문에 쓰인 if[whether]이다. (3) 'the restaurant'을 선행사로 하는 관계부사 where를 쓰는 것이 적절하다.

16 (1) if가 명사절을 이끌고 있으므로 미래는 미래시제로 나타내야 한다. will apologize가 되어야 한다. (2) 의문사가 없는 간접의문문에 쓰인 if[whether]이다. (3) 명사절을 이끄는 접속사 if[whether]를 이용하는 것이 적절하다. (4) 관계사 뒤의 절이 완전하므로 관계부사 where로 쓰는 것이 적절하다. (5) 'the evening'을 선행사로 하여 관계부사 when만 쓰거나 'in which'로 쓰는 것이 적절하다.

17 ② which → where ⑤ or not → 삭제 ⑥ does → will do

18 주어진 문장의 It에 주목한다. ④번 앞 문장의 Damnoen Saduak Floating Market을 받고 있으므로 ④번이 적절하다.

19 앞 문장의 내용을 가리킨다.

20 ⓑ와 ②, ③, ⑤: 계속 용법, ①: 완료 용법, ④: 결과 용법

21 Damnoen Saduak 수상 시장에서 여러분은 '배에서 직접' 현지 음식과 전통 선물을 살 수 있을 뿐만 아니라 여러분의 '배'에

서 내리지 않고서도 pad thai 같은 면 요리를 먹을 수 있다.

22 (A) 복수형 국가 이름에는 the를 붙여야 하므로 The Netherlands가 적절하다. (B) '대부분, 주로' 전동 트럭에 의해 움직인다고 해야 하므로 mostly가 적절하다. most: 최대[최고](의), 대부분(의), mostly: 주로, 일반적으로, (C) 꽃이 '도매로' 어떻게 거래되는지를 볼 수 있다고 해야 하므로 wholesale이 적절하다. retail: 소매의, 소매상의, wholesale: 도매의

23 ⓐ와 ②, ④, ⑤: 명사적 용법, ①: 형용사적 용법, ③: 부사적 용법

24 이 글은 '네덜란드는 국가의 약 70%가 해수면보다 낮기 때문에 네덜란드 사람들은 땅을 지어 올렸고 그것을 사용하는 효과적인 방법으로 꽃을 재배하여 팔았으며, 또한 세계에서 가장 큰 꽃 시장인 Aalsmeer 꽃 시장이 네덜란드에 있다'는 내용의 글이므로, 주제로는 ③번 '지리적인 약점을 강점으로 바꾼 성공 이야기'가 적절하다.

25 (A) that은 계속적 용법으로 쓸 수 없으므로 which가 적절하다. (B) 뒤에 완전한 문장이 이어지므로 관계부사 where가 적절하다. (C) 뒤에 숫자가 나오므로 for가 적절하다. during+기간을 나타내는 명사

26 일일 전통 공예 체험 또는 다양한 문화 행사를 경험하는 비용이 얼마인지는 대답할 수 없다. ① We can experience the traditional type of house in Korea. ② It costs about 15,000 won. ④ They are mandu and noodles. ⑤ Yes.

A Slice of History

Reading

| 확인문제 | p.118 |

1 T 2 F 3 T 4 F 5 T 6 F

| 확인문제 | p.119 |

1 T 2 T 3 F 4 F 5 T 6 F

| 교과서 확인학습 A | p.120~121 |

01 Slice
02 What do you like
03 Though, disagree on
04 It is sold
05 such a favorite food
06 have been eating
07 on hot rocks
08 Records show
09 It is believed, to name
10 was not born until
11 before, brought, from
12 make them sick
13 In time
14 where
15 from near and far, at any time
16 slices of pizza
17 so, that, for
18 as, on the street
19 world's first pizza shop
20 tried
21 that she loved most, that showed, on
22 went on to become
23 became known, moved to
24 brought pizza with them, at the same time
25 opened its doors
26 almost everywhere
27 from place to place
28 while
29 share two things
30 begins with, a slice of history

| 교과서 확인학습 B | p.122~123 |

1 A Slice of History
2 What do you like on your pizza?

3 Though you may disagree on the best toppings, you will agree that it is now a global food.

4 It is sold in fast-food restaurants or on the street in most parts of the world.

5 How has pizza become such a favorite food around the world?

6 Since the Stone Age, people have been eating pizza in one form or another.

7 Stone Age people baked flat bread on hot rocks.

8 Records show that the Greeks and the Romans started to put meat and vegetables on flat bread.

9 It is believed that the word "pizza" was first used in Italy to name the food over 1,000 years ago.

10 However, pizza with tomato toppings was not born until the 16th century.

11 There were no tomatoes in Italy before Christopher Columbus and other Europeans brought them from the New World.

12 When they were first introduced to Europe, people thought that tomatoes would make them sick.

13 In time, people learned that tomatoes were delicious and healthy.

14 In the 18th century, Naples was a large city where there were many jobs.

15 Workers from near and far came to the city, and what they needed in their busy lives was food they could eat quickly at any time.

16 Cooks in Naples began to put tomato and other toppings on flat bread and sold slices of pizza on the street.

17 The street food was so cheap and delicious that workers ate it for breakfast, lunch, and dinner.

18 They could buy slices of pizza and eat them as they walked on the street.

19 In 1830, the world's first pizza shop opened in Naples.

20 In 1889, Queen Margherita of Italy visited Naples and tried pizza.

21 The type of pizza that she loved most had tomato, cheese, and green leaf toppings that showed the three colors on Italy's national flag—red, white, and green.

22 After the queen's visit, pizza went on to become a truly national dish.

23 Pizza became known outside of Italy in the late 19th century, when many Italians moved to the United States.

24 Italians brought pizza with them, and Americans loved the flat bread topped with meat and vegetables because they could eat bread, meat, and vegetables at the same time.

25 The first pizza restaurant in the United States opened its doors in 1905.

26 Pizza is now enjoyed almost everywhere.

27 Of course, toppings differ widely from place to place.

28 Koreans love *bulgogi* on their pizza, while Russians like to have fish and onion toppings on their pizza.

29 However, all types of pizza share two things.

30 Each begins with flat bread, and each is a slice of history.

서술형 실전문제　　　　　p.124~125

01 disagree

02 (1) a slice of　(2) Stone Age　(3) near and far
　　(4) at the same time

03 (1) flat　(2) onion　(3) truly

04 (1) I usually bake a cake in my free time.
　　(2) Are you drawing a national flag?
　　(3) We took pictures from place to place.

05 People have been eating pizza since the Stone Age.

06 so, that　　　　　07 As → Though[Although]

08 such a favorite food　09 not until

10 크리스토퍼 콜럼버스와 다른 유럽인들이 신세계에서 토마토를 가져오기 전까지 이탈리아에는 토마토가 없었기 때문이다.

11 that 또는 which

12 (1) red　(2) white　(3) green　　13 topped

14 (1) 모든 피자는 납작한 빵에서 시작했다.
　　(2) 모든 피자는 역사의 한 조각이다.

01 주어진 관계는 반의어 관계이다. agree: 동의하다, disagree: 의견이 다르다

02 at the same time: 동시에, Stone Age: 석기시대, near and far: 사방, 천지, a slice of: 한 조각의

03 flat: 납작한, 평평한, onion: 양파, truly: 진정으로

05 사람들이 석기시대에 피자를 먹기 시작하여 지금도 먹고 있으므로 현재완료진행시제로 쓸 수 있다. since를 사용함에 주의한다.

06 so ~ that ...: 너무 ~해서 …하다

07 '비록 제일 좋아하는 피자 토핑에 대해 의견이 다를 수 있지만, 피자가 오늘날 세계적인 음식이라는 데에는 모두 동의할 것이다.'라고 해야 하므로, Though[Although]로 고치는 것이 적절하다.

08 such+a+형용사+명사

09 not ~ until[till] ...: …까지는 ~하지 않다, …이 되어서야 비로소 ~하다, 'not until'을 문장 앞으로 도치시키면 'be동사+주어'의 순서로 쓰는 것이 적절하다.

10 'There were no tomatoes in Italy before Christopher Columbus and other Europeans brought them from the New World.'라고 되어 있다.

11 ⓐ에는 목적격 관계대명사 that 또는 which, ⓑ에는 주격 관계대명사 that 또는 which가 적절하다.

12 (1) tomato topping이 상징하는 국기의 색: 빨간색, (2) cheese topping이 상징하는 국기의 색: 하얀색, (3) green leaf topping이 상징하는 국기의 색: 초록색

13 'which was topped with ~'에서 주격 관계대명사와 be동사를 생략한 것이므로, 과거분사 topped로 쓰는 것이 적절하다.

14 마지막 문장의 내용을 쓰는 것이 적절하다.

단원별 예상문제　　　　　p.126~130

01 (1) top　(2) national　(3) differ　(4) flag　(5) flat

02 ①　　　03 ①　　　04 ④　　　05 ③

06 (1) Now people enjoy pizza with different toppings all around the world.
　　(2) Visitors came from near and far to enjoy the local culture.

07 ⑤　　　08 ③

09 (1) That is the reason (why) I am angry with you.
　　(2) Wednesday is the day when I look ugliest.
　　(3) I want to know if[whether] she can sleep in this noisy place.
　　(4) He has not been practicing dancing since last Friday.
　　(5) She felt too hungry to keep walking.
　　(6) He danced so well that he won (the) first prize.

10 ②　　　11 why　　　12 ④

13 (1) I know a country where people speak Portuguese.
　　(2) Scientists studied the way(또는 how) those birds could fly so high up in the sky.
　　(3) We all know the reason why he failed.
　　(4) Do you remember the moment when you decided to become a singer?

14 ①　　　15 didn't　　　16 Italy's national flag

17 (A) How　(B) Since　(C) is believed

01 flag: 깃발, flat: 납작한, 평평한, differ: 다르다, national: 국가의, top: 얹다

02 무언가를 표면 위에 올려놓다는 'top(얹다)'이다.

03 flat: 평평한, 바람이 빠진, 펑크 난

04 topping: (음식 위에 얹는) 토핑

05 주어진 문장에서 record는 '기록'을 뜻하며 이와 같은 의미로 쓰인 것은 ③번이다. 나머지는 모두 '녹음하다'를 의미한다.

06 topping: (음식 위에 얹는) 토핑, local: 지역의, near and far: 사방, 천지

07 ⑤번은 '조건'을 나타내는 접속사 if가 적절하고 나머지는 모두 '~인지 (아닌지)'라는 의미의 명사절을 이끄는 접속사 if가 적절하다.

08 관계부사 how는 선행사 'the way'와 함께 쓸 수 없으므로 'the way'나 how만 써야 하며, 'the way in which'나 'the way that'으로도 쓸 수 있다.

09 (1) 선행사가 time, place, reason처럼 일반적인 뜻을 나타낼 때 선행사나 관계부사를 생략할 수 있다. (2) 선행사가 the day 이므로 관계부사 when을 쓴다. (3) 명사절을 이끄는 접속사 if[whether]를 이용한다. (4) 현재완료진행의 부정문을 이용한다. (5) 'so ~ that 주어 can't ... = too ~ to ...: 너무 ~해서 ...할 수 없다' 구문을 이용한다. (6) 'so ~ that ...: 너무 ~해서 ...하다' 구문을 이용한다.

10 ② She was so kind that everyone likes her.

11 선행사가 the reason이므로 관계부사 why가 적절하다

12 ① what → that[which] ② they 삭제 ③ the things what → the things that 또는 the things 삭제 ⑤ that → what

13 (1) 'a country'를 선행사로 하고 관계부사 where를 쓴다. (2) 'the way'만 쓰거나 'the way' 대신 how를 쓴다. (3) 'the reason'을 선행사로 하고 관계부사 why를 쓴다. (4) 'the moment'를 선행사로 하고 관계부사 when을 쓴다.

14 두 번째 빈칸 다음에 '주어+동사'의 절이 나오고 있으므로 원인과 결과를 나타내는 'so ~ that ...' 구문이 적절하다.

15 '왕비의 방문 이후로 피자는 진정한 이탈리아의 국가 음식이 되었다'는 말은 '왕비가 방문할 때까지는 피자가 진정한 이탈리아의 국가 음식이 되지 못했다'는 것과 같은 의미이다. not ~ until[till] ...: ...까지는 ~하지 않다, ...이 되어서야 비로소 ~하다

16 마르게리타 왕비가 가장 좋아했던 피자는 '이탈리아 국기'의 세 가지 색깔인 빨강, 하양, 초록을 나타낸 토마토, 치즈, 녹색 잎

채소 토핑으로 된 것이었다.

17 (A) '어떻게 해서 피자가 세계적으로 그토록 사랑받는 음식이 되었을까?'라고 해야 하므로 How가 적절하다. (B) '석기시대부터'라고 해야 하므로 Since가 적절하다. For: ~ 동안, Since: ~부터, (C) '~라고 알려져 있다'고 해야 하므로 is believed가 적절하다.

18 ⓐ와 ②, ③, ⑤: 부사적 용법, ①, ④: 명사적 용법

19 석기시대부터 사람들은 '여러 가지 형태로' 피자를 먹어 왔다.

20 not ~ until[till] ...: ...까지는 ~하지 않다, ...이 되어서야 비로소 ~하다

21 ⓑ 토마토, ⓒ 사람들

22 '크리스토퍼 콜럼버스와 다른 유럽인들이 신세계에서 가져오기 전까지 이탈리아에는 토마토가 없었다.'는 말은 '크리스토퍼 콜럼버스와 다른 유럽인들이 신세계에서 가져온 뒤에야 이탈리아에 토마토가 있게 되었다'는 뜻이므로 'after'를 쓰는 것이 적절하다.

23 (A) 뒤에 완전한 문장이 나오므로 관계부사 where가 적절하다. (B) 'they needed in their busy lives'가 불완전한 문장이므로 관계대명사를 써야 하는데 앞에 선행사가 없으므로, 선행사를 포함하는 관계대명사 what으로 쓰는 것이 적절하다. (C) 뒤에 명사가 없으므로 so가 적절하다. 'so+형용사+that' 구문: 너무 ~해서 ...하다

24 주어진 문장의 They에 주목한다. ④번 앞 문장의 'workers'를 받고 있으므로 ④번이 적절하다.

25 이 글은 '18세기에 다양한 직업이 존재하는 대도시 나폴리로 모여든 노동자들이 빨리 먹을 수 있도록 요리사들이 피자를 만들었다'는 내용의 글이므로, 제목으로는 ③번 '나폴리, 피자의 고향'이 적절하다.

26 앞에 나오는 내용과 상반되는 내용이 뒤에 이어지므로 However가 가장 적절하다. ① 그 결과, ③ 예를 들면, ④ 그러므로, ⑤ 다시 말해서

27 (A)와 ⑤: ~인 반면에 (부사절을 이끄는 접속사, 둘 사이의 대조를 나타냄). ①, ④: ~하는 동안, ② ~하는 한(as long as), ③ (짧은) 동안, 잠깐, 잠시(명사)

28 이 글은 '오늘날 피자는 어디에서나 즐길 수 있고 모든 피자는 역사의 한 조각이다'라는 내용의 글이므로, 주제로는 ④번 '전 세계적인 음식이자 역사의 한 조각으로서의 피자'가 적절하다.

Are You into Books?

시험대비 실력평가　p.134

01 independence　02 ④　03 ②
04 ②
05 (1) poet　(2) author[writer]　(3) publication
　(4) hometown　(5) turn　06 ④

01 주어진 관계는 반의어 관계이다. dependence: 의존, independence: 독립

02 나머지는 모두 동사와 명사로 짝지어져 있지만 ④번은 동사-형용사로 짝지어져 있다.

03 '무언가를 원하는 강한 감정'을 가리키는 말은 longing(동경, 갈망)이다.

04 look forward to~: ~을 기대하다

05 poet: 시인, poetry: 시, publication:출판, hometown: 고향, turn on: 켜다

06 주어진 문장과 나머지는 '표현하다'를 나타내지만 ④번은 '급행'을 나타낸다.

서술형 시험대비　p.135

01 borrow　02 hometown
03 (1) in a hurry　(2) by hand　(3) hang out with
04 (1) independence　(2) charge　(3) further
　(4) shine　(5) graduation
05 (1) Hong Kong gained independence from the UK in 1997.
　(2) I need to check my pictures before I publish my novel.
　(3) The forest is home to some rare insects and plants.
06 (1) The graduation ceremony is being held in the gym now.
　(2) The punishment was harsh and unfair.
　(3) I arrest you in the name of the law.

01 주어진 관계는 반의어 관계이다. borrow: 빌리다, lend: 빌려주다

02 '누군가가 태어나 자란 마을'을 가리키는 말은 hometown(고향)이다.

03 in a hurry: 서둘러, by hand 손으로, hang out with ~와 시간을 보내다

04 further: 더, 더 멀리; 더 이상의, independence: 독립, charge: 기소, 혐의, graduation: 졸업, shine: 빛나다

05 independence: 독립, publish: 출판하다, rare: 희귀한

06 graduation ceremony: 졸업식, punishment: 처벌, harsh: 가혹한, arrest: 체포하다

Conversation

핵심 Check　p.136~137

1 ②　　　　2 ②

교과서 대화문 익히기

Check(√) True or False　p.138

1 T　2 T　3 T　4 F

교과서 확인학습　p.140~141

Listen – Listen & Answer Dialog 1
Long, no, brings / a book report, recommend / about / show me / New Arrivals, popular / check, out / borrow

Listen – Listen & Answer Dialog 2
novel, book report / me see / borrowed / big fan, all / stop reading / what, has been made / interesting / come out, looking forward to seeing / together

Listen more – Listen and complete
Take a seat, How would you like / yearbook, cool / take / particular, mind / recommend / look good on / can't wait to see / sure

My Speaking Portfolio
real name / where you're from / usually / short story writer / special / well known for / recommend, surprise ending / recommend / who saves her life / can't wait

시험대비 기본평가　　　　　　　p.142

01 ⑤　　　　　　02 ①

03 She can't wait for the concert.

04 They will go to the Thunder concert this Friday.

01 ⑤번은 주문을 확인하겠다는 표현이며, 나머지는 모두 주문할 것인지 묻는 표현이다.

02 ①번을 제외한 나머지는 모두 추천해 주는 표현이다.

03 can't wait for 명사: ~이 너무 기대되다

04 James와 엄마는 이번 주 금요일에 Thunder 콘서트에 갈 것이다.

시험대비 실력평가　　　　　　　p.143~144

01 Can you recommend a good novel to read?

02 ⓐ Ken Kuller　ⓑ 22nd Street

03 ⑤　　　　　　04 ②

05 It'll come out next Thursday.　　06 ⑤

07 ⓔ seeing → to see　　08 ⑤

09 (A) you are　(B) known　(C) saves　　10 ⑤

03 대화의 내용으로 보아 학생과 사서 선생님과의 대화라는 것을 알 수 있다.

04 주어진 문장은 Ken Kuller를 아는지에 대한 대답으로 적절하므로 (B)에 들어간다.

06 ⑤번을 제외하고 모두 기대감을 표현한다.

07 can't wait to+동사원형

08 지호가 새로운 스타일을 보기 위해 얼마나 기다려야 할지는 알 수 없다.

09 (A)는 간접 의문문으로 '의문사+주어+동사' 어순으로 이어져야 한다. (B) be well known for: ~로 유명하다, (C) who가 가리키는 선행사가 an old artist이므로 saves가 적절하다.

10 O. Henry의 '마지막 잎새'를 추천한 이유는 뜻밖의 결말 때문이다.

서술형 시험대비　　　　　　　p.145

01 She recommends a new Ken Kuller book, *22nd Street*.

02 He can find it out in the "New Arrivals" area.

03 (A) the yearbook　(B) Dream & Joy Park

　　(C) to recommend a hairstyle for him

　　(D) seeing how he'll look in the pictures

　　(E) Jiho will look cool

04 (D) → (A) → (C) → (E) → (B)

01 서 선생님은 민준에게 Ken Kuller의 새 책, 22nd street을 추천한다.

02 민준은 '신착 도서' 서가에서 찾을 수 있다.

03 지호는 미용사, Mike에게 갔다. 지호는 금요일에 Dream & Joy Park에서 졸업 앨범을 위해 사진을 찍을 것이다. 지호는 마음에 둔 스타일이 없어서 마이크에게 헤어스타일을 추천해 줄 것을 요청했다. Mike는 하나를 제안했다. 지호는 그가 어떻게 사진에서 보일지 기대하고 있다. Mike는 지호가 멋있어 보일 것이라 확신했다.

04 (D) Ken Kuller에 대한 의견 표현 → (A) Ken Kuller의 소설이 영화로 만들어졌다고 소개 → (C) 영화에 대한 생각 표현 → (E) 영화 개봉일 설명 및 기대감 표현 → (B) 기대 표현에 대한 반응

교과서
Grammar

핵심 Check　　　　　　　p.146~147

1 (1) had just occurred　(2) had got　(3) met

2 (1) It　(2) that　(3) whom

시험대비 기본평가　　　　　　　p.148

01 ⑤

02 (1) had already left　(2) had been called

　　(3) It　(4) who　　　　　　03 ④

04 (1) I lost the backpack that I had bought two weeks before.

　　(2) He realized that he had lost the keys.

　　(3) It is the movie that everybody is talking about.

01 주절의 동사가 said로 과거이고 친구를 만난 것은 그 이전의 사실이므로 과거완료(대과거)를 써야 한다.

02 (1) 귀가한 것보다 그가 떠난 것이 앞서는 것이므로 과거완료가 적절하다. (2) 징집되었음(앞선 사실)을 말하는 것이므로 과거완료가 적절하다. (3) 'It+is/was+강조어(구)+that ...'의 형태로 특정 부분을 강조하여 나타낼 때 사용한다. That이 아닌 It이 적절하다. (4) 강조되는 어구가 사람으로 주격일 때는 that 대신에 who를 쓸 수 있다.

03 'It ~ that 강조 구문'은 'It is/was ~ that ...'의 형태로, 강조하고자 하는 부분을 'It is/was'와 that 사이에 넣고, 나머지 부분을 that 뒤에 써서 주어, 목적어인 명사, 부사(구/절) 등을 강조한다. that이 들어가는 것이 적절하다.

04 (1) 잃어버린 것보다 배낭을 산 것이 앞서므로 과거완료를 이용

한다. (2) 안 것보다 잃어버린 것이 앞서므로 과거완료로 나타낸다. (3) 'It ~ that 강조 구문'은 'It is/was ~ that ...'의 형태로, 강조하고자 하는 부분을 'It is/was'와 that 사이에 넣고, 나머지 부분을 that 뒤에 쓴다.

01 ②　　　　02 ③　　　　03 ①

04 (1) had ever made　(2) had presented
　　(3) had lived　(4) who　(5) when　(6) where

05 ④　　　06 ③　　　07 ⑤　　　08 ③

09 ④　　　10 ①　　　11 ②

12 Sherill found the box that Adam had hidden a
　　week before.

13 had played　　　　14 ②　　　　15 ③

16 (1) I looked at something I had never seen before.
　　(2) He remembered what he had read.
　　(3) It was the lamp that[which] someone broke in
　　　　the room.
　　(4) It was when Mike told his wife something that
　　　　she realized her mistake.
　　(5) It is in the school gym that we play basketball
　　　　every Saturday.

17 ④

01 ② She strongly insisted that she had not been there.

02 ③ 'It ~ that 강조 구문'은 동사를 강조하는데는 쓰이지 않는다.

03 첫 번째 빈칸에는 'It ~ that 강조 구문'으로 that 또는 which가 적절하다. 두 번째 빈칸에는 말한 시점인 과거보다 그전날 밤에 끝낸 것이 앞서므로 과거완료가 적절하다.

04 (1) 그때까지 계속해서 한 연설이므로 과거완료가 적절하다. (2) 목걸이를 찬 시점보다 사 준 시점이 앞서므로 'had presented'가 적절하다. (3) since(~이래로)가 있으므로 '1957년 이래로 살아왔다'는 'had lived'가 적절하다. (4) 강조하는 것이 Kate로 사람이므로 who가 적절하다. (5) 강조하는 것이 시간을 나타내는 부사 yesterday이므로 when이 적절하다. (6) 강조하는 것이 장소를 나타내는 부사구 'in the library'이므로 where가 적절하다.

05 말한 시점(과거)보다 살았던 것이 앞설 때 과거완료로 나타낸다.

06 ③ have met → had met

07 (A)에는 'It ~ that 강조 구문'으로 that이 적절하고, (B)에는 그가 지금까지 많은 책을 써 온 것이므로 현재완료가 적절하다.

08 <보기>와 ③번은 강조 용법의 that이다. ① 부사. (강조를 나타내어) 그렇게, 그 정도. 나는 그렇게 멀리 걸을 수가 없다. ② 대명사 [앞서 말한 명사의 반복을 피하기 위해] (~의) 그것. 중국에 있는 한 도시의 전체 인구는 한국의 세 개 도시의 전체 인구보다 더 많다. ③ 영어를 진정 문학적인 언어로 바꿔 놓은 이는

바로 Chaucer였다. ④ 접속사. [목적어를 이끌어] ~하다는[이라는] 것을. 네가 외국에 갔다온 것을 들었다. ⑤ 지시형용사. 저기 있는 저 남자 한번 봐.

09 집에 온 것보다 방을 청소한 것이 앞서므로 과거완료가 적절하다.

10 'It ~ that 강조 구문'은 강조하고자 하는 부분을 'It is/was'와 that 사이에 넣고, 나머지 부분을 that 뒤에 쓴다.

11 'It ~ that 강조 구문'은 강조하고자 하는 부분을 'It is/was'와 that 사이에 넣고, 나머지 부분을 that 뒤에 쓴다.

12 '찾은 것(과거)'보다 '숨긴 것'이 앞서는 시제이므로 과거완료로 나타낸다.

13 8살에 축구하기 시작했으므로 8살 이래로 축구해 왔다고 과거완료로 나타낼 수 있다.

14 ②번은 'It: 가주어, that절: 진주어'이고, 나머지는 모두 'It ~ that 강조 용법'으로 쓰였다.

15 <보기>는 계속적 용법이다. ① 완료, ② 경험, ③ 계속, ④ 결과, ⑤ 대과거

16 (1) 완료시제와 어울리는 것은 ago가 아니라 before이다. (2) 읽은 것을 기억했던 것이므로 'had remembered'를 remembered로, read를 'had read'로 고치는 것이 적절하다. (3) 강조하는 것이 'the lamp'이므로 who를 that이나 which로 고치는 것이 적절하다. (4) 강조하는 것이 'when Mike told his wife something'이므로 which를 that으로 고치는 것이 적절하다. (5) that 다음에 완전한 절이 나오므로 'the school gym'을 강조하는 것이 아니라 'in the school gym'으로 장소의 부사구를 강조하는 것으로 고치는 것이 적절하다.

17 '세상 사람 누구도 본 적이 없는'이라는 의미로 그때까지의 경험을 나타내는 과거완료를 이용한다.

01 had bought for me

02 (1) It was *gimbap* that Joanne ate for lunch.
　　(2) It is on Saturdays that I take a swimming
　　　　lesson.
　　(3) The police officer said Mr. Green had driven
　　　　through a red light.
　　(4) We had had that car for 15 years before it
　　　　broke down.

03 (1) He had never studied English before he went
　　　　to London.
　　(2) Daniel had never been to London until he met
　　　　Jane.
　　(3) He took items that he had given to Carolyn and
　　　　gave them to Dora.
　　(4) It was her wallet that[which] Judy lost on the
　　　　bus.

(5) It was on a small island that I was born.

(6) He drove his car carefully.

04 (1) had already broken　(2) It was a ladybug

05 (1) had opened　(2) had already left

06 (1) It was my brother who bought the cake at the store last night.

(2) My brother did buy the cake at the store last night.

(3) It was the cake which my brother bought at the store last night.

(4) It was at the store where my brother bought the cake last night.

(5) It was last night when my brother bought the cake at the store.

07 (1) It was at the age of six that[when] I learned how to read and write.

(2) It is my dad that[who] gets up earliest in my family.

(3) It is an egg sandwich that[which] I eat when I feel blue.

(4) Was it Nick that I saw at the bookstore?

01 과거보다 앞선 시제에 일어난 것을 나타내는 과거완료를 이용한다.

02 (1) 목적어 '김밥'을 강조하는 'It ~ that 강조 용법'을 이용한다.
(2) 시간을 나타내는 부사구 'on Saturdays'를 강조하는 'It ~ that 강조 용법'을 이용한다. (3) 경찰관이 말한 것을 과거시제로 하고 Green 씨가 빨간 신호등을 무시하고 운전한 것을 과거완료로 나타낸다. (4) 그 차가 고장 난 것을 과거시제로 하고 우리가 15년 동안 소유한 것을 과거완료로 나타낸다.

03 (1) 그가 런던에 가기 전에 일어난 일이므로 과거완료시제가 적절하다. (2) 그가 Jane을 만나기 전의 일이므로 과거완료로 고치는 것이 적절하다. (3) Carolyn에게 주었던 것을 Dora에게 준 것이므로 'had given'으로 고치는 것이 적절하다. (4) 강조하는 것이 'her wallet'이므로 who를 that이나 which로 고치는 것이 적절하다. (5) 'where I was born'이 완전한 절이므로 'a small island'를 강조하는 것이 아니라 'on a small island'로 장소의 부사구를 강조하는 것으로 고치는 것이 적절하다. (6) 'It ~ that ...' 강조 구문은 동사나 양태부사를 강조하는 데 쓰이지 않는다.

04 (1) 과거보다 앞서는 일이나 상태를 나타내는 과거완료(대과거)를 이용한다. (2) 목적어 'a ladybug'를 강조하는 'It ~ that 강조 용법'을 이용한다.

05 (1) 과거완료의 대과거 용법을 이용한다. (2) 과거완료의 결과 용법을 이용한다.

06 과거시제이므로 강조하고자 하는 부분을 It was와 that 사이에 넣고, 나머지 부분을 that 뒤에 쓴다. 이때 that을 사용하지 말라고

하였으므로, that 대신에 강조하고자 하는 것이 사람이면 who, 사물이면 which, 장소일 경우 where, 시간일 경우 when을 사용한다. 또한 'It is[was] ~ that ...' 구문은 동사를 강조할 수 없으므로 동사는 동사 앞에 do/does/did를 사용하여 강조한다.

07 'It ~ that 강조 구문'은 강조하고자 하는 부분을 'It is/was'와 that 사이에 넣고, 나머지 부분을 that 뒤에 쓴다. (4)번은 평서문으로 고친 후 강조 용법으로 쓰고 그것을 다시 의문문으로 바꾸면 쉽다.

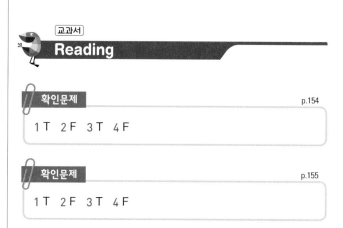

교과서
Reading

확인문제　　　　　　　　　　　　p.154

1 T　2 F　3 T　4 F

확인문제　　　　　　　　　　　　p.155

1 T　2 F　3 T　4 F

교과서 확인학습 A　　　　　　p.156~158

01 Who
02 where, in a hurry
03 fills
04 without a worry
05 count
06 Memory
07 another
08 Loneliness
09 Longing
10 for
11 for another star
12 these lines
13 part of, by
14 still remains, poems
15 was born
16 for his school
17 so, that
18 it was, that
19 a lot of poems
20 a literary magazine
21 copied, by hand
22 to have his own copy
23 to be a doctor
24 hung out with, where, lost country
25 To celebrate his graduation, under the title
26 three copies, by hand
27 was given to, another, the last one
28 advised against
29 followed, gave up
30 to study further, had studied
31 began to study
32 for taking part in
33 on the same charges
34 after harsh treatment
35 It was, that
36 they were finally published
37 was given, had thought of
38 are loved by, like

27

1 A Poet Who Loved Stars

2 In the sky where seasons pass in a hurry

3 Autumn fills the air.

4 And ready I stand, without a worry,

5 To count all the stars there.

6 Memory for one star,

7 Love for another star,

8 Loneliness for another star,

9 Longing for another star,

10 Poetry for another star,

11 And, oh, mother, mother for another star.

12 Have you read these lines before?

13 They are part of the poem "Counting Stars at Night" by Yoon Dong-ju.

14 The poem was written a long time ago but still remains one of Korea's favorite poems.

15 Dong-ju was born in 1917 near Yanbin, China.

16 As a young boy, he loved sports, and he was a soccer player for his school.

17 He also loved sewing so much that he sewed the numbers on all his friends' soccer uniforms.

18 However, it was literature that he loved most.

19 In elementary school he wrote a lot of poems.

20 He even made a literary magazine with his cousin, Song Mong-gyu.

21 In middle school he once borrowed a poetry book by a famous poet of the time, Baek Seok, and copied the whole book by hand.

22 He really wanted to have his own copy of the rare book.

23 His parents wanted him to be a doctor, but Dong-ju chose to study literature at a college in Seoul.

24 During his college years, he often hung out with other young poets and wrote poetry where he expressed feelings about his hometown and lost country.

25 To celebrate his graduation, he wished to publish 19 of his poems under the title, *Heaven, Wind, Stars, and Poetry*.

26 He made three copies of the book by hand.

27 One was given to his close friend, Jeong Byeong-uk, another was presented to his favorite professor, and the last one was kept for himself.

28 However, his professor advised against his plan because he thought the Japanese government would not allow the publication.

29 Dong-ju followed his advice and gave up the idea.

30 Dong-ju decided to study further in the country where his father had studied before.

31 So, in 1942, Dong-ju and his cousin began to study in Japan.

32 On July 10 the following year, his cousin was arrested by the Japanese police for taking part in an independence movement.

33 Four days later, Dong-ju was also arrested on the same charges.

34 In 1945, Dong-ju and his cousin died in prison after harsh treatment by the police.

35 It was just a few months later that Korea achieved independence from Japan.

36 In 1948, Jeong Byeong-uk brought Dong-ju's poems to the poet's brother, and they were finally published.

37 The book was given the title the poet had thought of many years before.

38 His poems are loved by people of all ages, and thus they still shine brightly in our hearts like the stars in the autumn night sky.

01 ②   02 ①, ④

03 favorite poem → favorite poems

04 ①, ③   05 (A) During   (B) other   (C) another

06 under the title, *Heaven, Wind, Stars, and Poetry*

07 ④   08 (A) poems   (B) a literary magazine

09 ⑤   10 in which   11 ③

12 participating in   13 sewing 또는 to sew

14 ③   15 ④   16 ②

17 ⑤   18 studying → to study

19 ③   20 ⓑ In 번 → On   21 ⑤

22 ③

01 ⓐ in a hurry: 서둘러, ⓑ by: ~에 의한(저자를 나타낼 때 사용)

02 (A)와 ①, ④: 경험 용법, ②, ⑤: 계속 용법, ③: 완료 용법

03 one+of+복수명사: ~ 중의 하나

04 동주가 그의 계획에 반대하는 교수의 충고를 따랐다고 했으므로, 그 생각을 '포기했다'고 하는 것이 적절하다. abandon = give up: 포기하다, ②, ⑤: 제의[제안]했다, ④ 설명했다

05 (A) during+기간을 나타내는 명사, while+주어+동사, (B) 뒤에 복수명사인 young poets가 나오므로 other가 적절하다. another+단수명사, (C) 책 세 부 중에 두 번째에 해당하므로 another가 적절하다. (세 개의 대상을 가리킬 때 하나는 one,

또 하나는 another, 나머지 하나는 the other나 the last one, the rest 등으로 쓴다.), the other: 둘 중에서 나머지 하나를 가리킴.

06 under the title: ~의 제목으로

07 ⓐ와 ④: ~일 때, ① ~한 대로, ② ~이기 때문에, ③ ~하다시피[~하듯이], ⑤ [보통 as ~ as ...로 형용사·부사 앞에서] …와 같은 정도로, 마찬가지로, (as ~ as …에서, 앞의 as가 지시부사, 뒤의 as는 접속사)

08 동주는 초등학교에 다닐 때 많은 '시'를 썼고, 심지어 사촌 송몽규와 '문학잡지'를 만들기도 했다.

09 동주가 필사한 시집의 제목이 무엇이었는지는 대답할 수 없다. ① He was born in 1917. ② He loved soccer. ③ Because he loved sewing so much. ④ In elementary school.

10 관계부사 where는 '전치사+관계대명사(in which)'로 바꿔 쓸 수 있다.

11 ⓑ와 ③: 혐의(명사), in court: 법정에서, ① (상품·서비스에 대한) 요금(명사), ② 충전하다(동사), ④ 비난하다, 고소[고발]하다(동사), prosecutor: 검사, ⑤ (요금, 값을) 청구하다(동사)

12 글그들은 독립운동에 '가담했다'는 이유로 일본 경찰에게 체포되었다. take part in = participate in: ~에 참가하다

13 love는 목적어로 to부정사와 동명사를 둘 다 쓸 수 있다.

14 주어진 문장의 However에 주목한다. ③번 앞 문장에서 바느질하는 것을 무척 좋아한다고 한 다음에, '그러나' 그가 가장 사랑한 것은 문학이었다고 해야 하므로 ③번이 적절하다.

15 동주는 '초등학교'에 다닐 때 사촌 송몽규와 문학잡지를 만들었다.

16 그의 교수는 일본 정부가 출판을 허가하지 않으리라 여겨, 그의 계획에 '반대하는' 충고를 했다고 하는 것이 적절하다. against: ~에 반대하여

17 ⑤의 his는 동주가 가장 좋아하는 교수를 가리키고, 나머지는 다 동주를 가리킨다.

18 choose는 to부정사를 목적어로 취하기 때문에, studying을 to study로 고치는 것이 적절하다.

19 주어진 문장의 Four days later에 주목한다. ③번 앞 문장에서 말한 그의 사촌이 독립운동에 가담했다는 이유로 일본 경찰에게 체포된 날로부터 나흘 뒤를 말하는 것이므로 ③번이 적절하다.

20 날짜가 있을 때는 전치사 on을 사용하는 것이 적절하다.

21 이 글은 '동주와 그의 사촌이 독립운동에 가담했다는 이유로 일본 경찰에게 체포되어 가혹 행위를 당한 후, 한국이 일본으로부터 독립하기 불과 몇 달 전에 감옥에서 사망했다'는 내용의 글이므로, 주제로는 ⑤번 '동주와 그의 사촌의 독립 운동과 불행한 사망'이 적절하다.

22 동사는 'It is ~ that ...' 강조 구문으로 강조할 수 없고, Jeong

Byeong-uk did bring Dong-ju's poems to the poet's brother in 1948.처럼 강조의 조동사 do(es)나 did를 사용하여 강조하는 것이 적절하다.

서술형 시험대비   p.166~167

01 where   02 in haste   03 These lines
04 (A) poems   (B) literary   (C) rare
05 it was literature that he loved most
06 bought → borrowed   07 was given
08 nineteen forty-eight   09 his poems
10 further   11 harsh treatment
12 He gave one to his close friend, Jeong Byeong-uk, presented another to his favorite professor, and kept the last one for himself.
13 졸업을 기념하여 그가 '하늘과 바람과 별과 시'라는 제목으로 자신의 시 19편을 출판하는 것
14 (A) literature   (B) a doctor

01 뒤에 완전한 문장이 이어지고 선행사가 장소이므로, 관계부사 where가 적절하다.

02 in a hurry = in haste: 서둘러

03 '이 시 구절들'을 가리킨다.

04 (A) 많은 '시'를 썼다고 해야 하므로 poems가 적절하다. poet: 시인, (B) '문학잡지'를 만들기도 했다고 해야 하므로 형용사 literary가 적절하다. literally: 문자[말] 그대로(부사), (C) 그 '희귀한' 책을 한 부 갖고 싶었던 것이라고 해야 하므로 rare가 적절하다. rare: 희귀한, common: 흔한

05 'it is ~ that ...' 강조 구문을 사용하여 it was와 that 사이에 강조하려는 말 literature를 쓰는 것이 적절하다.

06 동주가 중학교에 다니던 때 책 전체를 필사했던 백석의 시집은 그가 '산' 것이 아니라 '빌린' 것이다.

07 '책에는 시인이 수년 전에 생각해 두었던 제목이 붙었다'고 해야 하므로 수동태로 쓰는 것이 적절하다.

08 두 자리씩 끊어서 읽는 것이 적절하다.

09 '그의 시'를 가리킨다.

10 학업을 '이어가기로' 했다고 해야 하므로 further로 쓰는 것이 적절하다. far–farther–farthest: 멀리(거리), far–further–furthest: 더 이상의, 추가의(정도)

11 일본 경찰의 '가혹 행위'가 있었기 때문에 동주와 그의 사촌은 감옥에서 사망했다.

12 He를 주어로 하여 능동태로 고치는 것이 적절하다.

13 His plan was to publish 19 of his poems under the title, *Heaven, Wind, Stars, and Poetry* to celebrate his graduation.

14 그의 부모는 그가 '의사'가 되기를 바랐지만 동주는 서울에 있는 대학에서 '문학'을 전공하기로 했다. major in: ~을 전공하다

01 independence   02 ③

03 (1) poem   (2) whole   (3) rare   (4) loneliness

    (5) literature

04 ①   05 ⑤

06 (1) The robber was arrested near the bank.

    (2) Our team went through harsh training.

    (3) He tried his best to achieve his goal.

    (4) I want fair treatment.

07 (1) The professor advised against the use of

    sugar.

    (2) Let's celebrate our graduation and have a

    party.

    (3) Designers and editors try their best to make a

    gook book.

08 ⓔ to see → to seeing   09 ④   10 ②

11 What brings you here?   12 ⑤

13 (B) → (E) → (C) → (A) → (D)

14 ⑤   15 ⑤   16 ④

17 ⓐ, ⓓ, ⓔ   18 ①, ②   19 ⑤   20 ③

21 ②   22 ②   23 ①, ③, ④   24 ⑤

25 had thought   26 ①

01 '다른 나라의 지배를 받지 않는 상태'를 가리키는 말은 independence(독립)이다.

02 poet: 시인

03 rare: 드문, 희귀한, loneliness: 외로움, poem: 시, whole: 전체의, literature: 문학

04 check out: (도서관에서) 대출하다, come out: 나오다, hang out with: ~와 시간을 보내다

05 주어진 문장은 '주다, 제출하다'를 의미하며 이와 같은 의미를 나타내는 것은 ⑤번이다. ①, ②번은 '선물', ③, ④번은 '현재의'를 나타낸다.

06 robber: 도둑, try one's best: 최선을 다하다, achieve: (일·목적)을 이루다, fair: 공정한, treatment: 대우

07 advise against: ~에 반대하는 충고를 하다, graduation: 졸업, editor: 편집자

08 look forward to+~ing: ~하기를 기대하다

09 ④ Ken Kuller의 Four Eyes가 영화로 만들어졌다.

10 주어진 문장은 책을 추천해 달라는 요청에 대한 답변으로 적절하므로 ②번이 알맞다.

12 ⑤ '22nd Street'은 대출 가능하다.

13 (B) 언제 사진을 찍는지 대답 → (E) 마음에 둔 스타일이 있는지 질문 → (C) 대답 및 추천 요청 → (A) 제안 → (D) 반응 및 기대 표현

14 추천을 요청하는 표현에 '네 말에 전적으로 동의해.'라는 대답은 어색하다.

15 'It ~ that ...' 강조 구문에서 강조하는 대상이 장소의 부사(구/절)일 경우, that 대신에 where로 바꿔 쓸 수 있다.

16 He had already left when I returned home. 돌아오기 전에 이미 떠난 것이므로 돌아온 것은 과거로, 떠난 것은 과거완료로 써야 한다.

17 ⓑ had got → got, already began → had already begun ⓒ has → had ⓕ which → that[who] ⓖ That → It

18 ① Because she had not studied hard, she failed the test. ② It was in 2014 that my family moved to this city.

19 ⓐ 축구 유니폼 '위'에 번호를 바느질한 것이므로, 표면에 붙어서 '위'를 나타내는 on이 적절하다. ⓑ by hand: 손으로, 직접

20 이 글은 동주가 어린 소년이었을 때 운동을 좋아했고 바느질하는 것을 무척 좋아했지만, 그가 가장 사랑한 것은 문학이었다는 내용의 글이므로, 주제로는 ③번 '동주가 무엇보다도 가장 사랑한 것은 문학이었다.'가 적절하다.

21 동주가 어린 소년이었을 때 운동을 좋아한 이유는 알 수 없다. ① He was born near Yanbin, China. ③ He sewed the numbers on their soccer uniforms. ④ With his cousin, Song Mong-gyu. ⑤ Baek Seok's poetry book.

22 'he expressed feelings about his hometown and lost country in poetry'에서, 'in poetry'를 관계부사 where로 바꾸는 것이 적절하다.

23 ⓑ와 ②, ⑤: 부사적 용법, ①, ④: 형용사적 용법, ③: 명사적 용법

24 졸업을 기념하여 그는 '하늘과 바람과 별과 시'라는 제목으로 자신의 시 19편을 출판하고 싶어 했지만, 그 생각을 '포기했다.' ③ hang around with = hang out with: ~와 시간을 보내다

25 시인이 책의 제목을 생각한 것은 책에 제목을 붙인 것보다 먼저 일어난 일이므로 과거완료 had thought를 쓰는 것이 적절하다.

26 finally = at last = in the end = eventually − in the long run: 마침내, ① (여러 개를 언급할 때) 마지막으로

01 (1) take part in   (2) looking forward to

    (3) is well known for   (4) Give it a try

02 ④   03 ⓐ → a new book by Ken Kuller

04 ⑤   05 Can you recommend one for me?

06 ②   07 ③

08 Can you recommend a popular story with a

    surprise ending?

09 His short stories[They] are famous because of

    surprise endings.

10 It's about a sick girl and an old artist who saves

    her life.

11 (1) the U.S.   (2) short stories

   (3) surprising endings   (4) *The Last Leaf*

12 She was not upset because she had bought some extra balloons.

13 ④

14 (1) He showed me some poems he had written himself.

   (2) When I came back home, I found somebody had turned on the TV.

   (3) It was on the bus that[where] Judy lost her wallet.

   (4) It was in 1776 that[when] the U.S. gained independence from Great Britain.

15 ②	16 ①	17 ④	18 ①
19 ②	20 ⑤		

21 has studied → had studied   22 ②, ④

01 take part in: ~에 참가하다, look forward to: ~을 기대하다, be well known for: ~로 유명하다, give it a try: 시도하다

02 (A) stop+~ing: ~하던 것을 멈추다, stop+to부정사: ~하기 위해 멈추다 (B) 영화로 만들어졌으므로 made, (C) look forward to ~ing: ~하기를 기대하다

03 ⓐ를 제외한 나머지는 모두 영화를 가리킨다.

04 민준과 소라가 언제 그 영화를 보러 갈지는 알 수 없다.

06 위 대화는 미용사와 손님의 관계임을 알 수 있다.

07 지호가 마음에 둔 특별한 헤어 스타일은 없었다.

09 Mr. Henry의 단편 소설들은 뜻밖의 결말로 유명하다.

10 '마지막 잎새'는 아픈 소녀와 그녀의 목숨을 구하는 늙은 화가의 이야기이다.

12 시간차가 드러나도록 하라고 했으므로 앞서는 사건을 과거완료 시제로 나타낸다.

13 It is in the park that Patricia plays badminton every weekend.

14 (1) 그가 쓴 것이 보여 준 시점보다 앞서므로 과거완료로 나타낸다. (2) TV를 켠 것이 발견한 시점보다 앞서므로 과거완료로 나타낸다. (3) 'It ~ that …' 강조 구문에서 강조하는 대상이 'on the bus'로 장소를 나타내므로, which가 아니라 that이나 where로 써야 한다. (4) 'It ~ that …' 강조 구문이며 what이 아닌 that이 되어야 하고 that 이하가 완전한 절이므로 강조하는 대상이 1776이 아니라 시간의 부사구 in 1776이 되어야 한다. that 대신 when으로 써도 좋다.

15 첫 번째 문장에서는 빌려준 것이 잃어버린 것보다 앞선 시제이므로 과거완료 had lent가 적절하다. 두 번째 문장에서는 'It ~ that …' 강조 구문에서 강조하는 대상이 시간의 부사(구/절)일 경우, when으로 바꿔 쓸 수 있다.

16 앞에 나오는 내용과 상반되는 내용이 뒤에 이어지므로 However가 가장 적절하다. ② 그러므로, ③ 즉[말하자면], ⑤

그 결과

17 ⓑ와 ④: '(It is[was] … that ~'의 형태로 명사[대명사]를 강조하여) ~하는 것은, ① 보어절을 이끄는 접속사, ② 지시형용사, ③ [원인·이유] ~이므로, ~ 때문에, ⑤ 동격절을 이끄는 접속사

18 ⓐ for oneself: 혼자 힘으로, 자기를 위하여, ⓑ 그의 교수는 그의 계획에 '반대하는' 충고를 했다. against: ~에 반대하여[맞서], for: ~에 찬성[지지]하는

19 ②번 다음 문장의 the book에 주목한다. 주어진 문장에서 동주가 출판하고 싶어 했던 책을 받고 있으므로 ②번이 적절하다.

20 이 글은 '동주가 졸업을 기념하여 '하늘과 바람과 별과 시'라는 제목으로 자신의 시 19편을 출판하고 싶어했지만, 그의 교수가 일본 정부가 출판을 허가하지 않으리라 여겨 그의 계획에 반대하는 충고를 했고, 결국 동주는 그의 충고를 따라 자신의 생각을 포기했다'는 내용의 글이므로, 제목으로는 ⑤번 '시집 출판이라는 이루지 못한 소원'이 적절하다.

21 동주의 아버지가 공부한 것이 동주가 일본에 공부하러 가기로 결심한 것보다 앞서 일어난 일이므로, 과거완료인 had studied로 고치는 것이 적절하다.

22 take part in = participate in = join: ~에 참가하다, ① attend to: ~을 돌보다, 시중들다, ③ deal in: ~을 매매하다, ⑤ take into account: ~을 고려하다

서술형 실전문제
p.178~179

01 He is going to Dream & Joy Park.

02 He asks Mike to recommend a hairstyle for him.

03 He is going to take pictures for the yearbook.

04 (1) The witness admitted that he had not told the complete truth.

   (2) I learned that he had been sick since last week.

   (3) It was my parents that[who] got married in a small restaurant.

   (4) It was his endless efforts that[which] moved all the animals' hearts.

05 (1) My aunt knew London so well because she had visited the city many times.

   (2) It was *The Potato Eaters* that Vincent van Gogh painted in 1885.

06 (A) sewed   (B) that   (C) borrowed

07 a poetry book by a famous poet of the time, Baek Seok

08 Because he really wanted to have his own copy of the rare book.

09 (A) hung   (B) last   (C) followed

31

10 his professor advised against his plan because he thought the Japanese government would not allow the publication

11 He expressed feelings about his hometown and lost country.

01 지호는 이번 주 금요일에 Dream & Joy Park에 갈 것이다.

02 지호는 Mike에게 헤어스타일을 추천해 줄 것을 요청한다.

03 지호는 졸업 앨범을 위해 사진을 찍을 것이다.

04 (1) 목격자가 '진실을 말한 것이 아님을 인정했다.'라는 의미로 인정한 시점보다 진실을 말하지 않은 것이 앞선 시점이므로 과거완료로 나타내는 것이 적절하다. (2) since가 있으므로 '지난주부터 계속 아팠다'는 의미로 과거완료로 나타내는 것이 적절하다. (3) 접속사 없이 동사가 2개가 나온 형태이므로 'It ~ that ...' 강조 구문의 that이나 who를 넣어 주는 것이 적절하다. (4) 'It ~ that ...' 강조 구문에서 강조하고자 하는 것이 'his endless efforts'로 사물이므로 who를 that이나 which로 고치는 것이 적절하다.

05 (1) 잘 아는 것이 그 전에 여러 번 방문했기 때문이므로 방문했었던 것을 과거완료로 나타낸다. (2) 'It ~ that 강조 구문'은 강조하고자 하는 부분을 'It is/was'와 that 사이에 넣고, 나머지 부분을 that 뒤에 쓴다.

06 (A) 친구들의 축구 유니폼에 번호를 '바느질해' 주기도 했다고 해야 하므로 sewed가 적절하다. sew-sewed-sewn: 바느질하다, 깁다, saw-sawed-sawn: 톱으로 켜다, (B) 'it is ~ that ...' 강조 구문으로 literature를 강조하는 구문이므로 that이 적절하다. (C) 백석의 시집을 '빌려 와서' 책 전체를 필사하기도 했다고 해야 하므로 borrowed가 적절하다. borrow: 빌리다, lend-lent-lent: 빌려주다

07 '당대의 유명한 시인, 백석의 시집'을 가리킨다.

08 그는 정말로 그 희귀한 책을 한 부 갖고 싶었기 때문이었다.

09 (A) '다른 젊은 시인들과 어울려 다녔다'고 해야 하므로 hung이 적절하다. hang out with: ~와 시간을 보내다, hang이 '교수형에 처하다'의 뜻일 때는 hang-hanged-hanged로 변화하지만, 그 외에는 hang-hung-hung으로 변화한다. (B) '마지막 하나'라고 해야 하므로 last가 적절하다. last: 마지막의, latest: 최근의, (C) 그의 충고를 '따라' 그 생각을 포기했다고 해야 하므로 followed가 적절하다. refuse: 거절하다

10 'against'를 보충하면 된다.

11 그는 그의 시에서 '고향과 잃어버린 조국에 대한 심정'을 표현했다.

창의사고력 서술형 문제
p.180

|모범답안|

01 (A) a book report   (B) all of his mystery books
(C) has been made into a movie   (D) interesting

---

02 (A) Tommy   (B) washes his face
(C) black eyes   (D) jumps high   (E) in my bed

01 독후감을 위해 Ken Kuller의 새 책을 읽고 있는 중에, 소라가 내게 와서 Ken Kuller에 대해 이야기했다. 나는 소라가 이미 Ken Kuller를 알고 있으며 그의 모든 미스터리 책들을 읽었다는 것을 알게 되었다. 그녀는 내게 그의 소설 Four Eyes가 영화로 만들어졌다고 이야기했다. 내가 영화 포스터를 보았을 때, 그것은 재미있어 보였다. 소라는 그걸 보는 것을 기대하고 있다.

단원별 모의고사
p.181~185

01 (1) government   (2) publication   (3) literature
(4) literary

02 ⓔ → Can I check it out?   03 ⑤

04 (A) a good novel
(B) a new Ken Kuller book, 22nd Street
(C) among teens   (D) "New Arrivals" area

05 He borrowed it this morning.

06 Four Eyes has been made into a movie.

07 He thinks Ken Kuller is a great writer.

08 ③

09 I'm looking forward to seeing how I'll look in the pictures.

10 ⑤   11 ②   12 ⑤

13 (1) had gone   (2) had fixed

14 ③   15 ④

16 (1) It is fried chicken that I eat when I feel good.
(2) It was Mr. Brown that[who] saved the child in the river.
(3) She insisted that she had not been there the previous night.
(4) When the children arrived at the camp, their parents had already started cooking.

17 ①, ③, ④, ⑥   18 literary

19 He also loved sewing so much that he sewed the numbers on all his friends' soccer uniforms.

20 literature   21 ⑤   22 copy

23 Because he thought the Japanese government would not allow the publication.

24 ②   25 ③   26 living

27 plays, poems, novels, or cartoons

---

01 government: 정부, publication: 출판, literature: 문학, literary: 문학의

02 '타동사+부사'로 이루어진 경우 목적어가 인칭대명사일 때 '동사+대명사 목적어+부사'의 순서에 유의한다.

03 *22nd street*이 왜 영국의 십대들에게 인기가 있는지는 알 수 없다.

04 오늘 나는 책을 빌리러 도서관에 갔다. 나는 독후감을 써야 하는데 무엇을 읽어야 할지 몰랐다. 나는 서 선생님께 좋은 소설을 추천해 주실 것을 요청했다. 선생님은 Ken Kuller의 신간, '22번가'를 소개해 주셨다. 나는 이 책이 영국의 십 대들 사이에서 많은 인기가 있다고 들었다. 나는 '신착 도서' 서가에서 그것을 찾았다. 나는 이 책을 읽는 것을 매우 기대하고 있다.

05 민준이는 Ken Kuller의 새 책을 오늘 아침에 빌렸다.

06 Ken Kuller의 소설 중, *Four Eyes*가 영화로 만들어졌다.

07 민준이는 Ken Kuller가 위대한 작가라고 생각한다.

08 이어지는 대답에서 마음에 두고 있는 특정한 스타일이 없다는 대답이 이어지므로 ⓒ에 들어가는 것이 알맞다.

09 look forward to+~ing: ~하기를 기대하다

10 위 대화는 미용실에서 이루어지는 대화임을 알 수 있다.

11 주어진 문장은 주로 무엇을 쓰는지에 대한 대답으로서 적절하므로 (B)가 적절하다.

12 대화를 통해 '마지막 잎새'에서 늙은 화가가 어떻게 아픈 소녀를 구했는지 알 수 없다.

13 (1) 이미 가고 없다는 과거완료의 '결과' 용법을 이용한다. (2) 과거의 어느 시점보다 먼저 일어난 일이나 상태를 나타낼 때 과거완료를 사용한다.

14 It is the car that[which] James Bond drove in the famous films called 007.

15 주어진 문장과 ④번은 과거완료의 대과거 용법이다. ① 결과 ② 계속 ③ 경험 ⑤ 완료

16 (1) eat에 맞추어 'It is'로 쓰는 것이 적절하다. 또는 'It was'에 맞추어 ate로 쓰는 것이 적절하다. (2) 접속사 없이 동사가 2개가 나온 형태이므로 'It ~ that ...' 강조 구문의 that이나 who를 넣어 주는 것이 적절하다. (3) 그 전날, 거기에 없었다고 주장하는 것이므로 과거완료로 나타내는 것이 적절하다. (4) 도착한 시점보다 시작한 시점이 앞서므로 과거완료로 쓰는 것이 적절하다.

17 ② The train had left when I arrived at the station. ⑤ It was Uncle Ben that[who] broke Plum's toy. ⑦ It was the drums that[which] he played this year.

18 literary: 문학의, 문학을 쓰거나 연구하거나 혹은 이해하는 것과 관련된

19 so를 보충하면 된다. so+형용사/부사+that ~: 너무 …해서 ~하다

20 무엇보다도 동주가 가정 사랑한 것은 '문학'이었다.

21 앞에 나오는 내용과 상반되는 내용이 뒤에 이어지므로 However가 가장 적절하다. ① 게다가, 더욱이, ② 다시 말해서, ③ 비슷하게, ④ 따라서, 그러므로

22 one은 copy를 가리킨다.

23 '일본 정부가 출판을 허가하지 않으리라고 여겨', 그의 계획에 반대하는 충고를 했다.

24 ⓐ, ②, ⑤: 동명사, ①, ③, ④: 현재분사

25 동주와 그의 사촌은 1942년에 일본에서 공부를 시작했고 '다음 해(1943년)' 7월 10일에 그의 사촌은 독립운동에 가담했다는 이유로 일본 경찰에게 체포되었다.

26 동사 imagine의 목적어로 동명사 being과 병렬구조를 이루도록 쓰는 것이 적절하다.

25 '희곡, 시, 소설 또는 만화'를 가리킨다.

교과서 파헤치기

단어 TEST Step 1   p.02

01 인공적인	02 성가시게 하다	03 원인
04 안심이 되는	05 우울한	06 우정
07 도움이 되는	08 긍정적인	09 스트레스 받은
10 개선하다	11 외모	12 소리를 지르다
13 유명한	14 덜다	15 주장하다
16 인내하는	17 화학물질	18 그 외에도
19 방법	20 흔한	21 불안한
22 지루한	23 문제가 되다, 중요하다	
24 무서운	25 생산하다	26 효과
27 집중하다	28 짠	29 졸리는
30 깔끔한	31 효과가 있다	32 학교 공부
33 매체	34 남겨두다	35 ~하곤 했다
36 ~ 덕택에	37 동시에	38 우울하게 느끼다
39 ~에 따르면	40 의미가 통하다	
41 ~을 다루다, 처리하다		42 ~하는 한
43 ~에 어려움이 있다		

단어 TEST Step 2   p.03

01 media	02 relieved	03 produce
04 argue	05 helpful	06 sleepy
07 besides	08 focus	09 improve
10 scream	11 appearance	12 matter
13 chemical	14 scary	15 common
16 leave	17 nervous	18 stressed
19 patient	20 method	21 well-known
22 relieve	23 boring	24 salty
25 tidy	26 work	27 gloomy
28 artificial	29 bother	30 cause
31 positive	32 effect	33 schoolwork
34 friendship	35 according to	36 in other ways
37 as long as	38 forget to	
39 at the same time		40 instead of
41 deal with	42 break a promise	
43 used to		

단어 TEST Step 3   p.04

1 friendship, 우정 2 method, 방법

3 well-known, 유명한 4 artificial, 인공적인

5 cause, 원인 6 effect, 효과 7 gloomy, 우울한

8 improve, 개선하다 9 positive, 긍정적인

10 argue, 주장하다 11 tidy, 깔끔한

12 common, 흔한 13 appearance, 외모

14 bother, 성가시게 하다 15 scream, 소리를 지르다

16 focus, 집중하다

대화문 TEST Step 1   p.05~06

Listen and Answer – Dialog 1

talk, about, What makes, feel, stressed, About, answered, As, see, common cause, Over half of, stresses, Problems, took, with, Next, worries, get stressed because of, appearance

Listen and Answer – Dialog 2

What, doing / studying for, Grades / used to, way, too / know / a little stress, helpful / What makes, say / got stressed, at the same time, focus, try harder / help, in other ways / improve, memory

Listen More – Listen and choose.

talk, have to decide / Let, show, designs / choose, short sleeves / What makes, say / Because, wear / makes sense, about / cute / expensive, best one

Speak – Talk in groups.

like to talk, One, most well-known paintings

Speak – Talk in pairs.

spend / makes, say / make, around the world / makes sense

My Speaking Portfolio Step 3

like, good ways to relax, upset, take deep breaths, counting, drinking, Lastly, thinking, thoughts

Wrap Up – Listening & Speaking 1

talked, foods, are good, like to, healthy eating, slowly, to stop eating, full

Wrap Up – Listening & Speaking 2

don't, make / make / basketball, better idea / makes, say / we need

대화문 TEST Step 2   p.07~08

Listen and Answer – Dialog 1

W: Today, I'd like to talk to you about teen stress. What makes you feel the most stressed? About 9,000 teens answered this question. As you can see, schoolwork was the most common cause of stress. Over half of the students said schoolwork stresses them the most. Problems with friends took second place with 15.3%. Next came family and worries about the future. 8.2% of the students said they get stressed because of their appearance.

Listen and Answer – Dialog 2

W: What are you doing, Oliver?

B: I'm studying for the math test, Mom. Grades stress me out.

W: I understand. I used to feel that way, too.

B: Really? I didn't know that.

W: Yeah, but a little stress was helpful for me.

B: What makes you say that?

W: I got stressed when I had an exam, but at the same time it made me focus and try harder.

B: I see. Did stress help you in other ways?

W: Yes, it helped improve my memory.

Listen More – Listen and choose.

B1: Today, let's talk about the class T-shirt. We have to decide on the design.

G: Let me show you some designs on the screen.

B2: We have to choose a T-shirt with short sleeves.

B1: What makes you say that?

B2: Because we'll wear the T-shirt on Sports Day. It's in June.

G: That makes sense. What about this green one?

B2: I like it. The bee on the T-shirt is so cute.

G: And it's not expensive.

B1: Yes. I think it's the best one.

Speak – Talk in groups.

Hi. Today, I'd like to talk about Frida Kahlo. She was a Mexican painter. One of her most well-known paintings is *Viva la Vida*.

Speak – Talk in pairs.

A: I want to spend more time on social media.

B: What makes you say that?

A: I can make more friends from around the world.

B: That makes sense.

My Speaking Portfolio Step 3

I'd like to talk about some good ways to relax when you get upset. First, it's good to take deep breaths. Second, counting to ten is a great idea. Also, drinking cold water helps. Lastly, thinking happy thoughts can help.

Wrap Up – Listening & Speaking 1

W: Hello, teens. I'm Dr. Broccoli. Last time, I talked about different foods that are good for your health. Today, I'd like to talk about healthy eating habits. First, try to eat slowly. Second, it's important to stop eating when you're full.

Wrap Up – Listening & Speaking 2

G: Why don't we make a sport club?

B: Sounds good. Let's make a baseball club.

G: Well, I think a basketball club is a better idea.

B: What makes you say that?

G: All we need is a ball to play basketball.

본문 TEST Step 1   p.09~10

01 Goodbye, Stress

02 spend, with, feel low

03 Others, feel better

04 Still others, while   05 How, deal with

06 Here, suggest different ways

07 by saying, breaking, arguing

08 When, happens, horror   09 so, that, lot

10 screaming, top, lungs, feel

11 thanks, scenes, effects, bothers

12 been using, method, works

13 graduated from, ago

14 with, been looking for

15 stressed out, going fishing

16 gets upset, catch, fish

17 While, so, that, behind

18 Besides, be patient

19 sure, focusing on, forget

20 second-year, way, free from

21 seems, like, for, reason

22 because, number-one way, better

23 so, that, looks glommy

24 As, feel like, relieving

25 When, tidy, looks brighter   26 Let, tell, what

27 stressed, things, has, work

28 under stress, writes, calendar

29 takes, out, herself

30 reads, watches, talks

31 matter, as long as   32 been writing, on

33 Which methods, work for

34 Try, yourself, way, stress

본문 TEST Step 2   p.11~12

01 Say Goodbye

02 spend time with, feel low

03 Others, to feel better

04 Still others, for a while   05 deal with

06 suggest different ways

07 saying, breaking, arguing over

08 When this happens   09 so, that

35

10 at the top of my lungs helps, feel
11 thanks to, scenes, effects, what bothers me
12 I've been using, several months, works
13 graduated from, ago
14 he's been looking for
15 he's stressed out, always tries, by going fishing
16 gets upset
17 so, that, can leave, worries behind
18 Besides, to be patient
19 focusing on, forget something else
20 second-year, to stay free from
21 seems to like, for a good reason
22 number-one way to make
23 so, that, looks gloomy
24 As, feel like, relieving
25 looks tidy, looks brighter   26 Let, what
27 all the things she has to do at work
28 she's under stress
29 takes some time out
30 reads, watches, talks
31 matter what, as long as
32 I've been writing, feel much better
33 Which, work for you
34 to say goodbye to stress

1 스트레스와 이별하라
2 어떤 사람들은 울적할 때 친구들과 시간을 보낸다.
3 다른 사람들은 기분이 좋아지도록 특별한 음식을 먹는다.
4 또 다른 사람들은 그저 잠시 잠을 자기도 한다.
5 여러분은 스트레스를 어떻게 다루는가?
6 여기 다양한 방법을 제안하는 사람들의 이야기가 있다.
7 때때로 내 친구들은 나에 관해 나쁜 말을 하거나, 약속을 어기거나, 혹은 사소한 일을 두고 언쟁을 하며 내게 스트레스를 준다.
8 이럴 때, 나는 공포 영화를 본다!
9 훌륭한 공포 영화는 너무 무서워서 나는 소리를 많이 지르게 된다.
10 있는 힘껏 소리 지르는 것은 내 기분이 나아지는 데 도움이 된다고 생각한다.
11 또한, 무서운 장면과 음향 효과 덕분에 나를 괴롭히는 것들을 잊을 수 있다.
12 나는 지난 몇 달간 이 방법을 써 오고 있는데, 효과가 아주 좋다.
13 우리 삼촌은 2년 전에 대학을 졸업했다.
14 삼촌은 우리 가족과 함께 살고 있고, 얼마 전부터 직장을 구하고 있다.

15 나는 삼촌이 스트레스를 받고 있지만 낚시를 다니며 긍정적으로 지내려고 항상 노력한다는 것을 안다.
16 물고기를 한 마리도 잡지 못했을 때에도 삼촌은 절대 속상해하지 않는다.
17 삼촌은 "낚시하는 동안, 나는 아주 몰입해서 모든 걱정을 잊을 수 있어.
18 게다가 낚시는 나에게 인내를 가르쳐 준단다."라고 말한다.
19 한 가지 일에 집중하는 것이 다른 무언가를 잊는 데 도움이 된다고 나는 확신한다.
20 고등학교 2학년인 우리 누나에게는 스트레스에서 벗어나는 훌륭한 방법이 있다.
21 누나가 학업 때문에 많은 스트레스를 받지만, 그럴 만한 이유로 우리 어머니는 그 상황을 좋아하시는 것 같다.
22 그것은 바로, 청소가 누나의 삶을 향상하는 최고의 방법이기 때문이다.
23 스트레스를 너무 많이 받아서 인생이 우울해 보일 때, 누나는 방을 청소한다.
24 누나는 "방을 청소하면서 스트레스도 해소되는 것 같아.
25 내 방이 깔끔해 보이면 내 삶도 더 밝아 보여."라고 말한다.
26 우리 어머니께서 스트레스를 어떻게 다루시는지 소개하려고 한다.
27 어머니는 직장과 집에서 해야 하는 온갖 일로 인해 스트레스를 받으신다.
28 스트레스를 받을 때면 어머니는 달력에 '나만의 시간'이라고 적으신다.
29 이것은 어머니 자신을 위해 잠깐 시간을 낸다는 의미이다.
30 어머니는 책을 읽거나, 영화를 보거나, 친구들과 이야기를 나누신다.
31 어머니는 "내가 좋아하는 것이라면, 무엇을 하는지는 별로 중요하지 않아.
32 나는 두 달째 달력에 '나만의 시간'을 적어 왔고, 기분이 훨씬 좋아졌어."라고 말씀하신다.
33 어떤 방법이 여러분에게 효과가 있을까?
34 이 아이디어 중 몇 개를 직접 해 보고, 스트레스와 이별하는 자신만의 최고의 방법을 찾아라.

1 Say Goodbye to Stress
2 Some people spend time with friends when they feel low.
3 Others eat special foods to feel better.
4 Still others simply sleep for a while.
5 How do you deal with stress?
6 Here are some stories about people who suggest different ways.
7 Sometimes my friends give me stress by saying bad things about me, breaking promises, or

arguing over small things.

8 When this happens, I watch horror movies!

9 Good horror movies are so scary that I scream a lot.

10 I guess that screaming at the top of my lungs helps me feel better.

11 Also, thanks to scary scenes and sound effects, I can forget about what bothers me.

12 I've been using this method for the past several months, and it really works.

13 My uncle graduated from college two years ago.

14 He lives with my family, and he's been looking for a job for some time.

15 I know that he's stressed out, but he always tries to be positive by going fishing.

16 He never gets upset when he doesn't catch any fish.

17 He says, "While I fish, I'm so focused that I can leave all my worries behind.

18 Besides, it teaches me to be patient."

19 I'm sure that focusing on one thing helps us forget about something else.

20 My sister, a second-year student in high school, has a wonderful way to stay free from stress.

21 She feels a lot of stress from schoolwork, but my mother seems to like the situation for a good reason.

22 It is because cleaning is my sister's number-one way to make life better!

23 When she's so stressed that her life looks gloomy, she cleans her room.

24 She says, "As I clean my room, I feel like I'm also relieving stress.

25 When my room looks tidy, my life looks brighter."

26 Let me tell you what my mother does about her stress.

27 She feels stressed by all the things she has to do at work and at home.

28 When she's under stress, she writes "Me Time" on her calendar.

29 This means she takes some time out for herself.

30 She reads a book, watches a movie, or talks with her friends.

31 She says, "It doesn't really matter what I do, as long as it's something I like.

32 I've been writing 'Me Time' on my calendar for two months, and I feel much better."

33 Which methods will work for you?

34 Try some of these ideas yourself, and find your best way to say goodbye to stress.

구석구석지문 TEST Step 1 — p.19

Words in Action
1. stress, out, me more stress
2. Worry less, never helps
3. a lot of work to do
4. change, change my hairstyle
5. caught, a few, to fish

Speak – Get ready.
1. spend, less time
2. Working on, can be, helpful
3. watching, better
4. Having, part-time job, bad

Wrap Up - Reading
1. stressed, feeling low
2. some good news
3. A few, steps, help
4. outdoors, plenty of
5. According to, produce, in your brain, makes you feel
6. Another thing you can do
7. produce even more, happiness chemical
8. Try, simple tips, feel low
9. Instead of sitting, front, run around

구석구석지문 TEST Step 2 — p.20

Words in Action
1. Tests stress me out. Grades give me more stress.
2. Worry less, smile more. Worry never helps.
3. I work hard. I have a lot of work to do.
4. I need a change. I will change my hairstyle.
5. I caught just a few fish. I want to fish some more.

Speak – Get ready.
1. I want to spend more/less time on social media.
2. Working on a team can be difficult/helpful.
3. I like watching/playing sports better.
4. Having a part-time job as a teen can be good/bad.

Wrap Up - Reading
1. Are you stressed or feeling low?
2. Then here is some good news for you.
3. A few simple steps can help you!
4. First, go outdoors and get plenty of sunlight.
5. According to scientists, this helps produce a special chemical in your brain, and the chemical makes you feel happy!
6. Another thing you can do is exercise.
7. This helps produce even more of the "happiness chemical."
8. Try these simple tips the next time you feel low.
9. Instead of sitting in front of a screen, go outdoors and run around in the sun!

단어 TEST Step 1   p.21

01 살아 있는   02 인기 있는   03 쉬다
04 곧장, 바로, 직접적으로   05 선물
06 효과적인, 실질적인   07 원예
08 ~인지 아닌지   09 생산자
10 전기로 동력이 주어지는   11 도매의
12 상상할 수 있는   13 소화하다   14 조리법
15 건축가   16 번역하다   17 계산서
18 곤충   19 지속하다, 오래가다
20 운송하다, 실어 나르다
21 끌어들이다, 끌어당기다, 매혹하다   22 운송, 교통
23 현지의, 지역의   24 환경   25 주로, 대부분
26 제안하다   27 발견하다, 알아내다
28 주목하다   29 뜨다   30 그러므로, 따라서
31 사라지다   32 무역   33 방식
34 작동하다, 효과가 있다   35 ~와 잡담하다
36 낮잠을 자다   37 ~로 붐비다, 꽉 차다
38 ~한 공통점이 있다   39 ~에 유익하다
40 약속하다   41 ~이 풍부하다
42 유통 기한, 유효 기간   43 반드시 ~하다

단어 TEST Step 2   p.22

01 translate   02 imaginable   03 last
04 alive   05 float   06 architect
07 whether   08 insect   09 attract
10 carry   11 transportation   12 bill
13 disappear   14 wholesale   15 covered
16 work   17 suggest   18 discover
19 therefore   20 effective   21 environment
22 local   23 natural   24 mostly
25 experience   26 trade   27 gardening
28 notice   29 ship   30 directly
31 recipe   32 relax   33 digest
34 present   35 take a nap   36 be rich in
37 chat with   38 be crowded with
39 make an appointment   40 be good for
41 make sure to   42 have ~ in common
43 best-before date

단어 TEST Step 3   p.23

1 discover, 발견하다   2 disappear, 사라지다
3 architect, 건축가   4 recipe, 조리법
5 imaginable, 상상할 수 있는   6 tourist, 관광객
7 directly, 직접적으로   8 tradition, 전통   9 trade, 무역
10 wholesale, 도매의   11 ship, 운송하다
12 floating market, 수상 시장   13 insect, 곤충
14 present, 선물   15 attract, 끌다, 매혹하다
16 transportation, 운송

대화문 TEST Step 1   p.24~25

Listen – Listen & Answer Dialog 1

Welcome to, How, help / wonder if, tourist map / Is there, looking for / like to try, local / opens, five days, open / lucky, How can I get there / can walk, takes about, minutes / mark, way / Try, when, get

Listen – Listen & Answer Dialog 2

have, bill / Here, meal / good for your health / is rich in, digests / wonder if / want me to give, recipe for / be great

Listen More – Listen and complete

Excuse, help me with, milk / Read me, date / want me to tell, the best-before date / forgot, glasses / Let, see, by / I wonder if, lasts longer / found, one, until June 11 / one / welcome

Speak – Talk in pairs. 1

Excuse, wonder, around here / but, don't have one near / all right

Speak – Talk in pairs. 2

wrong / bored / want me to, with / be great

Wrap Up 1

feel hungry / How / want, to add

Wrap Up 2

look at, I wonder how much it is / Why don't, go in, check / didn't say, buy it for you, asking, price / course

대화문 TEST Step 2   p.26~27

Listen – Listen & Answer Dialog 1

M: Welcome to the Tourist Information Office! How may I help you?
W: Hi, I wonder if there's a tourist map of the town.
M: Sure. Is there a special place you're looking for?
W: Yes. I'd like to try some local food.

M: Then go to Jeongseon Market. It opens every five days, and it's open today.

W: I'm so lucky. How can I get there?

M: You can walk there. It takes about 10 minutes.

W: Great. Will you mark the way on the map, please?

M: Sure. Try gondrebap when you get there.

Listen – Listen & Answer Dialog 2

W: Can I have the bill, please?

M: Here you are. Did you enjoy the meal?

W: It was great. I liked the *gondrebap* very much.

M: Thanks. It's also good for your health.

W: Oh, really?

M: Yes. Gondre is rich in vitamins A and C. It also digests well.

W: Good. I wonder if I could buy some *gondre* here.

M: Sure. Do you want me to give you the recipe for *gondrebap*?

W: Yes, that'd be great.

Listen More – Listen and complete

W: Excuse me. Can you help me with this milk?

B: Sure. What is it?

W: Read me the date, please.

B: Oh, do you want me to tell you the best-before date?

W: Yes, I forgot my glasses.

B: Let me see. You should drink it by June 7.

W: That's too soon. I wonder if there's one that lasts longer.

B: Wait. I found one. This one is good until June 11.

W: Oh, I'll take that one. Thank you very much.

B: You're welcome.

Speak – Talk in pairs. 1

A: Excuse me. I wonder if there's a bank around here.

B: I'm sorry, but we don't have one near here.

A: That's all right. Thanks.

Speak – Talk in pairs. 2

A: What's wrong, Grandpa?

B: I'm bored.

A: Do you want me to play baduk with you?

B: That'd be great. Thank you.

Wrap Up 1

G: I feel hungry.

B: I'll make ramyeon for you.

G: How nice!

B: Do you want me to add an egg?

G: That'd be great.

Wrap Up 2

G: Dad, look at that cute bag. I wonder how much it is.

M: Why don't we go in and check?

G: Really? Thanks, Dad.

M: I didn't say I will buy it for you. We're just asking the price.

G: Of course.

본문 TEST Step 1   p.28~30

01 Travel Story   02 I am

03 have been writing, since

04 places, share, experiences with

05 Must-Visit, Around   06 July 15

07 Visiting, way, culture, country

08 places where, taste local

09 wonder whether, way, another

10 Grand, Turkey

11 where, long tradition, trade

12 natural place, markets like   13 was built, in

14 Back, traded goods, cloth

15 much, largest covered market

16 streets, shops under, roof   17 attracts over, every

18 almost, imaginable item

19 owners, carry, traditional, luck

20 make sure, try, traditional

21 Floating Market, Thailand   22 past, traded, on

23 beginning, floating markets

24 With, transportation, floating, disappeared

25 Since, however, back, alive

26 one, most popular, markets

27 crowded with, from, over

28 local, traditional, items, boats

29 wonder, had, meal   30 If, try, like

31 cook, pass, with, pole

32 Flower Market, Netherlands

33 means, low lands

34 As, suggests, below, level

35 built up, effective, grow

36 therefore, surprise that, largest

37 where, housed, bigger than

38 busy with, flower-filled   39 moved mostly by

40 around, traded, shipped, corners

41 wonder whether, buy, few

42 how wholesale, trading works

01 Travel Story
02 I am
03 have been writing, since
04 share my experiences with
05 Must-Visit, Around
06 July
07 Visiting markets, good way to learn
08 places where, taste local food
09 wonder whether, to discover another culture
10 Grand Bazaar
11 where, so, long tradition of trade
12 a natural place for, like
13 was built in
14 traded goods like cloth, gold
15 much bigger, largest covered market
16 more than, under one roof
17 attracts over
18 almost any imaginable item
19 if, traditional Turkish symbol, good luck
20 make sure to, traditional Turkish candy
21 Floating, Thailand
22 traded goods on
23 beginning of floating markets
24 With better road transportation, floating markets disappeared
25 Since, have come back, kept, alive
26 the most popular, markets is
27 crowded with tourists
28 traditional gift, directly from boats
29 wonder if, have, had
30 If not, like
31 with a long fishing pole
32 The Netherlands
33 means, low lands
34 As, suggests, about, below sea level
35 Thus, built up, effective way, to grow
36 therefore, no surprise, the largest flower market
37 where, is housed, bigger than
38 busy with, flower-filled
39 moved mostly by
40 around 20 million, traded, shipped, corners
41 whether, just a few
42 how wholesale flower trading works

1 Leah의 여행 이야기
2 저는 Leah입니다.
3 18세 때부터 여행 블로그를 써 왔습니다.
4 저는 여기저기 다니며 제 경험을 독자들과 공유하고 있습니다.
5 꼭 방문해야 할 세계의 시장들
6 20**년 7월 15일
7 시장 방문은 한 나라의 문화에 대해 배우는 좋은 방법입니다.
8 시장은 사람들을 만나고, 역사를 배우고, 또 지역 음식을 맛볼 수 있는 장소입니다.
9 다른 문화를 발견하는 데에 더 좋은 방법이 있을지 모르겠습니다.
10 1 터키의 Grand Bazaar(그랜드 바자)
11 터키는 동양과 서양이 만나는 나라이고, 그래서 오랜 교역의 전통을 가지고 있습니다.
12 터키는 Grand Bazaar 같은 대형 시장이 생겨나기에 자연스러운 곳입니다.
13 Grand Bazaar는 1455년 이스탄불에 지어졌습니다.
14 그 당시에 이 시장에는 큰 건물이 두 개 있었고, 거기서 사람들은 직물이나 금 같은 물건을 교환했습니다.
15 오늘날 Grand Bazaar는 훨씬 크고, 세계에서 가장 큰 지붕이 덮인 시장입니다.
16 64개의 거리와 4,000개 이상의 상점이 한 지붕 아래에 있습니다.
17 그 시장은 매일 25만 명 이상의 방문객을 불러 모읍니다.
18 그곳에서는 상상할 수 있는 거의 모든 물건을 살 수 있습니다.
19 추가 정보: 가게 주인에게 행운을 기원하는 터키 전통 상징인 'nazar boncuğu(나자르 본주)'를 파는지 물어보세요.
20 또한, 만약 맛있는 간식을 원한다면, 터키 전통 사탕인 'lokum(로쿰)'을 꼭 드셔 보세요.
21 2 태국의 Damnoen Saduak(담는 사두악) 수상 시장
22 과거에 태국 사람들은 강에서 물건을 교환했습니다.
23 이것이 태국 수상 시장의 시작이었습니다.
24 도로 교통이 개선되면서, 많은 수상 시장이 사라졌습니다.
25 그러나 1960년대 후반부터 일부가 다시 생겨나 전통을 이어 가고 있습니다.
26 오늘날, 가장 인기 있는 수상 시장 중 하나는 Damnoen Saduak 수상 시장입니다.
27 그곳은 전 세계에서 온 관광객들로 항상 붐빕니다.
28 배에서 직접 현지 음식과 전통 선물을 살 수 있습니다.
29 추가 정보: 여러분이 물 위에서 식사해 본 적이 있는지 궁금하네요.
30 만약 그렇지 않다면, 'pad thai(팟 타이)' 같은 면 요리를 드셔 보세요.
31 상인들이 배에서 음식을 만들어 긴 낚싯대로 건네줄 겁니다.
32 3 네덜란드 Aalsmeer(알스메이르) 꽃 시장
33 네덜란드는 '저지대'라는 뜻입니다.
34 이름에서 알 수 있듯이, 이 나라의 약 70%가 해수면보다 낮습니다.
35 그래서 네덜란드 사람들은 땅을 지어 올렸고, 그것을 사용하는 효과적인 방법은 꽃을 재배하고 파는 것이었습니다.
36 그러므로 네덜란드에 세계에서 가장 큰 꽃 시장인 Aalsmeer 꽃 시장이 있다는 것은 놀라운 일이 아닙니다.
37 시장이 들어선 건물은 축구장 120개보다 큽니다.
38 시장은 꽃이 가득 든 수천 개의 수레로 분주합니다.
39 수레는 대부분 전동 트럭에 의해 움직입니다.
40 매일, 약 2천만 송이의 꽃이 거래되어 세계 각지로 운송됩니다.
41 추가 정보: 시장에서 꽃을 조금 살 수 있는지 궁금할 겁니다.
42 애석하게도 안 되지만, 꽃이 도매로 어떻게 거래되는지를 볼 수 있습니다.

1 Leah's Travel Story

2 I am Leah.

3 I have been writing a travel blog since I was 18.

4 I go places and share my experiences with my readers.

5 Must-Visit Markets Around the World

6 July 15, 20**

7 Visiting markets is a good way to learn about the culture of a country.

8 Markets are places where you can meet people, learn history, and taste local food.

9 I wonder whether there is any better way to discover another culture.

10 1 Grand Bazaar, Turkey

11 Turkey is a country where East meets West, so it has a long tradition of trade.

12 It is a natural place for large markets like the Grand Bazaar.

13 The market was built in 1455 in Istanbul.

14 Back then, the market had two big buildings, and people traded goods like cloth and gold there.

15 Today the Grand Bazaar is much bigger, and it is the largest covered market in the world.

16 It has 64 streets and more than 4,000 shops under one roof.

17 The market attracts over 250,000 visitors every day.

18 You can buy almost any imaginable item there.

19 Extra Tip: Ask shop owners if they carry nazar boncuğu, a traditional Turkish symbol for good luck.

20 Also, if you want a nice snack, make sure to try lokum, a traditional Turkish candy.

21 2 Damnoen Saduak Floating Market, Thailand

22 In the past, Thai people traded goods on rivers.

23 This was the beginning of floating markets in Thailand.

24 With better road transportation, many floating markets disappeared.

25 Since the late 1960s, however, some of them have come back and kept the tradition alive.

26 Today, one of the most popular floating markets is Damnoen Saduak Floating Market.

27 It is always crowded with tourists from all over the world.

28 You can buy local foods and traditional gift items directly from boats.

29 Extra Tip: I wonder if you have ever had a meal on water.

30 If not, try noodles like *pad thai*.

31 The sellers will cook them on their boats and pass them to you with a long fishing pole.

32 3 Aalsmeer Flower Market, The Netherlands

33 The Netherlands means "low lands."

34 As the name suggests, about 70% of the country sits below sea level.

35 Thus, the Dutch built up the land, and one effective way to use it was to grow flowers and sell them.

36 It is, therefore, no surprise that the country has the largest flower market in the world: the Aalsmeer Flower Market.

37 The building where the market is housed is bigger than 120 soccer fields.

38 The market is busy with thousands of flower-filled carts.

39 They are moved mostly by electric-powered trucks.

40 Every day, around 20 million flowers are traded and shipped to all corners of the world.

41 Extra Tip: You may wonder whether you can buy just a few flowers at the market.

42 Sadly, you cannot, but you can see how wholesale flower trading works.

My Speaking Portfolio - Step 2

1. How, want to travel, wonder if, with friends, family

2. want to travel with

3. to visit museums, markets

4. if's, to learn about, local culture

After You Read

1. place where East meets West, long tradition of trade

2. country where trading on boats, long history

3. More than two-thirds, is below sea level

Wrap Up READING

1. Every Saturday, go to

2. the place where, coming week

3. all kinds of fresh vegetables

4. are usually picked, a few hours

5. also find, meet, home-made

6. Because, the items directly from, much cheaper than at other stores

7. local farmers, ready to share, recipes with

8. love going to, farmers' market

구석구석지문 TEST Step 2 p.44

My Speaking Portfolio - Step 2

1. A: How do you want to travel? I wonder if you want to travel with friends or family.

2. B: Well, I want to travel with my friends.

......

3. A: Okay. Do you want to visit museums or markets?

4. B: I want to visit museums. It's a great way to learn about the local culture.

After You Read

1. This country is a place where East meets West and has a long tradition of trade.

2. This is a country where trading on boats has a long history.

3. More than two-thirds of the country is below sea level.

Wrap Up READING

1. Every Saturday, I go to Oakville Farmers' Market.

2. That is the place where I buy food for the coming week.

3. There I find all kinds of fresh vegetables.

4. They are usually picked only a few hours before I buy them.

5. I also find bread, meet, and home-made jam.

6. Because I can buy the items directly from the producers, they are usually much cheaper than at other stores.

7. The local farmers are always kind and ready to share gardening tips and recipes with visitors, too.

8. I love going to the farmers' market .

단어 TEST Step 1 p.45

01 양파	02 폭넓게	03 아픈
04 값싼	05 맛있는	06 세기
07 모든 곳에서	08 팔다	09 건강한
10 다르다	11 (얇은) 조각	12 그러나
13 납작한, 평평한	14 소개하다	15 알다, 배우다
16 의견이 다르다	17 공유하다	18 멀리 떨어진
19 가지고 오다	20 고기	21 거의
22 국기	23 고명, 토핑	24 신세계
25 기록	26 국가의	27 아주 좋아하는
28 전 세계적인	29 ~ 이후로	30 유형
31 그런, ~와 같은	32 분주한, 바쁜	33 석기시대
34 채소	35 ~의 바깥쪽에	36 이윽고
37 ~로 덮여 있는	38 동시에	39 ~에 올려놓다
40 여러 가지 형태로	41 어느 때이든지	
42 ~하기 위하여 사용되다		
43 ~라고들 믿고 있다		

단어 TEST Step 2 p.46

01 busy	02 century	03 try
04 type	05 almost	06 while
07 as	08 since	09 delicious
10 national flag	11 onion	12 share
13 differ	14 widely	15 meat
16 shop	17 far	18 flat
19 global	20 however	21 name
22 bring	23 sell	24 cheap
25 national	26 disagree	27 healthy
28 everywhere	29 record	30 move
31 slice	32 such	33 topping
34 introduce	35 in time	36 at any time
37 topped with	38 so ~ that ...	39 go on to ~
40 at the same time		
41 be used to+동사원형		
42 around the world		
43 It is believed that ~		

1 shop, 상점   2 agree, 동의하다   3 century, 세기

4 global, 전 세계적인   5 bake, (음식을) 굽다

6 cheap, 값싼   7 slice, (얇은) 조각

8 introduce, 소개하다   9 onion, 양파

10 topping, 고명, 토핑   11 bread, 빵   12 flag, 깃발

01 Slice, History   02 What, like, your

03 Though, disagree on, global

04 sold, street, most parts

05 become such, favorite, around

06 Since, eating, form, another

07 baked flat, hot rocks   08 show, put meat, on

09 believed, used, name, over

10 with, born until, century

11 before, other, brought, from

12 introduced, thought, make, sick

13 In, learned, delicious, healthy

14 century, large, where, jobs

15 near, far, lives, time

16 other, flat, sold slices

17 street, cheap, delicious, workers

18 slice of, as, on

19 world's first, shop opened   20 In, of, visited, tried

21 type, leaf, colors, flag

22 visit, on, become, dish

23 became known, late, moved

24 brought, with, because, same

25 first, opened its doors

26 enjoyed almost everywhere

27 course, differ, from, to

28 while, have, onion, on

29 However, types of, share

30 Each, with flat, slice

01 Slice of History   02 What do you like

03 Though, disagree on, global food

04 It is sold, in most parts, world

05 has, become such a favorite food

06 Since, have been eating, another

07 on hot rocks

08 Records show, to put, on

09 It is believed, to name, over

10 However, was not born until

11 before, brought, from

12 were, introduced, make them sick

13 In time, delicious, healthy   14 In, century, where

15 from near and far, busy lives, at any time

16 put, on, slices of pizza

17 so cheap, delicious that, for

18 slices of, as, on the street

19 world's first pizza shop   20 tried

21 that she loved most, that showed, on

22 went on to become, national dish

23 became known outside of, moved to

24 brought pizza with them, topped with, at the same time

25 opened its doors in   26 almost everywhere

27 Of course, differ, from place to place

28 while, onion toppings   29 share two things

30 begins with, a slice of history

1 한 조각의 역사

2 여러분은 어떤 피자 토핑을 좋아하는가?

3 비록 제일 좋아하는 피자 토핑에 대해 의견이 다를 수 있지만, 피자가 오늘날 세계적인 음식이라는 데에는 모두 동의할 것이다.

4 피자는 세계 대부분 지역의 패스트푸드 식당이나 길거리에서 팔리고 있다.

5 어떻게 해서 피자가 세계적으로 이토록 사랑받는 음식이 되었을까?

6 석기시대부터 사람들은 여러 가지 형태로 피자를 먹어 왔다.

7 석기시대 사람들은 납작한 빵을 뜨거운 돌에 구워 먹었다.

8 기록에 의하면 그리스와 로마 사람들이 납작한 빵에 고기와 채소를 얹기 시작했다.

9 '피자'라는 단어는 이러한 음식을 지칭하기 위해 약 천 년 전에 이탈리아에서 처음 사용되었다고 알려져 있다.

10 하지만 토마토 토핑을 얹은 피자는 16세기까지는 존재하지 않았다.

11 크리스토퍼 콜럼버스와 다른 유럽인들이 신세계에서 가져오기 전까지 이탈리아에는 토마토가 없었다.

12 유럽에 처음 소개되었을 때 사람들은 토마토가 사람들을 아프게 할 거라고 여겼다.

13 시간이 지나며 사람들은 토마토가 맛있고 건강에도 좋다는 것을 알게 되었다.

14 18세기에 나폴리는 다양한 직업이 존재하는 대도시였다.

15 사방에서 노동자들이 이 도시로 모여들었고, 바쁜 생활 중인 그들에게 필요했던 것은 언제든지 빨리 먹을 수 있는

음식이었다.

16 나폴리의 요리사들이 납작한 빵에 토마토와 다른 토핑을 얹기 시작해 길거리에서 피자 조각을 팔았다.

17 이 길거리 음식은 무척 저렴하고 맛이 좋아서, 노동자들은 이것을 아침, 점심, 저녁으로 먹었다.

18 그들은 피자 조각을 사서 길을 걸어가며 먹을 수 있었다.

19 1830년에는 세계 최초의 피자 가게가 나폴리에서 문을 열었다.

20 1889년에 이탈리아의 마르게리타 왕비가 나폴리를 방문하여 피자를 맛보았다.

21 그녀가 가장 좋아했던 피자는 이탈리아 국기의 세 가지 색깔인 빨강, 하양, 초록을 나타낸 토마토, 치즈, 녹색 잎 채소 토핑으로 된 것이었다.

22 왕비의 방문 이후로 피자는 진정한 이탈리아의 국가 음식이 되었다.

23 19세기 후반에는 피자가 이탈리아 밖으로 알려지게 되었는데, 이 시기에 많은 이탈리아 사람들이 미국으로 이주를 하였다.

24 이탈리안들은 피자도 함께 가져갔고, 빵, 고기, 채소를 한꺼번에 먹을 수 있어서 미국인들은 고기와 채소를 얹은 이 납작한 빵을 좋아했다.

25 미국 최초의 피자 가게가 1905년에 문을 열었다.

26 오늘날 피자는 거의 어디에서나 즐길 수 있다.

27 물론, 토핑은 지역에 따라 매우 다양하다.

28 한국인은 불고기를 피자에 얹어 먹기를 좋아하고, 러시아 사람들은 생선과 양파 토핑을 좋아한다.

29 그러나 모든 종류의 피자가 두 가지 사실만큼은 똑같다.

30 모든 피자는 납작한 빵에서 시작하고, 각각은 역사의 한 조각이다

본문 TEST Step 4-Step 5   p.55~59

1 A Slice of History

2 What do you like on your pizza?

3 Though you may disagree on the best toppings, you will agree that it is now a global food.

4 It is sold in fast-food restaurants or on the street in most parts of the world.

5 How has pizza become such a favorite food around the world?

6 Since the Stone Age, people have been eating pizza in one form or another.

7 Stone Age people baked flat bread on hot rocks.

8 Records show that the Greeks and the Romans started to put meat and vegetables on flat bread.

9 It is believed that the word "pizza" was first used in Italy to name the food over 1,000 years ago.

10 However, pizza with tomato toppings was not born until the 16th century.

11 There were no tomatoes in Italy before Christopher Columbus and other Europeans brought them from the New World.

12 When they were first introduced to Europe, people thought that tomatoes would make them sick.

13 In time, people learned that tomatoes were delicious and healthy.

14 In the 18th century, Naples was a large city where there were many jobs.

15 Workers from near and far came to the city, and what they needed in their busy lives was food they could eat quickly at any time.

16 Cooks in Naples began to put tomato and other toppings on flat bread and sold slices of pizza on the street.

17 The street food was so cheap and delicious that workers ate it for breakfast, lunch, and dinner.

18 They could buy slices of pizza and eat them as they walked on the street.

19 In 1830, the world's first pizza shop opened in Naples.

20 In 1889, Queen Margherita of Italy visited Naples and tried pizza.

21 The type of pizza that she loved most had tomato, cheese, and green leaf toppings that showed the three colors on Italy's national flag—red, white, and green.

22 After the queen's visit, pizza went on to become a truly national dish.

23 Pizza became known outside of Italy in the late 19th century, when many Italians moved to the United States.

24 Italians brought pizza with them, and Americans loved the flat bread topped with meat and vegetables because they could eat bread, meat, and vegetables at the same time.

25 The first pizza restaurant in the United States opened its doors in 1905.

26 Pizza is now enjoyed almost everywhere.

27 Of course, toppings differ widely from place to place.

28 Koreans love *bulgogi* on their pizza, while Russians like to have fish and onion toppings on their pizza.

29 However, all types of pizza share two things.

30 Each begins with flat bread, and each is a slice of history.

12 loneliness, 외로움　13 poem, (한 편의) 시

14 publication, 출판, 발행　15 editor, 편집자

16 celebrate, 기념하다, 축하하다

단어 TEST Step 1　　　　　　　　　　　　p.60

01 도착	02 시인	03 문학
04 (책) 한 부; 베끼다, 복사하다		05 특별한, 특정한
06 기소, 혐의	07 문학의, 문학적인	08 표현하다
09 외로움	10 어린 시절	11 자유
12 출판하다	13 희귀한	14 더, 더 멀리
15 도서관	16 정부, 정권	17 이루다, 얻다
18 졸업	19 운동	20 (문학 장르) 시
21 기념하다, 축하하다		22 전체의, 모든
23 가혹한, 혹독한	24 남아 있다, 계속 ~하다	
25 바느질하다	26 (한 편의) 시	27 대우, 처리
28 지갑	29 선사하다, 주다	30 출판, 발행
31 독립	32 동경, 갈망	33 저자
34 편집자	35 포기하다	36 서둘러
37 (도서관에서) 대출하다		38 ~로 유명하다
39 ~와 시간을 보내다		40 ~에 참가하다
41 ~을 염두에 두다	42 ~에 잘 어울리다	43 시도하다

단어 TEST Step 2　　　　　　　　　　　　p.61

01 harsh	02 whole	03 arrest
04 loneliness	05 arrival	06 independence
07 charge	08 poem	09 literary
10 graduation	11 editor	12 yearbook
13 present	14 achieve	15 borrow
16 celebrate	17 longing	18 movement
19 freedom	20 rare	21 remain
22 further	23 government	24 author
25 poetry	26 publish	27 sew
28 literature	29 publication	30 treatment
31 childhood	32 express	33 poet
34 recommend	35 give up	36 put up
37 take part in	38 in a hurry	39 look good on
40 have ~ in mind	41 give it a try	
42 look forward to		43 hang out with

단어 TEST Step 3　　　　　　　　　　　　p.62

1 whole, 전체의, 모든　2 rare, 희귀한　3 poet, 시인

4 graduation, 졸업　5 literature, 문학

6 longing, 동경, 갈망　7 recommend, 추천하다

8 hometown, 고향　9 independence, 독립

10 sew, 바느질하다　11 harsh, 가혹한, 혹독한

대화문 TEST Step 1　　　　　　　　　　　p.63~64

Listen – Listen & Answer Dialog 1

Long, no, brings / have to, a book report, recommend, to read / about / heard of, show me / New Arrivals, popular among / check, out / borrow, for seven days

Listen – Listen & Answer Dialog 2

are, doing / novel, book report / me see / borrowed / course, big fan, all, mystery books / writer, stop reading / what, has been made into / looks interesting / come out, looking forward to seeing / together

Listen more – Listen and complete

Take a seat, How would you like / taking, yearbook, cool / take / particular, mind / recommend / Look at, look good on / can't wait to see / sure, look cool

My Speaking Portfolio

to meet, real name / where you're from / from / usually, write / short story writer, have written / special / well known for, surprise endings / recommend, with, surprise ending / recommend / about / who saves her life / can't wait

대화문 TEST Step 2　　　　　　　　　　　p.65~66

Listen – Listen & Answer Dialog 1

Minjun: Hello, Ms. Seo.

Ms. Seo: Hi, Minjun. Long time no see. What brings you here?

Minjun: I have to write a book report. Can you recommend a good novel to read?

Ms. Seo: How about a mystery? There's a new Ken Kuller book, *22nd Street*.

Minjun: Oh, I've heard of him. Can you show me the book?

Ms. Seo: It's in the "New Arrivals" area. It's really popular among teens in Great Britain.

Minjun: Thank you for your help. Can I check it out?

Ms. Seo: Sure. You can borrow new books for seven days.

Minjun: Okay.

Listen – Listen & Answer Dialog 2

Sora: Hey, Minjun. What are you doing?

Minjun: I'm reading a novel for a book report.

Sora: Let me see. Oh, is this a new book by Ken Kuller?

Minjun: Yeah, I borrowed it this morning. Do you know Ken Kuller?

Sora: Of course. I'm a big fan of his. I've read all of his mystery books.

Minjun: I think he's a great writer. I can't stop reading this book.

Sora: You know what? His novel *Four Eyes* has been made into a movie.

Minjun: Yeah. I saw the movie poster. It looks interesting.

Sora: It'll come out next Thursday. I'm looking forward to seeing it!

Minjun: Maybe we can see the movie together.

Listen more – Listen and complete

Mike: Good morning, Jiho.

Jiho: Good morning.

Mike: Take a seat, please. How would you like your hair done?

Jiho: Well, I'm taking my pictures for the yearbook. So I want to look cool.

Mike: When do you take the pictures?

Jiho: This Friday at Dream & Joy Park.

Mike: Sounds good. Do you have a particular style in mind?

Jiho: No. Can you recommend one for me?

Mike: Look at this. How about this style? It'll look good on you.

Jiho: Wow, I like it. I can't wait to see how I'll look in the pictures.

Mike: I'm sure you'll look cool.

My Speaking Portfolio

Jane: Nice to meet you, Mr. Henry. Is O. Henry your real name?

Mr. Henry: No. My real name is William Sydney Porter.

Jane: Can you tell me where you're from?

Mr. Henry: I'm from the U.S.

Jane: What do you usually write?

Mr. Henry: I'm a short story writer . I have written about 300 short stories.

Jane: Wow! You're great! What is special about your short stories?

Mr. Henry: They're well known for their surprise endings.

Jane: Can you recommend a popular story with a surprise ending?

Mr. Henry: Sure. I recommend *The Last Leaf*.

Jane: What is it about?

Mr. Henry: It's about a sick girl and an old artist who saves her life.

Jane: Oh, I want to read it. I can't wait.

본문 TEST Step 1　　　　　　　　　　p.67~69

01 Poet Who Loved
02 where, in a hurry
03 Autumn fills, air
04 ready, stand, without, worry
05 To count, stars
06 Memory, one
07 Love, another
08 Loneliness, another
09 Longing, another
10 Poetry for, star
11 for another star
12 Have, read, lines
13 part of, poem, by
14 written, still remains, poems
15 was born in, near
16 As, for, school
17 sewing so, that, sewed
18 it was, that, most
19 wrote, lot, poems
20 literary magazine with, cousin
21 borrowed, poetry, copied, whole
22 have, own copy, rare
23 doctor, chose, literature, college
24 hung out, expressed, lost
25 celebrate, graduation, publish, under
26 three copies, by hand
27 given, another, presented, kept
28 advised against, because, publication
29 followed, advice, gave up
30 study further, had studied
31 in, began to, study
32 following, arrested, part, independence
33 later, arrested, same charges
34 prison after harsh treatment

35 It, few, that, achieved

36 brought, poet's, finally published

37 was given, had thought

38 ages, brightly, hearts like

---

01 Poet Who

02 where, in a hurry

03 fills

04 without a worry

05 count

06 Memory

07 another

08 Loneliness

09 Longing

10 Poetry for

11 for another star

12 Have, read these lines

13 part of, by

14 was written, still remains, poems

15 was born in

16 As, for his school

17 sewing so, that, sewed

18 it was, that, most

19 wrote a lot of poems

20 a literary magazine with

21 borrowed, copied, by hand

22 to have his own copy, rare book

23 to be a doctor, chose to study literature

24 During, hung out with other young poets, where, expressed feelings, lost country

25 To celebrate his graduation, publish, under the title

26 three copies, by hand

27 was given to, another, the last one, for himself

28 advised against, because, allow, publication

29 followed, gave up

30 decided to study further, had studied before

31 began to study

32 following year, for taking part in, independence movement

33 later, arrested on the same charges

34 after harsh treatment by the police

35 It was, that, achieved independence

36 brought, to, they were finally published

37 was given, had thought of, before

38 are loved by, shine birghtly, like

---

1 별을 사랑한 시인

2 계절이 지나가는 하늘에는

3 가을로 가득 차 있습니다.

4 나는 아무 걱정도 없이

5 가을 속의 별들을 다 헤일 듯합니다.

6 별 하나에 추억과

7 별 하나에 사랑과

8 별 하나에 쓸쓸함과

9 별 하나에 동경과

10 별 하나에 시와

11 별 하나에 어머니, 어머니,

12 당신은 이 시 구절을 읽어 본 적이 있는가?

13 이것은 윤동주의 시 '별 헤는 밤'의 일부이다.

14 시는 오래 전에 쓰였지만 여전히 한국의 가장 좋아하는 시 중의 하나로 남아 있다.

15 동주는 중국 연변 근처에서 1917년에 태어났다.

16 어린 소년이었을 때 그는 운동을 좋아했고, 학교의 축구 선수였다.

17 그는 또한 바느질하는 것을 무척 좋아해서 친구들의 축구 유니폼에 번호를 바느질해 주기도 했다.

18 그러나 그가 가장 사랑한 것은 문학이었다.

19 초등학교에 다닐 때 그는 많은 시를 썼다.

20 심지어 사촌 송몽규와 문학잡지를 만들기도 했다.

21 그가 중학교에 다니던 때 한번은 당대의 유명한 시인 백석의 시집을 빌려 와서 책 전체를 필사하기도 했다.

22 그는 정말로 그 희귀한 책을 한 부 갖고 싶었던 것이다.

23 그의 부모는 그가 의사가 되기를 바랐지만 동주는 서울에 있는 대학에서 문학 공부를 하기로 했다.

24 대학 시절에 그는 종종 다른 젊은 시인들과 어울려 다녔고, 고향과 잃어버린 조국에 대한 심정을 표현하는 시를 썼다.

25 졸업을 기념하여 그는 '하늘과 바람과 별과 시'라는 제목으로 자신의 시 19편을 출판하고 싶어 했다.

26 그는 책 세 부를 손으로 만들었다.

27 한 부는 가까운 친구인 정병욱에게 주었고, 또 하나는 그가 가장 좋아하는 교수에게 선물했으며, 마지막 하나는 자신이 보관했다.

28 그러나 그의 교수는 일본 정부가 출판을 허가하지 않으리라 여겨, 그의 계획에 반대하는 충고를 했다.

29 동주는 그의 충고를 따랐고 그 생각을 포기했다.

30 동주는 그의 아버지가 예전에 공부했던 나라에서 학업을 이어 가기로 했다.

31 그리하여 1942년에 동주와 그의 사촌은 일본에서 공부를 시작했다.

32 다음 해 7월 10일에 그의 사촌은 독립운동에 가담했다는 이유로 일본 경찰에게 체포되었다.

33 나흘 뒤 동주 역시 같은 혐의로 체포되었다.

34 1945년에 동주와 그의 사촌은 경찰의 가혹 행위를 당한 후 감옥에서 사망했다.

35 한국이 일본으로부터 독립을 이룬 것은 그로부터 불과 몇 달 후의 일이었다.

36 1948년에 정병욱이 동주의 시를 시인의 동생에게 가져다주었고, 마침내 그것들은 출판되었다.

37 그 책에는 시인이 수년 전에 생각해 두었던 제목이 붙었다.

38 그의 시는 모든 세대의 사랑을 받고 있고, 따라서 그것들은 가을밤 하늘의 별처럼 우리 가슴 속에 여전히 밝게 빛나고 있다.

---

1 A Poet Who Loved Stars

2 In the sky where seasons pass in a hurry

3 Autumn fills the air.

4 And ready I stand, without a worry,

5 To count all the stars there.

6 Memory for one star,

7 Love for another star,

8 Loneliness for another star,

9 Longing for another star,

10 Poetry for another star,

11 And, oh, mother, mother for another star.

12 Have you read these lines before?

13 They are part of the poem "Counting Stars at Night" by Yoon Dong-ju.

14 The poem was written a long time ago but still remains one of Korea's favorite poems.

15 Dong-ju was born in 1917 near Yanbin, China.

16 As a young boy, he loved sports, and he was a soccer player for his school.

17 He also loved sewing so much that he sewed the numbers on all his friends' soccer uniforms.

18 However, it was literature that he loved most.

19 In elementary school he wrote a lot of poems.

20 He even made a literary magazine with his cousin, Song Mong-gyu.

21 In middle school he once borrowed a poetry book by a famous poet of the time, Baek Seok, and copied the whole book by hand.

22 He really wanted to have his own copy of the rare book.

23 His parents wanted him to be a doctor, but Dong-ju chose to study literature at a college in Seoul.

24 During his college years, he often hung out with other young poets and wrote poetry where he expressed feelings about his hometown and lost country.

25 To celebrate his graduation, he wished to publish 19 of his poems under the title, *Heaven, Wind, Stars, and Poetry*.

26 He made three copies of the book by hand.

27 One was given to his close friend, Jeong Byeong-uk, another was presented to his favorite professor, and the last one was kept for himself.

28 However, his professor advised against his plan because he thought the Japanese government would not allow the publication.

29 Dong-ju followed his advice and gave up the idea.

30 Dong-ju decided to study further in the country where his father had studied before.

31 So, in 1942, Dong-ju and his cousin began to study in Japan.

32 On July 10 the following year, his cousin was arrested by the Japanese police for taking part in an independence movement.

33 Four days later, Dong-ju was also arrested on the same charges.

34 In 1945, Dong-ju and his cousin died in prison after harsh treatment by the police.

35 It was just a few months later that Korea achieved independence from Japan.

36 In 1948, Jeong Byeong-uk brought Dong-ju's poems to the poet's brother, and they were finally published.

37 The book was given the title the poet had thought of many years before.

38 His poems are loved by people of all ages, and thus they still shine brightly in our hearts like the stars in the autumn night sky.

Communicate: Speak

1. look excited

2. looking forward to

3. on

4. curling match, can't wait

Before You Read

1. Last week, celebrated

2. put up, had lived, harsh times, tried to achieve

3. writers, had expressed, longing for freedom, literary works

Wrap Up READING

1. pomes, cartoons

2. different kinds of, differ in which kind they prefer

3. allow us to go beyond, where we live

4. come across, writers who lived

5. being, living, completely different place

6. In short, have never visited

Communicate: Speak

1. Tom: Hi, Sora. You look excited.

2. Sora: Yeah. I'm really looking forward to this Tuesday.

3. Tom: This Tuesday? What's on Tuesday?

4. Sora: There's a big curling match. I can't wait!

Before You Read

1. Last week we celebrated August 15 in our class.

2. We put up pictures of people who had lived through harsh times and tried to achieve independence.

3. Also, there was a talk on writers who had expressed their longing for freedom in literary works.

Wrap Up READING

1. Do you enjoy plays, pomes, novels, or cartoons?

2. They are different kinds of literature, and people differ in which kind they prefer.

3. However, all of them allow us to go beyond our own small world where we live.

4. When we read literature, we come across the ideas of great writers who lived long ago.

5. We can even imagine being someone else or living in a completely different place.

6. In short, literature opens up for us new worlds that we have never visited before.

MEMO

MEMO